CW00434403

PENGUIN BOO

ROMANCING WITH LIFE

Born in 1923, Bollywood's 'evergreen' hero Dev Anand was part of the Hindi film industry for more than sixty years. Starting his career as a complete unknown in pre-Independence India, he scored major hits in the 1950s as a debonair romantic hero in films like *Baazi*, *Taxi Driver*, *CID*, *Funtoosh*, *Paying Guest*, *Nau Do Gyarah* and *Kala Pani*. Dev Anand's success story continued in the 1960s with classics like *Kala Bazaar*, *Hum Dono*, *Tere Ghar Ke Samne*, *Teen Deviyan*, *Guide* and *Jewel Thief*. Most of his films were produced under the Navketan banner, the production house he had founded as early as 1950. With *Prem Pujari* (1970) Dev Anand turned director, and starred in the 1970s hits like *Johny Mera Naam*, *Hare Rama Hare Krishna*, *Gambler*, *Heera Panna* and *Des Pardes*. He continued to write, produce, direct and act in films based on socially relevant issues right till his death, his last film being *Chargesheet* (2011).

Dev Anand won the Filmfare Best Actor award twice (for *Kala Pani* and *Guide*) and was honoured with the Filmfare and Screen Lifetime Achievement Awards, the Dadasaheb Phalke Award and the Padma Bhushan.

He passed away in London in December 2011.

Romancing with Life

an
autobiography

Dev Anand

PENGUIN BOOKS

PENGUIN BOOKS
Published by the Penguin Group
Penguin Books India Pvt. Ltd, 11 Community Centre, Panchsheel Park, New Delhi 110 017, India
Penguin Group (USA) Inc., 375 Hudson Street, New York, New York 10014, USA
Penguin Group (Canada), 90 Eglinton Avenue East, Suite 700, Toronto, Ontario, M4P 2Y3, Canada (a division of Pearson Penguin Canada Inc.)
Penguin Books Ltd, 80 Strand, London WC2R 0RL, England
Penguin Ireland, 25 St Stephen's Green, Dublin 2, Ireland (a division of Penguin Books Ltd)
Penguin Group (Australia), 250 Camberwell Road, Camberwell, Victoria 3124, Australia (a division of Pearson Australia Group Pty Ltd)
Penguin Group (NZ), 67 Apollo Drive, Rosedale, Auckland 0632, New Zealand (a division of Pearson New Zealand Ltd)
Penguin Group (South Africa) (Pty) Ltd, 24 Sturdee Avenue, Rosebank, Johannesburg 2196, South Africa

Penguin Books Ltd, Registered Offices: 80 Strand, London WC2R 0RL, England

First published in Viking by Penguin Books India 2007
Published in Penguin Books 2011

Photographs courtesy of the author

The views and opinions expressed in this book are the author's own and the facts are as reported by him which have been verified to the extent possible and the publishers are not in any way liable for the same.

10 9 8 7 6 5 4 3 2 1

ISBN 9780143418566

Typeset in Sabon by Eleven Arts, New Delhi
Printed at Akash Printers, Okhla

I dedicate this book to life
as it is lived by people the world over
and to that special ray of sunshine
that makes life worth living

Acknowledgements

There are a few people I would like to thank:

Mohan Dewan, who read the first draft of the manuscript and offered his valuable inputs;

My publishers Penguin India, who brought the book to the world;

And my family and friends, and all my fans, as always, for everything.

Preface

Writing about your own life, for the whole world to read, can be easy as well as difficult.

On the one hand it is quite easy, because unlike fiction, in which you have to invent characters, create situations and incidents, and concoct a believable narrative, the story of your life has already been played out in front of your eyes, and you are intimate with its every detail. All you have to do is open the windows of your memory, and let the story run past, spool after spool—spicing it up a bit here and there, deleting bits that are unnecessary, and making it play to a rhythm that grips the reader, absorbs and inspires him throughout its unfolding.

On the other hand, writing about yourself can be extremely difficult, because you have to be honest and truthful both to yourself and to the events and personalities you're describing, even if the truth is sometimes not pleasant, and you have to lay yourself open, with all your strengths and weaknesses, before the reader, baring your soul to them as they read your book.

Writing an autobiography is tougher still when you are a public figure that the world has known and admired for over six decades, and has looked up to as a larger-than-life hero. Unless I can take my readers to a plane of absolute adoration for me as they read my book, the attempt will not have been worth it. And yet, my life has been an open book to my fans, and they must not feel that I am hiding something or glossing over some unsavoury bumps now that I have set out to write my autobiography. This is why the untarnished truth and complete honesty are the first pre-requisites to my writing about myself, rife as they are with the dangers of annoying or angering a few people who have rubbed shoulders with me on my journey along the path of life.

On some occasions, I have been accused of being 'narcissistic', and since this book is all about me, this is perhaps a charge I should answer to before I proceed. Perhaps those who have accused me of being focused almost obsessively on myself are right in a sense, for I, Dev Anand, am certainly the central point of everything I say and do. But my critics, I think, fail to see the reason behind this—that as a popular star, the image of Dev Anand is like that of a deity to his millions of fans. To honour that image, I must project myself as the best I can be in both my personal and professional life. For unless a man inspires himself to greater achievements, how can he inspire the world around him? His effort at raising his own status to the highest possible levels is not an act of self-gratification; it would seem that way only to the envious.

My life has been full of special moments and people, like thousands of sparkling jewels embedded in my mind in the form of precious memories. Most have continued to shine brightly; a few have lost their lustre a bit over time; and some, which turned out to be artificial, have faded or fallen off. But they all deserve to be remembered. And as I wrote this book I have remembered them all with great relish, never with regret. Not all of them may have been recounted in this book due to space constraints, but they remain vibrantly alive in my thoughts. So do the many people who have left their impressions on me over time. Not everyone may find themselves adequately represented in this narrative, but I hope they will not take offence at having to make cameo appearances, and enjoy their part in the larger story I have to tell. If anyone feels hurt, cold-shouldered or ignored as they read this book, I would like to assure them that this is not intentional in any way. Thousands of thoughts whirr around my brain every day; though you may have been mentioned only in passing in these pages, you may be the person I am thinking of with great affection and gratitude at this very moment, as you read this book.

Before I begin my first chapter, I must say a word about my fans, for they are the ones who have made me what I am, without them Dev Anand would not be what he is, and this book too would not have been written.

I love all my fans—all those I've met, and even those I haven't, but have only conversed with over long distances, delighting in the phone calls they make to me and the fan mail that they send. The extent of my fan mail has always floored me. If I had collected all of the mail I've received over my six-decade-long career, I would probably need to build a separate library for it. Instead, I've stored them all in the best place of all—in my heart.

I've replied to some of my fans on rare occasions, to people whom my fancy suddenly picked on at random, for no clear reason. Replying to every letter would be a full-time job, and I don't believe in the heartlessly impersonal method of having a secretary reply to letters people have written personally to you One response from me to a loyal fan resulted in his writing 3,720 more letters to me in the hope of receiving another reply. Another time, I replied to a teenager's flood of passionate letters by writing almost a dozen letters to her; but the day I stopped writing, she put all my letters in a neatly packed bundle and returned them to me along with a goodbye note, her heart broken.

How I wish I could write to all my fans, opening my heart to them the way I would like to.

This book finally gives me the chance to speak to each and every one of my beloved fans, one-on-one, like never before.

One

I wonder, as you start to read this book, how well you know me. If you do know me well, you will certainly come to know me better as you read on; if not, through these pages you will come to know me for who I am, and why I am what I am. I have been working ceaselessly for over sixty years now, with all my creative energies at my command, the excitement of creativity sprouting all the time inside me like so many seedlings, just the way they used to when I first launched myself all those years ago. This is my story, a story that has never been told before.

My mother used to call me 'Dev'; so did my family and the close circle of people around me. My father would call me 'Dev-aan', the 'aan' being an additional pampered prolongation of the three-letter name reserved by a doting father for his third son. He would always call out 'Dev-aan' when he got home in the evening, walking all the way back from his workplace. He loved the lingering resonance of the 'aan', the extension of the name he had made up for me.

When I was born, 'Dharam'—meaning faith—was prefixed to 'Dev' to form my full name, as ordained by the family 'pandit'. My name was never 'Devdutt' as some web sites will have it, refusing to rectify the error in spite of my repeated clarifications in the print and electronic media. I hung on to the 'Dharam' part of my name very faithfully all through my academic career, in school and in college, and in all official documents needed to further my presence in the world. My mates in educational institutions I went to preferred addressing me as 'DD', picking up the initial letters of the two words, making the name sound more familiar and 'pally'.

But as I stepped out into the world on my own to seek a foothold and recognition for myself, I dispensed with the 'Dharam' part of my name, and added 'Anand'—my family surname—instead to my identity, so that if ever I did achieve fame and glory, my family name should take its due part of the credit for my achievements.

Besides, I thought then as I do now, that a three-word name—Dharam Dev Anand—was too heavy a name for a simple man like me, and would have been too long and tiresome on the lips. 'Dev Anand' was just right, for it literally meant 'God of Happiness', and was aesthetically more appealing. So this was how I came to be known to all those who knew me. But after I became popular and ensconced myself deep in the hearts of the audience, many, in fact the majority, started adding a 'saab' to my first name whenever they addressed me, or even when they mentioned me in their conversation. I could never figure out why. Maybe it was because I had formed my own film company at a very early stage, and had thus also become my own boss and master, and started being looked up to as a boss, as somebody a notch above just a film star. Or perhaps it was because they found in my city-bred persona, wearing jeans and jackets, a touch of the western, as opposed to the dhoti-kurta-clad bumpkin from the Indian hinterland; the films I made were modern as well, slightly ahead of their times, and not the usual village or small-town sagas. It might even have been because I spoke English with the accent of an 'almost Englishman', a 'Brown Sahib'. Whatever the reason, 'saab' has stuck with me ever since, and has now become an inseparable part of my name, like rain and lightning to the clouds, waves to the sea, and stars to the sky—and I have got used to being called thus.

But those I am closest to, those who like and love me and I them, call me 'Dev', just 'Dev', short and sweet and possessive, godly and sexy, and intimate to the extreme, in bedrooms, in drawing rooms, in the streets and in public squares. I enjoy being owned by them thus, being possessed by them, loving me, admiring me, hating me, disliking me, making fun of me, throwing bouquets or brickbats at me in the same measure, sometimes raising me to the skies, at others pulling me harshly down to earth, tearing me apart viciously, only to raise me to the skies again . . . but never, never banishing me from their innermost thoughts.

Two

The main entrance to the Waldorf Astoria on 49th Street and Lexington Avenue leads to an escalator and a flight of steps. You can choose either, depending on your mood of the moment, to enter a corridor of elegant showrooms—one of which exhibits the pride of the American literary world, the works of Ernest Hemingway, James Joyce and Ayn Rand, encased in glass—and finally to reach the main lobby of one of the most prestigious hotels in Manhattan. Right at the centre of the lobby stands a dominating antique, a clock dating back to the nineteenth century, with Queen Victoria looking benignly down at you in silver. Below her are heads in bronze of some of the nation-builders of their times, Grant, Washington, Cleveland, Harrison, Lincoln, Jackson, Franklin, all ex-presidents of the United States of America, reminding you of the old times that have ticked away with relentless speed. It is night, eleven, says the clock, as the silver statue of the French lady—the Statue of Liberty—standing above them all, hails you with a wave of her hand. It is 23 March 2003, and though the hands of the clock keep moving ahead, time stands still for me suddenly. For America and its mammoth war machine have started emblazoning the horizons of Baghdad, the capital of Iraq, in multi-colours of red and orange and pink and yellow, as guns boom into the palaces of Saddam Hussein from the shores of the Mediterranean. I stand and pause over the names of the great people now dead and gone, who lived to change the history of the eras they represented. America grew with them, expanding from strength to strength, asserting its own notion of democracy over the rest of the world.

There is casual banter and laughter around me, as men and women move out of a cocktail party through the hotel bar. Young ladies flashing seductive smiles, and swaggering men holding their ladies by the arm, as their tail-coats flirt with the shimmering gowns that speak of the opulence of the moment. I find myself surrounded by the jovial crowd, yet beneath the joviality lies an undercurrent of sadness so poignantly emanating from the TV sets. News commentators race each other to bring to their channels the coverage of the massive attack, as men and women besieged with cannon strikes scream and shriek with horror. A child killed! A woman maimed! A man disembowelled!

Man killing man. It's been there through the ages, from the ancient ages to the very present, a time no less barbaric. I have seen and heard and read about it all, from as far back as I can remember. It had happened in 1942, when the Second World War was ravaging the world, and India was fighting for its independence from the British. When Pakistan and Bangladesh were non-existent and India was one, from the Bay of Bengal and the jungles of Burma to the high ranges of Kashmir and Afghanistan across the Himalayas. Mahatma Gandhi had given the clarion call, commanding the Englishmen to 'Quit India'. The British in turn had sent their tommies into the streets with tommy-guns and rifles. The peaceful Indian 'satyagrahis' were filling the jails in numbers, while the agitating nationalists resisting oppression were facing bullets outside.

As humanity wails on the TV, I stand beneath the clock . . . and pause, as I have never paused before. My mind stands still, refusing to race forward, a very rare phenomenon for me. For every second of my life that I have breathed, I have been moving on, speeding ahead, flying faster than the American missiles in Iraq. But now these moments that seem to freeze me also make me reflect backwards and inwards as never before. At that moment, I decide to write this book . . .

Three

My father was one of the leading lawyers in Gurdaspur, a district in the undivided Punjab, the land of the five rivers. I had passed with honours in English having taken my degree, Bachelor of Arts, from the Government College in Lahore, one of the most fashionable cities of India in those days. The students of the college were known to be the young 'elite' of the country, many of them going abroad to England for further studies. I too wanted to do my master's in English from the same college, and then prepare to go to England, across the 'seven seas', and be known amongst the ranks of those selected sons of India—bright and brilliant and polished—who could boast the badge of a foreign education pinned on their lapels, and therefore prove deserving of a high post in any field of occupation.

But it was not to be. My father was going through a very lean period in life. He had no money to spend on the luxury of his third son going for higher studies, and suggested a clerical job for me in a bank, after I got rejected for a commission in the Royal Indian Navy of the British Armed Forces. I shed a silent tear. A blank wall rose in front of me. It seemed that the river Ravi, on the banks of which Lahore prospered, had suddenly stopped flowing, and I was besieged by the thought of an empty abyss that was waiting to suck up a nonentity, who, before he could blossom, was about to fade away into nothingness forever. My mind revolted. My dreams took charge of the reins of my decision-making. I looked around me and felt in my pockets. All that I could come up with was a meagre thirty rupees. With that sum of money and a small bag of my most precious personal belongings, I found myself in the hustle and bustle of a third-class compartment of the Frontier Mail that

would take twenty-four hours to take me to the city of my dreams
. . . Bombay.

The train moved and with it the panorama outside sped along as
well. But my mind raced backwards in time even faster, clutching
at the snippets of memories that I was leaving behind.

I saw her running onto the platform, trying to board the train
along with me, struggling to get into the same compartment.

'Hold my hand! Hold my hand! I want to come with you!' she
was calling. But Usha Chopra was left behind, as the train whistled
away.

She was a beautiful girl . . . very beautiful. Born of an English
mother and an Indian father, who was professor of history in the
same college as I was, she was the only girl in a class of boys attending
the English honours tutorial headed by Principal Dickinson. She
always sat on a bench just ahead of me. Always the first to take her
place before the boys entered the room, and always the last to leave—
for she always had a question to ask the professor. She invariably
wore a sari that shimmered on her frame of white marble, standing
on high-heeled shoes that made her look even taller than she was.
I was enamoured of her, totally in love with her in secret, but always
too shy to confront her with my state of mind. I could never say
anything to her beyond a softly murmured self-conscious 'hello'.

My father always used to say I was more shy than a shy girl. He
had put me in a girls' school in Gurdaspur, and the girls ragged and
bullied me, but many would fall for me as I would run away from
them into the faraway seclusion of my shyness.

And then there was that awful, dark-skinned Florence, forever
clad in a short frock and black stockings, always a part of the crowd
that came out of the church behind our house after the Sunday
prayers. Whenever I hear church bells ring, I imagine Florence
chasing me. For she always chased me—in school, and in the
evenings as I went for walks in the municipal gardens. One day she
confronted me with a rose, simultaneously forcing a kiss on my
lips! I blushed to the tips of my ears and ran straight to my mother's
kitchen for a hot meal in front of the fire, entrapped in her thoughts.

Sitar and steel guitar
And luscious lips
Red as wine
Broke somebody's heart
And I'm afraid
It was mine.

She had recited the lines and then pushed this quaint romantic ditty on a slip of paper into my pocket, as I sat brooding one day outside the classroom. And then she ran away to look stealthily at me again from behind a pillar, with love and mischief in her eyes, waiting for my reaction. I, scared of her next attack, ran as fast as I could off the school compound, missing all the classes that day. But she was back at the company's gardens the same evening, popping out of a bed of flowers as I was about to pluck one that looked so beautiful and fresh. I ran away scared, but she followed. I ran faster. She was faster than I was, overtook me and pulled me towards her.

'No, Florence, no!' I resisted blushingly.

'I plucked for you the flower that you wanted. Take it,' she said, and held the flower in front of me. As I looked at it, she smooched me all over the face. Her red lipstick smelt good. Rubbing its marks off my face I ran, but stumbled on a rubble of stones and fell.

She laughed and teased me, 'I wanted to kiss you in the classroom this morning, but that stiff-neck Miss David had her eye on me!' She giggled naughtily.

I got up and ran as fast as I never had, in spite of the bruise on my knee, her giggles still ringing in my ears. I still remember, Florence always smelt of the perfume of sex.

My shyness always stood between me and Usha, with the result that it remained a one-sided romance that was the stuff of dreams. By the day, my eyes roved to look for her in the corridors, spotted her, admired her from a distance—and by night my heart ached for her. I wanted so much to be with her, to feel the warmth of her femininity next to me, to shower a thousand kisses all over her silken gorgeousness, each kiss opening a new vista of paradise that would engulf us both into its deepest ocean.

I had never seen the lusciousness of a naked female form, the mystery of which had intrigued and fascinated my imagination as I stepped out of my boyhood. I remember I had first felt the awakening of the man in me when Bhagoo and I were discussing the growing awareness of our coming of age. Bhagoo, short for Bhagwant, was my pal and next-door neighbour. We were each others' confidantes, and would often sit in his father's library in the hot sultry summer afternoons, and discuss all that was going on in our minds, chiefly a feeling of consciousness about what is known as sex, its possessive ache and its manifold unravelling revelations. During one such afternoon, we saw in the room across the narrow street, the face of a young girl in front of a big mirror hanging on the wall. She looked amused about something, looking at herself. Then she raised her blouse slowly to inspect and admire the young protruding pinkness of her nipples, running her fingers very delicately and languorously over them with the curiosity of an adolescent. Suddenly she seemed to sense some intrusion into her privacy, quickly lowered her blouse, and turned around to discover us watching her through the window. She strode to the window and shut it rather coyly.

A couple of seconds of still suspense! And then she half-opened the window again, to look at us, blushing and ashamed of having been caught at her self-indulgent act. Then she finally banged it shut for good.

That was the closest I came to seeing a female in her exciting nakedness. Usha was the only one with whom I might have hoped to achieve any sort of a female conquest—if only I had the bravado of a lover and could manage to tell her in one brave moment of confession how much I yearned to hold her in a quiet lonely corner, look into her eyes and into the whole universe in them, and then plant a kiss on her lips that would melt her whole being into mine. But my inhibitions always let that heavenly opportunity go waste. The last time I saw and actually talked to Usha was when I went to the college to collect my character certificate from Principal Dickinson, just before I left Lahore. She was standing in the corridor as usual, books and notebooks in her hand. As I came out of the principal's room, with the certificate in my hand, my most craved for 'Hello' greeted me. I turned to see her smiling her most beautiful smile.

'He-l-l-o-o!' I said, trying to peer into her eyes.

'Are you coming back to college, for your master's?' I found her asking me.

'Hello!' I said again. There was so much meaning in that little word this time—the beginning and the end of a declaration of love.

'Are you coming back to college?' she asked again.

'Are you?' I asked her back.

'Yes, I am,' she said.

'I . . . I . . . I don't know,' I kept looking at her, loving the moment.

'Do come!' her eyes seemed to say something else as well, as she continued, 'I have always liked you.'

'You have!' It was my most triumphant moment.

'But you never said you do,' she was ready to be conquered.

'What if I say it now!'

'So next time, when you see me in the corridor, say what you want to say!' she was her most charming self as she said smilingly. And then she vanished, for the principal suddenly passed behind her, giving her a look, his pipe dangling between his lips. She cast a quick glance at him and followed him hastily.

My eyes were glued to her, and to the principal, as they both disappeared behind the spires of the college.

'No—I will never say what I wanted to say to you, Usha,' I murmured, 'for I am not going to be in college again. Destiny has decided that I won't come back here.'

That evening, still thinking of her as I splashed water on my face, I looked into the mirror of my bathroom and laughed out loud saying, 'Not bad, not bad at all!' Beads of water were trickling down my face, assuring me—'Isn't this face pleasantly presentable? Didn't Usha confess she likes me? Didn't Florence kiss me hard? There is something about me—I am going to present myself to the world. I want the world to see me, to admire me. I am going to be an actor. Not just an actor—I am going to be a star! I am going to steer myself towards that goal. I am going to Bombay, the Mecca of films. The glamorous world of show business awaits me. I am going to grab the limelight.'

I was dancing with excitement. I took a quick joyful twirl and punched my fist hard into the mirror. Then laughed heartily at my own reflection and saw it laughing too.

I was still laughing in the train, as the Frontier Mail chugged along. It was July 1943.

Four

I mage after image kept appearing before my eyes, as I sat by the train window, my eyes fixed outside, looking steadily at nothing in particular. A montage of memories kept rushing in and out, with the same fleeting quickness of the blurry scenery outside. I felt sad that I had not told my father that I was going far, far away from him.

My father possessed wonderful oratorical skills, and had an insatiable appetite for knowledge. While he was very well versed in both Persian and Arabic, it was he who taught me the 'Gayatri Mantra', as also the Lord's Prayer. He was my best teacher during my most impressionable years, and would relish hearing from my lips prayers from diverse faiths. Himself an Arya Samaji and very tolerant, I frequently heard him reciting lines from the Quran to his Muslim neighbours. It seemed he enjoyed showing off his erudite Arabic accent. His uttering of 'Bismillah-ul-Rehman-ul-Rahim' still rings in my ears. And as his audience would praise him for his flawless rendering, he would suddenly, in a light-hearted mood, give vent to some Persian couplet, always a different one for a different occasion. Sometimes he would even throw in a quotation in Hebrew from the Jewish Torah. Through the years I attended the girls' school in Gurdaspur, during the summer holidays he would put me in an English convent, the Sacred Heart in Dalhousie, a hill station where he always took the whole family to get away from the burning heat of the plains. A very rich man at heart, he gave all his sons and daughters—nine in all (the tenth, a boy, had died very young)— the best education available at that time. While his eldest son did an MA in Sanskrit and then studied law to follow in his father's footsteps, the second one was sent to England to university, to compete for the ICS, the Indian Civil Services—then the highest honour for the topmost students of the country, who were selected for the most coveted posts after they returned from their studies abroad. But by the time I was ready for higher studies, my father had become financially poor, his law practice had dwindled, his resources were exhausted. My destiny perhaps dictated it that way, and I had to be pulled away from him into a distant city where there was not to be a meeting between father and son for years and years to come.

I missed him as I thought of him. Tears welled up in my eyes, and I saw through the mist of their dampness, each of my family members coming to me, one by one, like a series of images on a transparent celluloid. My two elder sisters who I had left behind in Lahore, one married to a doctor, another to a lawyer, and the eldest of us all, married and settled in Delhi. My two younger sisters, studying in Sir Ganga Ram School, Lahore. My eldest brother, practising law in Gurdaspur, but now in Lahore central jail for having offered 'satyagraha' in Gandhi's Quit India movement, as secretary of the district Congress committee in Gurdaspur. My second brother, who was now in Bombay. My younger brother was so attached to me and I to him that I always carried him on my back, as I went out in the evenings to play with my friends. Sometimes I would play cricket, at times hockey or 'gulli-danda', but mostly marbles—marbles of different sizes and hues, combinations of green and blue, and yellow, orange and brown, and the off-white of the soda water bottles. I had bagfuls of marbles that I had collected, having won them in games from my neighbours' sons, and pals in the street. They were my prized collection, for I was an ace at playing marbles. Every time I aimed at one from a given distance, it would hit the bill's eye, to the dismay of the other boys participating in the game. They were all jealous of my prowess. One day as I proudly jingled the marbles bulging out of my pockets, some of them spilled out, rolling down a slopy patch of ground. As I started chasing after them, I heard my father calling out 'Dev-aan', and there he was, turning the corner of the street towards the house. I left the marbles to their fate, drumming against one another, and quickly slipped inside, picked up my slate with sums and words of both Hindi and English written on it with chalk, and pretended to be a very studious lad. But my father was a sharp man, with a sharp eye; he had already glanced at the marbles, after almost tripping over them on his way in.

'I hear the neighbourhood gossips say you are a crack-shot at marbles!' he said.

'Of course I am,' I replied with a swagger.

'But I will be happy when you become a big shot in life!' he shot back.

'I will be. Just wait and see.' The words rushed out of my mouth.

'Not with these marbles as your only obsession!' he retorted.

'Don't you see I have been busy with my homework as well?' I was quick to answer, showing him the slate I was holding with a chalk in my right hand.

He looked at it and said, 'But it is the same as last evening's lesson—you have added nothing to it, nor erased anything off it.'

I gave him a sheepish look. Now he laughed affectionately, and giving me a few pats on the shoulder said, 'But I'm sure, being your father's son, you will be a big shot one day. Follow me now into the library for your evening lesson.' And he went straight in.

I did not want to leave the marbles all by themselves without their master, and they were soon back in the box that I always kept so well-guarded, next to my bed, at night. Counting them fondly, one by one, was my daily ritual before I closed my eyes.

They were my prized possession, a treasure I would never part with, until one day I picked up a fight with a boy while playing marbles with him. He hit me hard and I fell down on the gravel. As I got up to retaliate, my three-year-old younger brother, Goldie, eight years my junior, quickly clung to my legs, crying, scared, not letting me go after the boy, who swiftly ran away with all the marbles I had won for the day, in fact my entire booty lying in the box beside me, and disappeared into a street, along with some urchins who were waiting for him behind a cluster of houses.

'Leave me, Goldie. I want to chase the ruffians and teach them a lesson,' I pleaded with my little brother, trying to release myself from his affectionate grip.

'No—don't—don't—he is with so many others, from his own area—they'll all beat you up,' he said sobbing profusely, holding on tight to my legs, not letting me move.

'No—nobody can ever beat me. Aren't you with me? I am not alone!' I said.

He looked at me, tears rolling down his cheeks—but he calmed down, and smiled. His eyes shone, his long golden hair, with the evening sun directly falling upon them, looked absolutely mesmerizing with a particular ray enhancing the yellow gold of its colour. He seemed like an angel who had appeared straight out of a fairy tale. In fact my father had nicknamed him 'Goldilocks' from a children's book of fairy tales that he had brought for him, because of his long golden locks which were never cut for a long long time. I kissed Goldie and picked him up again on my shoulders, and as I walked back home, with him joyfully swinging along and enjoying the ride, we had both forgotten the nasty incident with that scoundrel from some slummy part of the town, and I, the marbles.

That night when I slept, there was no thought of marbles on my mind. I was at peace with myself. The chapter of marbles had been closed for good, and the next day was to be full of fresh excitements.

Five

The train raced along at terrific speed, snatching me away from the roots of my first nineteen years, unforgettable, but now dimming before the excitement of a novel newness. Yet, with every new blur of the receding landscape outside, snatches of the past came into focus before my eyes, to quickly diffuse and dissolve into others, all at random, with no continuity between them.

I saw my mother conducting the daily prayer in the courtyard of our house in Gurdaspur.. '*Om jai jagdish haré*,' she sang, with all the kids sitting around her, their hands folded.

My mother wrapping me up in heavy blankets during the severe winter, caressing me, saying, 'Time to go to sleep, my darling!' as I snuggled into the warmth of my bed. Then softly saying, 'And close your eyes as you say the Gayatri Mantra in your mind.' And, while starting to do so, I would suddenly drop off, leaving the prayer unfinished, flying off on a horse into the clouds in my dreams.

'It is time for you to have your milk,' she would shout through the window, as I was playing with my companions, out in the street.

My mother knitting a sweater in Dalhousie, sitting in front of the villa on top of a hill. The villa was owned by a Britisher, Mr Robinson, and was built on the highest point in town. My father always rented the villa during summer vacations, and the family drove up there by bus. A few passengers always vomited out of the windows of the bus as it climbed the steep heights, due to sudden vertigo. The bus would stop for a break in the middle of the journey, at a place called Bakloh, a British cantonment where English tommies roamed around in their khakis, wearing short knickers and long smart stockings and polished shoes.

My father suddenly appeared, and I saw him killing seven snakes, one after the other, as we checked into Clear Mount, the rented bungalow owned by Mr Robinson.

I saw the Englishman, old and scratching his skin—which was perpetually itchy because of some infection—laughing and telling me jokes, when he came and stayed at our house, in a room overlooking the street. He was my father's client and was fighting a legal battle with his Indian wife, a 'gaddan', meaning a hill-woman. The joke he narrated seemed innocuous to me then, but now I know it had something to do with a woman's private parts.

I saw myself walking into the Sacred Heart school in Dalhousie, with a schoolbag slung on my shoulder, stopping to look at the churchbells as they tolled. They sounded so resonant and rhythmic, with the whole valley reverberating with their music.

I was walking in the evening by the railings of 'Thandi Sadak'—the Cold Street—in Dalhousie, as the sun set in a breathtaking blaze. And then walking back by the 'Garam Sadak'—the Warm Street—as the afterglow of the sun played hide-and-seek with the fading blue sky. What a hill station Dalhousie was!

The train jerked to halt and I saw myself putting my ears against the electric pole by the side of a railway track, a couple of miles from our house in Gurdaspur, hearing the reverberating sound of an approaching train. Then the train suddenly flew past me, and the gates of the railway crossing opened behind it for the people and the held-up traffic to move across.

And that fast torrential gush of water through the bund of the Tibri, falling into the canal . . . I remember a pal of mine jumped into it from the high bridge, to show off his swimming skills! He suddenly went under in the foaming current, causing all of us to worry for several seconds, but then popped his head out with a broad victorious grin.

I saw myself, along with him and a few others, sucking honey-sweet mangoes, cooled in the icy waters of the Tibri Canal, followed by a glass of sugary-sweet lassi, made from homemade yoghurt, and soaked in pedas, a rich sweet made of creamy milk.

And that freshly made jaggery, straight from the hot oven, made of crushed sugar cane! And a cold glass of sugar cane juice, dripping from the crushing machine, blended with a mix of fresh orange juice! It used to be such an early-morning treat, immediately after dawn, as everybody shivered in their woollies, their teeth chattering in the cold-wave that had suddenly descended upon us.

My mouth watered even thinking about these things, and I saw myself buying vegetables and fruit from the market in the main bazaar, to carry them home in a bag, for my mothers' daily epicurean delights in the kitchen. On the way back home I would steal a few grapes, sweet and juicy, out of the bunch of the 'buys', and swallow them on the sly before I reached home.

The train jolted to a start again and sped along a fast bend. But I was ambling along in a jolting tonga, overloaded with luggage and packed with my younger brother and sisters, running across narrow dusty paths on the way to our village of Gharota, about twenty miles from Gurdaspur, to attend the marriage ceremony of one of my cousins. The horse clearly overburdened, yet trotting away, kicking blinding dust from its hooves on to another tonga following it!

I was sitting on the open terrace of my uncle's village haveli, in the darkness of the night, listening to a local villager's tales about the exploits of a robber in the vicinity, who would suddenly make his appearance and loot all that he could from the house, going to the extent of even murdering the inmates. I used to feel so scared then listening to the story, but I smiled now sitting in the train, at such a stupid fright, with a faraway look in my eyes.

Both my elder sisters, Kanti and Sheela, laughed as I let my memories run back and forth. Sheela, the younger of the two, was the more pampered and therefore the more aggressive, always nudging the older one out of her seat in the kitchen, as it was closer to the fire that burned in the hearth while my mother cooked and served dinner for the family during the winter. It used to be so cozy sitting by the fire. Cold weather is always welcome, more than the heat. You enjoy wearing soft warm clothes and basking out in the sun.

But it used to be so cold in Dharamsala, I reflected, the hill-station I studied in for my intermediate. And Principal W.A. Barnes! What a classy guy—a snob with his nose perpetually in the air, always clad in corduroy jackets! What a kind principal's smile he gave me when my father took me to his office on the first day, to ask him to take special care of his son's English. He instilled in me the 'propah' English, the right phonetics, pronunciation and articulation of words in the language, as also my love for the mountains and mountain climbing. And what a contrast there was between the two principals! The white Englishman Barnes, aloof and a stickler for discipline; and the brown, goatee-bearded Mr Shauq, a diminutive intellectual who always wore very smart well-stitched suits. Mr Shauq also had a crisp British accent, with an added habit of reciting Urdu couplets. Shauq replaced Barnes after there was a strike in the college against the principal. It was politically motivated, for there were hush-hush meetings under the shade of the pines around the college campus, and over the lush green valleys, against the backdrop of the gorgeous snow-capped mountains, radiating their splendour as the sun fell over them and the snow glistened.

Snow falling by the inches burying that small one-room tinny rest house, in the freezing cold of its whiteness! Our batch of students from the college had gone trekking, and got caught in a snowstorm and were forced to stay the night there. All huddled together in that small place, our bodies shivering in the sub-zero temperature, our hands locked inside folds of thin blankets, for there was no fireplace to light a fire in, as the lashing winds howled outside.

And the next morning as the sun rose against the clear blue sky, and its rays warmed our skins, I looked down from the heights of McLeodgunj at the small dotted houses looking like a miniature painting that was Kangra valley. There, one of the boys in the hostel said, lived the most beautiful girl in the hills. We had all fantasized about her the night before, as we struggled to sleep in the cold. What an innocent angelic face she must possess! And still envisioning her visage we fell off to sleep, dreaming of her in all her ravishing nakedness. She was still in our thoughts as we woke up. Now standing on that hill I tried to spot her, not knowing why, for I had neither ever met her nor ever seen and known the place she lived in, except that it was called Kangra. As I looked down at the Kangra valley now, she was the one in my imagination, representing the region. There was a trekker, holding up binoculars, standing next to me, a white foreigner, with shorts and long woollen stockings, and a Scottish tweed jacket, wearing a very distinguished-looking felt hat, with multicoloured feathers in it. He looked at me and smiled.

'Did you see what I saw through these?' he jocularly remarked.

'Your focus is sharp, while my view through my naked eyes is weak!' I smiled back.

He laughed.

'From England?' I asked.

'No.' He seemed to resent the suggestion. 'I'm Scottish!'

'Have a look!' He passed on his binoculars to me.

I looked through it down into Kangra valley; a young girl appeared from behind a house that the binos were focused on, disappeared instantly behind another, and appeared again, as fast as she had disappeared, to look up at the sun, her hair flying in the morning breeze. She looked fresh as the morning dew and pretty as a daisy. It seemed she was looking at me.

'That's the most beautiful girl from the hills that we all dreamt about!' I mumbled to myself with utmost delight.

'What?' asked the Scotsman.

'Look!' I handed the binoculars back to him. He stumbled while taking them from me, almost falling off into the deep precipice below.

The force of a gusty wind that dishevelled my hair, dislodged his hat too and it rolled off towards the deep valley, tumbling down and gliding in slow motion, dancing in the wind. It went lower and lower till I thought it must fall on the head of the girl, to entice her into looking up again at me. But it kept dancing a tango just above her head, as if serenading her, until the girl disappeared again, and the hat got stuck on the branch of a tree, its feathers separated from it, making merry, having achieved their freedom, flying in circles around it.

'Great show!' said the sporting Scotsman, laughing.

'And a frustrating one!' I said. 'For the girl never looked up.'

'There she is now!' He jumped with joy looking into the binoculars. 'She has come out and is looking up, and smiling!'

I waved at her, just for the heck of it, knowing full well I was too far away from her sight—not even a speck from her point of view. But the feeling was pleasurable and I shouted, my voice echoing through the valley, 'Come and pay me a visit in my college at Dharamsala. I'll walk down soon in time to play a game of tennis on its courts.'

I used to play tennis in college, was in its team participating in an inter-college tournament. But I was an awfully bad player. My elder brother Chetan was great at it. He had played at Wimbledon and lost. I always wanted to emulate his style, his bearing. He was waiting for me at the Bombay Central Station. But now as I thought of him, he was lying on the open terrace of our house in Gurdaspur, with just a swimming trunk on his well-shaped body, flat on his belly, sucking a sweet orange, basking in the wintry sun to tan his fair skin, having a mild verbal flirtation with a young and very pretty girl from the neighbourhood. Chetan was my parents' darling, and was at that moment in the same college where I went to years later. He was back home during the college vacations.

'Chetan, Chetan,' my mother called him from downstairs, but he was busy with his orange, and the good-looking girl standing next to him. She was fair and bosomy and pretty in her own way. But not as pretty as Usha, I thought—Usha was divine. I pictured her again as the train entered a bridge with huge steel girders and boulders on both sides of the railway track, jolting me back to my pet obsession—and then in another few quick seconds, as it jerked faster, I was pushed out of my past into a new fleeting expanse of water on both sides of the bridge. 'Sea!' somebody exclaimed.

Evidently, he was as new to the sea as I was. I had never seen it before. I suddenly felt my horizon broadening, I saw new vistas opening up before me, new resolutions emerging and speeding into my mind.

From now onwards, my movements have to be as fast as the train that's taking me to my destination, I told myself, my spirits as high as my dreams I came with. My will as strong as my desire to achieve, and my determination as deep as the ocean I am heading for.

A strange force was being lit inside me, thrusting me forward. I took a deep breath and saw the hand of my mother pushing me forward. 'Go on! Go on, my son!' she appeared to be saying. I heaved another sigh, and went back to her in my mind, snuggling close to her, almost in her lap, she giving me the warmth of a mother, sitting on the parapet of the top storey of our house. She was looking down, reflectively, at the passers-by in the street as they all stared in silence at a funeral procession at a distance.

My eyes too fell on the dead body being carried on a rickety cot, and I abruptly asked, 'Ma! What would happen to me, if one day you go away from this world, into the skies?'

'Don't be silly! Don't talk nonsense! Nothing of that sort will ever happen to me. I shall be alive for you all the time!' she answered, and hugged me affectionately, and in the folds of her sari, I felt good.

I felt very bad when my father slapped her one day, in an outburst of anger that was often evident in his dominating personality. I was not aware of the reason for his act. But my mother started crying, and I ran to her, as he moved out in a huff, and said clinging to her, in the same flow of emotion, 'When I grow up, Ma, and start earning, I will not let you stay with Father. I'll take you away from him. He slapped you so hard on the face!' I started sobbing.

'Don't cry, my son,' she said. 'This sort of thing often happens in a loving relationship between two people!' She smiled as she kissed me.

There was always a goatherd waiting for me outside in a corner of the street on which we lived, with his herd of goats, at an early hour of dawn. And I used to religiously rush to him for a pint of fresh goat's milk for my mother. She had been advised by her doctor to drink only goat's milk for she suffered from tuberculosis. She was seriously ill and in bed and was soon to be shifted to a sanatorium in the mountains for better treatment and recuperation. I was the only one there to look after her, along with my two younger sisters and a very young brother, attending to her needs. I often travelled by bus, all the way to Amritsar, the holy city of the Sikhs, about thirty miles away, along with my pal Bhagoo, in the burning June sun, to fetch medicines for her which were not available in Gurdaspur. On one such occasion, both of us were standing outside the Golden Temple, the holy shrine of the Sikhs, in front of a juice stall for a drink. We had ordered an icy cold sherbat made of almonds, our shirts dripping with sweat with the sun right above our heads. As the Sikh vendor at the stall stretched his hand out to me to offer the elixir of the moment that my parched throat so badly needed, his eyes got fixed on my forehead and he said in pure Punjabi:

'*Tere mathe de suraj heyga! Tu bahaut vadda banega!*' (You have the sun on your forehead, boy. You will be a very big man one day.)

I laughed off his statement as casually as he had made it, saying to myself, 'How could a small-town boy, a loner, from a middle-class family, with his father struggling to send him to college in Lahore, ever achieve even an iota of what this self-confessed prophet of a Sikh juice vendor predicted in a moment of sudden spontaneity?'

I mentioned the incident to my mother who was lying on her sickbed. She smiled and said, 'He is right!' And then clutching my hand, she said to my father, 'This son of mine has my blessings the most. He will be very big one day. He should always be happy and never wanting—send him to the college he wants to go to.'

I had not yet entered the portals of Lahore Government College. She was recommending my case to my financially poor father for a college that was beyond his means, besides wishing me all the heaven on this earth. I could see her blessing me even now, her hand on my head as I closed my eyes in remembrance.

I visualized her being lifted up by my eldest brother from her bed, her body reduced to a skeleton, with the disease that ate into her vitals, to be put into the car that would take her to a sanatorium. She was clinging hard to my brother, helplessly resisting, not wanting to be torn away and pushed into the vehicle, leaving her four young kids alone in the house—to their unknown fate.

She was crying, but hiding her face, for she did not want to be seen crying, but I could see she was, in spite of her effort to look controlled and not helpless. And I ran inside, hiding my face in the folds of a pillow that lay in a corner.

I was crying in the train now, as I saw a local shopkeeper in Gurdaspur, a friend and well-wisher of the family, barge into our compound, announcing to the four young kids who were living all by themselves—for my father was away to be at my mother's side—that she was no more. That she had died, in the sanatorium, and her dead body on the pyre lit into flames in the burning ghat of the dark forest. He uttered the words without any emotion, in a seeming casualness not befitting the cruel moment that sent piercing tongs into our beings.

'Oh Ma! Why did you say that you would never go away from me?' I screamed, and the four of us clung to one another and wept, and wept.

I was weeping in the train, and nature wept with me, for tears from the eyes of heaven were falling in torrents, splashing against the windowpanes that I must have closed, having noticed the initial raindrops that bore the signs of the coming monsoon onslaught.

Six

Rain was falling on the shutters of the Frontier Mail as it approached the Western Ghats, and continued to pour down with relentless fury as the train sped towards Bombay, now a few hours away. A fellow passenger who had boarded the train along with me at Lahore had become quite friendly. A mutual desire for company to shake off the tedium of loneliness, and a mounting excitement within us, anticipating our arrival in an unknown city, had brought us together. He started humming a melodious note to keep pace with the pitter-patter of the raindrops hitting the windowpanes. They rolled down the glass like so many naked female forms, writhing their bodies in a quivering dance, the lush green hills soaking themselves in the kiss of their romance.

A new chapter in my life was about to start, and as if to celebrate it, this Bengali gentleman now burst into a song of joy, written by Rabindranath Tagore, on the bounty of happiness that raindrops spread on parched human bodies and minds. He swayed as he sang, and I stood up, swaying too, leaning against the dancing figures of rain, marvelling at the composition of the great Indian poet. The downpour outside started lashing against the windows like the thunder of drumbeats, the sound of which became for me the symbol of the approaching city that was to be my home in the future.

I was standing in the doorway of the compartment as the train came to a halt at Bombay Central Station, its final destination. I looked for my brother, Chetan Bhaiji, who was to receive me at the station. He was already in Bombay on a brief visit, to spend his Doon School holidays in this creative city. We spotted each other, and as soon as I jumped out of the compartment, with a small suitcase in my hands, we were in each other's arms.

'Let's go *royally* by a Victoria. It'll be fun!' he said, beaming.

The Victoria-wallah slashed a whip and the horse jumped to a trot, swishing its tail as a signal to the bystanders to get out of its way. The Victoria rocked backwards and forwards, but I kept my head up, looking ahead and behind and sideways at the tall buildings and expensive structures passing by, that were a direct contrast to the much smaller ones in Lahore that I had left behind, and smaller ones still in Gurdaspur.

My brother was enjoying the thought of showing off the sights of this great cosmopolitan city to his younger brother, while I, with the curiosity of a child, was lapping up all that this huge city had to offer and teach me. I had always looked up to my brother. He was a model of everything I admired, handsome, intellectual, fashionable, England-returned, and now teaching in one of the most elite schools of the country, Doon School in Dehradun, that had a tradition of the best in all spheres of learning, catering to the classiest of tastes while keeping pace with the most modern developments in the western world. His appointment as a master in the school was a result of his erudite, polished, sophisticated personality. A tennis player, swimmer, a graduate of Lahore Government College who went for the Indian Civil Services examination to England, Chetan spoke fluent, flawless English and behaved in a manner that many dreamt of emulating. I often went and stayed with him in the elegantly furnished apartment allotted to him by the school. During those holidays with him, he taught me the manners of a proper Englishman. 'How do you do?' had to be answered with a 'How do you do?', not with an account of how you were doing.

Chetan taught me table manners, as he put me amongst the affluent, pick-of-the-upper-class students of Doon School, with their spick-and-span manners—breakfasting and dining on tables laid out for them by uniformed khansamas, eating with English-made cutlery that shone like silver, and with the soft hum of conversation flowing around, on Byron and Shelley and Keats, the great English poets, and the latest happenings at Lord's and at Wimbledon. He gave me his big leather boots, imported from London, as well as his woollen check-shirt, black and maroon, typically English, both of which I loved to flaunt as I joined Lahore Government College for my bachelor's degree. He was instrumental in giving me an entry into the westernized homes of the Lahore upper-crust society, then the most modern in the country, when he commissioned me to present an engagement ring on his behalf to Uma Chatterji, then his fiancé and later his wife, daughter of one of the most respected professors of philosophy in the college, and known for his intellect and oratory in English. He instilled in me a dream to be like him and, in fact, was my teacher in acting before I got my first break in the movies. He inspired a style that I made use of in my first films, though later, much later, as I became a star, and then a superstar, I outgrew it, and went far ahead of everybody else around me, to evolve a style that was hailed as unique and as entirely my own.

The horses' hooves stopped with a thud, as the Victoria driver slammed a caressing whip on its tail. We were on Walkeshwar Road on Malabar Hill, a very posh residential area of the city, with the Governor's residence right across at Land's End touching the shores of the Arabian Sea, and the 'Queen's Necklace', that semi-circular arch of Marine Drive, presenting a picture of great opulence and splendour with its glittering neon signs and lamp posts.

The flat we were going to was the residence of an old friend of my brother's from his college days, now a very high-ranking officer in the Bombay Customs. He had invited us to stay with him for a few days. It was on the third floor of a building. Every night, we would sleep on the floor on mattresses spread over tiles of marble, and every morning, musical strains from a certain Indian raga, heralding the dawn of the day, would wake us up from slumber. The melody would waft into the room with the whiffs of breeze through the transparent curtain of one of its open windows, and we could see through it, a fair figure of a sari-clad, heavily ornamented young lady, with golden bangles adorning her arms, a bright red bindi on her forehead, sindoor in the parting of her hair, sitting and strumming a tanpura, making the world around her aware of her presence.

She was, we were told by our host, the ex-secretary and now the young second wife of the most powerful film critic of the day. His was the most popular film magazine, taken seriously by the readers and the film community of the country. It carried colourful photographs of the reigning film stars of the day, stories about their lifestyles, their idiosyncrasies, their relationships—legal and illegal, marital and extramarital—along with the spicy gossip of the movie world. It was said his writings and comments could make or unmake a star, make a hit or a flop of a film. Known to be a terror and a bully, film-wallahs always sought his favours. When I was in the Quadrangle and then the New Hostel of my college in Lahore, the issue of that magazine in the very first week of every month was looked forward to by all the students, like they would look forward to their dates with their girlfriends, or to the opening of a much sought after star-studded film, and whatever the review a particular film got in its pages, irrespective of its merits or demerits, used to be taken as the gospel truth by the world of cinema-goers. It was rumoured that there was an inspirational woman behind the man who held such a sway over the film industry. She did all the thinking for him, did most of his writings, planned all the intrigues of enthroning or dethroning the stars on and off their pedestals. A woman he was head over heels in love with, who also wanted to be a star bigger than any other on the firmament.

As we stood behind the transparent curtains, fluttering sexily in the breeze, and sneaked a look at her charged with curiosity, we knew that this was the woman to whose tunes the powerful and glamorous world of Bombay danced. It was my first rub with the feel of moviedom in this Mecca of films that I had come to conquer. Here was a person who must know everybody who mattered towards the realization of my dream. So close—just the two windows between the two of us—at arm's reach, yet unapproachable, for our host did not know her, and hesitated encroaching upon her time for an introduction to a young fresher from the boondocks!

A few buildings ahead of the one we stayed in was the home of Motilal, a great star then. Raja Rao, the famed English novelist, also lived in the same building. Raja Rao was a friend of my brother's. They belonged to the same club of the intellectual elite who would often meet at the Parisian Dairy, a popular restaurant on Marine Drive, right opposite the promenade where the young and the old, the rich and the poor strolled around in the evenings, watching the sunset, or the mood of the sea waves that either longed to be receding towards the horizon, touching the vast expanse of the sea that they came from, or rushed with the fervour of jealous lovers to splash their romance over the parapet wall, on the smiling, laughing, loitering crowds of merrymakers. Parisian Dairy was the meeting point of this intellectual, artistic group, which used to congregate regularly to discuss future prospects, particularly in relation to their prospective contributions to the literary, theatrical and artistic life of this unique cosmopolitan city. They used to sit inside the café, or outside on the sidewalk, sipping tea, coffee or an alcoholic beverage, or a plain glass of cold or hot milk, which was my and my brother's favourite.

Raja Rao had lived in France, and spoke fluent French. He was immensely popular with some of the beautiful, happening female crowd that rotated with clockwork regularity from one party to another. He was a ladykiller—the very epitome of the tall, dark, handsome type from the Mills & Boon romances. He wore spotless white khadi dhoti-kurtas, very stylishly set in a Keralite fashion, with his long hair, always well-groomed and parted at the centre, falling over his shoulders. He smelt of a softly fragrant French perfume, and his spotless white handkerchief always displayed itself, sticking out of the side pocket of his kurta.

I never asked my brother how he knew Raja Rao, but I got to know him really well, and after my brother left, going back to his school in Dehradun, he offered to put me up in his small apartment until the time I made some useful contacts with the inner circle of those who could help me reach my goal, for which I had started to struggle. He knew Motilal, who was his next-door neighbour, casually, and often bumped into him, climbing up or down the flight of steps. One fine morning, Raja Rao woke me up from my sleep, as I lay as usual on the marble floor. He said he wanted me to meet Motilal as the latter came out of his apartment, all ready to go to work. I jumped at the chance.

'What brings you to Bombay from Lahore, young man?' Motilal asked me.

'The same reason that brought you here from Delhi, sir!' I was quick to answer.

'You want to be a star!' He looked me up and down.

'Like you!' I flattered him.

'Why not better than I am!' he quipped. 'Nice meeting you, keep your spirits up,' saying which he hastened down the steps that led to the street, shouting for his chauffeur to bring his convertible out of the garage. I came back to the room and peered from the window at the road, to see Motilal drive off into the skyline of Marine Drive, whistling in my mind the famous tune that he had whistled on screen in a movie of his that I had watched once in a Lahore cinema hall.

I fancied myself to be like him, a star, driving a convertible. Little did I know that many years later, after stardom kissed my feet, Motilal would be doing a character role, with me playing the main lead in the film *Asli Naqli*.

And that later, one day he would visit me in my house, wanting to know if I could help him by accepting a film that he wanted to direct. I so much wished I could, but I was burdened with my commitments, with my schedule for the whole year chalked out, and had to politely say 'No'. He accepted the 'no' sportingly.

Seven

Raja Rao's flat in Walkeshwar was twelve miles away from Khwaja Ahmed Abbas's place in Shivaji Park. Abbas was a very famous journalist. His column 'The Last Page' in the *Free Press Journal* was savoured by discerning readers, and later my association with him was a matter of great pride for me. Abbas had good contacts with some important movie folks. Raja Rao had called him to tell him that there was a young deserving aspirant trying to get into films who wanted to meet him. Abbas said, 'Send him over.' Next day I was at Samundar Tarang, his residence beside the beach. I had gone there for 'help', but I stayed on for three weeks. Abbas took a liking to me and let me stay with him until I got my first break. There was another young man, very good-looking, who often came to meet him. He was a pilot in the Royal Indian Air Force. I recognized him as Mohsin Ali, a very bright intelligent young student in my brother Chetan's tutorial group at the Doon School. I had met him there, when I had visited my brother during my vacations. Mohsin and I had become good friends then, and suddenly seeing each other again in a new city, our friendship grew. He made his visits more frequent, and both of us talked about our ambitions to each other. He said he wanted to work for the Reuters news agency, while I was hung up on movies. And all of a sudden a common interest developed between us. A young pretty Russian girl called Olga, living upstairs above Abbas's flat, seeing us together on the roadside from the balcony of her flat, would quickly stroll downstairs in the evenings, and after saying 'Hello' to both of us would amble along towards the sea. Our gaze always followed her. She would consciously look back, to cast a furtive glance at us, and then deliberately her steps would slow down. On one such occasion,

Mohsin took the lead over me, and hailed her as she approached the sea. She responded with a smile.

Mohsin looked at me and I at him. 'Let's see who gets to kiss her first,' Mohsin said naughtily.

'I think you will, for she is enamoured of your Air Force uniform,' I said.

'Don't underestimate yourself,' he retorted. 'You have such a great face!'

He followed her towards the beach, while I held myself back. Somewhere inside, I had guessed that Mohsin had previously made some advances towards her.

They were together on the beach for quite a while, while I lingered around to watch Lalita Pawar, the famous character actress, a neighbour of Abbas's in the next building, as she alighted from her car, followed and chased by a handful of street urchins, and went up to her apartment. The kids overtook her, bringing out bits of paper, empty cigarette packets and stained notebooks, for her autograph.

'I too shall be noticed and recognized one day!' I assured myself, and with that streak of optimism I picked up a pebble and threw it with great abandon at the rising waves. A young couple, looking at the sunset hand in hand, their backs towards me, turned suddenly. It was Mohsin and Olga. 'I can see you have beaten me to it!' I smiled.

He laughed and looked at her. She looked at him and laughed too.

I sauntered back into the compound of the apartment cursing my shyness that had always kept me clammed up in my shell.

First Usha. Now Olga.

I kicked the ground beneath my feet, swearing to myself: 'Learn to be bold, mister! Shyness has no place in your scheme of things.' A few dry and sunburnt leaves swept up from my boots and fell about me. I crushed them with my boots, enjoying the sadistic feeling. I decided there and then to set course for that very special day when a ray of sunshine would fall on me.

Bombay is a huge city, perhaps the largest in India, with its teeming millions constantly on the move throughout its length—by electric trains, double-deckers, buses in various stages of deterioration, taxis, trams, hand carts, and trudging on foot. Many of them are unemployed young men and women, always looking for adventures and escapades, a fling of some sort to add a few exciting moments to their otherwise dull, humdrum existence. I was one of them, without any work, at times on the borderline of starvation, seeking a glorious break in the glamorous city. My day used to start early. I would dress up, feeling smart, neat, tidy and handsome, and move out for a long day's journey full of expectation, either on top of a double-decker, or in a fast train, with no aim in particular, except that I must keep moving. For movement gave a fillip to my thinking, with humanity flying past me in all its colours and shades, its beauty and ugliness, teaching and provoking me and grabbing my attention, helping my growth.

One day I was in a suburban train, looking out of the window, totally immersed in my own thoughts. The train drew to a halt at a certain station. People scrambled out and in, and a young girl outside the window caught my fancy. In a flash, she clung on to the rail by the door, threw herself into the melee and, as my eyes eagerly panned to and fro to find out where she was, I found her jostling in the crowd, trying to find a place for herself inside the compartment, finally succeeding in squeezing herself into a seat, bang opposite mine.

'Beautiful and innocent, like a blossoming flower, ready to reach the peak of its glory,' I thought, and, turning more poetic, 'Like the sweet smell of freshness, or the flavour of a delicious chocolate!' I felt naughty inside, looking at her. She accidentally glanced at me and found my gaze fixed on her, became self-conscious and quickly turned away.

When she looked around again, I was sitting next to her. The train whistled and started moving.

I said, 'Hello!'

She looked at me, nodded bashfully, and looked away at the platform receding in the distance.

A little pause.

'Where are you going?' I began again.

She guardedly looked into my eyes this time.

'Where?' I repeated, taking the best smile out of my arsenal.

She now smiled, but looked away again.

'I am sorry if I offended you,' I found myself saying sweetly.

She turned again towards me, now a little relaxed, and asked, 'Why do you want to know?'

'I don't know,' was my spontaneous answer.

She seemed friendly now, and asked me back, 'Where are *you* going?'

'I don't know,' was my answer.

'You don't know where you are going!' she laughed, making fun of me.

'It all depends on where you are going!' My confidence was growing.

She smiled a smile that made her conquest complete—and looked away again.

'Has anybody ever told you that you are the most beautiful girl on this earth?' I tried to venture further, also convinced of every word that I spoke.

She could not resist looking back at me, blushing to the tips of her ears.

I blushed too.

'I am getting off at Churchgate station!' she told me.

'Now I too can tell you where I am going. I am going as far as Churchgate,' I said. She smiled, which conveyed a lot. Both of us looked away again.

'I thought I would alight at Marine Lines, a station ahead, and then saunter along Marine Drive . . . but now, Churchgate seems my destination.' I was Mr Courageous now.

And the train stopped at Marine Lines. She was not looking at me.

'Are you sure you don't want to walk with me down Marine Drive?' I asked.

She kept looking outside and did not reply. She was perhaps in a state of indecision whether to go along with my wild suggestion, or to rebuff me.

I laughed, making sure that she heard my laughter over the tumultuous din of alighting and departing passengers.

'I'll walk with you wherever you go from Churchgate station.' I was at my gallant best.

She was still silent.

'I mean to walk to your place—to see that you are safe and sound!' I seemed determined.

This time she looked at me. She was smiling with utmost charm and ease.

The train entered Churchgate station. There was an invasion of the crowd waiting to rush into the compartment. I held her by the arm, trying to protect her from being pushed about roughly by the impatient commuters swarming in and out of the train. She did not mind my holding her; in fact, she gave an impression that she liked the feel of my grip on her arm. I felt like Prince Charming, shielding his Cinderella from any harm that might befall her.

'How far is your house?' I asked her as we cut through the people in the rush hour of the station.

'It'll take a few minutes, more than five,' she said. I liked that. It would give me more time to spend with her.

'But my brother and his friends are going to be at the entrance of the house,' she said.

'You can introduce me to them,' I said nonchalantly.

She laughed, 'And my boyfriend, too, is going to be there, waiting for me.'

I was jolted. 'You have one?' I said. She smiled bashfully.

'Why not?' I continued, 'Every pretty girl deserves one!' As if I didn't care and could face any competition. 'And you deserve the best,' I added, looking deep into her eyes.

She seemed to agree with me.

I was on the way to my conquest, I thought.

'You won't like him,' she said.

'Why, is he not likeable?' I asked.

'He is the jealous type,' she said with a smile.

I smiled too.

'A strong muscular guy who fights anyone who comes close to me . . . See! Over there.' She pointed her finger as she stopped in her tracks. I stopped too. We both looked across the street. A few boys were standing outside a massive wooden gate, laughing amongst themselves.

'Which one is your boyfriend?' I was keen to see the guy who held an exclusive monopoly over this dainty girl I was falling for.

'Can't you make out? He stands out! The one with the most muscular biceps and triceps! His shirt sleeves pulled up.'

I looked with interest and a little jealousy at her boyfriend. His rolled-up sleeves made his muscles look prominent and strong. The front buttons of his shirt were left open to the navel. He had an extra-thin waistline, with a broad leather belt adorning it, and wore a pair of jeans clinging to his apparently strong thighs and legs, and high-heeled leather boots, presumably ready to kick any opponent who would dare touch his girlfriend. His motorbike was parked next to him, equally aggressive, ready to chase anybody who showed any signs of trying to take her away from him.

'He does seem very conspicuous,' I told her. For he was also laughing the loudest, as if proclaiming his presence to all passers-by.

And then I nodded, looking at her, 'He certainly deserves you.'

'You had better go away. I don't want him to see me with you.'

I let go her arm instantly. 'Go,' I said.

And she moved away from me, then stopped to look back and quickly whisper, 'You never asked my name!'

'Let it remain unknown for now!' I said with a smile. Blowing her a goodbye kiss, I compared myself, a skinny, frail-looking, gentle guy, always shy of baring his chest to the world, his shirt buttoned up to the neck to hide his delicate slimness, sensitive to the core, with a heart as soft as a lamb's, to the strong He-Man, the gym-going male, who she professed to be her boyfriend. I saw her running towards the group of boys, and kept looking at her for a while. She was being encircled by all of them, as if they all doted on her—and then they moved off to the left, and through the wide gate that opened for them, and disappeared behind it. Soon after, I saw her figure appear again through the slight opening in the gate, alone; giving me a tentative quiet wave, with one of the most fetching smiles I had come across in the city. I felt bigger and stronger then than that hunk of a guy, who would have easily sent me reeling across the traffic lights, yonder, with a single punch, had he known that I had dared to hold the arm of his girlfriend.

And with a confident smile of victory in my heart, I got lost again in the multitudes on Marine Drive.

Eight or nine years later, when I wore the crown of stardom on my head, a group of female fans cut through the police cordon controlling the unmanageable crowds in a hysterical frenzy to reach out to me as I came out of a premiere of a film, demanding my signature in their autograph books. The girl from Churchgate was one of them. As I signed my name in her autograph book, she thrust herself forward towards me, boldly kissed me on the cheek, jumped with joy and proclaimed, 'It's me, me! Remember?' The photographers flashed their bulbs, and my encounter with the young girl on the suburban train during my struggling days came to my mind in a flash as well.

'I am Nilofer . . . you never asked me my name then!'

'Nilofer!' I exclaimed. 'I too owe you a kiss in return!' And I kissed her in the full glare of the flashbulbs, before the cheering crowd.

'Where is your boyfriend—that muscular guy?' I asked.

'We were married, and then divorced! Will you cast me as your heroine in your next film?'

I laughed so loud that my voice was heard over the whistling, clapping mass of people even at the rear-end of Lamington Road, as shouts of 'Dev Anand', 'Long live Dev Anand' rent the air.

Eight

It seemed it would be a long wait before I could make my mark in Bombay, or even be spotted by a benefactor, a godfather. To impress people, I sang songs from the films I loved. I visited film studios, meeting important people. I knocked on doors that needed to be knocked, for some acceptance, some recognition, some breakthrough into the world I wanted to enter. I was liked by all, and was encouraged by the approving smiles on the faces of people whenever and wherever I met them, but that very special ray of sunshine that I waited for, eluded me still. I decided not to impose upon Abbas Saheb's hospitality any longer, for I realized that staying too long at the mercy of friends and well-wishers, enjoying their kind hospitality could lead to mutual dislike and contempt arising out of familiarity. I had started feeling embarrassed about my joblessness and could no longer bear the big burden of his generosity towards me.

I picked up my belongings one day, and told him I was leaving.

'Where are you going?' he asked.

'To a friend's place.'

'Where and who?'

'Only he knows where it is, and he wants me to stay with him. An old mate from my hometown.' It was a lie.

'I wish you luck,' said Abbas Saheb, encouragingly. 'Be in touch.' He got busy again with his thoughts, pouring them out for his next 'Last Page'.

I hardly had any money in my pockets. But an inner instinct told me this would not be a problem. The day was long, and my energy at its peak. To stoke my multicoloured dreams, I took a bus with the last few annas I had. I had grown fond of riding a double-decker, sitting on the upper deck, and if I could, in the front seat, right above the driver's, so that I could see, feel and inhale all that humanity on the streets had to offer towards my study of it. And being jobless, I would buy a return ticket from the starting point to the end destination, and travel back instantly to the same stop, not only enjoying the ride, but also giving vent to all my fanciful dreams along the way.

'Victoria Terminus!' shouted the conductor; I got off the bus and started walking towards Hornby Road. Suddenly, I felt a pang of hunger. I fiddled in my pockets. Maybe there was a spare coin hiding somewhere, in some fold of a pocket, to surprise me in my hour of dire need. But all the pockets were empty. There was nothing inside except for a handkerchief which, as soon as I took it out, breathed fragrance into the atmosphere. I had thrown the last few drops of Eau-de-Cologne onto it before I left Shivaji Park, emptying the bottle to be left on the table as a souvenir from me, for anybody to pick it up and look at the brand that conveyed taste and style. The fragrance invigorated me, but my hunger was on the rise. The small attaché in my hand seemed heavy. I looked at the passers-by, moving in both directions; shopkeepers on the pavements, selling their wares; a magician trying to attract my attention. A confectionary here, a fruit-seller there, all doing brisk business. My mouth watered, and money was the most urgent demand of the moment. As if from the blue, I saw a philatelist, a stamp-collecting vendor, displaying postal stamps from around the world, trying to bargain with a customer who wanted to buy some. A ray of hope, I thought, for I was carrying in my bag the most prized possession of my boyhood days, an album of stamps collected over the years, new ones and obsolete ones, all so precious, the only wealth I wanted to carry with me—besides the thirty rupees—when I had left home. This was the time to cash in on my precious property. I went and stood by the vendor, took out my album, and opened a page very boastfully to display the rare and costly items inside. He looked at it with interest, and then with a glint of greed in his eye asked me the question with a gesture of his head.

'You are selling yours! This one is on sale as well. Interested?' I asked.

'How much are you asking for it?' He snatched the album from my hands to have a close look at the extraordinary gems inside, leafing through the pages.

Hunger was gnawing inside me, and now thirst also started to overpower me. I looked at the lemonade and the orange soda next to it, lying in rows on the stall behind me. I could just pick up both the drinks, and drink them one after the other in two successive gulps, if only I had some cash to throw down on the counter they were gaping at me from!

My mind on the drinks, I told the vendor, 'I may sell a few, but not all, if you give me a good deal.'

'How much? I asked you!' he repeated.

'You tell me. But not for the entire treasure,' I replied.

'I don't buy piecemeal.'

He looked at me, and then back at my rarities.

'I am only selling out of necessity. You spell out the price, but only for a few pieces,' I insisted.

'They are not worth more than twenty rupees—the entire lot!' he said firmly.

'Twenty rupees! You must be joking!'

'Not an anna more! You can take it back.' He made as if to return my album.

'Thank you,' I said, and took the album back.

But behind me, the cold drinks were thirsting to be drunk by me. And that banana over there, in the other stall, so ripe! And tempting! Just waiting to be peeled! I had always loved that ripeness in bananas.

I looked at the stamp vendor again. Now he was feigning no interest, and took out a cigarette, deliberately looking away from me.

'Are you absolutely sure?' I could not resist asking him again.

He casually looked at me and asked, 'What about?'

'The stamps inside!' I pointed at the album.

'You won't even get what I offered you, from any other place. I am the only one who buys and sells this unknown commodity on the street like this,' he emphasized.

'They are rare!' I stood firm. He shook his head.

I started to move. He grabbed the album again from my hand, saying, 'Let me see once again—maybe there are some that can fetch a little money.' He started scanning them again.

'Five extra! Seeing your keenness,' he said, returning the album. 'Take it or leave it.'

I saw the stubbornness of a cunning businessman in him, and with the same stubbornness said, 'Ok—but only a few—not the whole album.'

He was stern—he shook his head.

'Goodbye then.' I picked up the courage to say so, against my desire, and moved away finally.

He stretched his hand towards me again, saying, 'Give it here', demanding the album. 'Thirty rupees for the entire deal. It's time for me to wind up and go home. You won't find me here another day.'

I let the album be grabbed by him. He took out thirty rupees, counting the currency notes and the annas, and thrust the money into my hands.

I turned on my heels and ordered, 'The lemonade—and that orange soda—both of them—quick—and you!' pointing at the banana-seller, 'couple of those, the ripe ones!'

I threw down the coins I had got from the stamp vendor on the counter, like one throws a tip at one's subordinates, grabbed the drinks, gulped down half the bottle of lemonade at one go, and then gobbled a banana, to come back to the drink again. I heaved a sigh of satisfaction, then had a quick afterthought of regret: 'My lifetime's fortune—gone with the wind! In a jiffy!' I grumbled to myself as I moved out on the street.

I had nowhere to go, no roof to rest my head under, in this vast city of Bombay, with its endless spaces and towering skylines.

'I shouldn't have told Abbas Saheb a lie; I could certainly have stayed at his place a little longer,' I was telling myself, standing in the middle of the road. I closed my eyes and thought of the Governor's residence at Land's End, on Malabar Hill. A huge mansion, with sprawling lawns! Surely, it could accommodate me for a few days— a deserving fellow from the most elitist college patronized by the government! Being an Englishman, he might get impressed by a man who could speak in his own crisp English accent, and carried a good-conduct certificate from Principal Dickinson—another Englishman! Who knows, they could be from the same university in England! All this was going around in my head, when a medley of horns and honking vehicles forced me to open my eyes. I found myself surrounded by taxis and buses and vehicles with their occupants swearing at me—

'Get out of the way, you scum!'

'How can you hold the traffic up—you skunk?'

'Throw him out!' There was a chorus of abuses for me, from all sides.

And in the midst of it all, a lone voice shouted, 'Dev!'

Confused and bewildered, I looked around to see where the voice had come from.

'Here! I am here! Dev—Dev!' The last was the loudest shout, as I apologetically got out of the way of the traffic, and stood looking for the voice.

'It's me, Dev! Tara!' And the voice was right behind me. I turned.

'Dev!' Tara repeated.

'Tara!' I exclaimed.

We both laughed and hugged each other—now on the sidewalk.

'What were you daydreaming about?' he asked, smilingly.

'Certainly not you—but how are you here?' I asked back.

'And you?' he asked the same question.

'Looking for a job,' I said.

'Let's find it together!' he exclaimed. He had also come to the city of dreams in search of a good job.

He and I were from the same district in the Punjab, had sat for the same examination together in school, in fact, we were distantly related in a way from our fathers' side, and were now meeting after a long time. Both of us were thrilled.

'Where are you staying here?' he asked.

'Don't know yet,' I said. 'I just picked up my bag and . . .' I stopped.

'To go where?' he asked.

'You tell me!' I sought his advice.

'I have a small room—a single. It's my brother's—he's in the Navy—I'm sharing with him,' he said.

'Where?' I egged him on.

'It's a chawl with scores of residents on the same floor. My brother comes and goes—to his duty on a ship.'

I listened silently.

'You can join us—all three of us can stay there—the more the merrier!' He meant it.

'He won't mind? Your brother?'

'You know him—he's elder to me—he'd be happy—he's very sporting,' Tara assured me.

'Of course! I've met him!' I remembered.

And the long lost pals shook hands heartily.

Nine

Krishna Niwas was a chawl occupying four or five floors opposite the KEM Hospital in Parel. Each floor had one-room tenements, each room occupied by a single family, with a common bathroom and toilets—to be shared by everyone living on the same floor. I spent a few months in that chawl with Tara and his brother. They were always kind, giving and helpful. Tara's brother would often be away on the high seas, so that the room was mostly left to Tara and myself. The only time Tara and I had to quit the place—and that too, for a matter of minutes—was when his girlfriend paid a visit for their love-making bouts.

There was an Udipi restaurant at the corner of the main street. Every evening, as Tara and I returned exhausted after our day-long futile trudging and bussing around looking for jobs, we enjoyed eating *garma-garam* idlis or masala dosas in that immensely popular and therefore always overcrowded eating joint.

The thirty rupees that I had earned courtesy my stamp album, started running out soon. Knocking at the doors of movie-employment bureaus bore no fruit, and, in a state of desperation, I was forced to offer my services as a clerk in an accountancy firm. The salary of eighty-five rupees per month was a humiliating proposition, but out of sheer necessity, to make both ends meet, I accepted the job. It kept me busy the whole day long, leaving me no time to look for something more lucrative and creative, suiting my temperament. Besides, I was miserable in accounts and did not understand its intricacies. Mathematics was never my forte. I chucked the job before I could be thrown out.

The Second World War was on. The British government had a

huge censorship department at Flora Fountain, occupying a multistoreyed building. An advertisement in the newspapers, asking for young, educated candidates well versed in the English language, came to my notice. I responded, and soon I was before an Army major for an interview. He asked me for my credentials. I mentioned my degree with honours in English from Government College, Lahore, and was instantly recruited.

Just then, my elder brother, Chetan, also resigned from his teaching job at Doon School, to seek greener pastures in the creative field of writing, acting and directing, areas towards which his heart was inclined. He, too, took a gamble, listening to the dictates of his creative conscience, and started his journey towards that goal. Though married and having a son, he landed in Bombay all by himself. Initially, he stayed with us at Krishna Niwas, having no other place to go. Now the four of us shared the small room in the chawl, probably the most crowded one in the city.

But later Chetan shifted to the very secluded environment of Pali Hill, Bandra, then a suburb of Bombay, along with his wife and young son. He rented a stylish, bohemian-looking wooden bungalow, perched on the sloping edge of a solid rock. The entrance to the bungalow was via a narrow road, climbing and meandering, winding its way to another road that led to a beautiful green meadow past a mango grove and ended in front of an Englishman's Golf Club. The bungalow was owned by a young Anglo-Indian couple, who lived on the upper storey, and being in need of money, rented out the lower two floors to Chetan. The couple had two very cute kids, a boy and a girl, and had a band in their house, with Anglo-Indian and Goan musicians, playing on the drums, dancing and singing most of the time to jazz, cha-cha-cha or tango. At that time most of the bungalows in Pali Hill belonged to Englishmen or to members of upper-class Indian society. It was a very posh neighbourhood.

My first assignment in the censor office was to censor letters, to and from Indian and British Army personnel, posted in India on Army bases, as also abroad on the war front. It was a very interesting job, for I could open and read all sorts of letters, written by officers and men of the British armed forces to their loved ones. It gave me an insight into the minds and temperament of those in 'active service', away from their homes and feeling lonely although in a crowd, living in constant fear of uncertain death. This was education for me! I was learning as I worked. Many of the letters were well-written, and they were in various languages. I was in the department which read the letters written in English and Hindi. Many of the letters were from lovelorn individuals, missing their wives, their girlfriends, fiancées or sweethearts. I was privy to their most private intimacies. We were ordered to excise only the portions that spoke of the low morale of the forces, or the ones that revealed secrets of their operations against the enemy, or mentioned the locations where they were positioned.

I was popular with my colleagues on the desk that I worked at. There were around eight or ten of us, on the same table, mostly ladies, young, educated girls in Army uniforms or in civilian clothes, selected from hundreds of aspiring candidates from all states and castes and religions. They looked very colourful. The ones in uniform oozed elan and elegance, and those who wore civilian clothes were in glamorous outfits that accentuated and enhanced their charm and appeal. I always made it a point to be there right on the dot, to cast an innocent, shy glance at them to see who looked better that day in their respective hair-dos. They all charmed me as they all worked with the precision of a disciplined, regimented group, under the hawk's eye of our immediate officers, a captain at the front table, a major at one corner, and a lieutenant-colonel at another of a very wide and expansive room. Out of the main entrance, a colonel occasionally walked in and out, twirling his whiskers, casting flirtatious looks at the lovely ladies, to make sure that everything was as he desired. The officers at times would pick on a beautiful girl and call her over. And I, too, whenever my spirits demanded, would be in a mood for a glad eye for someone that I thought looked more attractive than the others, at that particular moment, but never daring to ask for a date with her. They all knew I wanted to be a movie star, which I thought was my birthright and my ultimate ambition. And they all revelled in the thought that they knew, as I opened and read and censored some of the hottest love letters. We were all a team, outwardly working on the letters we read, but inwardly fantasizing amorously about some person or the other whom we fancied. During lunch break, some of us would go and sit together, and hobnob at a coffee-shop next door, at Kala Ghoda, discussing topics of the day, or a popular English film running in the theatres. It was the golden period of Hollywood, the era of MGM and Fox and Paramount and David Selznick and Universal, and other famous movie production houses, and of internationally famous reigning stars of the day like James Stewart, Gary Cooper, Spencer Tracy, James Cagney, Ronald Colman, Robert Donat, Clark Gable, Paul Muni, Ingrid Bergman and Greer Garson. I would try and copy some of them, speak and act in their style, and enact some of the well-known and popular scenes that the audiences had seen and enjoyed and remembered.

One day, during one of the few stolen moments away from the supervising gaze of the officers, as they left their seats to go into a faraway corner for a short coffee-break for themselves, I whisperingly asked those on my table, 'What sort of a letter is each of you reading right now?'

'A love letter!' one of the girls whispered back.

'Love!' they all repeated in chorus.

'Me too!' I said. 'And what ecstasies!' I pointed to the letter. 'And by the way, who is the most exciting lover currently on the screen?' I asked.

'Cary Grant,' somebody said.

'Clark Gable!' said another.

'Charles Boyer!' came from a third girl.

'Yes!' they all unanimously agreed in a chorus. His *Gaslight* was running in town to packed houses.

'Have you seen it?' they all asked one another. They all had, and enjoyed it. And I rattled off a few lines of Charles Boyer from the film, as he had held Ingrid Bergman in his arms, imitating his style and soft accent.

'Wow!' All the girls were very impressed, while the lone other man on the table also nodded in appreciation. I felt on top of the world at a self-indulgent thought, as I went back to reading the letter in front of me, that all the girls on my table were thinking of me romantically.

'How is it going on your table?' came the voice of our immediate officer, the captain, as he passed from behind our table to go back to his seat on the front desk.

'Never better, sir!' I replied and turned to look at him. He was eyeing the girls with total fascination, as they all smiled in their sleeves!

Ten

I was a hit with the ladies' crowd at the censor office, and I grew conscious of it. Every morning I would get up as the cock crowed, dress 'to kill' in my best casuals, groom my hair properly with an accentuated puff on the right that everybody in the office seemed to admire, give myself a final look in the mirror, and confidently walk down Pali Hill 'Naka' to stand in a long queue of people waiting for a certain faded blue-coloured single-decker bus that would take us Pali Hillers to the Bandra station. More often than not, there used to be a dusky attractive girl with sultry eyes, standing ahead of everybody in the queue. She also worked in the censor office. I had noticed her almost every day, sitting at the faraway last table touching the wall of the long sprawling office. She always carried a small silk umbrella in her hand, distinguishing herself by wearing a short skirt that showed her legs to advantage, and long black stockings that added sheen to the exquisite shape they covered. From her looks and demeanour, she appeared to be a Goan Christian.

Every time I reached the bus stop, we looked at each other. She would cast a quick glance at me, a shy half-nod or a courteous 'good morning', and look away. And as soon as the bus arrived, she would almost always be the first to jump into it to occupy the most comfortable seat, leaving me to struggle with the rest, and with a desire to know her better.

From Bandra, a train would take us all to Churchgate station in half an hour, with a single stop at Grant Road. In the train she was lost from me in the overcrowded rush. From Churchgate all of us would walk briskly to our destinations. I was in the group going towards Flora Fountain. It used to be a very well-groomed, disciplined bunch of men and women, hordes of us, walking fast and silently, looking steadfastly in the distance, like an army on the move—each person immersed in his or her thoughts, with only the activity of the day ahead of them on their minds. No conversation at all amongst us, no noise or chattering, except that of the shuffling of feet, of boots and shoes and sandals, over the concrete road, eager to get to our seats in office. Both the Goan girl and I were conscious of each other's presence in the caravan of marching people. She would casually look round at me and then quicken her step. I too would, at times, try to catch up with her, to make my presence felt. But the moment she turned to give me a look, I ended up with a weak and winsome smile, that meant to convey a lot but meant nothing to her. The same shy syndrome, standing in my way! I needed to take a bold decision for a date with her, for one enjoyable evening together. But it took time to pierce the layers and layers of inhibited shyness and ask for a private meeting. And every day we both ended up entering the precincts of our office with nothing said, losing ourselves thence to the company of others and in the work on our respective tables.

The political situation in the country was very volatile. India was demanding independence and the Englishmen ruling the country were enacting laws that suited them according to the times. The ongoing war threw up dramatic information every day about who was winning and who was losing, and how and where. Indian soldiers were fighting beside the British Army on all fronts. As we would come out of the offices after work, we would see copies of the *Evening News* and the *Free Press Journal* and all the other tabloids in the vernacular and in English selling out in seconds, as soon as they hit the stands. There was no television then, and not much radio either, except at news time. Therefore, the headlines on the front pages of newspapers, and the editorial comments inside, were devoured by the population hungry for the latest news. The nation about to be liberated from the yoke of the British Raj was on tenterhooks expecting the heavens to fall. Riots, processions, defiance of law, and satyagrahas were the order of the day, and suddenly, during the

Indian Naval mutiny of 1945 in the dockyards of the city, there was an explosion that shook the entire multistoreyed office building, along with many others in the vicinity, to the deadly shrieks and screams of people around. All the floors trembled violently, with tremors that shattered the glass doors and windowpanes into smithereens, with the sound of a deafening blast sending shivers through all working inside. People ran helter-skelter in panic, as if there was an enemy air-raid. Nobody could guess what had happened. Suddenly the uniformed army officers commanding the office were not on their seats, their chairs and tables toppled, and papers and files and letters scattered all over, mixing with the glass splinters and flying everywhere. One officer was trying to speak desperately on the phone, the wires of which did not respond. The telephone instrument of another had flown out of its hook, hitting the ceiling and smashing itself. A third officer was coolly taking out a cigarette from his pack standing in a far corner, trying to fathom the phenomenon that had sent sheets and sheets of letters, hundreds of them, pouring out of their envelopes.

I found the pretty, unknown companion of my daily journey from Pali Hill to the office, sitting quietly, cosily in her corner, cool as a cucumber, her legs caught inside the overturned table, her back against the wall, looking at me through the littered bundle of letters, clutching her umbrella. I saw something in her eyes that prompted me to say, 'Are you ok, miss?'

'Maria,' she said, 'you never asked my name.' She smiled as she conveyed her grudge. Her expression said so much. I smiled back—and kept smiling.

'Has something shaken you? Or not yet?' she asked.

'What?' I was intrigued.

'It had to be this explosion, and now, to say what I always wanted to say to you!' Maria said looking at me.

I did not fully understand.

'You are beautiful—and . . . I . . . like you!' she said in soft undertones, as I walked towards her, stepping over the crunching broken, splintered glass, holding out my hand to her.

We went to the cinema later in the evening. We held each other's hands throughout. I kissed her behind her ear, and she responded with a kiss on my cheek in the darkened auditorium of the cinema hall. My lips touched hers—as Clark Gable was kissing his leading lady in a passion that set the screen on fire.

We travelled together by train to Bandra, huddled close to each other in the bus that took us to Pali Hill. We were the last to get out, as the conductor rang the bell very loudly, calling and reminding us: 'Your destination.'

'Where do you stay here?' she asked, getting off the bus.

'On top of the hill—over there—in a beautiful wooden house. And you?'

'Behind that house at that street-corner!' she answered, pointing at a house, a little distance away, with her umbrella. The high heel of her sandals tripped over a stone. She almost fell. I held her, saying, 'May I walk you to your house?'

'No, thank you,' she answered, very sweetly. 'My boyfriend is inside, waiting,' she added, looking at me.

I relaxed my grip on her shoulder.

'I am, as you know, already late,' she said, still looking at me.

I was both amused and confused.

'Thanks to you!' her sultry eyes smiled again.

'Thank you,' I conveyed everything in those two words, and couldn't resist adding, 'See you tomorrow in the bus again.'

'I'm afraid not,' she said, moving away.

I did not like the answer.

'I am off to Goa tomorrow—we are getting married there!'

I laughed, went close to her and shook her hand and said, 'I wish you a very happy married life, Maria!'

'And I wish you a far bigger stardom than Clark Gable, Dev!' She genuinely meant it.

Then she abruptly turned and was gone. I kept looking at her receding figure, as the wave of my hand remained frozen in midair.

Then she disappeared for good behind the house she had pointed at.

Eleven

It was 1945, the war had just ended. Unemployment was everywhere. It was a period of transition, as the country recovered from the long-drawn-out war and prepared for its impending independence. The pent-up energies of creative thinkers were impatient to explode into the dramatic arts, music, theatre and cinema. Chetan's home, 41 Pali Hill, was the intellectual hub for many such people in the city, thanks to him and his wife, Uma Didi to the family. They used to encourage gatherings of people who had something to say to the world and were waiting for their breaks. The place used to be full of restless minds, sharp and high on talent, bubbling to pour forth and create new vistas. They were all without work, which gave them greater resolve to harness themselves for their future contributions to the literary and the artistic world.

I was the youngest of them all, but the richest. While most of the artists' pockets were empty, I, with my salary of one hundred and sixty-five rupees from the censor office, was a king by comparison. Though they had all their train passes, taken out for their movements about the city, I would very often come to their rescue, doling out cash to them for their small necessities, on a returnable-when-able-otherwise-forgettable basis, sometimes treating them to a meal at the famous coffee-house, which was their usual venue for brainstorming and intellectual debates. Several people in the group professed to be readying themselves to 'revolutionize' the film industry and rid it of the staleness that had set into it; they were out to restructure the repetitive pattern of things that they felt needed total overhauling. And often, late in the evening, the Pali Hill bungalow would resound with chatter and recitations of poetry and qawwali sessions, even, at times, reverberate with the soul-stirring strains of a sitar played by Pandit Ravi Shankar, or a sarod strummed by Ustad Ali Akbar Khan.

Zohra Sehgal and her younger sister Uzra Mumtaz, both popular stage actresses and working with Prithviraj Kapoor, the doyen of actors, at his Prithvi Theatres, also lived in the same premises, and often added glamour to the gathering with their starry presence, while Chetan and Balraj Sahni, who had returned from England after a stint as an announcer with the BBC's foreign service, along with his charming wife Damayanti—'Dammo' to friends—vied with each other to be the first to hit the marquee and achieve countrywide fame.

No one took me seriously. I, to them, was just a 'kid', but someone whose presence they could not ignore because of his inherent effervescence and pleasant persona. Chetan soon started his first film *Neecha Nagar* which went on to win the Golden Palm in the very first year of the Cannes Film Festival, right after the Second World War was over. Khwaja Ahmed Abbas, with his leftist leanings, was ready to start his *Dharti Ke Laal*, and though both knew about my inclinations to act, neither had a role in their films that would suit me. I did not mind, for I was always carefree and took everything in my stride, always waiting for that 'very special ray of sunshine' to fall upon me. That ray was still eluding me, and I was sure the game of hide-and-seek was taking so long because I was the best. I had only to wait for the right moment.

But my job at the censor office was bogging me down, preventing me from forging ahead towards where my destination lay. It was taking too much of my time, just sitting at a table, reading what other people had to say of their likes and dislikes. It left me no time at all to plan and meet those who I knew were waiting to be met. Destiny never comes to you. You have to reach out to your destiny. I grew very restless. During one of my introspective moods, as I was reading a letter from a high-ranking Indian Army officer to his wife, one of the lines in it struck me. The Army officer was mooning over his wife, as he wrote: 'I wish I could chuck this job right now, and rush straightaway into your arms.'

'Chuck this job'—the words gave a resolution to the fickleness of my thoughts, and pushed me into taking a decision that I was only half-considering till then.

'I am going to chuck my job to chase and woo my destiny,' I suddenly decided, and inwardly thanked the brave colonel fighting on the front for this inspiration.

I walked to my immediate officer, Captain Simeon, a handsome Anglo-Indian from Allahabad. We had become very friendly, because both of us had studied in a convent school and thanks to our English-medium college degrees, spoke fluent English with a proper accent.

'I want to leave,' I said.

'Some urgent work?' he asked.

'No. I am giving up the job!' I said.

'Don't like it any more?' he was curious.

'No—I hate to leave. It's beautiful out here!' I said, pointing at the table I worked on. 'The best of the girls are at my table.'

He laughed, looking across at them working.

'But I am stuck here,' I continued.

He reacted with an enquiring look.

'The ray of sunshine that I'm expecting to fall upon me is eluding me in this place,' I said.

He silently nodded, waiting for more.

'I want to chase it—and I cannot do that here.'

'I understand,' Captain Simeon said. 'You have often told me about it—have you got the break?'

I shook my head. 'Not yet—but I am quitting on instinct.'

He nodded, saying, 'I will not stand in your way.'

'My resignation will be on your table, sir. And it's been great working under you!' I found myself saying.

He stood up and shook my hand. 'Good luck!' he said.

I mentally saluted the captain. Then I went and stood near my seat, next to my colleagues. They all looked at me.

'Goodbye. I am leaving,' I said a little emotionally.

'No!' they all said together.

'Yes,' I said, 'I shall miss you all.'

'We shall too!' they said.

'Going to be a star?' one of them asked.

'You have always given me your good wishes,' I answered.

'Don't forget us,' another one in a khaki uniform said in a friendly tone.

Many years later, she was a receptionist in the studio where I filmed most of my pictures. I had become a star by then.

It was raining outside and I was in a railway compartment again. '*Badal dhara*!' That Bengali gentleman singing the Tagore song who had travelled with me to Bombay on the Frontier Mail, came to my mind. Where could he be? He was also coming to Bombay with the glint of a dream in his eyes. Had he achieved it?

I chuckled as the train came to a halt. Outside, on the platform, Ashok Kumar stared at me from a huge banner for his latest movie. My favourite movie star! All of us in the New Hostel, Lahore, had rushed to see him and shake hands with him when he made an appearance at the Plaza cinema, where his film *Bandhan* was celebrating its silver jubilee. He had come all the way from Bombay for the occasion. But the crowds were so enormous and the frenzy so overwhelming that we could hardly stand in a queue to buy tickets for the special show in which he was to appear on stage for a 'darshan'. It had been a frustrating experience. Ashok Kumar was inaccessible! Unapproachable! A star in the heavens that one could only see, but could not reach! And here he was on the banner, and in the same city where I was now. Surely I should be able to meet him, I thought to myself. The train moved and a man came and sat opposite me.

'I was looking for you, Dev!' he suddenly said, seeing me.

'Hello! Musurekar!' I shook his hand.

'There's great news for you, and I am glad I found you,' he said excitedly.

'What?' I asked, equally excited.

'Prabhat Film Company is looking for a young handsome man to be cast in their latest film, already on the floors. There couldn't be a better choice than you!' He looked admiringly at me as he said this.

My excitement increased.

'Go and meet the boss right away!' he said.

'But we are in a moving train. Right away—where is the boss?' I enquired.

'You have to go back to Opera House, to the Famous Pictures office, bang opposite the theatres, across the street. His name is Baburao Pai.'

My excitement was mounting. 'What sort of a man is Mr Baburao Pai? Will he agree to meet me?' I asked.

'Anybody would love to meet you—just go,' he encouraged me.

I looked at his watch. I never wore one since I could not afford one. It was six in the evening.

'Meet him tomorrow—when his office opens,' he egged me on.

'Thank you, Musurekar.' I liked him. He was an amateur singer of sorts, not holding down any particular job, always in a tie and a jacket, and carrying a black umbrella. I had met him during my lessons in vocal music from a local music teacher near the Opera House, who charged ten or fifteen rupees a month from a bunch of us for lessons given in a small room, which he called his school. Next door was a small walled structure, which people called a hall, in which a newly formed People's Theatre group used to assemble to rehearse plays. These plays were irregularly performed for the Hindi- or Urdu-theatre-loving audience.

Musurekar was often found there, and I, too, started visiting it off and on, with the hope of earning a part in some play, even a bit one. This common interest in the arts brought Musurekar and me together. He had, therefore, got to know of my great ambition to touch the stars.

I got up earlier than usual the next morning, and as the office of Famous Pictures opened, I was there, outside the door of Mr Pai. I wanted to be the first caller, lest he went away on some urgent mission, not to return at all for the whole day. The orderly outside demanded to know who I was.

'Mr Pai knows,' I said nonchalantly.

He still wore the same question on his face.

'He'll know when he sees me,' I elaborated.

'You may have to wait,' the orderly was trying to brush off my eagerness.

'How long?' I was anxious to know.

'Only the boss knows. He may not come at all. It happens for days and days.' This time, he was not looking at me.

I was disappointed and had more or less resigned myself to a long wait when, all of a sudden, he turned and gave a big 'obediently yours' salute to a short-statured, dark-skinned, bespectacled man in a dark brown suit. His well-set hair was combed sideways with a parting to the left. His gait conveyed he was the boss. He went straight towards his office, not caring to look at the person so eagerly waiting to have an audience with him. But he paused abruptly at the doorway, threw a quick glance at me, and then went in. The orderly followed him.

My moment of reckoning had arrived. The orderly came back soon and said, 'The boss will see you now.'

I rushed in. There he was, the famous owner of Prabhat Film Studios, who could with a nod of acceptance decide the fate of a twenty-one-year-old, who was waiting on the threshold of a big career. He took off his specs, gestured to me to sit down, and then asked, 'What's your name?'

'Dev Anand, sir,' I said very respectfully.

'Just Dev Anand! No surname?' he was curious.

'Anand is my surname, sir—and Dev is the first name.'

'Very short and sweet,' he mumbled to himself.

'It was longer and more complicated, for "Dharam" was added before "Dev" by my parents. They named me Dharam Dev, but seeing many problems that religious faiths create in the world, I eliminated the "Dharam" part of it from my personality, and am happy to be just "Dev" now,' I said smilingly.

He laughed heartily, looking into my eyes.

'But that does not mean I am not religious. I am. But in a moderate way. Religion is in my heart, not necessarily in temples, or mosques, or churches,' I continued.

'I like your attitude and philosophy,' he said very attentively. 'What can I do for you?'

'I am sure by now you know why I am here, sir.'

'I want you to say it, go on,' he encouraged me.

'You are looking for a young lead player in your new film, and there cannot be a better choice than me. I present myself.' I was a picture of self-confidence.

He looked deep into my eyes.

'I am ready and prepared,' I added.

He laughed again. His laughter was sharp, prolonged and aristocratic.

'But it is the director who usually makes the choice. And in this case, he is certainly the one who will,' he was emphatic.

'I'd love to go and meet him, wherever he is,' I pleaded.

He kept looking at me.

'With your kind introduction, and—your recommendation,' I was persuasive.

He smiled. 'Come tomorrow, Mr P.L. Santoshi will be here at one o'clock,' he said.

'I shall be here a few minutes earlier, sir.' I thanked him, and left.

At one o'clock sharp the next day, a roly-poly man, very short and stocky, was at the door of the Famous Pictures. The shine on his bald pate matched the shine on his shoes. As the orderly raised his arm for a salaam, I knew it was the director. He grinned broadly as he nodded, showing a small gap in his front teeth that made him look a bit like a naughty urchin. A handkerchief stuck out of the breast-pocket of the suit he was wearing. The moment he crossed us, and before I could say 'Hello' to him, he took it out, wiped his face with it and entered Mr Pai's office, placing the handkerchief carefully back in its place with a flourish. The corridor was instantly suffused with a fragrance, and I inhaled its freshness with a deep long breath, getting ready to face my test inside.

'How are you, sir, this morning?' I heard him say to his boss, Mr Pai.

'I have somebody here you may want to meet,' I heard Mr Pai say, and then the bell rang on the table.

The orderly outside stood to attention and walked in, and came out quickly to tell me, 'Saab wants you.'

Santoshi evidently took a liking to me, but he seemed in a hurry.

'Time is of the essence, you have to be in Poona, at the studios, for an audition at the earliest, for the set is held up and waiting to be shot in,' he said.

I listened, waiting to be told more.

'A young man who was doing the lead has been thrown out for

his bad behaviour and ill manners, and has to be replaced,' he continued.

'I would certainly fit in the most gentlemanly way, and make you happy,' I was about to say, when he continued, 'Are you prepared to go to Poona tomorrow?'

'Whenever you command, sir, I am at your beck and call,' I took no time in replying.

'We shall get you a ticket for the Deccan Queen. Have you travelled by it?'

Before I could answer, he hurriedly said, 'The studio's station wagon will be waiting for you at the Poona station.'

He did not let me say 'Thank you', and rushed to add, 'The studio will have all the arrangements made for your audition, and I shall personally take your test on camera, watching you minutely from behind it.'

Since I had already said 'Thank you' in my mind earlier, I just gave a prolonged 'Yes, sir' nod of acceptance and gratitude. Though I was excited, I was a little nervous now at having been asked to face a test, so clearly pronounced by Mr Santoshi.

'Where do you live in Bombay?' he enquired now.

'Pali Hill. A very peaceful and exclusive place,' I said in style.

'You speak good English. Where were you tutored?' he was keen to know.

'In the best college this side of the Suez, sir!'

They laughed. Santoshi suddenly seemed to relax, and showed the gap between his teeth again.

'Lahore Government College,' I said with pride.

They knew about the college and were impressed.

A first-class return ticket to and from Poona, by the Deccan Queen, promptly arrived at my Pali Hill residence the very next morning.

Twelve

I was new to the profession. I had never been to any school or academy for acting. If I had to learn anything about performing, I would have to be my own teacher, and use my own instinct and intelligence to figure out the 'whats' and 'whys' and 'hows' of the business.

For a creative desire to grow inside you, you do not always need a teacher. You must look deep inside yourself and draw out the passion for your chosen field. Teaching helps a little. But it ceases to be a guide after a certain stage, sometimes even becoming a hindrance. And finally you are as good or as bad as you can be. Talent goes hand in hand with presentability, which is the keyword for the world to recognize you.

I knew I had that quality, for my mirror always told me, as it lit my reflection in it every time I looked into it, with a chorus of angelic voices, 'Wow, let the world see you!'

This is no boast, nor any pampering of my ego, both of which can be terribly disastrous and self-annihilating, but a confession of my own confidence. I looked forward to my audition in Poona. My moment had arrived. Destiny had clutched my hand, and I'd make sure that it never left it. I was about to set out to face a challenge.

Victoria Terminus, that gorgeous architectural present from the British, and then the Deccan Queen, another gift from our colonial rulers that snaked and glided through the Western Ghats, embracing its favourite beau, the monsoon.

I have always associated Bombay with its rainfall. The monsoon with its various moods and idiosyncrasies, sometimes drizzling softly, sometimes lashing threateningly, at times cooling and life-giving, at others devastating like a cruel storm, drumming on roof-tops, and drubbing the flooding streets as thousands and thousands of black umbrellas opened over the heads of people running away from its fury, made a poetic picture for an inspired painter to paint.

Monsoon flirts with Bombayites, and the rains of 1943, when I had my first brush with the city, was like a never-ending affair. I enjoyed and revelled in the newness of a feeling I was encountering for the first time. It rained every day for weeks and weeks, incessantly and regularly, clouds emerging from the sky to fall into the lap of the sea in the form of rain with a thunderous roar, as the waves rose and fell, making love to the foaming sands, pebbly beaches, craggy rocks and whatever else came their way. Their passion never seemed to end, and the clear rays of the sun had to wait for a long time before they were allowed to appear on the skyline.

But now, as I travelled by the Deccan Queen through the Western Ghats, the monsoon was enhancing the majesty of the surroundings. The Queen enjoyed passing through the lush green mountainous terrain, dripping with the waters of torrential rains, carrying The Prince—that was me—with her, through tunnels and valleys, as I feasted my eyes on this new experience, admiring the great beauty of the ghats which they say are the oldest hills in India—even older than the Himalayas!

And then Poona station! And the station wagon ride to Prabhat Studios which made films the whole country loved and remembered! I would watch them on the first day of their release in the overcrowded, jam-packed cinema halls of Lahore.

I was there now. The studio was situated amidst beautiful surroundings, at the foot of a hill overlooking the small township of Khadakvasla, where years later the famous Indian Defence Academy would be built, to become the pride of the armed forces.

I was ushered into a make-up room where some of the greatest actors of their times must have sat for hours and hours putting on greasepaint, or whiskers, beards, or wigs, according to the requirements of their roles. An expert make-up man started working with his fingers on my face. I felt important.

'Good, very good,' the make-up man kept murmuring as he rubbed foundation on my face. And then, saying 'fine', looked finally at my face through the mirror, thoroughly satisfied with his handiwork.

A dress-man brought in a dhoti-kurta for me to wear. I gave the dress a thorough look and smiled. I had never worn a dhoti before. But now that I was going to be an actor, I knew I would be required to get into all sorts of garb! I liked the look of the dhoti-kurta. My father always used to wear desi clothes. For him it was a kurta-pajama with a long khadi coat worn over it, and a turban adorning his head. He was so Indian, and yet so English—for he looked up to western education which, according to him, was the best form of learning, along with the Vedas. My boyhood and youth had seen me dressed in knickers, half-pants up to the knees, and later pants and trousers. Now, for a change, I relished the idea of wearing a dhoti-kurta. The director wanted me to wear it for the lead role I was being tested for. It was that of a Hindu boy, not a Muslim or Christian. So, the dhoti-kurta was ideal, along with a small tikka on my forehead, which the make-up artist took no time in applying with an expert flick of his middle finger. This made me feel even more important. I was being anointed!

Going inside the studio, I saw that it was littered with cables of all shapes and sizes, plugged into a huge switchboard in a corner. Large lights hung from the ceiling and from the sides, along with smaller ones; they called them the Brutes and the Babies. It seemed they were all paying attention to me. A movie camera was in front of me, with its 'crew', a band of technicians around it, all gaping at me, their keenness focused on my personality. I felt I was the man of the moment. The cameraman threw a Brute at me, along with a few Babies on both sides of my face. The soft lights kissing my cheeks, my face got beautifully lit—as I saw in a mirror kept in front by the make-up man. And I knew that the 'very special ray of sunshine' I had been waiting for had finally fallen on me.

'Do you remember any lines from the play that you worked in? You said you played a part in Abbas's play called *Zubeida*,' Mr Santoshi thundered from near the camera, and then grinned as I looked at him.

'Give me a second, sir.' I closed my eyes to remember, and as I did, I also thought, 'Here's my chance! In the People's Theatre, I had never been given a big role, for they never trusted my ability, brushing me aside as a mere "bachcha", a kid. I am now going to leave them all far behind, and in a few seconds leap into the limelight the likes of which it'll take them years to reach!' I was not being inimical, I was just enjoying the thought.

I opened my eyes and said, 'I am ready, sir! Are you?'

'Ready?' the director asked the cameraman.

'Ready!' came the reply.

'Roll!' ordered the director. And I reeled off all the ten lines of the only scene given to me in *Zubeida* in one breath. The lines referred to the old, aging mare being decorated with bright red reins and colourful feathers. But I galloped like a young stallion, rattling off the lines like an automatic machine gun that fires nonstop once you pull the trigger.

'Cut!' said the director and he and the technicians around smiled with joy.

'Good! You have the confidence!' he couldn't help saying.

'Very good eyes, and a smile that conquers!' I heard the cameraman whisper into the director's ear.

The director nodded.

The cameraman whispered again, 'Take him.' I was extra attentive to what they were saying.

'But we shall have to give you a filler between your teeth,' said Santoshi. 'If it is ok by you, you can report for work.'

I ran my tongue over my teeth and confirmed the presence of two gaps on either side of my front teeth. I had never thought this would be a drawback.

'But I suppose I have to listen!' my good sense prevailed. I nodded my consent.

'When do I report for work?' I enquired.

'At the earliest. We cannot wait,' Santoshi said.

'But I have to go back home, to get my belongings,' I answered.

'How long would that take?' he persisted.

'As long as it takes!'

I shook his hand. It was a warm handshake. He held mine tight and grinned. That grin seemed to be his eternal companion and made him look very friendly, except when he would be grim and put a cigarette between his lips, nervously lighting it. At those times I could tell, after working with him, that he was having a problem with his creative thinking, or with the leading lady.

'Go upstairs before you leave.' He pressed my hand again, more warmly, quickly released the grip and walked away quickly into a corner. He had walked fast at the Famous Pictures' office as well, and I realized that walking fast was also a very prominent trait of his personality.

Upstairs, only one floor up, a typed letter was waiting for me in the studio manager's office, offering me a three-year contract at four hundred rupees a month.

'Oh boy,' I jumped at the thought. I had suddenly become rich, richer than the richest man in the world. The warm rays of the sun had certainly started to shine on me.

Back in Pali Hill, I was so excited that I ran a high fever. I took seven days to recover, during the course of which I had two urgent calls from the studio, to report immediately. I felt big and wanted. Reporting for shooting, and filming for the first time were the first steps on the long ladder I was getting ready to climb.

Thirteen

I was on a high, on my way to Poona to report to Prabhat Studios. Not by the Deccan Queen this time, but by a night train. I was all alone with a compartment all to myself, sitting like a Lord by a window. Outside a lone star twinkled in the skies, in the darkness of the night.

'Twinkle, twinkle, little star,' I called out, weaving my own starry fantasies. The star blinked at me in response, and then suddenly hid behind a dark cloud; the cloud covered up the sky, making the night look darker, and more sinister. The train came to a halt and its door was flung open. A broadly built woman, perhaps in her thirties, entered the compartment laughing naughtily, followed by a man in a suit. She was dressed in a pink sari, worn Parsi style, a large shining brooch on her blouse. They were exchanging very intimate pleasantries with each other and joking away. She looked around and then pointed to the upper berth. The man jumped up on it, and pulled her up as well, and soon, both disappeared from my sight. The train started with a jolt. The door slammed shut. As the train gained speed, I could hear the man and the woman giggling to each other overhead, soon followed by her mumbling, 'Faster . . . faster!'

I, too, was enjoying the fast speed of the train. My mind had wandered off into faraway reveries when there was a sudden burst of laughter from above. It was the man this time, saying, 'Don't tickle me! Please!'

My curiosity was aroused. They were probably making love to each other! I had never made love to a woman, except in my imagination. What was it like? To have a woman in your arms— just the two of you together? What would one be expected to do?

The train entered a station, and the man alighted from his perch and his short-lived togetherness with his lady-love, jumped off the train and waved goodbye to her. The door closed, and the train started moving again on its nocturnal journey, leaving Lonavala behind.

I looked up and found the woman smiling at me seductively. She was lying flat on her chest, her face bent downwards, and now she was saying, 'You are a very lovely young boy!'

'Thank you, ma'am,' came my natural answer, polite and courteous.

'Why don't you come up on this berth, for me to sing you a lullaby?' she teased.

'No, thank you ma'am!' I blurted out, embarrassed.

'Don't you like women?' she flirted on.

I blushed.

'I will give you the kind of pleasure that no young woman can!'

I blushed even more.

Half revealing her body, with just a transparent sari-pallu covering it, she slid backwards and lunged forward, her arms stretched towards me, cajoling, 'Come.'

I froze.

'Come! Are you not a man?'

'Of course I am!' I thought to myself.

'I am an experienced lady—come, I shall teach you,' and her hands almost touched my face as I sat still looking up at her.

'Of course,' I said to myself, 'There is so much to learn about sex!' I looked at her hands; there were diamond rings on her fingers and a gold bracelet on her wrist.

She pushed herself forward towards me again. A few loose strands of hair had fallen on her face, and her hair-clip came unclasped and fell on her bulging breasts, even as I looked. Then it fell off the berth and into my hands, as I kept looking at her breasts.

'Don't just look, feel me!' She was getting more erotic.

I was feeling curious. She had invaded my shyness. I looked at her clip in my hands.

'Give it to me!' she said.

As I stood up to give the clip back to her, she pulled me towards her, her face inches away from mine. She had now completely uncovered her femininity. I closed my eyes.

'Eyes are meant to see, not to be closed when you're in paradise!' She was lusting for me.

I opened my eyes, and she threw the soft gorgeousness of her sari over my head, closing me in from the outside world. Both of us were closeted inside that transparent curtain now, and her face was smothering mine.

'What a beautiful boy!' she was moaning to herself.

Almost involuntarily I climbed up into her berth, and found her engulfing me, caressing me, covering me with kisses.

'Come, here!' She offered me the opening to her ecstasy.

And I came.

'You young boys of today!' she gasped frustratedly. 'Did you see that man who got off at the last station? That Anglo-Indian? They are strong! What a capacity. And you . . .'

The train was grinding to a halt.

'But you will learn fast. You were strong, as I held you,' she said, fixing her hair up with the clip. Her brooch clasped back on her sari, she quickly tidied her appearance to look like she did when she first entered the compartment at Khandala, and rushed towards the door as the train drew into Kirkee.

'God bless you, my boy!' she said with a wave of her hand. 'Reach your destination safely.'

Her expensive high-heeled shoes clicked away into the darkness.

The door to the compartment closed again. And I sat there, having been taught the first lesson on the stirrings of manhood, though the lesson had remained unfinished. Now I was ready for the first ever filming of my career!

On the very first day of filming in Poona I was with one of the reigning stars, the great actress Durga Khote, who was a favourite of mine. She played my mother in the film. I was awed by her presence on the sets. It took me some time to compose myself. After our initial introduction to each other conducted by the director, I complimented her saying, 'I have carried your name right here in my heart all the time, as a fan, waiting for the day when . . .' and found I was lost for words, admiring her silently.

She broke the awkward silence, by complimenting me as well. 'Santoshi has made a marvellous choice in you,' she said, and saved me the blushes for not being able to complete my sentence. Santoshi grinned his broad grin, and the atmosphere turned friendlier and more relaxed.

Durga Khote was a source of great inspiration while working, guiding me and encouraging me whenever I fumbled, stumbled, stammered or forgot my lines. Whenever I got stuck with my expressions or dialogues, she was patient. When I gave a good shot, she applauded. I was gradually getting into my element. But the artificial fillers that had been inserted between the gaps of my teeth by the dentist made it difficult for me to deliver my lines properly. I slurred a bit and they affected the natural flow of my speech, since I was always conscious of a foreign object in my mouth. One day I took Santoshi into confidence, and he grinningly agreed that I should get rid of them. From that moment onwards, I was totally myself on screen, with all my strengths and weaknesses.

And suddenly, everyone started to feel that the weak point that had been spotted during my audition and screen test was, in fact, my forte, for it made me unique. I was happy that I had been accepted for myself.

The filming of *Hum Ek Hain* was a very rewarding period for me, both as an actor and as a person. I learnt as I worked. I kept growing every day, maturing and progressing in terms of knowledge and understanding. As an actor, having started from scratch, every time I came back at the end of the day, I would analyse my day's work in front of the camera, and try to improve upon it in my mind. As a person, my awakening as a man, who must know his power, to conquer, to charm, to dominate, came into sharp focus within myself.

I had put up in a guest house. In the same guest house stayed a young lady, only a big hall and a dining room separating our rooms. We became friendly. She was very fair in complexion, slightly plump, with round greenish-grey eyes that sparkled with a come-hither quality, and a smile that was irresistibly friendly. We met in the dining hall, conversed, and were taken with each other. I looked forward to the evenings for our dinner meetings. One night, however, as I came in, expecting to see her in the dining hall, the bearer-cum-cook said, 'Miss saab is not eating here tonight, sir.'

I was frustrated.

'She is eating in her room, and I have sent her food there, along with yours!' he continued.

I looked across to her room. The door was slightly ajar. I saw movement inside.

The bearer-cum-cook continued, 'She wants you to eat in her room tonight—she had something specially cooked for you.'

I loved the idea. 'Thank you, Kulkarni,' I told the cook.

'Good night, sir. I am closing the kitchen for the night—see you tomorrow.' He walked away.

'Good night,' I said to his back. Then I saw her peep through the opening of her door, beckoning to me, with a look and a body language that conveyed all that had to be conveyed!

She was gorgeous, voluptuous, every inch of her desirable, and kissing, kissing, kissing me again and again, like a woman passionate and possessed, holding me, caressing me, unbuttoning my shirt. I hid myself in her bosom, as she let go her apparel, undressing herself. I took hold of her breasts, kissing her pink nipples over and over again, tasting the flavour of their honey, and she bent downwards until she reached my manliness, erect and hard, and sucked its nectar. Then she lay flat on the bed, silken and slippery, her legs spread wide on its edge, revealing her inmost velvetiness, arms spread out towards me, ready to engulf me and take me deep, deep into the ocean of sighs and ecstasy of joy.

We lay motionless, our bodies intertwined, I, like a child in its mother's womb.

Man is born for that pleasure! I understood the meaning of living and existence at that moment. I grew overnight, matured suddenly, became knowledgeable. I forgot Usha and Maria and everybody else from the wide world who had ever come into my wild thoughts.

Next to us on the table lay our dinner in the trays. But it was left untouched. We were hungry only for each other.

She obsessed me. I was intoxicated with her amorous sexuality, and during the day stole moments to sneak into the nearby fields of corn and sugar cane, where she lay in wait for me away from the eyes of the world, to hug me, to drink of me, to pamper me, to assure me, again and again, that I was the greatest of them all, of all the lovers on the screen who had spread their magic on the minds of audiences the world over.

Living in Poona then was like floating in a dream, like living in a city built on rainbows, on which I stood, with the widest horizons to look at and reach out to, and beyond.

'Put on your best shirt tomorrow when you come and meet me,' she said one day, very lovingly, in the dining hall.

'Don't I wear my best shirt every day?'

'But better than the best!' she ordered.

'Why just tomorrow?'

'It's my birthday—and I am going to wear my best sari!'

'Wow! I shall give you the best present ever given to the best of sweethearts!' I wanted to kiss her, but the cook was nearby, serving on another table. 'What do you want besides me?' I whispered.

'No present. For I shan't be here,' she said.

'Where then?

'Back in the sugar cane fields! My husband is coming back,' she said in a matter-of-fact tone.

'Your husband!' I murmured, shocked.

'To spend the evening of my birthday with me,' she added.

'You are married?' I could not help asking.

'Yes. But he loves another girl—and it's just a put-on, a façade now, between us,' she said.

'I suddenly feel I am cheating him,' words rushed out of my mouth.

'What if I didn't tell you?' she said.

'You shouldn't have!' I was still hurt.

'I'd be dishonest then!'

She was right. I reclined in my seat, thinking.

'Don't think. He's going to leave me for another girl,' she tried to put me at rest. 'And as a parting gift, he insists that he spends the evening with me on my birthday, the day we got married!'

'That's sentimental rubbish,' I declared.

'A whim—which all love is!' she laughed. 'So I want to be with you, during the day.'

I looked at her. She looked so kissable, more than ever before. I asked, 'Where?'

'Where else! Our favourite spot!'

'With our best clothes?'

'With our best clothes!' she repeated.

'When?'

'Just as the sun is about to go down.'

The next day I was looking inside the cupboard for my best shirt, but it wasn't there. I called my elder sister, who was staying with me in Poona then.

'It's there, your shirt,' she pulled it out from the cupboard.

'But that's not my shirt,' I insisted.

'But this is the one the washerman brought back,' she said.

'And that was the only one that went for washing. I wonder . . . Perhaps the washerman has brought me back the wrong shirt! And I have to wear that today,' I murmured, half-cursing the washerman.

'Wear this one then, looks just as good, and seems to be your size,' she suggested.

'Not bad—looks as good!' I thought.

I entered the portals of the studio in the afternoon, with somebody else's shirt on.

A young man roughly my age and almost the same build was leaving as I entered. As we crossed each other, he stopped to say, 'Hello.'

'Hello,' I responded.

'You are the new leading man they are all talking about in the studio?' he was curious to know.

'You have recognized me!' I said with humility.

'Well, you look like one,' he flattered me.

'Thank you,' I said.

'My name is Guru Dutt; I'm assisting Mr Bedekar—I'm his assistant director,' he introduced himself.

'Hope to see more of you, Mr Guru Dutt,' I said, and we shook hands.

'Sure,' he said, and was about to move on when he stopped abruptly to look at me.

I looked back.

He was looking at the shirt I was wearing. I looked at it too, and then suddenly at the one he was wearing.

Our eyes were glued to each other's shirts. Then he raised his eyes, and said, 'I like that! It is beautiful!' pointing to the shirt I had on.

'That is beautiful, too,' I said, pointing to the shirt he was wearing.

'Where did you buy it from?' he was keen to know.

'You tell me, where did you buy that one from?' I asked too.

'I stole it, for it is so elegant,' he smiled.

'And my washerman presented mine to me!' I joked back. 'To wear it on somebody's birthday,' I said on the side.

We both laughed like we had never laughed before. We hugged each other, wearing each other's shirts, and became the greatest of pals, for all times.

As the sun was about to go down, and its orange rays fell on the corn fields, the two lovers were hiding in the shadows of the tall corns, in a world of their own. The birthday of one of them was being celebrated in style.

'You can take me wherever you want. I gift myself to you on this day.' I was madly in love as I said this.

'I shall say my final goodbye to him, and then come to you . . . he'll be at the guest house till tomorrow evening.' She was all love too.

'I shall wait. I have a special invitation from a man called Guru Dutt, to celebrate our new friendship, over a glass of beer at the Lucky restaurant,' I said as we left.

Next day when I went into the dining hall, looking for her, she was not there. I looked at her door, but it was locked. Disappointed, I sat in a corner, and then heard a car stop at the guest house entrance. She came out of it, accompanied by an affluent-looking fatso.

'Go and wait for me in my room—I shall join you soon,' I heard her tell him. Then she walked into the dining hall, looked around and spotted me. I stood up. She ran to me and held my hand, eager to say something. But instead she closed her eyes and heaved a sigh.

'Something wrong?' I sensed something was amiss.

She opened her eyes, let go my hand, and sat down holding her face in her hands while I stood still.

'You won't mind?' She raised her face, started to say something and then held herself back again.

'What about?' I asked.

'He's made up with me! And he swears he'll never ditch me ever again for another girl—and . . . and begs me not to leave him.'

I kept looking at her—frozen inside.

'What shall I do?' She stood up, facing me, looking into my eyes.

'Your conscience is your best answer,' I said, as dampness welled up in my eyes.

'And I have a child in Panchgani school. Five years old.'

'You don't meet him?' I asked her.

She heaved a sigh again and looking down, confessed, 'I do. He's missing his mother and father terribly,' she continued, her eyes closed again.

'Hello!' I tried to be my cheerful self.

She looked up. We looked at each other for a couple of seconds—and then, I picked up my courage.

'I wish you, your husband and your child the greatest happiness and future together,' I said, and kissed her hand for the final time.

She stifled a sob, and forced a smile on her lips. I moved away to the corner, and very slowly poured water into a glass from a jug. As I drank, I guessed she must have gone away.

She had, from my life.

Guru Dutt and I were on the same wavelength. He wanted to make some great films, and I wanted to be a great actor, a great star. We both had a passion for cinema. We saw masterpieces of outstanding film-makers together, both of us earnest to make our marks on the sands of time. We were inseparable. Together we tramped and cycled the streets of Poona, looking for books and magazines that excited our creativity. Together, we spent our evenings visiting restaurants, riding in tongas, walking on the main thoroughfares, sitting in cinemas, even sharing an innocent flirtation with a dancer from Bombay, brought by the studio in Poona for a song number for the film. We joked and exchanged notes on how far each of us was getting as we made our advances towards her.

Often for hours we would climb up the hill, struggling through rough patches of overgrown grass and wild jungle flowers, to watch the gold on the horizon melt into the pale yellow of twilight, our dreams dancing back and forth, getting ready to form a shape that the world would take note of one day.

While in Bombay, he would bring his camera and would go on clicking pictures with me as his model in the solitude of Pali Hill. We discussed our plans, our varied interests. We would travel by bus to go to his house in Matunga, where his very beautiful mother cooked for us, and we sat around her in the kitchen as she served hot chapattis, and narrated tales of our daily adventures to her as we ate.

In a mood for a solemn pledge, one day he clinked his glass of beer with mine and swore, 'You'll be my star, Dev, when I become a director!' And I, with equal bravado, clinked my glass with his with an even stronger force, pledging more solemnly, 'And you will be the director of the film that I produce, Guru Dutt!'

One day, as we were travelling together by train in Bombay, Guru Dutt suddenly gasped, looking at a poster on the station platform.

'That's you!' *Hum Ek Hain* was about to be released. The posters were up.

By the time I looked back, the local train had moved on, and I could only see the poster as it passed out of sight. I could not register anything of its contents.

'It'll probably be boring for you, but I'd like to get back, and see myself hanging at a railway platform, like I had seen Ashok Kumar's banner once!' I told Guru Dutt.

He agreed to indulge me. We came back in the same train without getting off, and postponed the proposed destination we were off to, to a later time.

Standing at the railway station, watching my face on a movie poster for the first time, with a few people staring at it with pleasant curiosity, was a thrilling experience. I looked at Guru Dutt—he smiled and simply said, 'Good.'

A couple of young girls who were passing by stopped, looking at the poster as well. They went forward to have a closer look.

'How does he look?' asked Guru Dutt of them.

'Very good!' they answered in the same breath.

'Would you like to meet him?' he provoked them.

'Yes!' They were keen.

'Then go and see his film!' I picked it up from there.

They looked at me, then at the poster, then back at me again, and smiled at each other, shyly mumbling something in whispers.

I turned away, took Guru Dutt's hand, and together we ran fast to catch the train which had started to move.

They kept looking, wonderstruck! And I kept waving to them from the train, and saw them waving back until they disappeared from my sight.

Time passed quickly. *Hum Ek Hain* was released, and was soon behind me. By and by I started discovering that I had been accepted by the audience. And acceptance by the people erases all of one's flaws, drawbacks and shortcomings. The ladies in the crowds thought the gaps between my teeth looked cute; I was told quite a few mooned in secret whispers: 'Kissable.' Santoshi, my director, the great grinner, also with a gap in his front teeth, was in fact the one responsible for shaping the people's verdict, for he had allowed me to throw the artificial fillers into a dustbin!

I had 'arrived' as a newcomer. I just had to keep moving ahead. In strict confidence, I thought I was utterly stupid in my first film—disastrously uncouth and absolutely immature, rattling away my lines in an incoherent fast monologue. But perhaps the world was wiser in its judgement, and that was what mattered at the time.

I started getting offers, but was extra-choosy. I did my second film called *Aage Badho* as per my contract with Prabhat Film Studios, this time opposite a famous actress named Khursheed. She was a big star of her days. When I was in college in Lahore, she and the great K.L. Saigal created a musical sensation, appearing together in *Tansen*. The hostel I was staying in reverberated with songs sung by both of them in that extraordinary hit. When I starred with her in Poona, K.L. Saigal was already dead, but Khursheed was still a star and a rage.

Fourteen

The theme of *Hum Ek Hain* was based on Hindu–Muslim unity, Santoshi's clarion call of the day. But the irony was that the unity of the country was being destroyed by a communal virus, inflamed by fundamentalist lobbies that only wanted division, even if it meant igniting and unleashing a terror of hatred that made demons of human beings, made them kill each other like animals.

Jinnah talked of a separate Muslim state called Pakistan, which, at that moment, we all thought was a big joke. For how could you take a family out of its household, make an enemy out of a neighbour, by suddenly declaring separate identities for each community in a huge multi-racial, multi-religious country like India, where we were used to living together harmoniously? But Jinnah's genius succeeded in forming it. And our Indian leaders, in a hurry to achieve 'freedom', accepted the formula of partition, rather than waiting a little longer for a better solution. It never came into their heads, perhaps, that English domination was going to end in any case, because its time had come. They would have to 'Quit India' with the least resistance, for they would have no longer been able to hold on to their colony, which was resisting them at every step with its strong moral fibre and resolute determination, when their own country was crumbling. The Second World War had created havoc in Britain, devastating the land and paralyzing the morale of the British people. It had mauled them, reduced them from being a world power to playing second fiddle to the USA, which emerged the strongest after the War. The Britishers' homes were in shambles, bombarded, broken, reduced to scattered bricks and rubble. Their nation at the end of war was on the verge of starvation, with no eggs for breakfast and no proper meals for sustenance. There was not enough petrol for their vehicles, or fuel for their mills and their factories, only barren chimneys through which fumes of soot had ceased to emanate. Everything was rationed, and the sun that never used to set on the British Empire now started to hide behind dark clouds that forebode and foresaw their doom as a strong nation.

The Indian leadership, if it had the vision and the foresight to see what the sun in the heavens was seeing, would have resisted the temptation of the settlement it made with a declining power. But haste and hurry was in the veins of our overzealous and overambitious leaders, quick to grab seats of power. They succumbed to the guiles of the British, who would rather see India partitioned and divided before they left. For, the subcontinent of India united would have been too powerful for the disintegrated West. The mere thought of it was not easy for them to digest. So they were happy and content with the formula they doled out to the Indian leadership, which in turn became a willing party to a sad arrangement that resulted in the greatest exodus the world has ever seen in the history of mankind.

The country was carved up, as if by a sharp knife, into three pieces, West Pakistan, East Pakistan, and the rest of what used to be India sandwiched in between and dangling out to the east, mourning the loss of its dear, departed ones who had suddenly become threatening neighbours it had to guard itself against.

Hundreds of thousands of people were slaughtered as human hatred was let loose by the slogans of bigoted fundamentalists on either side of the borders. Man killed man. Trainloads of dead bodies, killed and massacred with guns and rifles, their throats slit with knives and bayonets, would land on the Indian side of the border almost daily, and a similar caravan of equally horrifying baggage would arrive on the Pakistan side of the border, as the tricolour of the Indian flag and the newly invented moon and crescent of the Pakistani flag fluttered merrily, teasing each other, the winds of revenge blowing ominously over them. Even the prayers and fasts of the saint on the Indian side, who had earlier vowed that the partition of the sacred land called India could only take place over his dead body, could not hold back the *tamasha* of evil.

Freedom, that most sought after right of man, desired by man from man, from one of his own species, had ultimately arrived in India. Thousands cheered as our first prime minister, Pandit Jawaharlal Nehru, received the greetings and applause of his people standing in an open jeep alongside the giver of freedom, Lord Mountbatten. Both looked very dignified and handsome, garlands of flowers around their necks, Panditji wearing his Gandhi cap, his immaculate sherwani and churidar, and the viceroy in his bowler hat and a very commanding outfit, as all of humanity showered petals on their motorcade in Bombay, chanting 'Pandit Mountbatten ki jai'.

Panditji was being sidelined in the chant as the ex-chief commander of the allied armed forces in South East Asia was being hailed. There was an irony in all this, for Panditji was the beloved leader, the sweetheart of the nation! And the red rose in his button hole was the flower of his destiny.

I was in the crowd too, holding the new flag of our nation and waving vociferously along with the rest, as their jeep went past.

I did not know then, that one day, years later, I would be sitting next to Lord Mountbatten, at a dinner reception hosted in his honour by Madame Vijayalakshmi Pandit, the then Governor at the Raj Bhavan, Bombay.

I travelled by the local train in the small hours of 15 August 1947, after having heard the very historic and inspiring 'tryst with destiny' speech of Panditji, a masterpiece both in its content and its mastery of the English language, delivered in an impeccable crisp accent by the prime minister as his first official address to the nation, at the stroke of midnight, when India awoke to freedom.

I toasted the new Indian dawn, downing a glass of beer, cheering along with the crowds around me at the Ritz Hotel, and got up with the same spirit to catch the gloriously illuminated train starting from Churchgate station. The train was dressed in colourful lights, in saffron, white and green, from top to bottom and from end to end, symbolizing the bright beginning of a newly born independent country, eager to march into the comity of nations that had their spirits freed from all shackles of slavery and subjugation. The train lit the faces of people, already lit with delirious joy, their thought filled with patriotic fervour, '*Jana-Gana-Mana*,' the new national anthem, and '*Vande Mataram*', the pre-Independence one, combining with each other to give Iqbal's '*Saare jahan se achcha*' a new meaning. Yesterdays had dissolved into the Now, and the nation was ready to move ahead on the newly built rails.

I reminisced, as I sat amongst the madly joyous crowds in the illuminated train, transported in my thoughts to the Frontier Mail that had first brought me to the metropolis. I could not have believed at that time that the 'Frontier' which the train had derived its name from, would no longer be India's frontier in a few years' time. That Peshawar, the frontier town the train started from, and Lahore, the city from where I boarded the train, and where I spent the most impressionable and memorable part of my youth, were to become alien cities in Indian geography books. And that the peaceful town of Gurdaspur where I was born and brought up, would become a border town between the two countries, India and Pakistan, who from now on would constantly be training their guns at each other.

Fifteen

A woman plays a great part in moulding and shaping a man into who he ultimately becomes. It starts with his mother, who carries him in her womb for nine months, and influences him profoundly as a baby, with all that she does and thinks. The child comes into the world crying; as she mothers him, that mothering becomes his confidence, his strength, and helps him. Again, as adolescence turns into adulthood, it is a woman who plays a major part in his life, in awakening his desires as a male. He looks up to her, and he looks forward to all his wild fantasies coming true—and this is what spurs him on.

'If you have a good wife, you have heaven under your hat,' goes a saying. I would go a step further, and say, 'If you have a strong, yet gentle woman beside you, to support you, to influence and balance your thinking, you have the makings of a conqueror.'

One such woman crossed my path at this very crucial stage of my life and career. I began to see in her my mother, my sister, my beloved, my wife, for she was my inspiration. I started looking up to her, and she radiated all that an ambitious young man, looking for unlimited horizons and undiscovered pastures, wants to find in a woman. Petite, charming and very pretty, she exuded sex-appeal of a very endearing nature. She had gradually come closer to my heart, and now I found her irresistible. I fell for her, before she fell for me. Together, we went to the movies, travelled by train, hired hotel rooms to spend time together, and lay together for hours and hours, cut off from the world, amidst the growth of weeds in the wilderness, in the stillness of the night, with only the moon and the stars above us, and our dreams inside. She put me on a pedestal from where she made me look at myself as the most handsome man of the day, imbued with a talent that would flower out in all directions. I started believing her, and in myself, and when I think back, it was very important for me to believe. For, after all, what is stronger than one's belief? Belief in oneself is what winners and victors are made of. And then who defines handsomeness? How does one tell who is the most handsome? It is all in your perception—in how you look at a man.

She had a great intellect, and influenced by her, I swam in a current that was both energizing and intellectually stimulating. I have never written love letters to anyone like I wrote to her. When she was away, every third day a blue envelope would reach me by post, and most of my time was spent reading it, or looking forward to another one, or planning what to write back in reply. The eloquence and language that I poured into my confessions on paper matched the best of literary writers, I thought. My creative strength grew with my imagination and my dreams started touching the sky. I was flying high in my mind, feeling very rich, though I was still travelling by train in real life, with a monthly pass in my pocket. Buying a car was a distant dream.

One day as I was boarding the train, a voice called to me from inside a compartment. I stopped to look. It was Shahid Lateef, an Urdu writer and later a film director. I had met him at Abbas's place during the days of my ramblings in the city. His wife, the renowned Urdu writer Ismat Chughtai, was sitting next to him. He asked me what I was doing.

'Getting into the train,' I said.

'I mean workwise,' he smiled.

'Movies, as you know—but . . .'

He cut me short. 'Come to the Bombay Talkies studio tomorrow.'

'Anything up there?' I was inquisitive.

'Just come!' he repeated.

I looked at Ismat aapa.

'Yes!' she encouraged me.

I could see that they had made up their minds about something, as they saw me on the platform.

'What time?' I asked.

'Any time after eleven in the morning.'

Bombay Talkies was in Malad, a suburb of Bombay. One had to get off at the Malad station, then take a tonga that would trot along to the main gate of the studio that had produced some of the biggest and the most popular hits of that era, with Ashok Kumar, then the reigning star of the country, starring in almost all of them.

A little after eleven, I was inside the gates of Bombay Talkies for the first time. The magic of the banner had always mesmerized my consciousness, and now I was standing right there, looking around at every nook and corner. Shahid saheb took me to the canteen of the studio for a cup of tea, then telephoned somebody from there, and asked, 'Shall I send him in?'

I wondered, who could be this very important person, as was evident from his respectful and awestruck attitude, that he was sending me to?

'Who is it?' I asked him in confidence.

'Just go into the room and you'll know!' He took me to the main door. It looked like the office of the boss of the place. Shahid saheb waited outside.

I entered the anteroom, and then knocked.

'Come in!' came a familiar voice.

And I found myself face-to-face with my idol—Ashok Kumar!

I had missed shaking hands with him in Lahore, when he had come for his jubilee celebrations, and now there was just the two of us, in the same room! He looking very authoritative, with his trademark cigarette in his hand, smiling his usual broad smile in the form of a 'Hello'. I felt shy, quite overwhelmed by his personality, very respectful and excited standing in front of him. We paused to look at each other, then he signalled to me, with a typical Ashok Kumar gesture, to sit down, and drew on his cigarette.

'I hate to call you sir, for I know you so well from your movies, sir.'

The word 'sir' slipped out of my lips, out of sheer reverence for him, in spite of the fact that Ashok Kumar to me was someone to adore and befriend, not just a star to be held in awe and looked at from a distance.

He exhaled smoke in a fashion typically his, laughed, and said, 'You don't have to "sir" me!' and laughed again. There was such friendliness in his laughter. It was exactly like I had seen him on the screen, and I laughed too.

'Doing my film?' he asked me.

I was bowled over, and looked at him in amazement.

'How many films have you done?' he asked.

I kept looking at him with the same charmed expression.

'Would you like to do a Bombay Talkies film?' he repeated.

'I cannot imagine you asking me.' I was still amazed.

'Why?' He put the cigarette again to his lips.

'For . . .' I fell short of words.

He puffed out smoke and smilingly said, 'Can't I ask you to do a film for me?'

'Is that,' I laughed and repeated, 'is that why you asked me to come?'

'That's why you are here!' Shahid saheb completed the sentence, suddenly emerging behind me.

I looked at him. 'And I am directing it!' he continued. 'And you are sitting in the room, right in front of the producer!'

I turned towards Ashok Kumar. 'For his approval,' Shahid saheb finished the thought.

Ashok Kumar, amused, stubbed out the cigarette in the ashtray, and looked at Shahid, saying, 'I am asking for *his* approval!' He looked back at me, and laughed again.

'Now you are making fun of me, Dadamoni,' I said. I had heard that people called him thus with respect, and I called him the same.

He took another cigarette out of the pack and asked, 'Do you smoke?'

'Not yet,' I replied.

He laughed again and asked, 'How much would you like to be paid for the film?' and lit the cigarette.

'Don't embarrass me, Dadamoni. You just make a good actor out of me. That is the price I want to charge for the film,' I said in all humility.

Ashok Kumar puffed out smoke, very happy with me.

'The letter of arrangement is ready—everything's in it,' said Shahid. 'He just has to sign it.'

With a look of gratitude in my eyes for having cast me in *Ziddi*, my first big film, to play the central role of the novel written by Ismat Chughtai, I now shook hands with Ashok Kumar, my new mentor. Then I strolled around the studio which was now to be my temple of learning, where I would share the limelight with some of the 'greats' of that era: Kamini Kaushal, my leading lady in *Ziddi*, the very beautiful Meena Kumari who played my sweetheart in *Tamasha* and later in *Baadbaan*, film directors Phani Mazumdar, the most gentlemanly of them all and in whom I confided the most, and Amiya Chakrabarty, the hit-maker in whose *Patita* I starred with Usha Kiron.

As I got out of the studio compound, stuffing the contract into my pocket, Nasir Khan was walking in. We were great friends. He was also an actor, having got his first break with Filmistan, before I got mine at Prabhat in Poona.

'What are you doing here in Bombay Talkies, Dev?' he asked, surprised.

'I just signed a film with the studio,' I said very excitedly.

'Which one?' He seemed a bit perturbed.

'*Ziddi*,' I said.

His face fell, but he covered up by saying, 'I am so happy for you. It is a great part!'

'And what brings you here?' I enquired.

'Just came to congratulate you!' He was hiding his embarrassment with a forced smile, and shook my hand complimenting me.

I got to know later that Nasir Khan was also in the running for the same role, and had come to meet both Shahid Lateef and Ashok Kumar, when he bumped into me instead.

Nasir Khan and I had known each other much before both of us got our respective breaks in movies. I had met him standing in the queue for the Pali Hill bus that would take us both to Bandra station in the same fashion that I had met Maria. He always wore a good-looking felt hat that suited his face, and a very well-starched full-sleeved shirt. He always stood quietly in the line of passengers, looking at me—and when I looked at him, he would look away. This happened so many times that I felt like breaking the ice one day and asked, 'Where do you stay?'

'Here,' he said. 'And you?'

'Here!' I said.

'I am the oldest Pali-Hiller,' he said with pride.

'It shows in your confidence, the way you stand, waiting for the bus,' I told him.

He smiled a boyish smile.

'This suits you,' I said, pointing at his hat.

'Thank you!'

'I thought you were a foreigner, you are so fair!' I complimented him.

'I am a Pathan, and a Punjabi,' he said with pride again.

'Me too—a Punjabi—though not a Pathan,' I said and laughed. He laughed with me, and we became good friends. Our friendship lasted for many years until he married a Pakistani girl and disappeared to Pakistan.

His father was a fruit merchant at Crawford market, and from Peshawar, which explained his very healthy looks and physical bearing. Both of us struggled together for a place in the sun. Both of us had dreams in our eyes for the world to recognize us. Almost every evening, we sat by the seashore, behind Pali Hill, looking at the rocks being hit by waves and the waves in turn being overrun by the sea. And after the sun went down and the stars shone in the sky, we would climb up the winding path leading to our homes. One day, outside his home, he introduced me to his elder brother, who stood there looking very striking in a white shirt and white pants. He was doing his first film for Bombay Talkies at the time. His name was Yusuf Khan. The world knows him better as Dilip Kumar, the biggest and the most charismatic star of the Indian screen.

Sixteen

*Z*iddi was a milestone in my career, since it was the first film that brought me into the limelight as an actor to reckon with. It brought me very close to Ashok Kumar and his youngest brother, Kishore Kumar, who had just arrived from his hometown Khandwa clad in his kurta-pajamas, with a phenomenal singing voice that years later was going to hypnotize the world with its resonance. The very first song of his career was sung by me on screen in *Ziddi*; it was a ghazal composed by a renowned poet, Prem Dhawan:

Marne ki duayen kyun mangoon
Jeene ki tamanna kaun kare
Yeh duniya ho yaa woh duniya
Ab kwahish-e-duniya kaun kare.

Why should I wish to die
And who wishes to live
Whether it's this world, or whether it's that
What is left in worlds to desire.

The song became a hit, and people started associating Kishore's voice with mine, and his playback singing with my acting on screen. We complemented each other. He always sang my songs with an eye on how I would perform them, and gave the necessary nuances to his voice with my acting style in mind. His famous yodelling, which he pioneered in Indian films, was encouraged by me; it sounded like the cry of a solitary voice in the loneliness of the hills, a call for romance. After he became a star–actor, and the artist in him grew in great measure, Kishore never sang for anybody except for me, barring a few exceptions. Whenever I needed him to sing for me, he was ready to play Dev Anand in front of the microphones in the recording studios. He always asked me in what particular way I wanted to perform the song on the screen, so that he could modulate and style his singing accordingly. And I would always say, 'Do it with all the pep you want, and I shall follow your way.' There was that kind of rapport between the two of us.

He was a great funster, though this was not apparent to the outside world. Since we were both childlike, we made jolly good friends. He often confided in me, like a child in his elder brother. Before he got married to his first wife, he asked me if marriage was a good idea. I told him, 'If you like the idea, and are in a mood for it, it is the best thing in the world.'

But Kishore remained an enigma to me, a very loveable enigma. A great singer who never learnt singing professionally from a master, a great comic actor who never went to a training school, a reasonably good director who conceived and directed his own movies, having never been an assistant to any director. And finally, one day, without giving any warning, he was gone, suddenly.

He was recording what was to be the last song of his life for me, in one of my films called *Sachche Ka Bol-Bala*, when he called me into the recording booth and said, 'Dev bhai, I'm going abroad for my last concert. This time it is my wish that you too come along, to make an introductory speech to the audience. It is everybody's wish in America.'

'I would love to do it for a darling like you, Kishore. Do let me know when,' I responded. But the darling changed his mind and left us all, leaving me stunned along with the rest of the world.

I stood by his dead body in his bedroom all alone, closed my eyes and silently sang all the songs he had sung for me, in a deep moment of sorrow. Then I rushed back to my car outside, and cried and cried, crying all the way back home.

In the words of the song Kishore had sung for me in the film *Munimji*:

Jeevan ke safar mein rahi
Milte hain bichhadh jaane ko
Aur de jatein hain yadein
Tanhai mein tadpa ne ko.

Travellers on the road of life
Meet only to part
And parting leave behind memories
To torment the lonely times.

Seventeen

The filming of *Ziddi* also brought me close to Dilip Kumar. Sitting next to each other on the local trains, boarding them from the same station on our way to the studios to report for work, was almost a daily routine. He would get off at Goregaon, heading for Filmistan where he was filming *Shaheed*, while I proceeded along to Malad. The daily discussions of common interest, and the recounting of funny happenings that are always prone to take place whenever and wherever groups with varied temperaments work together, especially on a film set, laid the foundations of a mutual trust and an emotional relationship between the two of us. During that period, I was also offered and accepted my first film with Suraiya, who was then at her peak. I bought my first car from the first installment of the remuneration I earned from Pratap Rana, the producer of the film. It was a Hillman Minx. Rana had also taught me how to drive earlier. And he was the one who drove the car out of the Dadajee Dhackjee showroom at Chowpatty, with me sitting next to him, learning about the mechanism, its gears and various gadgets.

As the Hillman reached the road outside, he made me sit at the wheel. And I raced it, jerking forward as it lurched, making quick left-right, right-left turns, narrowly avoiding banging into a moving truck, then zig-zagging again, missing a paan-shop by a whisker, cutting through a bunch of stragglers who were gaping at my rashness, hurriedly crossing a red light at a traffic signal, the policeman on duty blowing his whistle hard, trying to stop me, but the car vrooming on and on, my foot on the accelerator, as I threw a quick, sneaky look behind me at the fast-receding image of the policeman still blowing on his whistle furiously, the sound drowned out by the din of my car horn. I could vaguely see the policeman trying to put on his specs to note the number of my car, before he completely vanished from my sight in the thick crowds of the busy street, and I disappeared into a turning. By now, I had got the hang of it. There could not have been a better rehearsal for me than the moments that had just gone by, and I suddenly discovered that I had mastered the functioning of my car, and was driving confidently and laughing. Pratap Rana was laughing as well, though he must have been scared that his head would be smashed to bits any minute. He threw me a 'Shabaash!', and patted me on the back.

I dropped him on the way and sped straight off towards Khandala, enjoying my newly acquired machine and its great racing capacity. I now knew how to handle it to its advantage. Soon I reached the main highway. Though there wasn't a highway around that would allow the speed I wanted to go at, with cows and buffaloes, bullock-carts, street urchins and villagers carrying burdens on their heads obstructing the tempo, I was humming with a new joy that kept pace with the buzzing of the racing Minx on the bumpy roads. The vehicular traffic passed by in fast motion, as birds flew overhead flapping their wings, applauding the spirit of the man who was at one with his machine.

I was unstoppable. I didn't even stop at Khapoli, where drivers almost always take a break for a cup of tea or coffee and the famous dahi-vadas before they start the climb on to Khandala. My car would only rest at the hotel in Khandala. It climbed the ghats with the ease of a flying machine, waving to the receding townships down below, and to the city of Bombay, left far behind. I stopped finally with a big jolting jerk in the vast compound of the hotel. The sun was still hot and bright in the sky. I opened the door, got out and looked up, searching for that special ray that had thrown its shine on me—but all I could see was a ball of blinding light. I leaned against the car, closed my eyes and saw the ray come to me suddenly in a single flash, accompanied by the chorus from a symphony that said: 'Keep moving forward, your past has gone into oblivion, your present dominates you, and the future is your horizon.' I bucked up, and as if out of the blue the face of that Sikh sherbat vendor outside the Golden Temple who had discovered the sun on my forehead came to mind. I opened my eyes and thought, 'If he gives up his juice-shop to settle down as a clairvoyant or an astrologer, there is no reason why he shouldn't make millions!'

I hired a driver, an equal car enthusiast. With him next to me, I drove into the compound of Bombay Talkies. Luckily, the main gate was wide open, as if waiting for me, and I didn't have to slacken the speed of my new acquisition. Looking ahead, I saw Dadamoni's car parked in a corner. I headed straight towards it, to park mine at its side. The studio staff was moving around and I blew the horn loudly to make sure that people noticed who the new car belonged to.

Everyone exclaimed, 'Dev, you have bought a car!'

I honked two more times to say, 'Yes, yes,' and came out laughing. 'And I am already in make-up, ready to walk straight on to the sets,' I declared.

'But the studio is closed today,' they said.

'Why?'

'Don't you know, Gandhiji has been assassinated!'

A sudden pall of darkness fell upon me and I could hear

Ishwar Allah tero naam
Sab ko sanmati de bhagwan

Gandhiji's famous prayer sung in that divine melody being chanted all around. The moment took me back to my early days in Bombay, when as a part of the multitude, I saw Gandhiji from a distance. I was standing on the sands of Juhu Beach. Gandhiji was conducting his evening prayers sitting on a wooden platform, with his flock surrounding him, as the sea beyond framed by the gold of the sunset became a part of the inspiration that he was for his countrymen. Now his dead body lay on a similar wooden platform, riddled with bullets, draped in bloodstained white khadi sheets, his spectacles and watch by his side, the tri-colour hung down in sorrow, the nation plunged into darkness, mourning their Mahatma.

The 'naked fakir', as Winston Churchill had derisively called him, was loved by millions of his countrymen, revered and worshipped. He would walk clad in just a khadi dhoti with a lathi in his hand amongst the masses, with his childlike smile and a face so benign that it struck a chord with the most innocent, yet radiated the confidence of a sage out to redeem his poor yet magnificent country from the bonds of slavery and domination. Nobody had ever dared to lift a hand on him, but, a few hours earlier, as he was at his evening prayers, asking the people to chant with him, one of them, with violence and hatred writ large on his face, aimed his revolver at him at point-blank range and shot three bullets at him. The heart-rending report of the bullets hung in the air, blending with Gandhiji's dying words, 'Hey Ram', and then the apostle of non-violence and peace fell to the ground in eternal sleep.

Gandhiji's dying a violent death at the hands of an assassin in a country where non-violence was the first code of social and political conduct was a riddle that could not be answered. It did not happen to him before the country achieved Independence, but only after it was free. What was the evil lurking in our land now? And why? These were the questions on everybody's lips. Whether they asked them openly, or silently in their minds, they made the atmosphere foreboding.

Dark clouds overshadowing the golden rays of freedom, dimming their shine!

Eighteen

Suraiya was a huge star, while I was new to the industry, on the lower periphery of stardom, when I was cast opposite her. She was the reigning singing film actress, because her rival Noorjehan, her senior, had opted to settle in Pakistan after Partition, and had become a rage there.

Songs sung by Suraiya sent the audiences into waves of hysteria. They also went crazy when her American Buick or Lincoln passed the streets in their midst.

I was nervous the day I was to face the camera for the first time with her as my co-star. I was moving my fingers at random on the keys of a piano that I had to play in the shot, just to get a feel of it, before she appeared on the sets for shooting. Everybody had remarked earlier that Suraiya hardly needed any rehearsals, and I did not want to cut a sorry figure while performing with her.

When Suraiya arrived, everybody stood up. All the attention was diverted from the spotlight of the arc-lamps in the area of filming, for which lighting was being arranged, to her entry into the studio. I could sense the aura she created around her. I glanced at her from where I was sitting, on the piano stool. She had quite a retinue accompanying her: her make-up man and maid, feeling very important; her granny, entering majestically, smoking a cigarette held between her third and little finger; and, as I was told, her uncle, carrying his tin of expensive cigarettes and two thermos bottles, one carrying juice, freshly squeezed from fruits, containing all the vitamins to sustain the 'baby' of the family for the entire day, and the other containing steaming hot flavoured tea of the best brand to energize her whenever she needed.

Suraiya giggled as the filming crew surrounded her for a welcome. Far above us some of the lighting men were enjoying the spectacle as they sat on top of the set, on wooden railings and planks, handling the big lights, their legs dangling. I saw one of them lighting a beedi on the quiet, as he looked at the heroine from an awkward angle.

'You must meet our new hero, Suraiyaji,' I heard the director say to her, pointing towards me. Her eyes turned towards me. I rotated the piano stool and stood up as she reached me, and before the director could say anything, I took the initiative.

'Everybody calls me Dev here. What would you like to call me?' I said smartly.

'Dev,' she answered with a giggle. Both of us relaxed.

'You are going to be singing a song,' I reminded her.

'While you play the piano,' she completed the sentence for me.

'And I don't know how to play it, I was just trying to get familiar with it,' I confessed, and tinkled on it with a single finger. She finished the note with a quick flourish of her fingers, with great expertise, and giggled again, looking at me, adding, 'You see! It's so easy!'

'Now I know it will be very easy to work with you!' I said.

She giggled again. I looked into her eyes, and smiled a deliberate smile, my charming best.

'What are you looking at?' she was keen to know.

'Something in you!' I said.

'What in me?' Her curiosity grew.

'I'll tell you later.' This could have gone on for some time, but the director intervened.

'Suraiyaji! You have to walk into the frame from that side. As the camera follows you, put your arms around him, as you sing and he plays. Then ruffle his hair.'

She looked at the puff of my hair and giggled again, and said, 'I'm ready—make-up man!'

She moved aside, to touch up her face in the mirror which her make-up artist, quick to her command, produced out of his bag, with his assistant holding the paraphernalia. Her hairdresser fiddled with a few strands of her hair with a brush, handed over to her by another maid, who was Suraiya's special on-duty maid. While they all fussed over her, I, too, gave a last look at my hair, thinking to myself, 'The dream girl of the country, reigning in every heart, putting her arms around me would be a lensman's delight. Are there any around?' I scanned left and right, and saw a still photographer, standing with his camera, waiting to capture the moment. Inspired, I swept a strand of hair that had fallen on my forehead back to its place with a flick of my finger and announced, 'I'm ready.'

'Me too!' She left her mirror and waked to my side.

'Please! Be a little careful about my hair, as you ruffle it!' I pleaded with her.

'Yes, I know, I won't disturb your puff!' She giggled for the fifth time. 'Take!' she announced.

The song played, the camera rolled, and she was in her element. I felt the warmth of her breath as she sang and hugged me from the back. I turned to look at her as I played the piano. The camera trolleyed to our faces, catching us in a big close-up. I kissed her hand, let it go, then threw a most charming kiss at her. She reciprocated with a kiss too on the back of my head, then ruffled my hair, making sure my puff was intact. The director, very pleased, said, 'Ok! Great! Next shot!'

'Not yet!' The photographers, three or four of them now, screamed, jumping into the frame and clicking away. It seemed that they always followed Suraiya wherever she went.

'Kiss her again, Dev,' they requested.

'Suraiya?' I asked her.

She nodded. I kissed her on the cheek this time, a little more genuinely. The photographers went berserk.

Her seat next to her granny and her uncle, with 'Suraiya' embossed on it, was waiting. But she kept standing next to me near the piano.

'Now?' She giggled again.

'What now?' I asked.

'You were saying something about . . .' She abruptly stopped, holding herself back.

I looked at her.

'What was on your mind about me?' she finally asked what was playing on her mind.

'I don't want to flatter you,' I flirted.

'I want to be flattered!' She was enjoying it.

'You'd take me seriously if I said what I was thinking?'

'Absolutely!' she shot back.

'Your eyes are like glittering diamonds, on a queen's face!' I said.

She liked this, and giggled again.

'But . . .' and I hesitated.

'But what?' she insisted.

'Your nose, though pretty, is a little too long!' I was frank.

'Oh yes! It is,' she confessed, touching it.

'Though it goes well with your face,' I said, compensating her. 'It tempts me to give you a nickname!'

'What?' She was amused.

'I always nickname the girls I work with,' I said.

'You have worked with many?' she wanted to know.

'Not yet—very few,' I said. 'But selected ones,' I added with a deliberate cheekiness. 'Selected by the directors, of course!'

Her beautiful eyes smiled. 'So, what do you want to nickname me?'

'Nosey!' I prolonged the word fondly, giving her a soft, endearing punch on her nose.

This time she had a definite reason to giggle again as she said softly, 'Sweet!' also prolonging the word, looking into my eyes.

The first phase of our romance ended there.

On the outdoor location next day, she remarked, 'You know who you look like?'

'Who?' I asked.

'Hasn't anybody told you?' She had mischief in her eyes.

'I don't know.'

'Gregory Peck!' she said, and watched my reaction.

'Oh come on! It's old hat. They have been saying so for a long time. I don't like it,' I said.

'Why not? He's so good looking,' she complimented me.

'I am more good-looking,' I said jestfully.

I had given her a reason to giggle again. 'I admire your confidence,' she said. I could sense she had started to like me.

'Give me a better name than Gregory Peck,' I said, radiating more confidence.

She started thinking in amusement.

'Though I know he's your favourite, I want to be your bigger favourite,' I said, only half in jest.

We were both called for a shot. As soon as it was over, I pursued the conversation.

'Some name for me in your mind yet—Nosey?' I put a lot of emphasis on the 'Nosey'.

She called for the mirror, which instantly came to her. She looked into it, and I could see she was looking at me through it as she powdered her nose, as I stood behind her.

'The shot is ready!' came a voice.

In the shot, she had to go and stand by a bed of flowers. I had to go behind her, pluck a flower and present it to her, saying a sweet something.

'Let's do it straightaway, as it comes spontaneously, and naturally. No rehearsals!' I suggested.

'Yes.' She was ready.

The camera rolled. She went and stood by the flower bed. I sneaked from behind, plucked a flower and threw it up in the air. As it came down, I caught it between my lips. She plucked it from between my lips, and kissed it. The camera caught the action, the director was happy, and everybody clapped.

Both of us were pleased with ourselves, and as she walked away, she threw me a hint to follow her, while the unit got busy setting up the next shot.

As I joined her, she turned and said, 'I will call you Steve.'

'Steve! Why Steve?'

'Just like that! It struck me. I like it.'

'That's what matters—then I like it too. Nosey and Steve! Hmmm, good friends?' I wanted to make sure.

'Good friends!' she repeated. We shook hands, and let the handshake linger. I pressed her hand. She pressed mine back.

From good friends to close friends, and then to lovers.

The film magazines started gossiping, and the readers relished the gossip. The rumour mills worked overtime. And our love affair became the talk of the town, nay, of the whole country.

Nineteen

Chetan's first film *Neecha Nagar* was hailed at the Cannes Film Festival, the very first festival held immediately after the end of the war, winning the Golden Palm. But it could not find any patronage in its own country. It did not even see the light of day, for no distributor came forward to buy it. All the money invested in it by its producer got sunk in a venture that though artistic was not commercially viable. Nobody was prepared to take a risk with the film, with theatres charging heavy rentals, and the actors in it not known to the audience. Chetan, a brilliant director, got frantic and desperate, looking for an avenue to further his creativity and a source of income. My stature was growing as an actor, and I thought of a plan.

Without telling my brother I went into the office of one of my producers. He stood up seeing his charismatic actor walking in without any prior appointment. 'Dev!' he said.

'I have a favour to ask of you, sir,' I said.

'Favour! What can I do for you? Ask for anything,' he was obliging.

'Nothing except what is my right.'

'Let's sit there,' he said, pointing to a sofa in a corner.

'No, it won't take long. I need some extra dough, if you can manage it, out of my remuneration, for a great new beginning.'

'It shall be done!' he quickly responded. He was rich and on the share market. 'But won't you share with me the secret—the beginning you are making?' he was curious to know.

'You shall automatically know when it happens.' I gave him a smile of thanks.

'Fly the flag,' I told my brother.

'Flag?' he asked.

'Name the banner under which you want to launch it!' I enjoyed the moment.

'What?' His curiosity was mounting.

'Our first film together!' and I laughed.

'How?' He wasn't convinced.

I pulled out a bundle of currency notes. He looked mystified.

'A part of this will go to Suraiya, and she is going to be your leading lady,' I said.

He still looked puzzled.

'And I'll be your leading man; that is, if you approve of me.'

Now he burst out laughing and hugged me in joy.

He had performed a play for IPTA, which he had also written, based on the Russian author Nikolai Gogol's *The Inspector General*, a satirical comedy which was a hit with the audience. Both he and Balraj Sahni had played the lead in it on stage, and it was my turn now to do the same in the screen version.

Suraiya was signed for it, and was crowned the first leading lady of the production company the two brothers floated together, called Navketan, meaning 'new banner'. The flag started to fly as the pundit put a red tikka on our foreheads at the muhurat. The name of the film was *Afsar*.

There was not a day when Suraiya and I did not meet or talk to each other on the phone. I was in love. Not that I hadn't fallen in love before. I had been physically and emotionally involved before, and had my share of love-affairs. But they were with women already married, with a past of their own. This time it was as if two eligible beings, suited for each other, had got together, lighting a torch for young love, openly in the public eye, with the approval of their admiring fans.

My visits to her place came with clockwork regularity. If I missed any rendezvous with her, she'd be unhappy, and the day I didn't get to see her I felt cheated. Religiously, I would take the local train from Bandra, to get off at Churchgate station, and then walk across to Marine Drive to ring her doorbell. We huddled together in a corner, under the scrutinizing hawk eye of the family, cooing and wooing each other, whispering in each other's ears.

Our affair caught the attention of a particular lobby that started showing their resentment after they discovered its seriousness and its consequences, for she and I were secretly talking of getting engaged. This leaked out as a suspicion at first, that consolidated itself with the way both Suraiya and I looked at each other as if we were made for each other, excluding the whole world around us.

It soon became a touchy and thorny issue for the self-proclaimed suitors of Suraiya, who came and sat every evening in her drawing room, each luring her family into a proposal for marrying her, and also poisoning their minds against me, giving our affair a communal twist, thereby instigating their religious sentiments. A Hindu marrying their Muslim daughter was sacrilegious! They kept on hammering the thought into the minds of all her family members, during their daily tête-à-tête with them. The granny who controlled the ethical, moral and religious code of the family, as also its purse strings, became the main opponent to our relationship, though I always felt that Suraiya's mother was sympathetic to our cause and did not disapprove of the idea of her daughter's emotional involvement with me. She secretly liked and admired me. But hers was a lone voice in a babble of tongues that wagged in the evening get-togethers at Krishna Mahal, Suraiya's ground-floor abode.

Soon, I realized I was no longer welcome at her house, and that Suraiya was a silent prisoner in her family's hands. Several persons from the movie industry would be sitting there, watching my entry into the drawing room, then cold-shouldering my presence, as the great durbar of her sycophant admirers, her ex-directors as well as current ones, and future hopefuls, cast unfriendly glances at me. I became an unwanted visitor and stopped going there altogether.

Suraiya's grandmother's open resentment came to the fore one day, on the sets of *Afsar*. She started monitoring our movements on the set, making sure that the lovers did not get an opportunity to communicate with each other, except to speak and perform the lines required of them in the scenes. She also forbade any physical contact between us in any scene to be shot.

In an intimate scene, I had to kiss Suraiya on the eyes, a soft innocent kiss in praise of the eloquence of her eyes. Her granny, watching the goings-on with an eagle's eye, got to know about this, and kicked up a ruckus. She would not allow it to happen. The lights had to be switched off for a long, long time, waiting for her temper to cool down. She was adamant, and did not move an inch from her position, sitting on the spot where the scene had to be enacted, glaring at the working unit that surrounded me and Suraiya, making sure the kissing moment did not happen. Ultimately, we had to devise a shrewd plan to cunningly whisk her away from the studio for a brief while, thanks to a member of the unit who was very friendly with her. And during that brief interlude, we hurriedly took the shot, to everybody's delight and amusement.

To me, the whole exercise proved a point, that Suraiya had no say in her own life; its sole arbiter was her granny. But the more I was forbidden to meet her, the more my craving grew to have a union with her. The forbidden apple now seemed to be more desirable and most delicious, being out of my reach. It turned me mad. I felt lost, totally disinterested in anything, like a Romeo without his Juliet or a Majnu without his Laila. The only occasions when I could meet her were when we both were on the sets, and that too during our shots with arc-lamps on our faces, her granny and uncle sitting at hand scrutinizing every moment, along with some other people who now started joining them on the sets daily, as if to guard their 'princess' from the greatest 'villain' who had the evil intention of kidnapping her.

And as I saw that I was not allowed to utter a single word of a personal nature to Suraiya, outside the ones written in the script for both of us, my yearning for a contact with her reached a stage of such desperation that I started seeing myself as a man rejected by the girl who was by now most important to me. My ego and self-respect at stake, I now understood why young people committed suicide, craving for each other, but not being able to meet because of forces beyond their control.

But I was made of a different mould and sterner stuff: forever on a plateau of excitement and eternally riding the crest of an optimistic wave. I decided to confront my obsession. I had to be bolder and more demanding. I devised a plan of writing to her and getting Divecha, the cameraman on the sets of *Jeet*, who was very close to her and her family, to pass the letter on to her.

As Divecha passed by, adjusting another Baby on me, he teased me, 'Hey, lover! How much more handsome do you want to look?'

'The lover has a request for you,' I whispered into his ears.

'Anything for a friend,' he whispered back.

I sat in a quiet corner and scribbled a hurried note to Suraiya.

She was sitting like a forlorn lamb besides her granny and her uncle who were sipping tea and laughing away with a couple of cronies who looked like bodyguards. Divecha played his game very well and by pack-up time, my note was inside the bag that Suraiya carried.

Next day, when Divecha passed by me again, checking the light on my face for a solo close-up, he put an envelope into my pocket stealthily and whispered, 'Should be hot stuff, for it is a quick response, buddy!'

Standing in a corner I read the note scribbled back by Suraiya. It read, 'I cried as I read your letter. It is mutual. I love you. I, too, am dying to meet you. Call me tomorrow at 7.00 p.m. I shall be near the phone.'

Next day, I called her exactly at the time she had given. She picked up the phone. As I heard her 'Hello', joy coursed through my veins.

'Nosey,' I poured all my love into the word. But I heard granny's voice reply instead, saying, 'Who's that?' and a weeping shriek from Suraiya in the background, while the phone got disconnected. I did not let my determination die down though and called again; the phone was picked up; I repeated, 'Suraiya!'

'Suraiya is not at home!' The granny shouted and banged the phone down. I persisted and rang again. Granny who picked up the phone now said threateningly, 'Next time I hear your voice, you will have the police talking to you.' Then came a loud banging down of the phone, this time more violent. Frustrated, I closed my eyes, sat down, holding my head in my hands; but I did not give up. I let a little time go by, about an hour, during the course of which I again thought of the futility of existence without my lady-love. Then I rang her number again.

Somebody picked up the phone. I listened quietly to the voice. It said 'Hello' very softly. It wasn't Suraiya's voice, and it certainly wasn't the granny's either. I guessed it could be Suraiya's mother.

'Is that Mummy?' I whispered.

'Yes Dev.' I heaved a sigh of relief.

'Can I speak to Suraiya?'

'She's been crying,' her mother said.

I was emboldened. 'Can I speak to her?' I repeated.

'No, she cannot, her granny is close by,' she said in a soft whisper.

'But I must meet her!' I was desperate.

'She, too, wants to meet you.'

'Then?' I asked eagerly.

'Call me exactly after one hour, I shall arrange a meeting.'

I called exactly after one hour, and her mother said, 'Don't call Suraiya. But you can meet her tomorrow.'

I was in heaven. She continued, 'But very late at night. A little after eleven-thirty.'

'Eleven-thirty tomorrow night?' I reaffirmed.

'She'll be up on the terrace of the building. You can take the staircase, as you enter from the main building, and climb straight up,' she said, and put the phone down.

'Is this a ruse—to trap me?' I wondered.

'I don't think so. I should take the risk!' the determined part of me said.

'What if I am caught? I'll be proclaimed a sneaky scoundrel in all the newspapers,' the cautious side of me warned. 'I could even land in a lock-up.'

There was a hell of a debate raging inside me. But the lover in me had the final say, 'How can I not trust Suraiya's mother? She is the only one in the family who is fond of me. I have to believe her.'

I opted for my historic and fairy-tale rendezvous with the love of my heart and took my friend, Tara, now an inspector in the police department in Bombay, along with me.

Much before the appointed time given by Suraiya's mother, we both stood on the parapet by the sea, at a spot that provided a view of the top of the terrace. Tara pushed a small torch into my pocket.

'In case of any mishap, just flash this torch towards me from above. I shall flash mine getting your signal, and then rush upstairs to your rescue. I am carrying a revolver,' he said. I felt safer and protected by the strategy planned by the policeman, which was straight out of a movie thriller.

After a seemingly long, impatient and nerve-racking wait, the hands on my gold-bordered Rolex watch, newly bought from the Army and Navy stores, in keeping with my current star status, showed eleven-thirty. I climbed up the stairs to the open terrace, five or six storeys above the ground, as fast as a cat.

Panting for breath as I stood at the doorway while my eyes roved for her, I discerned her turning towards me. She was sitting by the water-tank. I rushed forward to meet her. She stood up, holding out her arms towards me. We held each other in a long, hot embrace. She did not utter a word, nor did I. After a long silence that said everything, we looked at each other. As I stroked her hair, she held her lips up to me, ready for a kiss. The kiss lingered till eternity, as the angels serenaded us from above. And then she wept. I consoled her, and she smiled a smile that fairies would envy. I wanted to protect her from all the evil that ever befell her. 'Will you marry me?' I asked.

She hugged me again and nodded, mumbling, 'I love you! I love you! I love you!'

Down in the street waiting by the sea, with the tide rising, was Tara, my friend, looking up at the terrace. But the light from the torch never flashed.

I went to Zaveri Bazaar and bought one of the costliest rings that would adorn her finger. I called Suraiya's number, but the granny picked up the phone. I recognized her gruff voice and put the phone down, and called her again after another hour. Again, I recognized the granny's voice. I repeated the call in the evening, and got the same inimical 'Hello'. Now I knew she was guarding the telephone and screening the calls.

I called Divecha, my cinematographer friend, in distress. He answered the phone and on hearing my voice immediately asked, 'A love-note again?'

'No, an engagement ring this time,' I said.

'Where is my bottle of Black Label?' he joked.

'You shall have as many as you want,' I joked back.

He took my ring to her house.

When he got back from Suraiya's house, he was very happy for me, and said, 'She was charmed by the ring, took it quietly inside her room to treasure it in a box, and came out to tell me how much she loved you.'

I was in seventh heaven. We were now engaged! I longed for her, more and more; but I did not hear from her. Our filming episodes with each other were over, and there was no way we could meet. Days turned into weeks and there was no news from her. No written note, no call, no message. I checked with Divecha, and he promised to find out. But this time he was not allowed into their house. The granny shut the door on his face, saying, 'We are not welcoming even the best of our friends for reasons we need not divulge.' But he too became inquisitive, and being a reliable information gatherer, very close to the gossiping tongues of the film industry, he soon found out that there was a severe rift in Suraiya's family, nobody taking her side on the issue of her personal emotional involvement except her mother. If she chose to go against the wishes of the family, either she would be eliminated, or the granny would kill herself. Apparently, Suraiya had wept and wept and finally yielded to the pressure mounting on her.

They prevailed upon her. She took a solemn oath to throw me completely out of her mind. Later, as an act of desperate frustration, she took the ring I sent her to the seaside, and looking at it for the last time, with all the love she had in her heart for me, threw it far into the sea, to sing songs about our romance to the rising and falling tides.

Divecha was sad and sympathetic as he narrated all this. Then he philosophized, 'Shakespeare will be reborn to give your tragic love story immorality in another play that will beat his own *Romeo and Juliet*.'

My heart sank, and my whole world shattered. There was no meaning to existence without her. But then not living meant killing myself, which would be a negation of all that my inner strength stood for. Finally, I ended up crying on the shoulder of my brother

Chetan, who knew the extent of my involvement with Suraiya. He consoled me and said, 'This episode will only make you stronger, more mature, to fight bigger battles later.'

I looked across to the distant horizon. The evening sun that was still aglow threw the special ray it reserved for me in my direction. It brightened my face anew. I kept looking at it, as my brother continued, 'Life teaches its own lessons at every step, chapter by chapter. This chapter is closed for you forever, and you must start a new one.'

Twenty

Afsar, Navketan's first film, was a comedy, a satire on corruption, probably the first in its genre. Though the bane of corruption has always been there in society, it wasn't so evident in India during the nascent years of our independence, but became a cancerous reality soon thereafter. The film was very well made, and established the new banner. It enhanced the name of Chetan, reaffirmed my status as an actor, and brought into our fold a musical genius who was later to weave his magic spell in film after film, and become a strong pillar for Navketan—the one and only S.D. Burman. The audience enjoyed the film, and was in splits at some of its hilarious situations; but it failed to ring in the cash registers at the box-office.

The company formed to give a new dimension to the world of entertainment had to keep the flag flying high. We made a silent promise to ourselves to provide a new beat to the orchestra we had started to play for the world. What next? I thought of my pledge to Guru Dutt and gave him a call to come over.

He came, lit cigarette in hand, sat in front of me, and I said, 'Before you exhale, hold your breath.'

He held his breath and waited. I broke the news. 'Remember, we had dreamt a dream together on the hill-top of Poona, looking down at the world?' He nodded, still holding his breath.

'Let the world see our dream now. You are going to direct a film for Navketan.'

He let out the smoke in short measured puffs with a broad smile straight on my face. I inhaled it, for it smelt of a coming success.

He stretched his hand towards me and I shook it. Chetan was standing right behind us, saying, 'Congratulations, Guru Dutt!'

I had come through a phase of great emotional strain in my life that had drained me, wrenched me from inside, and now that I was free from my bondage, I felt like a bird flying in the air, flapping its wings, humming to the wind, 'I am free, I am free, I am free.'

Chetan arrived one day and wanted me to get ready to meet my new leading lady for the film which was to be called *Baazi*. Her name was Mona Singha, and she was fresh from St. Bede's College, Simla. Chetan renamed her Kalpana Kartik, and organized a photo-session of us together at Ambalal Patel's studio on Hornby Road. We picked her and her mother up from the YMCA hostel where they were staying. After the photo-session was over, we all drove to Juhu beach in my car. Mona was new to Bombay, and being an upcountry girl, she was enjoying the feel of the city for the first time, and loved the beach.

It was her first encounter with the sea. Coming from a ladies' college that turned out bright, smart students, she was lively, extremely mischievous, and a prankster, full of beans.

On the beach, she held her sandals in her hands, looked at me with a glint of mischief in her eyes and ran fast towards the sea. 'Let's see who reaches the waves first!' was her command, delivered loud and clear.

Quick to respond, I reached her equally fast, and she splashed water all over me, drenching me playfully. Reciprocating, I drenched her in the same measure.

Laughing with great youthful exuberance, enjoying the feel of dripping water on her face, its beads adding to the sparkle of her innocence, she now turned towards the mound of sand piled up next to where the waves touched the shore. As I followed her, she was grabbing handfuls of sand to plaster my face with. Before my hands too could gather up sand, I heard some stragglers on the beach who were watching laugh, looking at my face. I must have been looking funny, with my eyes popping out of a mask of sand. Mona having done the mischief was laughing too like a naughty schoolgirl, pointing at me.

I kept the laugh-riot alive by parking myself on the mountain of sand, deliberately sinking deep into it, both my hands now kicking the sand up in the air in all directions, grimacing like a buffoon!

'Chase me,' came another command from her, this time more boisterous, and she was now running her fastest behind a thicket of shrubby seaweeds. 'Where are you?' I shouted back with the same boisterousness, definitely looking away from her, giving her ample time to hide behind the bushes.

'Find me,' came her voice again, as she stealthily and naughtily brought her face out in childlike joy through the opening of two tiny twigs, holding out her hand that held her sandals.

'I know where you are!' I crooned back, pampering her like I would a child.

'I saw your film *Afsar*,' she now said from behind the twigs.

'Did you like me in it?' I asked her with the same zest, wiping the sand off my clothes.

'Sort of. But in this one, you will be better, for I'm in it,' she declared.

'Of course!' I said.

She came out of hiding and dashed off again into the waves, expecting me to go after her. Which I did.

'You get a lot of fan-mail?' she asked, splashing water on me.

'Sort of,' I said, repeating exactly what she had said earlier.

She laughed and kicked a blast of water at me this time, hitting my face directly. I enjoyed the moment immensely.

Soon, Mona became an important part of my life. She started conquering me, and I willingly let myself be conquered. Navketan made her shift from the YMCA hostel to a guest house behind Eros cinema. I visited her every day, parking my Minx right beneath her window that looked out on the road. The musical horn of the car would bring the waiting Mona joyfully to the window, to wave and indicate she was ready to prance instantly out of her room and sit next to me in the car.

Soon the musical horn changed its tune to a 'lover's horn', as I decided to trade my Hillman for a flashier convertible, an olive green Triumph. I had become a little richer and could afford to sit in a more noticeable open car, so that I could wave my kisses to the growing number of admiring fans as I swished past them, being helloed at and helloing back with a little more distinction. I walked into the showroom that had given me my first car, and saw a tremendously elegant beauty parked in the lot. It looked as if she was smiling at me, ready to receive me in her arms. The manager of the place, seeing my interest, praised the car to the skies; it had a 'lover's horn' inside, he said, which, once set off, would inspire all the female beloveds in the world to come out throwing flying kisses at their calling lover. I liked the way he put it, more so when he said, 'This princess is meant just for you, sir.'

I willingly gave in to his flattery and was immediately in a mood to sit in the driver's seat, as he held the door open for me. Once inside, I could not resist pressing the most provocative part of the 'Princess', the 'lover's horn', and the music emanating from it brought all the sales girls working in the showroom out of their seats, from different directions, in one grand show of interest, all muttering a soulful 'Wow!' in unison.

'What did I say?' said the manager to me.

As I looked at him, all the girls repeated in chorus, 'Meant just for you, sir!'

I believed them and, feeling like a prince, glided the Princess away, out of the showroom, onto the road, heading straight for Mona's guest house. Looking at the Triumph from her window and hearing the melody of its horn, she too screamed a soulful 'Wow!' And as she excitedly jumped into the car, the first thing she did was to press the horn, for the sheer thrill. The windows of the building she stayed in, along with the ones of those that surrounded hers, opened in quick succession, bringing out the faces of people, as if responding to a call from the car down below. We both waved at them and they waved back, enjoying the sight of two young people nestling close in the magnificent car, and then driving it triumphantly away and out of their sight.

'Where do we go?' I asked Mona.

'The whole city is waiting,' she said boisterously.

We drove off to Juhu beach, where I had taken her for the first time when she first arrived in the city. From Juhu beach back to the city, waving to all those who waved, jumping and screaming like a prince with the girl he fancied sitting by his side, the Princess driving them both. The car needed to show more of its prowess, so we drove it the next day to Khandala for coffee, then to Lonavala to buy honey-sweet chikkis which we munched all the way back to Bombay, to a cinema theatre where it rested in a parking lot making all the cars around it salute its new grandeur. Every evening the neighbours in Mona's guest house would come out on to the balconies and peer from the windows, hearing the lover's melody coming from the Triumph, watch Mona get into it, and then regally speed away from their gaze with me into the joys of the universe.

I started finding in Mona an anchor, which I so badly needed. Both of us became great companions and the green convertible became a symbol of our togetherness.

Twenty-one

The character in *Baazi* was specially written for me. A hail-fellow-well-met loveable scoundrel, a tramp, a have-not, on the wrong side of law, but with a heart of gold, who does and acts in a manner that endears him to the common man. It gave me an image that stayed in the minds of people, and made a genuine star out of me. For the first time I felt and saw what stardom was in terms of adulation and fan-following.

It all happens in the dark. In cinema halls there is a strange, inexplicable chemistry that works on the minds of the audience when images of lifelike yet fairy-tale characters flicker on the screen, as reel after reel unfolds itself, imprinting its images on the viewers. That sudden, spontaneous, magical reaction to a face or a personality and his or her behaviour on screen is what stardom is all about. People fall for it. They love it, they would pay any price to be close to it, to touch it, to feel it, to scream, yell and whistle at it, as if they have all of a sudden found their long-lost beloved. An actor who can have this maddening effect on the audience is a true star.

· Of course there are many stars and superstars, all shining with their brilliance in the starry firmament at any given time. Some are like meteors, like shooting stars, blazing across the sky; and some like tiny galaxies, glowing luminously year after year. I did not know which category I belonged to. But I did start twinkling, as I saw people looking at me, whenever I passed by, with beaming smiles on their faces.

I became a phenomenon after the release of *Baazi* and faced heady intoxicating moments of hysteria, let loose by groups of young girls, who blocked my exit from the theatre where the movie was released, as I was coming out after the premiere. I was on purpose wearing the same beret cap I had worn for my role in the film, as a double reminder of my presence amongst the opening-night viewers. They loved my gimmick, and had noticed me from a distance as I came out to the lobby. They charged towards me, lifted me by my waist, as the rest of the crowd around me also helped them in their exercise, and threw me up towards the skies. Somebody jumped to grab the cap off my head, screaming 'I love your beret too!' but before she could do so, I threw it up in the air myself, with a great force and bravado, then blew a long-drawn flying kiss to everyone around. A wave of teenagers rushed forward, with scores of hands simultaneously going up into the air to grab and possess the precious souvenir. A pitched battle followed. Hands struggled, and a sensuous mouth lunged forward to rub her lipstick on my laughing but bashful face, with a smooch that engraved the moment forever in my memory. But before I could taste its flavour, a pretty little face was running away with the grabbed treasure. She quickly looked back, put on my beret and threw me a kiss so special that it became the second kiss of the evening that was frozen in my mind.

The cap had become synonymous with my personality. And the girl carried my trademark on her head.

The more hysterically rowdy the audience inside and outside the theatre where the movie is released, the more 'starry' the star of the movie is. I had become one such star!

Mona was in Delhi—not attending the premiere at the Swastik cinema in Bombay. She called from there after midnight. I was in raptures, saying the film had clicked.

'What do you mean it's clicked?' she innocently asked.

'Means, it is a hit. A sixer, as circket-wallahs would say!' I was in a jocular mood.

'Who made *Baazi* into a hit?' she asked like a child, enjoying the news.

'We together,' I said with pride.

'No! I made it into a hit, for I worked in it!' She was a great teaser.

'Of course! Without you, it would not have been possible!' I agreed.

She always had her own way—and we laughed.

A hit film is like God's hand on the heads of its makers, and everyone associated with it. Overnight, Guru Dutt started riding a big horse. Balraj Sahni, who had collaborated on the screenplay and written the dialogues, smiled a smile that said 'I knew it'. S.D. Burman created a niche for himself in film music. Sahir Ludhianvi, the famous Urdu poet, joined him in forming a team that started spelling magic amongst moviegoers. Geeta Bali and I scored as a great performing couple. And Mona was dancing in her heart, having given the gift of success to Navketan, the flag of which had started flying high.

Half a century later, as I was walking out of my dentist's clinic after being attended to for a tooth problem, I hit myself against a glass door installed between the clinic and its waiting room. The glass was so thin and transparent that it looked like an open space, more so to a man lost in his thoughts, and in a hurry to move out.

One of the significant traits of my character is that I am always in a hurry, and hate laziness of any sort. There is always a terrific pace bubbling inside me. I think fast, I move fast with my decisions. I talk fast and I walk fast. It was only after I smashed into the glass, breaking it into smithereens, big and small pieces scattered all around with me in the centre covered in shards and glass dust, standing mute and motionless and frozen to the spot, that I realized my stupid folly. It was a moment of great shock. All the patients in the waiting room were panic-stricken; they stood up, speechless, afraid to ask whether I was ok or injured or indeed dead. But the accident that could have been near fatal had the hand of providence protecting me, thanks to the customary cap I was wearing on my head that bore the brunt of the impact. To my amazement, there was not a single scratch on my body. I wasn't hurt at all. I calmly shook the pieces of glass off my body, as well as those resting on my head.

'Miraculous escape!' remarked a shocked onlooker.

'Your cap saved you, Mr Dev Anand,' said another in a similar stage of shock.

'That's why I wear it!' I humoured them.

'Thank God you were looking down, as you thrust your head forward cutting into the glass,' came another nervous comment.

'Yes, I was looking down—instead of ahead—stupid of me—I

wouldn't have banged into it otherwise,' I humoured them again, now having gained my self-composure, still looking down and at the sharp broken pieces littered all over the floor that could have cut into my veins. One of the assistants in the clinic came rushing forward, wiping my jacket and my trousers, with the dentist profusely apologizing, imploring me to sit down for a while to recover from the shock. They all brought a chair for me to sit down, and four or five youngsters who were waiting for some dental treatment came out with school notebooks, seeking my autograph.

'Are you all from Mumbai?' I asked them. For by that time there was no Bombay any more—the city had transformed itself into Mumbai.

'Yes. And my grandmother is your biggest fan,' one of them said.

'Yes? Give her my love,' I reciprocated, scrawling my signature.

'And she has preserved the cap you sent flying into the air at the premiere of *Baazi*,' she said excitedly.

'Ye-e-ss?' I looked at her. 'Is the cap still there?'

'Kept in a showcase,' she answered. 'My grandma was the one who grabbed it out of so many chasing it.' She was full of pride for her grandma.

I tried to remember the girl. She quickly appeared before my eyes and I enjoyed the feeling.

'And she says she'll die only after she's met you again!' The girl had a sentimental choke in her voice.

'Tell your grandma I shall never meet her, for I don't want her to die,' I said.

They all laughed.

'And give her this from me,' I signed another, a very special autograph for her. 'And a kiss on my behalf!'

The girl smiled happily.

That's what *Baazi* did for me.

Twenty-two

Guru Dutt and I were seeing an Italian film together at the Excelsior, and we both fell in love with it. He took out his cigarette, lit it and said, 'I am basing my next film on this.' 'I am with you.' I was also inspired.

The film was *Bitter Rice*. The male lead, Vittorio Gasman, a roguish character, had all the shades of villainy in him. I did not mind doing that type of a role for a change.

The film Guru Dutt made was called *Jaal*, and he cast Geeta Bali again opposite me. Its filming took us to Malwan, on the Goa border.

Geeta Bali was a very bright actress, with a sparkle in her eyes, and a rhythm in her body that made her a great dancer and an actress to watch. Casting Geeta Bali in *Baazi* had been Guru Dutt's idea. It was an inspired piece of casting, and she won the hearts of the audiences with some musical numbers that became a rage with cine-goers at the time. Now Geeta and I were together again, in Malwan.

Malwan was a very picturesque fishing village. Its coastline was very attractive, with the sea waves touching the fringe of the village. While the waves kissed the corner of the village in high tide, the villagers got high on feni, a local brew.

The film's crew stayed in Malwan for a fortnight. It was a very colourful stint of filming for me. One day as Geeta and I were filming on the beach, actor K.N. Singh, the 'uncle' of the industry, who loved to hit the bottle in the evenings, invited me in from a hut. I asked Guru Dutt if I could go.

'Sure,' he said, for he was taking a few independent shots of Geeta Bali.

Inside the hut, K.N. Singh was jovial and grinning, a little tipsy.

'It looked so beautiful from here—you and Geeta near the sea,' he said. 'I was watching through the door, what a glorious camera angle from here! And this is to that.' He raised his glass and drained it.

'What are you drinking, Uncle? Certainly not your favourite whisky at this time of the day?' I asked.

He showed me a white bottle, with a white drink in it. 'Feni,' he said. 'Far more delicious than whisky. Take a swig!'

'No, thank you. You know I don't drink, Uncle,' I replied.

'But this is not a drink. This is elixir!' he was persuasive. 'A few drops!' he insisted. 'And then watch the pep. You'll be in high sprits in front of the camera!'

I yielded, 'Just a few drops then.'

He started pouring. 'That's it!' I tried to stop him.

'That's not it. It is nothing. Just an essence of cashew nuts. Goa is famous for it. Very healthy. You shall never fall ill.' He kept on pouring, and by the time he handed the glass over to me, it was almost full. I looked at it and hesitated.

'Young men like you!' he challenged me. 'Just gulp it down. That much cannot affect you, unless you let the whole bottle go down your throat. Look at me!'

He poured another large one for himself, downed it in one gulp, and giving his head a big shake, mumbled to himself, 'The most delicious stuff in the world!'

Both his act and words tempted me, and I drank it all.

'Look, nothing has happened to you!' he assured me.

'Nothing,' I repeated.

'Aren't you feeling more invigorated?' he asked triumphantly.

'Maybe,' I nodded, feeling myself.

'Another one won't affect you either!' He poured another large peg into my empty glass. In a show of bravado, I drank that too, conveying an exquisite relish on my face, trying not to let the 'uncle' down in his estimation of me.

'Delicious?' he asked.

'Delicious,' I repeated. 'Thank you!'

'Devji?' came the voice of the assistant director from outside. 'Your shot is ready.'

I rushed out, galloping like a horse.

'No time to rehearse,' said the director. 'The tide is rising, and we must shoot quickly.'

'Certainly!' I agreed.

'It's all arranged. Just hold Geeta's hand and run into the water; as soon as you reach ankle-deep water, look towards me, near the camera. I shall cut the shot then,' Guru Dutt gave me his final instructions.

'Yes, easy,' I responded very confidently. 'Geeta,' I said, 'Your hand.'

'Here it is,' she offered it to me like a tomboy. I held it and gave the arm a couple of swings.

The camera was switched on, and I pulled Geeta along, running into the waters of the sea.

'That's it!' shouted Guru Dutt. But we were running further and further into the sea.

'That's it!' Guru Dutt shouted again, now at the top of his voice. But I was happy with the high waves of the rising current that were making Geeta flow with me! The water came as high as our waists.

'THAT'S IT!' Guru Dutt yelled. He panicked and started running towards us.

Suddenly an undercurrent swept us off our feet with terrific force. It is going to wash us away to the Persian Gulf, I thought, and conveyed this with great effort to Geeta, in an attempt to boost her sinking morale. But she hardly responded to the humour, with salt water now entering our noses and mouths.

On the beach, Guru Dutt was screaming himself hoarse, 'Are you ok?'

'Ye-e-e-e-s. N-o-o-o.'

Sound of gurgling water. We were about to drown.

But since both of us had the will to live and walk on the earth again . . . Suddenly a violent wave hit us and propelled us shorewards, sweeping us along with it, and thrusting us straight into the hands of Guru Dutt and a few other members of the film unit who were rushing towards us in panic.

I was still laughing thanks to the feni, though I felt dazed, and Geeta too laughed with me, trying to keep a brave front. She was such a sport, with the vitality and vigour of a Punjabi rustic. All our clothes were soaked. My gold Rolex, having bathed in the salty waters of the Arabian Sea, had became timeless, time for it having stopped at a certain momentous second. Soon the façade of boisterousness excited by feni, the Indian vodka, started dying out. My head began to swim. Guru Dutt sportingly ordered pack up.

At nightfall, I found myself in bed in my room, still wearing the clothes in which I had dipped myself into the sea. They had yet not dried up, and I smelt of salt and fish.

I suddenly discovered Geeta through a little opening of the door, trying to look inside to fathom whether everything was ok with me. Her eyes met mine, and after making sure I was fine she teased, 'Game for a night out?' and laughed.

'I am—come in,' I said, and opened the door fully for her. She laughed heartily this time, and threw her hand towards me. I slapped mine on it. She said, 'There is some drama in the village tonight.'

'A better one was enacted this afternoon,' I retorted.

'I mean a play, in the best traditions of Maharashtra. The man performing the lead is their best stage actor!' she exclaimed.

'Who is he?' I asked, and as she was about to mention his name, Guru Dutt arrived on the scene and said, 'We must see the play. He is most famous for the role he's playing, that of an alcoholic.'

The three of us went and watched the play. By the time it finished, it was two o'clock. The filming in Malwan had finished and the unit was scheduled to catch a boat for Bombay at six in the morning. Geeta was to travel with them, but knowing I had my big Chevrolet driving me back at a more convenient time, she asked if I could accommodate her as well. I agreed gladly.

Twenty-three

Driving together from Malwan to Bombay was fun all the way. I was at the wheel, Geeta sitting next to me, her legs raised on the seat, her hands on her knees, her sister and my driver in the back seat. We started before daybreak, saw the sun rise, and then felt the day gradually getting warm.

Geeta was naughty and playful, full of jokes and pranks, and I at my likeable best. We were constantly on the move, stopping on the way only for sugar-cane juice.

'Keen for breakfast somewhere?' I asked her.

'No, only at Poona. Let's see you break the all-time speed record!' she provoked me.

I sped the car onwards at seventy—seventy-five—eighty miles.

'More!' she was enjoying the thrill. I pressed the accelerator down. 'Eighty-five!'

'More!' she challenged me, while her sister in the back seat looked terrified. 'Slow down!' she kept saying, as the driver showed all his teeth in a broad grin, in a non-committal reaction.

Mile after mile of the road were being chewed up in seconds by my rusty-brown Chevy. I was set to create a record. Geeta, boisterous as ever, broke into song after song, a medley of all that came into her head, matching the mood of the moment, with the straight empty road receding fast behind us. The windows of the car were open; her hair was flying as she sang with great abandon. So was mine; my cap rested on her knee.

Outside, the sun was getting hotter, but the breeze that blew inside the car was cool and sleep-inducing. The lusty songs of Geeta started becoming a humming lullaby. Then she gradually began to doze off. Her sister was already snoozing away, and the driver was snoring. My eyes too were tempted to close for a second or two. But I jerked my head, and looked at the milestone speeding by. It said: 'Poona—35 miles.'

'Thirty-five miles, in less than twenty-five minutes!' I said to myself and looked at my watch. But it had stopped functioning after its immersion in the sea. I looked at Geeta. Her eyes, the cool breeze fanning them, had drooped into a sweet slumber; her hair was dancing a ballet in the air; one of her hands held my cap, and the other rested over it, with a dainty watch on her wrist showing the time, a little after noon!

'In time for lunch in Poona. I shall give them all a surprise, after having parked outside the best restaurant!' I delighted myself with the boastful thought, looking outside: 'Poona—34 miles.'

The milestone was in an immense hurry to recede, and another one hazily sped towards me from a distance. The vista suddenly went out of focus. The car swirled, whirled and jolted off the road into a deep precipice, banging against a huge ancient tree trunk. I violently jerked my eyes open, and saw the Chevy had turned turtle and was lying at an odd angle, its front wheel still rotating at a terrific speed, while the sound of the crash still reverberated in my ears. I was pinned between the steering wheel and my seat, my chest crushed with the impact of the mighty hit. I looked at Geeta through the mirror. Her forehead was bleeding.

'I offered her a ride, not to end up with a scar on her forehead,' I thought guiltily. I looked behind with an immense effort. Geeta's sister was in a state of shock, invoking her gods. My driver, also safe, but in a similar state, could hardly mutter 'Saab?' to find out how I was. I realized I could not move but managed to ask Geeta from the same position, 'Are you all right?' She looked at herself in the mirror and smiled, 'Yes. Just a little adornment on my head. But are you ok?'

'I can't—can't—can't get up.' It was an effort to try to speak. The steering wheel was jammed against my chest. I could not extricate myself, and any movement caused me severe pain, as if some part of me had cracked or broken. Luckily, the steering wheel that was crushing my chest was also my saviour, for if I had hit the windscreen instead with the same impact it would have severed my head.

There was dead silence around. It was a lonely road, not a soul to be seen anywhere except a few small birds that were chirping away, breaking the silence of the sunny afternoon, and a crow that was cawing for our rescue. Finally, a huge station wagon came our way. It slowed down when it saw the twisted, dented vehicle hanging between the edge of the road and a tree. The two occupants—both men—rushed out.

I could hear one of them say, 'Is that Dev Anand?'

'And Geeta Bali?' the other one asked himself.

'They were shooting only the other day at Malwan!' said the first one.

'How did it happen?' they both asked us now.

'Before we ask any questions, let's rescue them first!' came the first voice.

'Let's put them in our station wagon and take them to the hospital in Poona,' said the second voice, as they saw Geeta bleeding and me stuck in a helpless posture.

'Come out, Mr Dev Anand, into our wagon,' one of them said.

I shook my head. 'Can't.'

'Make an effort!' he pleaded.

'I—just can't,' I closed my eyes with pain, as I tried to pull myself out. My torso was jammed between the steering wheel and the seat, and my legs trapped between the clutch and the brake.

I was slowly lifted out of the car with great care and caution, and then shifted into their station wagon. The rest also joined in, with the station wagon now covering the rest of the distance to Poona, my Chevrolet bemoaning the absence of its master for all times.

'Drive—slow—very slow—no jerks please. It hurts—inside—with an—acute pain,' I mumbled breathlessly, as the wagon moved forward at a snail's pace.

My eyes could not resist drooping and I saw my mother opening hers. She was sitting next to me, my head in her lap.

A debate raged inside me. My will-power was on one side, fighting to survive, and my physical being on the other, slipping into the unknown.

'This son of mine is going to be a very big man!' my mother was saying to my father. 'Very big!'

'But I am not that big yet. I've only started being recognized, getting into the popularity charts,' I said to myself. 'And that's not being "very big"—I still have to go a long way. I cannot die so soon. My mother cannot be wrong. She is now with God, and God is protecting me,' said my will-power.

'Then why am I floating towards death?' I asked myself.

'Damn it, don't talk about death. It means annihilation of the self, to go to nothingness,' my will-power said. 'I am not nothing. I am me—an achiever, on my way up, with a strong mind, and an overpowering will.'

'But I am helpless now—I'm being helped. I cannot move. I can hardly breathe. I had to be lifted!' my 'self' was saying.

'Oh come! You are going to pull through,' my will-power struggled.

'But it is tough—very tough, Dev,' the pain in my body was taking over.

'Stupid! Fight it out. Aren't you a fighter? You have always been one. And you are going to remain one. Tell yourself: I shall fight! I shall fight! I shall fight!'

I opened my eyes. I could see and feel pillows around me, cushioning me from bumps and jerks on the road, and from being jostled around.

And then the warmth of a hand gripping my shoulder. 'You are fine!' Geeta said.

'I am . . . but I cannot forgive myself for that . . . that . . . that blood oozing from your forehead!' I spoke with difficulty.

'It's just a scratch!' she tried to brush it away.

'What if it leaves a scar?' I was concerned.

'Even the moon has a scar, and is yet beautiful.' This was typically Geeta. She laughed.

I tried to laugh too. She was a darling of a colleague, and a great pal. My eyes closed again.

I heard someone say, 'We are right in front of the Sassoon Hospital in Poona.' As I opened my eyes again, I saw hundreds of faces above mine, lining either side of the stretcher that was taking me through the corridor of the hospital to the X-ray room. None of my fans had ever seen me from such close quarters and in such a condition.

On the X-ray table, my first question was, 'How is Geeta?'

'Fine,' someone said.

'Where is she?' I asked.

'Very safe,' said another.

I heaved a sigh of relief. The doctors administered anaesthesia. I had passed out by the time they X-rayed me. When I came to I found myself on a hospital bed in a ward specially given to me for my two weeks' stay for treatment. My chest was in plaster. I was surrounded by doctors. Sreeram Lagoo, later a famous Marathi stage artist and equally famous character actor in Hindi films, was one of them.

'Just a contusion of the ribs,' a young doctor told me.

'It is often the shock of a serious accident that hits a patient that kills him, more than the grievous hurt. And in your case, it was certainly your will-power that made you survive,' another doctor said.

In Bombay the news spread like wildfire. The filming of *Aandhiyan*, a Navketan film, was cancelled, and concerned people were already on the highway crossing the ghats on their way to the Poona hospital. Newspapers had flashed the news all over the country. People were enquiring whether I was dead or alive. I thought of my family. I thought of Mona and there she was, walking towards me, her eyes full of tears, from behind the green curtain that partitioned the room from its main entrance, my brothers Chetan and Goldie with her.

'All's well that ends well,' said Chetan Bhaiji, putting his hand on my forehead, while Goldie kept his hand on mine, Mona next to him, a tear falling from her eye.

'Mona!' I was thanking her for coming all the way and so soon. 'How are you?' I mumbled.

'Not well! Looking at you,' she said, and wiped her tears.

My eyes fell on a telegram Chetan Bhaiji was holding in his hand.

'It's from Frank Capra,' he said. 'Wishing you a speedy recovery.'

I thanked Frank, thinking of him. The world-famous film director was leading the American film delegation at the first-ever international film festival held in India, which had been inaugurated in Bombay. An ardent fan of his work, I had watched his latest film *It's a Wonderful Life* twice in a theatre in Bombay, once with Guru Dutt and another time alone. At the opening of the film festival, I had made friends with him. We had both got on very well together. I had driven him in my car to my favourite Army and Navy stores, bought him a pair of swimming trunks and taken him to Juhu beach for a swim. Then for dinner we had landed up at my brother's shack. We had promised each other a dinner in Delhi again, where the festival was to shift from Bombay. But now that was out of question. I told my brother to thank him for his telegram.

Mona wanted to stay in Poona to look after me. But I persuaded her to go back to Bombay, along with my brothers. She was obstinate, like always, but I prevailed, saying it wouldn't be long before we met again, because stout was found aplenty in Poona, and it would help me recuperate fast. Stout is a brown beer, made in England, a little bitter but frothier and more healthy than the usual brew. Mona and I loved it. From the quota of liquor granted to me on my legal permit by the state government in Bombay during its prohibition days, stout was the only drink I bought. She laughed at the mention of stout, and agreed to go back to Bombay. I held her hand and pressed it hard. She pressed mine too. And I was already on my way to recovery.

Twenty-four

'I'm regaining my strength fast. Putting on extra weight, thanks to the daily consumption of Guinness, and no exercise—and I have never been pampered so much as by the doctors taking care of me,' I was telling my eldest brother Mohan Bhaiji who was visiting me from Bombay. He insisted on not leaving me alone and wanted to stay in Poona for as along as I was in hospital, but I persuaded him to return to look after other responsibilities at the Navketan office, and as he parted with the most affectionate hug, he also left behind a flood of memories for my idle mind to ramble back into.

He was my father's first-born child, and was very close to me during my boyhood in Gurdaspur. A lawyer by profession, following in the footsteps of my father, he also possessed a brilliant mind. An MA in Sanskrit, a poet and a dreamer, he would compose and recite Hindi poems at public mushairas held in the town off and on. After his marriage to a very beautiful girl from Rohtas, he started living separately from my father, having acquired his own space for living, good enough for a newly married couple, with his own law practice to support him. I used to go to him for my Sanskrit lessons; in between he would pick up a harmonium and switch over to teaching me the fundamentals of the seven musical notes. I enjoyed running my fingers over the keys of the harmonium much more than imbibing the grammar of the Sanskrit language.

Mohan Bhaiji had the most romantic and bright smile. The image of him that I remember the most was when he was arrested by the British government in Gurdaspur during the Quit India movement for having offered satyagraha. The entire neighbourhood had come out into the street to give him a warm send-off to jail. Standing in a spotlessly white khadi dhoti-kurta, he turned to everybody with hands folded to say goodbye with a smile so loving that he won the hearts of everybody. That smile had turned very special for a particular young girl in the gathering, a neighbour's daughter, perhaps the prettiest in town, who was standing a little aloof at her doorway, and who switched on her most winning smile too in return. She was also in a white khadi salwar-kurta, and I could not help noticing the most eloquent pause of the moment as their eyes met for an exchange so subtly intimate.

He was incarcerated in Lahore Central Jail, where I went with my father to meet him during the interview hours granted to the inmates. He was a very ardent fan of Mahatma Gandhi, and being an educated intellectual was made the secretary of the Congress party in Gurdaspur. Later on, after Independence, he switched his loyalties to the Jan Sangh, and left his law practice to join a local bank as its manager. He and my father often exchanged views on political philosophy. My father too had been in prison during the pre-Independence era, having spoken publicly about his patriotic views after the Jallianwalla Bagh massacre in Amritsar. He often took pride in telling his family that the first president of the Indian Republic, Dr Rajendra Prasad, had spent a night as a guest at our house during the days of his party's struggle for India's liberation from British imperialism.

He often narrated many such anecdotes, mostly during the intervals of his long-drawn-out luxury of a bath under the cold water drawn out of a manually handled water pump operated by his young son Dev-aan, that is me, smiling wide-eyed and hanging on to every word that his father, the most intellectual amongst men in the town had to say. He also loved sucking the ripest and the sweetest of mangoes and melons in the season that coincided with the onrush of the monsoon in the town.

From the window of my hospital room I could see the rain falling in torrents outside, the sound of which lulled me to sleep, dreaming of the Gurdaspur that I had left behind.

Twenty-five

Chetan Bhaiji had been marking his time, waiting to give Navketan a hit. He was his own creative person and never compromised by plagiarizing i.e. taking somebody else's idea for his own films. I had great faith in his talent, and had initiated the launching of our banner because of my total belief in him as a dynamic film-maker. He had decided on *Aandhiyan* as his next film and I had consented blindly. But the part written for me in it did not do justice to the stature I had acquired as an actor after *Baazi*. I did not ask any questions and went along with my brother's decision. The only worthwhile sequence for me in the film was the courtroom drama at the end. I worked hard on it and everybody remarked that I stood out. But when the film was released, Chetan and I saw the audience walking out during the court scenes. It turned out to be the anticlimax of the film. The film flopped all over the country. Its only redeeming feature was the low-key dark black-and-white photography, meant only for the critics, and the very classical music composed by the great Ustad Ali Akbar Khan, the famous sarod player, again appreciated only by the connoisseurs of art, but ignored en masse for lack of its popular appeal to the common man. The other consoling factor was that the film became India's official entry to the Venice film festival. But the print that went to the festival was drastically cut to suit the requirements of the festival and the international audiences. The courtroom scenes were removed since they were lengthy and contained a lot of dialogue, natural to a courtroom drama; they were redundant to an audience not understanding the language. Chetan was right in taking the sequence out of the film, though I did feel disappointed and frustrated. Being a performer and having performed well in those scenes, their absence from the film was bound to create resentment in my mind, and that was the first time there was some discord between me and Chetan, the two partners in Navketan.

Both of us went to Venice with the film. It was my first trip abroad. Therefore, the excitement of it compensated for my grumpiness at Chetan's truncating the length of the film.

We first flew to Rome. While in Rome, the name of Benito Mussolini, the Italian dictator who ruled his country with an iron fist a little less than a decade ago, came to my mind, for his memories were still fresh in the world then. I was thrilled to see the square in which that majestic structure is situated from the balcony of which he stirred his nation to sanctify his association with Adolf Hitler, the great dictator of Germany, on their diabolic plan to annex their docile neighbouring countries. While he conquered the hearts of his people with his oratorial skills standing on the ramparts, it was the same place where he was humbled, humiliated and annihilated by his countrymen, when he met his doom after the war.

I drank deeply of the beautiful city of Rome and adored every inch of it. The Italian style, the Italian fashion, the pretty Italian girls, the sidewalk cafes, especially Via Veneto, where classy Italian wine flowed from table to table, with sensational-looking Italian hostesses serving you with glints in their eyes more intoxicating than the glasses of wine they served. I quickly learned to say 'grassi' in Italian, which means 'thank you', and every time I picked up a gin-martini, my 'grassi' was more and more inspired with a desire for a rendezvous, which was granted at times.

While in Rome, we also met and lunched with the famed Italian film director, Vittorio de Sica, who had created waves internationally with his award-winning *Bicycle Thieves*.

We drove to Venice from Rome by car, owned and driven by a very hospitable cultural attaché from the Indian embassy. He spoke impeccable Italian and I wished I could do the same. On the way we stopped over at Florence. Florence is a beautiful city of fine vintage steeped in history, with paintings and architecture that have a certain age-old charm. As we drove through the mountainous Apennines, we stopped over at a village, from where the Indian Embassy representatives had to pick up the ashes of an Indian Sikh soldier called Banta Singh, who was killed in action there, fighting bravely for the allies against Mussolini's forces during World War II. This was in 1952, and the war had ended in 1945. For so many years the ashes of the brave Sikh soldier were lying there, reminding the Italians of India's heroic participation in that grim battle, and now it was time to send the remains back home to his family in India.

To me, it made a great stirring story for a film.

Venice was a city floating in water, full of gondolas and extremely expensive and sleek hotels, and of beaches on which attractive young European women lay with their bare backs, apparently tanning them, hiding their frontals in the mounds of sparkling sands in the afternoon Mediterranean sun. The tan of their bodies lured international photographers and cameramen with strong lenses. The Italian paparazzi was as well known as the Italian mafia, and Sicily, where the latter thrived, was just a stone's throw away. The nights glittered during the festival time. The lobbies and dance-halls of every five-star hotel resonated with the sound of flashbulbs going off, as movie moghuls, renowned film directors and glamorous stars danced and dined, talked about their forthcoming ventures, and struck deals for new cinema projects over amorous kisses and embraces.

Aandhiyan, in which I was starring, was shown in Venice. I was in the auditorium at its screening. I waved at the beaming appreciative audiences from one of the boxes of the balcony reserved for the participants of the film being screened at the festival, and the people stood up and welcomed the man they had just seen on the screen with clapping hands. Clapping for long is a customary tradition in the West that speaks of a finely groomed social etiquette.

Aandhiyan did not create any waves, but the experience of being at a festival of that stature, that too as a star representing my country, was reward enough. We had become very familiar with Venice, or with Venezia as the Italians call it—especially with the spectacular St Marco Square where hundreds of pigeons feed themselves on grain that is constantly thrown at them by the tourists, and where the local guides work ceaselessly to earn their liras from the whims and fancies of extravagant lovers—and we were sad to leave.

Twenty-six

Back in Rome, I spotted a film unit shooting on the famous Spanish steps. I pointed it out to Chetan Bhaiji, who was sitting next to me in the car, but before he could say anything, I exclaimed, 'Gregory Peck!'

I had earlier met Mr Peck in Bombay, at the Willingdon Club, in a party hosted for him by J.C. Jain of the *Times of India*. He was passing through Bombay on his way back from a stint of filming in Ceylon, and was keen to meet a cross-section of his fans. At the club, we had exchanged some pleasantries in a very informal atmosphere. Now, seeing him filming on location in Rome, before the curious and admiring glances of onlookers, I wanted to seize the opportunity of meeting him again.

We stopped our car. I got out, diving into the crowd of passers-by that had collected in large numbers to see a movie being shot. I pushed my way through to the front. Peck was sitting on a canvas chair reserved for him, facing the street. I walked a couple of steps further, to single myself out from the rest, in the hope of being recognized by him. He casually looked at me. I waved. He nodded in the same casual way as he would at any other in the crowd and looked away. I got hold of the girl with a copy of the script in her hand, breaking all the rules of discipline, and said to her in an undertone, 'I know Mr Peck. Can I have a word with him?'

'I am afraid not here—he cannot be disturbed,' was her curt reply.

I felt despondent. A policeman was asking me to step back, but as luck would have it, Peck looked at me again. I waved vigorously this time. He smiled, nodded his recognition and waved back.

I picked up courage. 'May I? Just for a second, Mr Peck!'

He responded, 'Come on over.'

The Willingdon Club meeting was remembered, the present meeting welcomed, and a future one, whenever, looked forward to by both of us. All this happened in precisely a couple of minutes, after which I said 'Bye', and his attention was focused on the extraordinarily beautiful Audrey Hepburn, a future Oscar winner but at that moment absolutely new to Hollywood, playing the princess to Peck's ordinary newspaperman in the film which was *Roman Holiday*. William Wyler, one of my most favourite directors, was directing.

My first trip abroad had to have Paris in its itinerary. While Chetan had to come back to Bombay, I had visas taken out for some more European countries. Paris being Paris, France was the first on my list. To be able to enjoy the enchanting 'Parisian way' one has to be alone, especially for the first time. You have to give yourself a chance to get lost in its breathtaking beauty; and you cannot get lost in the way you must with another person sharing your time and experiences and at times imposing his or her preferences of likes and dislikes according to his or her temperament.

Walking in and around the illuminated flashiness of Champs-Élysée by night, or climbing up the Eiffel Tower to see and admire the expansive gorgeousness of Paris from its apex, rubbing shoulders with the community of tourists from all over the globe, or rambling into the stylish arcades of the Lido that take you into the famous bar, opening its hospitality to you as a prelude to the extraordinariness of the world-famous stage show there, have their charm intensified when you are all by yourself. You can stop wherever you want to, pause and look at where and what your eyes feast on, buy at leisure what pleases you, lazily seek whatever fancies you, whether it is a bottle of sparkling French champagne, or one of the lithe Moulin Rouge dancers, or a young hostess at one of the bars, or a thickly painted damsel offering you an hour of pleasure in her bed for a few hundred bargained francs!

I conquered Paris alone. I devoured it. Being in a crowd or with a companion would have left me like any other curious onlooker, marvelling only at the great art museums and the architectural wonders of the most beautiful city of the world, without getting beneath its skin. And I came back with impressions that have lasted.

The luxury of a visit to the Lido bar, where the tempting hostess sits next to you with two bottles of champagne on the table in ice buckets, wrapped tenderly like pubescents on the verge of blooming into their full youthfulness, till they are poured by the stylish nail-polished hands of the hostess to serve you in a manner that outclasses the heady effect of the drink on you, before the curtain goes up for the performance of the evening, is unforgettable.

The show at Moulin Rouge is another painting alive in my memory, where the can-can dancers lift their skirts to show off their shapely legs that quickly capture your interest—their underpants peeping at you in all their naughtiness. They arouse and entice you, making you eager to see more and more of them, and as you involuntarily rise from your seat to have a closer look, the skirts are hurriedly thrown back swirling on your face, making you scream for a repeat performance.

And I remember the craziness of Crazy Horse, where the visuals of the numbers performed on the stage left an eternal imprint. The sexy dancers, their bodies bare to the maximum possible, with large wooden crosses hanging loosely over their naked breasts just covering their nipples, danced so exquisitely to the rhythm of the psychedelic lights falling upon them, that as the crosses swayed over their nakedness in the flickering multicoloured extravaganza, it brought sex and God closer to each other. The artist in the choreographer was making a statement of universal truth. 'Isn't sex your God when you reach an orgasm?' and 'Isn't God your sex when you crave for His realization?'

Going from Paris to Geneva and Zurich in Switzerland is like travelling next door. But it is another country, with another language, the Alps, snow and skiing, and hilly-billy songs that remind you of India's own Pahari strains, and valleys and dales the scenic beauty of which is like so many picture postcards, competing with each other in picturesqueness.

It snowed in Interlaken, where I spent a night in a velvety bed of thick quilts thrown over me, as the snow fell outside like tiny cottonballs dancing to the winds. I saw a lovely girl by the light of a lamp in her room opposite mine. She was looking at my window from her own, and at the falling snowflakes. I lit my lamp on the table so that I could be seen by her. She waved back and switched her light off. I switched off mine. And we both shivered and slept.

Next day, at the breakfast table of the hotel, the two of us were together, just the two of us in the large dining room, alone again, perhaps lonely. She was from Britain, a student, on a tour of Switzerland. So we could speak the same language. Together we went on mountain trolleys, and together we bought dainty little souvenirs. She presented one to me. I presented one to her. And Switzerland, the land of clocks and watches and chocolates, of hospitable, innocent, industrious people with a very colourful sprinkling of kissable young maids in local costumes, stayed in the minds of both of us.

London was my last destination. Though it was my first trip, I felt more at home there, for language was neither a problem nor a barrier. There is so much we have adopted from the British, including our Constitution and our judicial system, and the way our administration works, and so much of theirs we have adapted ourselves to, especially where manners and etiquette amongst the top echelons of our social strata are concerned. And there is no shame in that, for, after all, aren't societies the world over an outcome of some adoption and adaptation from some source or the other? Culture is a great traveller, and one habit rubs on to another. Aren't we also similarly influenced by the Mughals, the Persians, the Arabs, and the Mongols?

My first priority in London was to visit Oxford and Cambridge, the great seats of Western education from where, for centuries, some of the best brains have sharpened and embellished their thinking, and contributed towards the growth and progress of mankind.

My guide to these temples of learning was a very young and pretty English girl, owner of a car company inherited from her departed father. She drove me in her Mercedes Benz herself. A student for ever, my hunger for knowledge and learning has never been satiated. And Elizabeth, the owner of the car rented by me, was a great tutor on my visit to these universities. At every nook and corner of the cobbled streets of the two university towns that we roamed, there was a new thought to be discovered, a new wave of thinking weaving its way into my inquisitive mind. She even took me to the top of the tallest buildings in Oxford and Cambridge, to have a panoramic view of the spots where some of the immortals of arts and science walked and worked, romancing with their ideas. I in turn entertained Elizabeth with my own childlike curiosities, as we sat over cups and cups of coffee in overcrowded cafes frequented by young students in their college blazers. Elizabeth loved coffee, and I too became a great drinker of the brew along with her.

My fascination for scarves took me inside a dainty curio shop, where university scarves of wool hung in abundance in all their colourful splendour. I picked up a couple. Elizabeth picked up one of a combination of colours, and threw it around my neck, saying, 'My choice!'

I picked up another and threw it around her. 'A present from me!' I said.

Momentarily, we imagined ourselves as university students.

On our way back to London, Elizabeth told me of her jilted love affair, and laughed her guts out, as the brakes of her car screeched outside the Londonderry House Hotel I was staying in.

After I paid her for the car rental, I took out an extra handsome tip for her excellent services rendered, but she declined. 'My best tip would be when you hire my car again on your next trip,' she said gently, and drove away waving a long, enduring goodbye.

My next impression of London was the English pub, an institution by itself, where, between six and eleven in the evenings, people discussed everything under the sun, from politics to movies, from stately kings and queens and their love affairs to drunken bums and whoring wenches. Apart from my favourite stout, I got used to lager, and to a particular pub with a lot of character, and to one of its pony-tailed buxom bartenders with a bottle opener constantly hanging around her neck, fitting itself sexily into her cleavage. She was a great charmer, quick-witted, sporting and outgoing—pouring the beer into large mugs straight from the wooden barrels in style as if all the breweries in the land belonged to her. The mug she handed me was always overflowing with froth streaming down its sides, and I enjoyed licking the frothiness of it, eyeing her as she looked deliberately amused, reciprocating my gesture with a flirtatious smile, at the same time winking at a British 'Charlie' sitting on the bar-stool next to mine, swearing at her for a kiss!

Twenty-seven

Chetan seemed depressed. Both his directorial ventures had failed to leave any mark on the box office. As I was sitting in the recording booth of a film studio during a break in filming for one of my outside projects, a friend of mine from my struggling days suggested, 'Why don't you make a film on a taxi driver? His is always a very down-to-earth, rough and tough character. Should suit your image, especially after *Baazi*.'

It seemed to me a good box-office thought. I told my brother, who at first smiled it away casually, but immediately afterwards, seeing that there was a chance to make another film, jumped at the idea.

Goldie, my younger brother, was entrusted with the job of writing the script, his first foray into film writing. He was brilliant, studying in St. Xavier's college, and already making a name for himself in the dramatic society of the college. He was writing and directing plays which were admired by his fellow students.

Since the finances of Navketan were drained, *Taxi Driver* was launched on a shoestring budget, with a very small working unit. It was mostly shot on locations in Bombay, with a very handy French Eclaire camera. We would all leave early in the morning, slog the whole day long, canning the maximum footage possible minus the soundtrack, leaving the dubbing of dialogues to be done at the post-production stage, and come back home late in the evenings. It took us less than thirty-five days of filming to complete the project. Survival of the company was the motivating factor, and lack of funds drove us to work at breakneck speed. The result was phenomenal. *Taxi Driver* turned out to be a superhit, and drove home an old truth, that big money does not necessarily make a big film. While big money can help structure a big film project, with glitter and shine, it cannot give it the spine it needs to be a hit. A good story is the soul of a good film, not the artificial glamour surrounding it. A great thought can be worth a million, but millions without a great thought are like so many pieces of diamonds hidden in rubble.

Mona was superb in *Taxi Driver*, enjoying her role to the hilt. She was already a part of Navketan, sailing along with it. In fact, she was Navketan's and Navketan's only. She had started getting outside offers; I felt good for her, but she told me, 'I shall take the best as and when it comes to me!' and hugged me.

I understood what she meant. 'But where is the hurry?' I asked her.

'You don't want me to be lost to you!' she put it across smilingly.

'Certainly not!' was my answer.

'Then give me a commitment, and I shall not take any other offers. I mean professionally,' she added.

I looked at her, trying to figure out whether she meant it.

'Make a commitment—and I am yours, not only for now, but for all times,' she said.

I pondered and said, 'Give me a little time, and I shall commit fully.'

'Now!' she insisted.

We went for a drive, parked the car by the seaside, and stood outside, looking at the setting sun, watching it go down. My decision was still not forthcoming.

'How long will you take to decide?' she asked.

I picked up a few pebbles and threw them into the sea.

She also picked one up and threw it up in the air.

I came back and sat in the car. She followed and sat beside me. I was contemplating. She was waiting for my answer, and put her head on my chest, cosily entrenching herself, listening to my heartbeats.

'Your heartbeats are getting faster,' she teased me.

'For it is a life-long decision—let's go!' I said.

'No, we decide and then go.' She was adamant.

'What if I don't decide now?' I asked.

'I won't let you drive.' And she clung to me. I raised her head and kissed her, a long, long kiss that endured forever. She yielded herself to me, and cried.

'Mona!' I mumbled. She did not stop crying.

'Mona!' I lovingly repeated, a little louder. She stopped crying and looked at me. The innocence in her face was absolute, and so winning! I loved her the most then, more than I loved myself.

'I have decided,' I said.

'What?' she asked.

'Have you forgotten?' I said.

'I don't care, as long as we are like this forever—and ever and ever.'

'Forever—and ever and ever,' I repeated, and then continued, 'We are going to get engaged tomorrow!'

'No, not tomorrow,' she said.

'When, then?'

'No engagement,' she said.

'But I have a beautiful ring in my mind for you,' I enthused.

'The ring would be worn the same day that we pledge ourselves to each other in marriage,' she said.

'And not tell the world that you are my beautiful secret!' I turned poetic.

'Don't tell the world!' she agreed.

'No fuss in our marriage!' I said.

'No fuss,' she repeated.

'No music except that of the dancing in our hearts,' I continued.

She closed her eyes and swayed as she enjoyed my statement.

'No guests and no parties.' I hadn't finished yet.

'You shall be my guest and I shall cook.' She was now full of an inner joy.

'Yes!' I beamed a smile. 'And I shall be yours as you feed me.'

'Did you like the chicken I specially cooked for you the other evening?' she asked excitedly.

'It never tasted better than that evening. Look, my mouth has already started watering,' I laughed.

'Let's go to my little place, I am going to cook for you,' she said, and made me start the car.

We registered a date for our marriage with the Registrar of Marriages. The notice hung on the wall of the court for two weeks. Exactly after two weeks, we were on the sets of *Taxi Driver*, and there was a small break in-between for the cameraman Ratra to light the shot. I looked at my watch and winked at Mona. She got the hint and walked out. I followed a few seconds later, into the art department's room, where she was waiting. We walked across to the Registrar of Marriages. I took out the ring, put it around her finger. She hugged me shyly. Then we both signed the register and were husband and wife.

Nobody knew except our confidants. They had to for the marriage required two witnesses, one on each side, to verify that we were the same persons mentioned in the affidavits.

After the stolen moment, we went back silently to the sets. The world was ignorant as to what had just taken place. But Ratra, the cameraman, an intimate friend of both of us, noticed the ring on her finger as Mona was giving an independent shot for a love-scene.

'But it wasn't there in the previous shot!' he blurted out to himself.

'I shall hide it in the shot!' Mona discreetly and quietly motioned to him. He guessed what might have happened, and looked at me in amusement, for rumour had it that Dev and Mona would marry secretly one day.

'Maybe they have!' he started suspecting, and wanted to be the first to pull the cat out of the bag. But I hastened to hush him up with a subtle gesture of my hand. He understood, nodded a stealthy nod, and became the only person besides the two witnesses and the registrar and his assistant to know that the leading lady of *Taxi Driver* was now Mrs Dev Anand!

But the well-kept secrets of a popular figure very much in the news are very often destined to be leaked out by the wagging tongues of the gossip circle. And one day, my father who was visiting Bombay and staying with my elder brother Chetan walked across a couple of streets to see me. It was a heart-to-heart meeting between the two of us after many years.

'You never told your father about your marriage,' were the first grudging words he uttered. He was right, for he had the right to know, and it was his privilege as a father.

'I didn't tell anybody,' was my answer.

'With a Christian girl?' he continued.

'Does it make a difference?' I asked.

He paused for a while, the victim of a debate in his mind, and then said, 'It might. I shall ask you much later—if I am still alive.'

'Don't condemn my marriage,' I told him.

'There were thousands of beautiful girls wanting to marry you,' he said.

'I got the one I wanted,' I retorted.

'You are a child.'

'Naturally, for I am talking to my father.'

'You are bound to have a clash with her.'

'That can happen with any other girl as well.'

'A clash of values—of each other's background and upbringing and culture.'

'We are two human beings—and a bond of love has similar values,' I was now quite stern.

'Don't be headstrong. Listen to what your father is going to say,' he said, half-angry, half-cajoling.

'Why?' I cut him short. 'Did you listen to me when you wanted me to serve as a clerk in a bank? Did you listen to me when I wanted to do my master's in English Literature at Lahore?' The words rushed out in one long breath.

'You know I was poor then. I could not afford that.' He was apologetic.

'So how can you now afford to dictate to a son who did not even take his train fare from you, to come all the way to struggle in this cut-throat, cold-blooded city, to join the ranks of millions unemployed here?' I was rude and ruthless.

He heaved a long sigh.

'That's destiny, my son. Yours, as well as mine. But always remember my words.' He walked out slowly and in great turmoil, sad and broken. I felt sorry for my outburst but my ego stopped me from calling him back. I let him go.

Taxi Driver was released with great fanfare. At its opening, outside the theatre situated at the end of a busy thoroughfare, one could see an unending line of taxis, as the city's taxi drivers in all their strength were sitting in the hall watching the premiere, with the chairman of their association in attendance as well, as the chief guest.

'It is our film,' they all took pride in proclaiming, and pronounced me their hero.

One of our unit members gleefully announced that there was no taxi available for any passengers that evening, as all the taxi drivers were having a gala time in the theatre in which the movie was released, and that the only taxi driver who could be had for the most needy was Mr Dev Anand, at the cost of a million rupees for a ride to a limited destination!

It was true that my screen persona of a taxi driver had become something of an extension of my real-life personality. During the filming of *Taxi Driver*, I was constantly in the minds and eyes of people, who would see me in various streets of the city driving a taxi, in a taxi-driver's uniform, with a taxi-driver's docket hanging from my khaki jacket.

During a shot once, I was offloading a passenger outside the Taj Mahal Hotel. As soon as the take was over, a foreigner with a couple of cameras round his neck hastily entered my taxi and ordered, 'To the red-light district, please.'

I looked at him through the rear-view mirror. 'Red-light district!' he repeated.

I turned and looked at him, raising my cap this time.

'Red-light district—I'm sure you know where it is. I am in a hurry,' he said.

The crowds watching the shooting outside started laughing boisterously. And a couple of rowdies rushed forward to tell him he was talking to a popular movie star.

'What?' He was amazed.

'Good afternoon, sir,' I addressed him now, taking off my cap. 'I'm sorry, but you have to take another taxi. This one is not for hire.'

'Is it not?' he asked quizzically.

'For a movie is being shot in it!' I said.

'What's your name, sir?' He suddenly started sirring me, getting ready to get out of the taxi, not taking his eyes off me.

'Sir, if you get to see an Indian movie called *Taxi Driver* in your country, you'll get to know the name of the guy you just met!' I said, getting out first and holding the door open for him.

He looked wonderstruck, and seemed to have forgotten all about the red-light district.

Twenty-eight

The year 1954 was an eventful year for me. I got married that year, and catapulted to fame with *Taxi Driver*. I had the experience of a lifetime in the Soviet Union, and another rewarding one, a three-hour-long historic meeting with the inimitable Charles Chaplin, one of the greatest actors and directors in the history of world cinema.

After World War II, the Soviet Union under Stalin had closed its doors to the outside world, having regimented its society, trying to build up its economy, which was in shambles after the war, and its system of authoritative communism amongst the fourteen republics that formed the Soviet Union. In 1954, for the first time, it lifted the iron curtain and allowed visitors from the outside world. The movie industry in India was asked by the Ministry of Culture to send a delegation of prominent and popular movie stars to hobnob with their counterparts in the USSR, to have a first-hand knowledge of the goings-on in that forbidden part of the world. Khwaja Ahmed Abbas, with his leftist leanings, was asked to select and head a fourteen-member delegation to travel to the USSR as guests, to acquaint itself with the Soviet Union's experiments with communism. I was chosen as one of its members, along with Chetan, Balraj Sahni, Bimal Roy, Raj Kapoor, Nargis and Hrishikesh Mukherjee. It was a momentous trip.

On our way to the Soviet Union, we stopped for a couple of days in Geneva, before taking a flight to Prague, then the capital of communist Czechoslovakia, from where a Soviet aircraft would fly the delegation to Moscow.

Charles Chaplin at that time had settled down in Switzerland, in Vevey near Montreaux, after having been dubbed a leftist by the

American government and asked to leave the country for his involvement in 'un-American activities'. He had acquired a palatial mansion a few hours' drive from Geneva, which he called his White House, having made it look like the exterior of the American presidential palace in Washington DC, thus getting his own back at the American government. The leader of our delegation, K.A. Abbas, had sought a meeting with the great comedian, who had agreed to meet us for an informal chat over cups of coffee in his villa.

As a student in Lahore, I had seen Charles Chaplin in *The Great Dictator*, in which he had lampooned Adolf Hitler, the German dictator of the Third Reich who had overrun Europe to bring the peoples and governments of that continent under German subjugation, his Nazi armies goose-stepping over their freedom, striking terror into the hearts of all European nations. Chaplin's portrayal of the double role of the dictator and his lookalike, a Jewish barber, was a masterpiece of cinematic acting. We all looked forward to a meeting with the great legend.

There is a scene in the film in which the dictator kicks the globe of the world with the heels of his boots. That scene had always stood out in my mind. As I got out of the bus outside the entrance of his Swiss villa along with the other members of the delegation to be met, received and welcomed by Chaplin himself, I could not resist saying aloud, 'Hail Chaplin!' with my arm raised in the same fashion as the Nazi soldiers did to salute their leader.

Chaplin laughed heartily, fully understanding why I did so, said 'Thank you' and then adding jokingly, 'And now, welcome to my White House.' He raised his arm in a salute too, this time copying me! He escorted us all through the main hall of his elegant villa, out into the portico, in front of the lush green lawns that looked out over a very picturesque Swiss valley. Every time a tourist bus passed that landmark, the conductor of the bus pointed at the famous Chaplin mansion with great glee and pride.

In a corner of the main hall that we crossed, on our way to the portico, sat a piano, with a very elegantly dressed lady playing it. She casually nodded hello to us as she played. I guessed she must be Chaplin's latest wife Oona, daughter of the famous playwright Eugene O'Neill. A toddler, evidently her daughter from Charlie, was reclining on her knees. The sonata that she played set the background for our meeting with the great philosopher comedian. We squatted around him on the grassy ground as he reclined in his easy chair. He spoke of the philosophy of his life, the humour he brought to his films, of romance, of poetry, of affluence, of his disillusionment with America, to which he said he had given the best years of his life. He was ready to answer all that we wanted to know. Raj Kapoor literally sat at his feet, being his best disciple—he had consciously or subconsciously been following Chaplin's style as an actor.

I had met Danny Kaye, another famous comedian, earlier, during his brief visit to Bombay when he was the UN ambassador. The difference I found between the two was that while Danny was a comic even in his behaviour towards his fans, always playing to the gallery, Chaplin struck a serious chord as a man. While Danny Kaye in his talk and mannerisms conveyed the personality of an entertaining joker, Chaplin imparted an impression of a great thinker, who always philosophized on the frailties of man and society. Danny made people laugh with his buffoonery while Chaplin added quiet chuckles of wit and cheer.

The three intimate hours we spent with 'Charlie' were as good as reading all his biographies written the world over. The goodbye kiss he blew us when he saw us off at the front door of his villa, stayed with us through the rest of the trip. We carried his aura with us on our trip to the world of communism we were about to visit. As the bus taking us back to Geneva drove away, and took a turn, taking the diminutive figure of the giant of an artist, thinker and comedian away from view, Raj Kapoor was heard shouting again and again: 'Goodbye little fellow, goodbye little fellow, goodbye little fellow', as he hung out of the window of the bus.

Twenty-nine

At Prague we were received by a group of Czech officials who were commissioned by their masters to look after us during our brief stopover. Two amongst them struck me with strong personalities that could stand out in any crowd. One of them, apparently the leader, looked like a killer, and I thought he must be carrying a gun in his pocket, with a couple of henchmen handy around him all the time. It was a scary thought.

The second person, who fascinated me immensely, was Allena, an interpreter. She was a picture-perfect image of beauty. Probably just out of her teens, she was slim as a young girl should be, without being anorexic; tall as a young girl should be, but not so much as to be labelled mannish; very fair, without the chalky whiteness of a European; and soft and cuddly, with a smile in her eyes. If I was not married already, I would there and then have proposed to her and taken her back with me to India.

Allena became friendly as we briefly danced together at a small party thrown by our hosts, under the vigil of the leader, who, though he looked like a ruthless killer, turned out to be a very polite host, giving all the attention and assistance to the first-ever foreign delegation on communist soil.

My six-week trip to the Soviet Union was a great lesson on the working of Soviet society and the people who lived under that system. Two films I starred in, *Aandhiyan* and the English version of *Rahi*, directed by K.A. Abbas, were official entries at the film festival. All the invited Hindi films were dubbed in the various languages of the Soviet republics, and eight hundred prints of each were released simultaneously all over the Soviet Union. This could only be possible in a state-controlled society. Each one of us was asked to choose the places and republics he or she wanted to visit during our tour, besides Moscow, which was the starting point of our trip. I chose Leningrad (now St. Petersburg), Tbilisi in Georgia, Stalingrad and Sochie, the Black Sea resort. Tashkent, in Tajikistan, was of course a common place that all of us visited, for the Soviet aircraft took us there first, it being the first stopover on the way to Moscow.

We were given interpreters who knew English, as well as Hindi, and who saw to it that we went only to those places which were planned for us to visit and see, and with proper escorts. We were kept busy all the time, never left alone to ourselves, neither for sightseeing, nor for any private or public meetings. Being a state guest in the Soviet Union was a rare privilege and honour in those days. Not everybody could enter that world. The Russians were very friendly, affectionate people, and very outgoing. Their hospitality overflowed with generosity and a genuine desire to impress the outside world about their system. They gave us roubles to spend, for there was no money exchange system; took us to their largest department store in Moscow called Gum, state-owned it goes without saying, where one could buy, as a Russian put it, 'anything from one's body to one's soul'; to the Bolshoi theatre in Moscow, where once the famous Anna Pavlova maddened audiences with her ballet performances; and to their museums and their universities, and showed us with pride the reconstructed showpieces of post-war development.

Some of the landmarks of their valour and fighting spirit, which they were keen to show us, told us tales of their bravery, both by patriotic civilians and the armed forces, when their collective might had overthrown the powerful war machine of their deadliest enemy, Adolf Hilter. In Stalingrad, we were taken to the hill on which the last hand-to-hand combat took place between the Soviet forces and the Nazi army, in which hundreds from both sides were killed. That was the last bastion of Hitler's militia, from where his soldiers started retreating as the Soviets started advancing, until they oversaw his end and his final annihilation as he found himself hounded like a rat in its hiding place, to be discovered dead in his bunker.

As we stood over the hill named after Stalin, our hosts dug out pieces of broken and twisted metal from the bombs that had been blasted on both the sides, bombs that were reminders of a not so distant past. Underneath the rubble lay buried the remains of the maimed bodies of both the victors and the vanquished. A part of the World War was enacted before our eyes as decorated Soviet heroes of that grim tragedy shook hands with us, flaunting rows and rows of war medals shining on their jackets over chests that had been wounded and scarred, reminding us of each conquering step that they had marched towards their final victory on D-Day. We were all impressed by the fast pace of their recovery and projects of reconstruction.

Vodka flowed like the waters of the Volga. Toasting over vodka was customary and a ritual that opened the gates of friendship and bonhomie. Large-hearted gregarious Russians would embrace us with affection and kisses and hugs, like long-lost relations from a previous birth. Young, pretty schoolgirls, the Pioneers as they were called, would appear from nowhere to pin badges on the lapels of our jackets, and wrap red scarves around our necks. 'Dasoidonya' (thank you) and 'Tovarish' (comrade) became pet words in our daily vocabulary. In umpteen receptions in our honour, followed by dances, we could with total courtesy and politeness pick up a partner from amongst the gathered invitees. A spirit of revelry and open-mindedness was in the air.

In a party one evening two attractive young Russian girls kept looking at me, whispering something into each other's ears. Fascinated, I approached one of them for a dance, to which she readily agreed, to the visible disappointment of the other. As soon as the number finished, I beckoned to the other as well, who jumped onto the floor with a rhythmic gusto that went well with the music. No words could be exchanged with any of them, language being a handicap, but our eyes did all the talking, with the tempo of the moment swaying us along with it. As soon as the second dance ended and the music came to an abrupt halt, both girls wanted to say something friendly and intimate, but it appeared they were being watched by someone from amongst the crowd, and they suddenly disappeared out of sight. I never saw them again in any other party or reception in our honour. It was evident that no one Russian invitee in a get-together was repeated in any other. I had heard about people being policed in communist regimes. Now I saw it with my own eyes.

People fell for us, and wanted to make friends and build contacts, but were kept away from doing so, being constantly watched by a hidden eye of the State vigilance department. Was it the KGB? I wondered. No one ever gave us his or her visiting card, or invited us home, though it was abundantly clear that a sudden surge of joy had swept into the humdrum, regimented, overdisciplined lives of these people with the visit of members of a colourful entertainment industry from a friendly Asian country, and they wanted to add to that joy by welcoming us with open arms.

I spent my thirty-first birthday in the midst of a large cocktail-cum-dinner reception. The hostess was an important Soviet official. She emphasized the importance of the evening in her opening speech, toasting me with a glass of vodka, as everybody in the party cheered and congratulated me, for my birthday coincided with the release of *Rahi* the same day in the theatres. Many present in the gathering were already familiar with my face and personality. As I saw the glasses of vodka raised towards me, I too picked up mine, clinked it with the ones on my immediate right and left, said 'cheers' in Russian, which expression by now came easy on my lips, and gulped the contents down in the same vein as they all did theirs. As soon as I emptied my glass, there was another toast to me, this time for my performance in *Rahi*. My glass was refilled, another round of glasses was raised and I drained my glass again, as they all looked at me admiringly. I shook my head and felt the heady warmth of the vodka coursing through me, and found a need to speak and say 'thanks'. I rattled off a few lines in a deep, grainy, vodka-soaked voice, and then stopped for the interpreter to take over and translate the gist of what I said. That was followed by a round of applause so heartening that I immediately came out with an addition to my earlier vote of thanks, coining and inventing phrases more forcefully endearing to their hearts, which when interpreted again brought even brighter cheer to their faces and elicited still more claps. Feeling more heroic, I continued the speech process for as long as I could, more and more thunderous applause bucking me up. By the time I finally ended my speech, the hall was reverberating with sounds of 'Bravo, bravo'.

Pleased with myself, I felt as important as a member of the Soviet politburo!

I had started with 'Tovarish', and ended with 'Long live the people'. The vibrant crowd raised the glasses for the third time with a resounding chorus of 'Dev Anand', and etiquette demanded a similar gesture on my part. My glass refilled again, I gulped the vodka down for the third time, and got down to exploring the inspiration behind the speech that had delivered itself so eloquently. Was it the world-famous Russian vodka? Was it the plump attractive lady with the black flowing evening dress and well-coiffeured auburn hair who had set the ball rolling for the evening with a kiss on my cheek? Or was it the good-looking and seductive Marina, my Georgian interpreter, who kept on eyeing me with a 'Happy Birthday' smile from amidst the crowd, her hand holding her vodka raised the highest, above the hands of the rest? Or the adoring, admiring faces of the gathering, their minds fresh with images of me from the film they had seen? Or the thought of Mona, my wife, remembering me on a day when I should have been exclusively with her? Perhaps all the factors combined together to give meaning to an evening that was charged and heady with the intoxication of the moment.

The people of the Soviet Union were used to seeing only those films that were made by their ministry of culture, on themes and subjects that needed to be propagated by the State, to further its ideology. Anything from outside that could influence them to the contrary was strictly prohibited, and banned if necessary. For the first time, like a wave of fresh breeze, the escapist Indian music-and-dance extravaganzas and sexy love fantasies found their way into their theatres, and the Soviets pounced upon them with the joy of a child in wonderland. They filled the theatres and sang our songs, and followed our movie stars and movie makers like teenage autograph hunters.

Raj Kapoor ended up being the most popular figure and his film *Awara* became something of a cult phenomenon. The song '*Awara hoon*' was on everyone's lips, being sung everywhere as if it was the national anthem of the country. Wherever we went, there was a demand for Raj Kapoor to sing his song, and he willingly and valiantly sang it whole-heartedly, playing to the gallery, sitting on a piano stool with glasses of vodka being offered to him from all sides, as his own glass of whisky lay emptied on the piano, waiting to be refilled. As he sang, men and women participated in the song, dancing and screaming and reeling with drunken delight. He was the hero and commanded such a following that the Russians often asked Indians who visited their land long after the delegation had left their shores, 'Are you from the land of *Awara*?' Even Pt. Jawaharlal Nehru, when he later visited the Soviet Union, the very first official visit ever of an Indian prime minister there, developed a Raj Kapoor complex when he heard the popular Indian movie star being mentioned wherever he went.

My farewell to the Soviet Union came with a beautiful red rose pinned on my buttonhole, and a red souvenir scarf hung around my neck. I carried both back home in my bag. The rose had withered inside the pages of a favourite book I was reading by the time I returned. But the scarf must still be lying amongst my vast collection of scarves.

A Russian friend of mine, a journalist from the Tass agency, New Delhi, was on a holiday in his country, resting in a sanatorium in Sochi, a port on the Black Sea. It is a scenic resort in Caucasus, in the mountains of which, the saying goes, live the most luscious-looking fairies, tempting men with their heavenly looks. I was visiting Sochi as a member of the delegation. My Russian friend invited me to the sanatorium for an evening, having sought permission from the authorities concerned, to celebrate my visit to his country. It turned out to be the celebration of their national drink. He first toasted my visit, then my health. Two glasses of vodka down our throats, I reciprocated by toasting his country, the great political and social system they had adopted, and their brave people who stood the test of time to become a world power. With those five toasts, one after another in quick succession, accompanied by slices of butter to counterbalance the heady effect of alcohol in our system, the stage was set for another bottle of vodka to be opened. It seemed we could go on drinking, with the flow of conversation getting warmer and warmer, uniting Russia and India on a common platform of vodka. Suddenly a young pretty Russian girl emerged with a red rose and a scarf matching the colour of the flower, planted a kiss on my cheek, put the rose into my buttonhole, and decorated my neck with the red scarf, adding a 'fairy' touch to the moment that was imprinted on my mind even as it swam in vodka.

Everything that happened after that remains a total blackout. At ten-thirty the next morning, I discovered myself on the bed in the hotel room with a terrible hangover, with Balraj Sahni trying hard to wake me up, literally thrashing me, saying, 'Don't you remember that Ambassador K.P.S. Menon is having breakfast with all of us here in the hotel? We are all waiting for you.'

I rubbed my eyes, my head splitting, the red rose and the scarf still a very loving part of my person.

My second trip to the Soviet Union was several years later, as a member of the jury for the Moscow Film Festival. King Vidor, the famed American director, headed the jury as its chairman. While deliberating on the winners, we watched the first moon landing on television. There was an expression of triumphant glee on the faces of the Americans at America's victory over the Soviets in putting a man on the moon, while the Soviets chuckled ruefully, accepting defeat in the race. It was a great study in human moods for me.

Thirty

Russia was always in the forefront of world cinema. Its great pioneers and masters Eisenstein and Pudovkin became world famous, contributing to the growth of the medium. Their cinematic work was considered as textbooks for future film-makers to learn from. Eisenstein's book *The Film Sense* was accepted as a Bible for all students of cinema, along with Stanislavski's *An Actor Prepares*. Chetan was a great admirer of their work.

When Pudovkin visited India along with one of the great actors of their early period, Cherkasov, they saw *Afsar* in a private screening especially organized for them. Cherkasov had played the role I played in *Afsar* on stage in Russia. After seeing the film he felt very nostalgic.

When the Indian film delegation alighted from a train in Leningrad, Cherkasov was the person commissioned to receive and welcome us. As soon as the train whistled to a stop, his searching eyes looked for and spotted me, and he shouted 'Dev Anand!' in a voice as booming and dominating as his imposing figure. He then presented me with his autobiography written in Russian in which he had mentioned me, with a picture of him and me together taken in Bombay after the screening of *Afsar*. I thought it was a great honour. Chetan, who had often enthused to me about the pioneering work of Eisenstein and Cherkasov as an actor–director team, was equally thrilled to meet the great actor again.

When we came back to India, Chetan was possessed with an overflowing creative energy, and dived deep into the making of *Funtoosh*, a fun film. I enjoyed playing a farcical comedy to the hilt this time, opposite Sheila Ramani, who had also starred in *Taxi Driver*. Once a Miss Simla, she was great fun and a great sport. She had danced her way into the hearts of people in *Taxi Driver*, and was now in great touch, wooing and swooning over a buffoon that was me in the film. The songs were again a highlight of the film, and the one that stood out was '*Dukhi man mere, sun mera kehna*', which to my mind is one of the greatest songs that Navketan has given the world, for the sheer simplicity of its lyrics, as well as the sweet sadness of its melodious strains. The song was sung with great feeling by Kishore Kumar, and in fact is one of the best rendered by him; it touches one's heart, pulling at the heart strings.

Funtoosh was fun, fun, fun all the way. On my way back from the Karlovy Vary film festival in Czechoslovakia, when a bus took all the delegates back to Prague after the closing of the great event, each one of us sang the national anthem of his or her country. When my turn came, after having started our own '*Jana-Gana-Mana*' with great feeling, I suddenly got stuck both with the words and the musical notations, and quickly switched over to singing '*Ai meri topi palat ke aa*', a popular musical number from *Funtoosh*, to the utter joy and delight of my co-passengers, since the rhythm of the song matched the fast speed of the bus. After I finished singing, there was applause and demands for an encore, with people clapping lustily, but I confessed apologetically, 'Ladies and gentlemen, this was not my national anthem, but a song from my latest film!'

After his first commercial success in *Taxi Driver*, Chetan wanted to branch off on his own, to do something away from Dev Anand, the established star. He was right in his own way. Breaking away from the shackles of his younger brother's image, desiring to achieve something on his own was a natural corollary that followed his acceptance as a viable box-office proposition. While in Navketan he had to make films only for me because of certain moral and box-office compulsions; outside, as an independent entity, he could branch out more happily on the steam of his own creative desires. He revealed this openly in a letter to his wife. I don't ever read other people's letters unless asked to. But a handwritten letter by him to his wife lay open on the dining table one day, waiting to be put in an envelope and then posted. Accidentally my eyes fell upon it, my name in it written boldly. My curiosity aroused, I could not resist reading the line: 'There is a lot I would like to do in this company, but Dev is my problem.' I did not read further. It pained me to know I had suddenly become a 'problem'. But as a sensitive human being, I fully understood Chetan's creative necessity, not to be forever tied down to his younger brother, whose popularity was growing day by day. I started preparing myself for an emotional and heart-searing moment when my brother would suddenly walk out of the company that I had helped him form so that he could make movies.

And when the confrontation actually happened, after I heard that he was secretly planning his own film and his own company, I was neither shocked nor unhappy. My eyes had already fallen upon Goldie. He was extremely intelligent, had written the script for *Taxi Driver* and had partly participated in writing and directing *Funtoosh* as well along with Chetan. I was certain he was equipped to jump into the arena the moment I asked him to. One day, fully aware that Chetan's concentration was being divided between Navketan and his own about-to-be-formed company, I chose a moment to show my intense affection for my younger brother, and looked at him with a question in my eyes. He quickly understood what my eyes conveyed and immediately said, 'I have a script ready.'

And *Nau Do Gyarah* was launched with me and Mona starring, and Goldie directing.

The film began with me at the wheel of a truck going from Delhi to Bombay, the camera sometimes following me, sometimes running ahead of me and making a photographic survey of the countryside, from state to state, as we travelled along. Rural India kept pace with us, waking out of its lazy slumber, as we, on our nonstop journey of filming, kept smiling and waving at curious passers-by trying to guess what we filmwallahs were up to. We went over the highways and through shrubby pebbly muddy pathways, over bridges and through tunnels, through forests of eye-pleasing gulmohar trees and dangerous-looking dacoit-infested ravines, through sunshine— with the burning heat of June scorching us—and through cloudy weather—with drizzling, sprinkling showers cooling our nerves.

Staying in dak bungalows at night and eating at dhabas on the way was a part of our cinematic adventure, as our caravan marched on, singing and dancing its way into the hearts of our countrymen, villagers and townsfolk alike: turbaned passers-by, their backs laden with bags of crops fresh from their fertile fields; village damsels with anklets around their bare feet and heavy pots balanced on their heads, their arms adorned with copper and silver bangles, swaying to the rhythm of our songs being played back for the artists in the movie; little children, naked from head to toe, begging for a few annas, running alongside the truck, inventing their own dance movements to the beat of the music that fell on their ears; and braided young schoolgirls in their uniforms, holding out notebooks, running along with us as if they had joined the bandwagon, seeking autographs, occasionally having a sneaky peep into the camera for their cute, pretty faces to be captured by it as well. It all made for a great road show of mirth, gaiety and revelry, as we kept on canning footage for the movie. It was a long-drawn-out picnic of great joy and creative satisfaction—a three-week-long adventure!

One evening in a dak bungalow in the Chambal area, an outsider alerted us about a planned attack by the local dacoits. I told the guy who informed us to tell the scoundrels to bring their autograph books along with them, as well as their cameras, for a once-in-a-lifetime photograph with their idol! The message was duly conveyed. Next morning, as we were on the road for filming, a bunch of ruffians surrounded our unit. I stood up on the truck and asked them in a very loud voice, 'How are you, my countrymen?'

'Arr-e-e? Dev saab! We are here only for your darshan,' came a barrage of voices, and soon they were all around me. After the usual warm handshakes and overindulgent embraces, a voluptuous village belle was seen running towards me through the tall grass, shouting 'Don't let him! Don't let him go!' in her own village dialect. From the reception they all gave to her sudden appearance amidst them, it was evident they were all her lovelorn suitors, each one of them desiring to be the most privileged one to win her over. She ordered everybody around and sought a solo photograph of me with her, taking a small camera out from inside her blouse and thrusting it into her favourite beau's hand. Before one could say 'Jack Robinson', her arm was around me. I reciprocated too in a very chivalrous way, squeezing her hand in mine. The photographer clicked the shot, capturing the man of the dacoit-girl's dreams clutched in her possessive grip. After the great melodramatic act was over, she ordered her band of ruffians, again in her local dialect, 'Now let them all go—you skunks!'

What had seemed to hold the possibilities of a dramatic encounter with the dreaded Chambal dacoits turned out to be the most 'filmy' of episodes. And we were back on the road again, filming.

By the time our film unit reached Khandala on the Western Ghats, more than half of *Nau Do Gyarah* was finished. The film had some of the best musical compositions of S.D. Burman, this time with Majrooh Sultanpuri as his lyricist. When the film got released, Goldie, now known by his proper name Vijay Anand, was hailed as the brightest young film director ever on the Indian film scene. Meanwhile, Mona declared that this was her last film. She now wanted to take charge of the home, which was her priority.

Goldie was made a partner in Navketan, as Chetan willingly quit after both of us agreed to disagree and part. Goldie got ready to call some of the most memorable creative shots with me on screen. He was all set to compete with the best in the field. Together we were destined to produce some work that would go down in history.

Thirty-one

As soon as *Nau Do Gyarah* was released, we started work on *Kala Pani*. It was directed by Raj Khosla, my coffeehouse friend from the days I was working at the military censor office. Raj had a deep grainy voice and was a blind admirer of K.L. Saigal's singing. He had also wanted to be a singer originally. I had put him on to Guru Dutt, then about to direct *Baazi*, and he had made him his assistant. That was the beginning of the movie career of a man who later gave some memorable hits. Together, we made a finely tuned team that lasted for a long time.

Raj would often drop in at my place without notice, ask for a harmonium and sing songs that would delight us both. After having set the pace for a prolonged musical soirée, he would suddenly open the briefcase he always carried to dig out a bottle of scotch hiding amidst his numerous files, and take a swig.

Later, when he directed Hema Malini and me in *Shareef Badmash*, a Navketan film, I could discern that his concentration was divided between the making of the film and his constantly nagging desire for a drink. That craving for alcohol became a part of his existence at the fag end of his career and proved fatal for him. Though he died of a sudden fracture that never healed, I am sure it was his addiction to liquor that drowned him in the abyss which is the final resting place for all mortals.

Kala Pani was memorable for various reasons. It gave me my first Filmfare award for best actor, along with a best supporting actress award for Nalini Jaywant. We received our awards from Al-Nasser, the late president of Egypt.

Kala Pani also gave the world a story about me that has been circulating amongst my fans ever since—that I am forbidden to wear black, for women swoon when they see me dressed in that colour. A stupid myth! But I went along with it, humouring my fans. The yarn, perhaps, originated from the fact that I wore black throughout *Kala Pani*. The father of the character I played was undergoing 'kala-pani', a life sentence, for a crime he had never committed. And the son had sworn to himself that he'd always be dressed in black, symbolizing mourning, until the time he freed his innocent father from the clutches of the law.

Kala Pani also brought the late President Sukarno of Indonesia on our sets to watch it being filmed. While shooting one day we got a call saying he would be visiting us. All excited, I meticulously rehearsed a shot for the famous song '*Hum bekhudi mein tumko pukare chale gaye*', and waited for his arrival. But he did not turn up for two hours. Fed up of waiting, we took the shot. However, as soon as the take was okayed and canned, a message came across that Sukarno and his entourage had entered the gates of the studio. I quickly warmed up again and readied myself for a repeat performance, as if for a royal court. After he arrived and was given a warm welcome befitting the stature of an acclaimed foreign statesman on our soil, I went back to face the arc-lamps along with my co-star Nalini Jaywant.

The director asked, 'Are you ready, Dev?'

'Ready,' was my instant reply.

'Camera!' he ordered.

'Rolling,' responded the cameraman.

And I sang through the entire stanza of the song without a break.

The director shouted 'Cut'. The lights were switched off. The honoured guests clapped and I went rushing back to the great leader to receive more accolades from him. The Indonesian president felt very pleased and flattered to have actually seen us shoot. I was happy at having entertained him, and the studio workers were most amused at the mock filming staged exclusively for the honoured guest.

But above all, I remember *Kala Pani* the most for Madhubala, its leading lady, the most beautiful of all the heroines in the fairyland of films, with her natural looks, always as fresh as morning dew, sans heavy make-up, false eyelashes, contact lenses or scanty dresses fashioned by designers to impart artificial glamour that would titillate male curiosity. Her childlike innocence was accentuated by the most noticeable trait of her character, her famous giggle. Every time I think of her, I hear her giggle outside my make-up room, followed by a knock at the door that announced her arrival.

'So you have arrived! Ho-ho-ho!' I would greet her.

And her 'Yes, I have' was always substituted by another giggle. She was forever giggling at the slightest pretext. Nobody knew when the next bout of giggles would come, and once it did, how long it would last!

Many times she would suddenly start giggling during a take when the camera was on. The lights had to be switched off indefinitely and tea ordered, until she was able to get a hold of herself and rein in her mirth.

The great giggler was perhaps laughing at the world around her that did not know that she had a damaged heart, and would die quite young.

Thirty-two

Our first child was born in Switzerland, in a nursing home. I was shooting for *Paying Guest* for Subodh Mukherji, enacting a drunken scene, when the news arrived that Mona had given birth to a son. I was in such high spirits that I gave a brilliant shot, probably my best in the film. I called the nursing home in Zurich as soon as the shot was canned; a nurse answered the phone and congratulated me.

I joined Mona a fortnight later; both of us were invited to attend the Karlovy Vary film festival in Czechoslovakia. We carried Suneil, our child, in a little basket with us to the festival, and everybody there, the delegates as well as the citizens of that cute town famous for its hot water springs, were amused at the sight of the two-week-old child being carted around in a basket all over the place. One of the delegates at the festival was a white-bearded eighty-six-year-old man. The press, always on the lookout for an interesting story, photographed him with Suneil, and put their picture on the front page of a local newspaper, with the caption: 'The oldest and the youngest delegates at the Karlovy Vary film festival.'

The newspaper was brought to me by Allena, the same girl who had been our Czech interpreter in Prague when we were on our way to Moscow. She was in Karlovy Vary as well, again as our interpreter. We were meeting each other after a gap of about two years. She was intrigued and very charmed at our carrying our baby in the basket wherever we went, and often took the basket over from us, to carry it herself and play with the baby.

During our meeting in Prague she had expressed a keen desire to visit India, which she could never do all alone, being under the yoke of the communist regime. People travelling outside their country needed a sanction from the State, unless invited officially or sponsored by somebody in the country they wanted to visit.

'Anybody would love to do that for a pretty girl like you,' I had jocularly remarked, 'but the danger is you will never be able to come back to your own country.'

'Why?' she had asked.

'For you'll find so many suitors there,' I had said.

'I shall stay there then,' was her reply.

'Would you prefer that?' I had asked.

'Anywhere, where there is freedom,' was her answer. She was being stifled in her country, and she wanted to get out.

'Are you married?' she had abruptly asked me. I already was, but preferred not to answer, some innocent mischief tickling me. I waited instead for her next query, which came instantly.

'If I go to India and if you asked me not to come back here, I would stay on there,' she put it across very frankly.

There was a hint of flirtation in her eyes and tone, which enamoured me. I kissed her hand.

'I shall write to you,' she continued.

I scribbled my address on the diary she put in front of me. As she put the diary back in her handbag, she was interrupted, getting a call from her officer to quickly move the delegation to the airport, to catch their flight for the Soviet Union.

Back in India, a couple of months later, I received a light-blue envelope by post. It carried a Czech postmark. As I opened it, a very sweet fragrance breezed out of it, along with some dried rose petals. There was nothing written on the matching blue writing paper inside the envelope, except a big question mark, filling up the entire page. There was no sender's name. I was intrigued, but guessed it could only be Allena.

I kept asking myself, what could it mean? Did she want an answer to the question, 'Will you marry me?' Or was she asking for an invitation to the country? Perhaps both. I felt elated, since the letter did convey a certain amount of intimacy. I put it in my drawer, and then forgot all about it.

In Karlovy Vary I was reminded of that letter as Allena escorted us here and there. One day, when I was alone with her, I mentioned the letter to her. She confirmed having written and posted it, and said she was sorry since she did not know I was married. The chauvinistic male in me instinctively asked, 'Do you still wish I wasn't?'

'I do,' she confessed openly. I looked into her eyes. There was a desire in them, a longing.

'How long will you be here, at the festival?' she asked.

'As long as Allena is there!' I said, the flirt in me rising to the bait.

'We shall meet,' she said, and left hurriedly on an assignment.

Back in our hotel suite, Mona threw a tantrum. 'Who is that girl?' she fired a straight question at me.

'You know her, she's our interpreter,' I answered.

'You are lying! It's quite clear you knew her earlier,' she said through clenched teeth.

'I first met her in Prague, before I went to Russia,' I came out with the truth.

'Met her! It looks like you know each other quite well!' She had perhaps watched us talking to each other from a distance. 'I don't trust you. You send me back immediately. I don't want to stay here any longer,' she exploded, and started crying.

'Come on, Mona! Be calm. You are making a mountain out of a molehill,' I tried to calm her in soft undertones, trying not to be heard outside our door.

'I just cannot stay. I feel so humiliated—so . . . ignored!' she shot back, louder this time.

I was scared of a nasty showdown in the making that people would hear and gossip about.

'I am not ignoring you,' I whispered very softly and lovingly, imploring her to quieten down.

'Yes you are!' she screamed as she wept.

'Quiet, somebody might be listening, Mona!' I cajoled, but she kept on crying.

'This is not our home, it is a foreign land. Don't you realize?' I was almost begging in a hush-hush tone.

'I want to leave!' she shouted at the top of her voice—turning towards me.

I sat and cursed my fate, kicking myself for that conversation with Allena.

Mona started sobbing to herself. I let her, giving her time to cool down. Could it be that she had secretly seen Allena's anonymous but fragrant letter to me, having pulled it out of my drawer out of curiosity, and put two and two together when she saw us talking to each other? I closed my eyes in deep introspection, and suddenly heard the young Suneil let out a cry.

Both Mona and I walked up to his basket. He looked up at me, then threw his arms up and smiled.

'Look—he too is smiling at the big joke!' I smiled at Mona. She picked the baby up. And together, we fondled him.

That was the second big display of hysterical anger that I saw Mona make. Once before, she had shown a similar outburst of temper in front of her mother and her eldest brother. He was a group captain in the Indian Air Force and was in England on a mission with the Royal Air Force of Britain. Mona was, as he had casually mentioned, the most petted and pampered child of her family. Being the youngest she always had her say in all matters. Her brothers, all five of them, doted on her, as did her parents and two elder sisters. The group captain had brought a bottle of French wine from the services canteen and served her a little as well, along with me. She always loved a drink and never hesitated if someone she knew offered that hospitality. After she finished the wine offered to her by her brother, she wanted to pour more into her glass.

'No more,' her brother politely said, and took away the bottle from her.

'Why not? I want some more!' she insisted.

'Anything that my younger sister asks me—but no more of this. You've already had more than you should.' He held on to the bottle.

'I want more!' she ordered.

'Look at Dev. He is not taking more than he's had. Why are you so obstinate?' he said.

'I insist!' she thundered.

'You cannot insist in all matters,' her brother said quietly.

'I have always insisted. Haven't I?' She would not relent.

'This time you don't!' He was equally stubborn, yet smiling at his younger sister.

'I shall break the bottle!' She threw him a challenge.

'Break it, if you want to.' He kept it on the table.

She grabbed the bottle and threw it on the floor, smashing it. The wine spilled all over, and splinters flew in all directions.

Mona ran out of the room shrieking.

'Come Mona. Don't cry. Let's go for a drive,' I called, trying to pacify her.

Returning from Karlovy Vary, Mona and I landed at Santa Cruz airport in Bombay, carrying Suneil in the basket. The entire team of Navketan and friends and well-wishers were waiting with flowers and bouquets. *CID*, my latest film, had already been proclaimed a hit.

'Do you want to meet our little son?' I raised the basket over my head, in which Suneil was in another world that only he knew about, completely oblivious of what was going on around him. Everyone was jumping up and down with excitement and curiosity to have a first look at the new Prince. I raised the basket a little higher, prolonging their suspense, involving the people around in a game of hide-and-seek, as their inquisitive eyes tried desperately to catch a glimpse of the bundle of joy hiding inside, and the airport staff also joined in playfully. Finally, I put the basket down on the counter. People surrounded it at once and a rain of comments started pouring in:

'Cute.'

'Handsome.'

'Like both of you.'

'More of Mona.'

'More of Dev.'

'How many pounds did he weigh?'

'Beautiful thick eyebrows,' Chetan was saying.

'A carbon copy of Dev and Mona.'

I did not pay heed to what they were saying. My eyes were on the tiny tot wrapped very royally in a soft woollen blanket, with his red face peeping out, a monkey cap on his head, a twenty-six-day-old piece of oddity, struggling and kicking with his hands and legs, trying to search and explore the world he had come into, perhaps trying to fathom what shape and form he was likely to take.

Devina, our second child, was born three years later in Bombay, though Mona and I were absolutely sure she was conceived in Zurich, Switzerland, where Suneil was born. It was almost a deliberate move on our part, sinced we nursed the fond feeling that both our children should have the blessings of the Swiss Alps at the time of signalling their arrival into the world.

Mona and I were on a holiday in Europe. I owed her a foreign trip, for we had not gone anywhere for our honeymoon, as newly married couples normally do. Our honeymoon was spent in our familiar surroundings, in the home that we lived in, where we enjoyed the bliss of each other's closeness—and that's what honeymooning is all about anyway. During our European holiday, we spent a few days in Zurich, which held lots of memories for both of us. Mona had stayed there alone earlier, walked its streets, felt its fresh air, arising out of the snow-capped mountains around it, glistening in the warm sunshine, carrying and nursing her first baby in the protective sheath of her inner being. She was sentimental about the place. So we selected Zurich as one of the very important points in our itinerary.

A very popular Italian restaurant by the side of the lake became our favourite eating place. Every evening we went there for dinner at a fixed time, by the clock on the square that tolled the hours out in music. The waitress, sensing our arrival, always kept the same table reserved for us, and instead of the menu card always had the same question on her lips, 'Poulet a la rouche?' to which we always politely nodded with a sweet smile. As she would walk away with the order, another attendant would step in with the same brand of famous French red wine every evening to pour into the glasses in front of us, a larger quantity into Mona's glass, and a much smaller one into mine.

A great understanding between two couples, the guests and the hosts, foreign to each other, in a foreign land!

Normally, I am a vegetarian; but Poulet a la rouche was a deliciously cooked dish of chicken, and since Mona had cooked chicken in a similar fashion when she served me a special meal at her place on the day we pledged wedding vows to each other, this particular preparation of chicken added a special flavour to my taste.

And clinking wine glasses to each other's happiness for all times in a quaint Swiss place, with memories tugging at our heart strings, was worth an eternity.

One evening, as we held our glasses of wine, Mona said, 'Let's get a little high, and do something naughty!'

'Aren't we naughty every night?' I asked.

'Let tonight be a naughtier night.' She drank down the wine and winked.

I partly understood her meaning. She clinked my glass again with the naughtiest of smiles. I drained my glass at one go.

High on the classiest French wine, we made love to each other that night, on an extremely luxurious bed, and produced another baby whose name was derived from that of ours: Devina.

I doted on Devina. Not that I hadn't doted on Suneil, but Devina always wanted to be carried by me, and I was always available to do so. She was a doll. As soon as she spotted me arriving home, she would raise her arms, to be picked up and pampered. Having been picked up, she would cling to me, her arms thrown tightly around my shoulders, making me feel equally important in turn.

One day, a glass splinter hit her, resulting in a deep cut on her forehead. She burst out crying. I cried with her, and carried her instantly to the hospital. As the doctor cleaned and stitched her wound, she cried louder and louder, throwing her arms desperately and repeatedly towards me, to come to her rescue. I couldn't bear the sight, closed my eyes and turned away.

'NO!' she screamed.

She thought she was being left alone. That heart-rending scream was like the stab of a knife through my heart. I thought the doctor was slaughtering my daughter and hated him at that moment. After she was properly bandaged, she was back in my arms, sucking her thumb and going to sleep. She always sucked her thumb as a child.

I made the little Jasbir, calling herself 'Janice', in *Hare Rama Hare Krishna* suck her thumb as her childhood habit as well. The audience loved it.

Thirty-three

Stardom brings prosperity which makes for a comfortable lifestyle, with an accent on a little extra luxury, for people are watching you now. When you are ordinary, nobody has the time to look at you twice. But when you achieve star status, the world goes out of its way to watch your every move, what time you go to bed, what sort of bedroom you go to, and with whom. There is always a roving eye monitoring you. And to make yourself feel big in other people's eyes, you want to go for an expensive, expansive extension of your living standards. That's why stars are so often seen moving into palatial mansions right after they've scored a hit.

All that we needed, however, was a little more space in our bungalow. We got hold of a clever architect to design a floor above the existing structure. While it was being constructed, we rented an exclusive bungalow right on Juhu beach, and shifted there until the time our original residence was remodelled and ready.

The new bungalow gave us an advantage that was spiritually uplifting. It had a room with a terrace on its top level, with two windows facing opposite directions, the east and the west. Every day we enjoyed the pleasures of both the sunrise and the sunset sitting in that room. I savoured the shades and colours of both of these grand spectacles of nature. Living a life full of work had left me no time for such sights. Now I suddenly came alive to the drama of God's creation, and that room assumed great significance for me.

One evening, while I was watching the sunset and smiling in ecstasy at its changing colours, I got a call from a very dear friend, Sunil Dutt. I had earlier known him as Balraj and as our friendship grew, we switched over to calling each other 'Graen' (one belonging to the same place). He was a regular visitor to our home, coming over ever so often. I had encouraged him to join films as well, for he had a pleasant, strong personality with a boyish charm, and a typically north Indian demeanour with a strong Punjabi accent. He had not only got his break but was now doing a very big and important film, *Mother India*.

He had not come to our house for quite some time, and this long overdue call conveyed a lot of eagerness and excitement on his part to meet us.

'Come over!' I said.

'At twelve sharp, we shall be at your doorstep.' His keenness was intriguing.

'Why twelve sharp?' I asked.

'Just a kink in our minds,' he replied joyfully.

We? Our? Who was this other person? I was curious, and asked.

'You will see, you will both meet her then!' he said, and hung up.

We could partly guess, for some rumours were afloat about his hot romance with his leading lady.

At the stroke of the midnight hour, our doorbell rang. I opened the door.

'Nargis!' I exclaimed.

'My wife now!' he said. 'We just got married!'

So the cat was out of the bag. And Mona and I were the first persons to whom Sunil Dutt broke the news. Nargis had been my co-star as well in one film. She was the one who introduced me to Frederick's Hotel in Mahabaleshwar, when we were shooting there for Gajanand Jagirdar's *Birha Ki Raat*. Whenever I go to Mahabaleshwar, I stay at the Frederick's and Nargis often comes to mind. For she and I once sat at the Frederick's bar, she with a lemonade and I with a glass of beer, as I toasted the 'lucky guy' who would be her paramour, and one day her future husband. Now I was seeing the 'lucky guy', my own 'Graen', before my eyes, making Nargis the happiest girl in the world.

'Congratulations! And great timing!' I said to both of them. 'We have Fateh Ali, the great Pakistani qawwal, coming for a qawwali session to our house tomorrow evening. Let's combine that occasion with the announcement of your tying the knot. I shall prepare a special guest list. We'll have a big celebration with the great Fateh Ali and his group of qawwals serenading your nuptial joy!' I was really enthused.

But Nargis and Sunil had different plans, and the Fateh Ali session was left to a gathering of qawwali lovers, our friends in town and colleagues in the movie industry, who attended in large numbers. He sang until the wee hours of the dawn. Fateh Ali was accompanied by his little nephew, a very young child, along with the rest of his troupe. That little boy later shone on the international music scene as Nusrat Fateh Ali Khan.

When I reminded Nusrat about my date with him as a child at my home in Bombay in the late fifties, decades later at a film award function, he reciprocated by saying he was equally excited to meet me, for his late uncle Fateh Ali often mentioned that one of the greatest musical evenings of his career had taken place at the home of the famous Dev Anand in Bombay.

As I was sitting out on the terrace one evening, again watching the sunset and listening to the steady rise and fall of the sea waves, a voice called out from the beach revelers, 'Mr Dev Anand—Sivaji Ganeshan is here and wants to call on you!'

'Send him up!' I replied with great enthusiasm.

'He is not here now, but he'd like to meet you tomorrow—he called your other number and nobody responded.'

In Madras, I had done a film for Sivaji called *Amardeep*, and we had become friends. He came over next evening and stayed for dinner. Together, we watched the sunset, and talked until the full moon was high in the sky.

I respected Sivaji Ganeshan a lot. For his golden jubilee celebrations in Madras, with the chief minister Jayalalitha in the chair, and the entire south Indian movie industry honouring him, I was especially invited from Mumbai to be one of the main speakers in a huge stadium, and I obliged. Years went by, and the *Indian Express* group of newspapers invited me to Madras to confer upon me the 'Star of the Millennium' award. While I gave my thanksgiving speech to the vibrant gathering at the venue, Sivaji was watching me on television. He called me later at my hotel, and invited me over for a cup of tea with him at his place, before I left for the airport.

As I entered his residence I was welcomed by a garland so huge that the moment he put it around my neck I was literally bowed down by its weight. Humbly, I offered a long, revered 'namaskaram' to Sivaji for his generosity. He was ailing then, and that was my last and final 'adieu' to him.

Thirty-four

'*Do ka char, do ka char, do ka char.*'
    '*Paanch ka dus, paanch ka dus, paanch ka dus.*'
    Those were the going rates for tickets to the premiere of *Mother India* at Liberty cinema. Enthusiastic crowds had queued up in front of the booking windows, but the show was House Full. Tickets costing two rupees were being sold at four rupees, and those costing five for ten in the black market. The leader of the gang of black marketeers, moving amongst eager, inquisitive cinemagoers, tempting them with better seats for bigger money, was me, playing the lead in my new film *Kala Bazaar*. Standing behind the camera fitted with a zoom lens and installed on a high platform was Goldie, the director.

As star after star arrived in his or her limousine at the entrance to the theatre to attend the premiere, Goldie switched on the camera, signalling to me with a wave of his hand, while I moved from behind or in front of those alighting from the cars, whispering to the fans who were anxious to see the film in such august company, rubbing shoulders with their favourite stars. The more stars there were, the better the sale of tickets. It was a very brisk and risky business, demanding quick reflexes and a cunning eye, to avoid being noticed by the policemen on duty.

This was the opening sequence of the film, and is remembered for its originality and deft execution. My role again had negative shades, but with likeability of a sort that endeared itself to my fans. I never really cared what I played, as long as the character I was cast in was central to the story. From a black marketeer in *Kala Bazaar* to the double role of Captain Anand and Major Verma in *Hum Dono* and then *Tere Ghar Ke Samne* in which I was a Romeo again, and then on to being a 'Guide' and later a 'Jewel Thief'—my graph of stardom rose steadily, along with Goldie's reputation as a writer–director. He had become a great asset. I was completely relaxed with him behind the camera, and he too felt easy and confident with my presence on the sets. We complemented each other. Together we became an unbeatable team of writer–director and star, the cause of great envy to the rest of the film industry.

The banner of Navketan was flying high. It made a bigger star out of me with every new film, sparing no effort to make its leading light shine brighter than ever before. Very challenging roles were created for me.

In *Hum Dono*, besides playing a captain of the army, I also played his lookalike major. For this role I put on the haw-haw British accent and mannerisms suiting his carriage and bearing, all of which went down marvellously with the audiences. I patterned the character after an almost similarly mustachioed major I had known in a British army cantonment at Kirkee, near Poona. I had often dropped by at his military bungalow on weekends for a glass of beer, and emulated his style in my portrayal of Major Verma. The performance got so strikingly imprinted in the hearts of my fans, that wherever I am amongst them, in India or abroad, they never fail to remind me of that image of me that had stayed in their minds. This is especially the case with those in the army themselves. Whether it is in Gangtok in Sikkim which touches the border of China at Nathula pass, or in Ladakh, where the Indian army has the highest military post in the Himalayas, officers as well as jawans salute me and stand to attention whenever I am in their midst, in appreciation of my performance in the film. They always see Major Verma in me, and surround me for autographs and handshakes, offer glasses of beer or rum, while their superior officers look on admiringly, standing a little distance away.

In an army hospital somewhere in the border area, an amputated jawan got up from his bed as I was visiting the patients, and said with great pride, 'I still have one leg to walk on,' referring to Major Verma's famous line in the film, when he is on his crutches. The doctor attending on him told me later that he found the jawan's morale boosted after meeting me, and his spirits restored enough to encourage him to move out of the hospital.

The popularity of Major Verma's character rose to phenomenal heights. I specially invited Lt. Gen. Chaudhary, the General Officer Commanding Southern Command, Poona, to attend the premiere of the film at the Eros cinema in Bombay. Seeing Major Verma perform on the screen, he could not help breaking all norms of decorum and social etiquette when he shouted at the top of his voice in the middle of a scene, 'Doesn't he remind you of ____?' And he mentioned a certain army officer's name, simultaneously letting out a guffaw aping Major Verma as rowdily as any front bencher would. Everybody in the balcony looked at the general, pleased to see he was enjoying himself.

The philosophy of Captain Anand, played by me as well, also touched the hearts of people when he sang:

Main zindagi ka saath nibhata chala gaya
Har fiqr ko dhuye mein udaata chala gaya

I kept on giving life my company
And blew every weary thought away like smoke-rings

They took inspiration from those lines, so stirringly written by Sahir Ludhianvi, and often quoted them back to me in private or public gatherings. I came to be associated with this wonderfully philosophical attitude towards life, which rings true for everyone who believes that life is worth living.

All the songs of *Hum Dono* had a rare ageless quality and came from the depth of the heart. The composer–lyricist duo Jaidev and Sahir wove a special magic with each song. Rafi and Lata and Asha, singing at their best, made the songs immortal. '*Allah tero naam, Ishwar tero naam*' will always stay on people's lips as long as the spirit of the divine stays in their hearts. And '*Abhi na jao chhod kar ke dil abhi bhara nahi*' will be sung as long as romance lives in those very hearts.

Filming of the army scenes in *Hum Dono* were done under the guidance and supervision of an army officer on location, for reasons of authenticity; so we were committed to the defence ministry of the Government of India for its approval before the release of the film along with the censor certification. V.K. Krishna Menon was the defence minister at that time. He saw the film along with his friends and relatives in New Delhi. I had known him since he was in London as the first High Commissioner of India.

After my visit to the Soviet Union, I had gone to London for a short trip and had called on him, to pay my respects to the man I admired. He took a liking to me and asked me to accompany him to a meeting he had organized for Indian students studying in England. While there he suddenly announced that I would speak to them on my experiences in the Soviet Union, which I willingly did.

Later, when he was brought to India as a minister without portfolio in Pandit Nehru's cabinet, the movie industry canvassed for him as he stood for parliament from a Bombay constituency. We participated in his public rallies and gave him all our support, ensuring his victory at the polls. He got elected to the Lok Sabha with a thumping majority, and was appointed the defence minister of the country.

Whenever he came to Bombay on a short official tour, my home would often be a venue for a small gathering of Krishna Menon's friends. He was a very powerful orator, and did a lot for the armed forces. His arrival in the city was always heralded with great fanfare, with tight security measures, army and police jeeps piloting and following his black Ambassador car, the national tri-colour fluttering on its bonnet, his fellow countrymen lined up on the streets saluting and salaaming him, waving at his entourage as it moved on.

But the day he fell from grace, and had to resign in the aftermath of India's defeat at the hands of the Chinese aggressors on our north-eastern borders, Krishna Menon was made to look very small in the eyes of his countrymen. A shining star on the political firmament suddenly became a complete nonentity, like a shooting star fizzling out into nothingness.

One night, as I was standing at the first-floor window of my house, I saw a frail old figure at the wooden gate below, trying to knock at it with his stick. He was wearing a white dhoti in a south Indian style. As my chowkidar rushed forward to confront him, I recognized Krishna Menon. He was alone. I ran down to greet him. He looked very lonely, his dishevelled and unruly hair flying in the breeze. There was no police or army jeep accompanying him, no bodyguard to protect him. He was the picture of a lost, forlorn, deserted man.

As I respectfully 'sirred' him, trying to get over my astonishment, he stopped me from saying anything further and said, 'I didn't mean to disturb you, Dev. It is already eleven-thirty at night. I tried to call on your neighbour, Mr Menon, for he is a friend. But he is not there.'

'Why don't you come in, sir?' I said.

'No, thank you. I have to catch my flight back to Delhi, and thought I might as well say "Hello" to you while I am here.' He seemed undecided.

'I know you love tea, sir, and my cook will make a cup as fast as I order him,' I tried to persuade him.

But a little distance away, a car honked.

'No, it's time for me to leave. Look after yourself, Dev.'

And he walked back and got into the car, waving his stick at me. It was a very old ramshackle car, with just a driver inside, busy smoking a cigarette, not bothering to come out to open the door for the person who was once India's defence minister.

That was the last time I saw Mr Krishna Menon. After a few days, I read that he had died.

Fame, power and money are the three factors that make you great in the eyes of the world. The moment these desert you, you are like a particle of dust under one's feet.

Thirty-five

There was a marriage in our household. While my marriage to Mona was a quiet celebration of the coming together of two minds, a full-fledged marriage ceremony with all the trappings of pomp and grandeur now took place for the first time at our Iris Park cottage.

My younger sisters had grown to be of marriageable age. They were under the protective umbrella of their elder brothers in Bombay, and Bonie, the elder of the two, immediately younger to me, selected her own groom on a prolonged trip to London, and announced her decision to us. I had met her fiancé, Raj Sarin, in London, had approved of her choice and followed up my meeting with him by drawing up plans, in consultation with the elders in the family, for a Hindu-style wedding in Bombay and a grand reception for the bride and the bridegroom at the famous Cricket Club of India. It was a huge affair with almost everybody in the city and our entire circle of friends attending, to give their blessings to the married couple.

My little daughter Devina was the darling of the party, always insisting on being lifted by her papa, enjoying sucking her thumb, amused at the affectionate and loving crowd around, trying to talk to and pamper her, feeling important, being the centre of attention, while Suneil, my son, would come and hold my finger when the lensmen came requesting him for snaps with some of the celebrities gathered together for the occasion.

My father had also come from Punjab. He had forgiven me and I, him. We had both silently made up with each other.

He had never seen an Indian film, and therefore never seen, met or known a movie star. Nor did he have any desire to do so. But being in the midst of so many of them, and that too the topmost reigning ones of the day, he was adding to his own encyclopaedic knowledge of the world. Curious and inquisitive, as he saw them being surrounded by admiring fans, glittering lights flashing on them with a riot of cameras clicking away, he could be seen enjoying himself with a childlike excitement. An epitome of simplicity himself with the wisdom of years and experience written on his face, he was the focus of attraction of all the cameramen, who are always looking out for an offbeat personality for an unusual photograph. They had their prize shot of the evening when the famous Dilip Kumar sat with me on the ground, with my father right behind us in a chair, and the two newly-weds sitting on either side of him. I admired the very down-to-earth Dilip Kumar then, making himself appear a part of my family. He made everybody around proud of him.

My youngest sister Usha was now the only one left amongst my sisters who had to settle down to married life. She later found her beau and got married in the same gala fashion to a surgeon, Prithvi Madhok. As she was sitting in front of the sacred fire with the pundit reciting shlokas to the couple about to pledge their life to each other for a lifetime, my thoughts went back to her growing-up years in our hometown. She was my favourite sister as a child, a little girl in a frock, also thumb-sucking like my daughter, rushing out fast barefoot to the lane outside our house, at the call of the 'dal murmura' vendor. And as soon as she had brought me pocketfuls of these tasty, crunchy lentils, she would wait with equal interest for the next street vendor to announce his arrival, with his familiar sing-song melody—'Bissey de chholey!' The gram cooked with Punjabi masala was relished by everyone in the family.

Those days of carefree childhood, of fun and pranks, of rain and sunshine, of monsoon mangoes, ripe, sweet and juicy, and melons as sugary as honey, and all of us, the kids and parents huddled together at night by the kitchen fire in the winters, and upstairs on the terrace in summers, with the cool breeze wafting over us from the mango and jamun trees kissing us to sleep, the stars above serenading us! Those days will never return, for when people grow up they all go their separate ways, pulled apart by their own destinies. And their moments of childhood remain their most precious memories, like golden studs in their armour.

Thirty-six

For me, the biggest reward for making *Hum Dono* was that it became India's official entry at the 1962 Berlin Film Festival. I took a team of persons associated with the film along with me to the great city, ravaged by World War II. The first thing we noticed when we arrived was the destroyed dome of a beautiful church in the centre of Berlin's main street, targetted repeatedly by the allied bombers. The dilapidated structure was now a tourist attraction, deliberately not restored and left in its devastated state as a testimonial to the evils of war.

On the opening day of the festival, I was presented on stage and introduced to the audience together with my counterparts from Europe, UK, the USA and the rest of the film-making world. I felt part of a truly international community, surrounded by stars. I met Shirley Maclaine backstage and formed an acquaintance with her. We also met Jimmy Stewart accidentally in the hotel elevator; he was heading the American delegation and promoting his latest film. Having been an ardent fan of his ever since I joined the movies, Mona and I were thrilled to find him in the same elevator as us. 'Mr Jimmy Stewart!' I could not help exclaiming aloud, partly to him, partly to myself, with the joyous adulation of a teenager for a huge star. He nodded and smiled his starry smile at us. I introduced myself and invited him to the party we were throwing that night for the international delegates. He graced the party with his usual warmth, and added an extra glow to the evening. Maximilian Schell and his sister Maria Schell, both Academy Award winners, James Mason, the very fine British actor, and Christian Doermer, a young, handsome German lead player, along with a host of other international celebrities from cinema, also attended our midnight bash. Our party contributed towards the growing popularity of tandoori chicken, which was specially flown in from India courtesy Air-India.

Barbara, an intensely sexy German blonde, with searing blue eyes, enticing hair and buck-teeth that looked ready to bite, was our hostess for the evening. She had been assigned to us by the German ministry of culture. Besides Mona, our stars, Sadhna and Nanda, Amarjeet and Goldie, who had done such an outstanding job with the script and the making of the film, Barbara was the one looking after the guests, interpreting our thoughts to the foreign delegates who did not speak English fluently. The party lasted till the early hours, with many saying 'Good morning' when they left, as they saw the dawn breaking outside.

The Polish–American director Tad Danielewski was also in the party. He was representing his and Pearl Buck's film company from New York, and a film directed by him based on Jean-Paul Sartre's famous play *No Exit* bagged one of the awards at the festival.

Tad Danielewski had earlier met me in Bombay along with Pearl Buck, the Nobel Prize winner for Literature. Both of them showed interest in casting me in an American film based on an English novel by an Indian author, and made me read the book. But I eventually declined the offer. I told them that keeping my star status in India in mind, I would accept a role only if it was really challenging and aroused my interest.

Tad's presence in my party further strengthened our mutual desire to do a film together. It set me thinking seriously about going international, both as an experiment and to let my own growth as a star–actor continue. I started searching for a subject that would take me across to the other side of the Atlantic.

I was in London after the festival was over, for Mona had come back to Bombay to be with our kids. Somebody suggested a book called *The Guide*. I had not read it but felt curious. So I went to Foyle's, the largest bookstore in London, and asked for the book. They did not have any copy left, but the sales girl at the counter promised me she would procure one for me if I left my address in London with her, which I did. The very next day, the receptionist at the Londonderry hotel called to say she was sending a parcel up to my room. I opened it to find *The Guide*, waiting to be devoured by me. I read it at one go, sitting on the balcony of my suite which overlooked Hyde Park. I thought it had a good story, and the character of Raju, the guide, was quite extraordinary. Then I suddenly remembered, the novel had won the Sahitya Akademi award as the best work of fiction in the English language. R.K. Narayan, the author, was a very distinguished novelist, and had also made a name in the Western literary world.

I called Pearl Buck at her country estate in Connecticut. She picked up the phone, and I said, 'It seems we can join hands on a project.' She was immediately interested.

'On a book by R.K. Narayan,' I continued. She had heard his name.

'It's called *The Guide*,' I said.

'Of course!' She was familiar with it. She said, 'I believe there was a play based on it, performed off Broadway.'

I did not know this, but said, 'I have read the book in one long sitting, and find it exciting, worthy of a film.'

She was eager. 'Fly over to the States right away,' she said. 'Let's talk about this.'

'I can't go to the USA, for I have no permission from my government to visit that country,' I told her.

'Isn't that stupid?' she commented.

'According to the regulations of my country, I need an invitation from your side, to enable me to reach you,' I explained.

She immediately posted an invitation to my London address and soon I was on a British Airways flight for my first trip to America.

Manhattan looked dynamic, overpowering and breathtaking, with its gigantic sky-scrapers towering against the sky. I checked in at a hotel, and called Pearl.

'Come over,' she said, 'we are sending a car to pick you up.'

Both she and Tad were waiting. We discussed the book and the possibility of the project over cups of coffee, sitting on the lawns of her sprawling estate. I left the novel with them, and went back to my hotel.

His father

His mother

His first double-role: shaking hands with himself as a boy

With his sisters

In his youth

With Suraiya

One of the gatherings at 41 Pali Hill in 1950, full of future luminaries

Baazi (1951): on the sets with director Guru Dutt (above),
and with Geeta Bali (below)

Chetan Anand directing *Afsar*
(1950)

With Meena Kumari in
Baadbaan (1954)

With Kalpana Kartik in
House No. 44 (1955) (left) and
Nau Do Gyarah (1957)

In *Taxi Driver* (1954) with Sheila Ramani

With the cast and crew of *Funtoosh* (1956) in Khadakvasla

Dressed in black in *Kala Pani* (1958)—with Madhubala

In *Bambai Ka Babu* (1960) with Suchitra Sen

In *Kala Bazaar* (1960) with Waheeda Rehman

'Dil ka bhanwar kare pukar' —with Nutan in *Tere Ghar Ke Samne* (1963)

Hum Dono (1961): Captain Anand and Major Verma (above) and with Sadhna (below)

The Big Three—with Dilip Kumar and Raj Kapoor

With the 'down-to-earth' Dilip Kumar at his sister's wedding

With 'lookalike' Gregory Peck

with Mona and good friends Sunil Dutt and Nargis

The hill connection: with the Chogyal of Sikkim and his wife (above)
and with King Mahendra and the queen of Nepal (below)

The prime ministers' man: with Jawaharlal Nehru (above)
and with Indira Gandhi (below)

With Pearl S. Buck, who scripted the English version of *The Guide*

With Vijay Anand at the premiere of *Jewel Thief*

With Shirley Maclaine, looking at the *Screen* issue on *Jewel Thief*

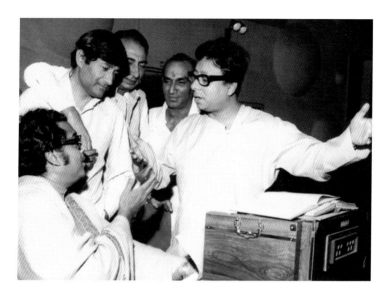

Making melodies: with Kishore Kumar, Sahir Ludhianvi and
R.D. Burman, with Yash Chopra looking on (above),
and with S.D. and R.D. Burman (below)

The famous smile; (inset) with his children Suneil and Devina

Mobbed by his fans

A couple of days later, I heard from her and Tad. They too had liked the book and agreed it would make excellent cinema, with a great part for me.

'Do you own the rights to the property?' they enquired.

'No,' I answered, 'but where there is a will there is a way. I shall follow it up.'

I checked through my sources about R.K. Narayan's whereabouts. Somebody confirmed that Mysore was his hometown, and that he visited the States off and on. We started conjecturing whether he would be in the country at that point of time, when another acquaintance of his said he was definitely in Mysore, and that 'somebody' in California positively knew his telephone number there. We called that 'somebody' in California, and the answering machine rattled, 'I am out of town for a couple of days.'

I had planned to go to California as well. For being in the USA for the first time and not visiting Hollywood was unthinkable. I got Narayan's number from the California contact, and called him from Hollywood.

The receiver was picked up and I heard a voice say, 'R.K. Narayan here.'

'Dev Anand!' was my reply.

'Dev Anand!' He was curious. 'Which Dev Anand?'

'Dev Anand, the actor!' I clarified.

'Are you sure?' He did not seem to believe me.

'Yes, it is me,' I assured him.

'Nice talking to you, Mr Dev Anand,' he said warmly. 'Where are you calling from, Mr Dev Anand?'

'I frantically tried to get hold of your number in New York . . .' I said.

'You did!' he interrupted me, getting interested when he heard the word 'frantically'.

'Couldn't get it from anyone, but now I am calling from Los Angeles, California,' I finished.

'I see.'

'Hollywood,' I emphasized.

'Hollywood?' he said quizzically.

'A name associated with the best of show business!' I enthused.

'Of course, Mr Dev Anand.' He played with my name and gave a friendly laugh. 'Tell me, what can I do for you?'

'We could shake hands on a project that can conquer Hollywood!' I remarked.

He listened silently.

'We want to put your story on the screen, for the world to look at, and admire your work,' I said.

'What do you mean by "we"?' He was inquisitive.

'Have you heard of Pearl Buck?' I asked.

'The famous author? Who hasn't?'

'She and I are keen to film your great work of fiction!' I flattered him.

'Which one?' he asked.

'*The Guide*.'

'*The Guide*?' he laughed. There was a triumphant note in his voice.

'*The Guide*,' I repeated. 'And I want to play the guide.'

'I like the idea,' he said.

'But have you the rights? Somebody mentioned it was being performed as a play off Broadway!' I said, wanting to clear this up.

'I gave them only an oral consent,' he said. 'That can be sorted out. No problem at all, you can go ahead!'

'But I need your blessings,' I said. Seeking 'blessings' appeals to the Indian emotion, no matter how harsh and tough the person from whom it is sought might be.

'I am with you.' He was immediately patronizing.

'Your whole-hearted blessings, besides your assurance that you will sell the rights to me for filming the book as we want.' I spelt out my immediate requirement.

He gave a prolonged pause and then asked, 'When are you coming back to India?'

'Whenever you say. I have finalized the deal verbally, but without your signed approval, nothing can move further,' I indicated the urgency.

'I am going to be in Mysore the next few weeks. When you come to Bombay, give me a call at the same number.'

'Wonderful, Mr Narayan,' I thanked him.

'You fly down from Bombay, I shall drive down to Bangalore from Mysore. Do you know Bangalore at all?' he asked.

'Very well. I always stay at the West End there.'

'We meet at the West End then. I shall be waiting for your call.' The receiver was put down with a bang, which seemed to indicate his excitement.

I was whistling with joy too, already filming *The Guide* in my thoughts.

Thirty-seven

Tad Danielewski and I finalized the details of the partnership between Stratton Productions of New York and Navketan International. Then, I flew back to Bombay, where the film industry was agog with the news that R.K. Narayan's famous novel *The Guide* was to be an Indo-American co-production, to be shot simultaneously in Hindi and English, that the world-renowned writer Pearl S. Buck was collaborating on the script, and that Dev Anand was to star in both the versions.

Pearl and Tad arrived in Bombay soon after. I hosted a big reception for them at the Sun-n-Sand Hotel, in keeping with Pearl's stature. Important people from different walks of life were invited and they all turned up to meet her. I also held a press conference for Pearl at the Taj. The entire journalist 'elite' of the city attended. Later, at Nagpur, I was a special invitee for an All-India Congress Committee session, and was asked to sit next to Pandit Nehru. I broke the news of my new project to him, and he gave me a pat on the back.

Tad and I dived headlong into the casting for the film. The role of the dancer Rosie finally went to Waheeda Rehman. She had already worked for Navketan in *Kala Bazaar*, and was a natural choice for the central role. Pearl Buck took charge of her English diction, and having her as a tutor was a matter of great pride for Waheeda.

Tad and I went all over the country on a location-hunting spree, and after all the meticulous details of 'when', 'where' and 'how long' to shoot were finalized, *The Guide* was launched in grand style, with both the floors of the best studio in Bombay booked in advance for a few weeks for a non-stop filming schedule.

I had persuaded Chetan to shoot the Hindi version. The idea was to film the scenes common to both versions simultaneously, a

Hindi shot to be immediately followed by the same shot in English, to save time and money. But it did not seem to work out smoothly, with two different personalities wielding the megaphone. There were differences of opinion between the two directors on the placing of the camera. A clash of creative egos began to come to the fore—resulting in my feeling the strain psychologically and emotionally, and reflecting in my own performance. Besides, a discussion before every camera set-up was a colossal waste of time when every moment wasted meant extra burden on the film's budget, which was already huge. While we were shooting in Udaipur, thousands of spectators had flocked at a busy thoroughfare to participate in a holi sequence that was to be shot. People had turned up in their Sunday best, eager and keen to be caught on camera along with their favourites on screen, not caring that they would all be drenched repeatedly in the coloured waters of holi for the few seconds on screen that would capture the spirit of that Hindu festival. As soon as Waheeda and I, standing on a slightly elevated stage, waved to them, waves of deafening applause rang in the air with thousands of hands hailing us. That very moment had to be recorded on camera. But the camera did not roll—for the directors had differed on where it was to be placed, and were still whispering to each other, an expression of disgust with the goings-on writ large on their faces. To me, a great moment of spontaneity failed to be registered—a moment of authenticity that the camera always looks for, especially with crowds, and all because of two clashing viewpoints!

Disappointed and frustrated, I quickly took a bold decision. I decided to shoot the English version first, and the Hindi one later, after the former was finished. I told both Tad and Chetan of my decision. It brought sudden relief to the two warring directors, and soon Fali Mistry, the ace cameraman, was ready to roll the camera and immortalize the city of Udaipur on screen for world audiences.

My decision to go along with the English version first gave Chetan the opportunity he was looking for to abandon the project, for the finances for his own film *Haqeeqat* had just been sanctioned, and he wanted to put his heart and soul into his own creative venture rather than hang on to one which he was doing under compulsion, firstly because he badly needed work and money, and secondly because he did not want to let his brother down. He was honest when he confessed this to me; I hugged him and wished him luck for his own film.

The passage of time proved that it was the right decision. Later, while *Haqeeqat* was justly acclaimed, *Guide* became a milestone for Goldie and took him to the zenith of fame. As soon as Chetan walked out, I had persuaded Goldie to step into his shoes. Goldie was a little hesitant at first but later became a big part of the project. We arrived at a mutual understanding that for the betterment of the Hindi version, the entire English script of the film would have to be rewritten from scratch. We needed a new screenplay to suit the Indian ethos and the sensibilities of the Indian mind. Not a single shot taken in the English version would be repeated or included in its Hindi counterpart. The story outline was to be the same but the treatment completely different. It meant doing the same film twice, for two diametrically opposite tastes, the eastern and the western. It also meant playing with a budget that reached astronomical proportions, and that too for a film the subject of which was adultery, which is inherently taboo to the Indian psyche. But now we were going in for a revolution! Perhaps it was a mad thing to go ahead with, to an outsider. But all great works of art are born out of madness. You have to have a streak of madness in you, to break away from the shackles of accepted norms, for an achievement to go down in history. I instilled all my confidence and enthusiasm in Goldie, convincing him of the great hidden potential in the theme of *Guide*. He was charged up and picked up the gauntlet, and started rewriting the script from a new angle.

In the meantime, Tad and I kept on with the filming of the English version, without any break, whether it was indoor shooting or outdoors. The filming finished on schedule, and the entire exposed footage was flown to Pathe Laboratories in New York, to be processed, printed and then to be edited there. We gave a grand send-off to both Pearl Buck and Tad Danielewski. Everybody rejoiced that evening, delighted with the fact that the baby that was being nurtured in the womb for so long was now delivered for the world to see. Waheeda gave Pearl a prolonged hug, and Pearl kissed her on both cheeks for being such an obedient student on the sets and delivering her lines in English in a proper accent and pronunciation!

After seven or eight weeks of continuously living with *The Guide*, emotionally and spiritually, in and out of the studios, with the whole country reading and talking about it, or watching it being filmed, I was now ready for Goldie, who was raring to go, and to dive into the Hindi version. Bigger in canvas than any of the Navketan films so far, *Guide* was to set new trends in every aspect. A new film altogether, certainly not on the lines of the English one of the same name, the Indian version had its own interpretation of the story and the characters. It had never happened anywhere in the annals of cinema that the same story was filmed twice from two different perspectives with the same actor, one immediately after the other.

People started gossiping and tongues began to wag. Waves of sympathy started flowing around for me, for everyone reckoned I had embarked on a foolhardy misadventure, a reckless attempt that would lead to naught. Busybodies and idlers started whispering maliciously to each other that I was throwing my money down the drain, and that soon I would be on the verge of bankruptcy—that I would have sold my last shirt before the film could be completed. Everyone was convinced that adultery and a woman's infidelity to her man were themes repulsive to the Indian audience, and they would dump all our efforts into the dustbin marked with their revulsion, scorn and disdain.

We were shooting on the dry river bed of river Baramati in Gujarat, near Limbdi, and the Swami played be me was fasting unto death to bring the rains down from the heavens, to save the parched humanity from the throes of famine. This gave the rumour mongers more fodder for a slanderous campaign. My detractors started saying that a sophisticated star like Dev Anand with a romantic image playing a shabby, unshaven sadhu in an ordinary, crumpled, dusty khadi kurta-pajama would be very hard to swallow. To top it all they had already passed the verdict that by making the sadhu die at the end, I had signed the death warrant of a popular star, putting an end to his innings as a leading man!

But the more the murmurings of adverse propaganda against *Guide*, the more I enjoyed being on a creative high. The more the

sham of a world pitied me for my plight, the greater was the esteem
for the Swami on fast amongst the common masses on location.
Day after day, hundreds, and then thousands, and then tens of
thousands started congregating on the expansive open space directly
under Nature's eye, where the Swami was praying for a miracle to
happen for the sake of his people, with his hands folded and eyes
closed in total communion with his inner God. I became both the
temple and the God for them. Men and women, tramping barefoot
on burning parched earth, travelling on bicycles and motorbikes,
covering miles and miles on bullock carts, whipping their animals
to go faster, packing into overcrowded buses, hanging outside or
clutching on to their rooftops, truck loads of humanity from
neighbouring villages and towns, converged and gathered on the
spot where their 'Mahatma' was fasting, to sit at his feet and touch
them, like they would a saint's on a pilgrimage.

The rival groups had written me off, drumming up their anti-
Guide wave. But I had become what the guide says when he is on
a spiritual high at the end of the film:

> *Na dukh hai na sukh hai*
> *Na din na duniya*
> *Na insaan na bhagwan*
> *Sirf main, main, main!*

> There is neither joy nor pain
> No days, no worlds
> No man, no God
> There is only me, me, and me.

I had transcended all human emotions, making the 'self' in me
the sole conqueror. The ascetic in me was totally in tune with my
performance during those glorious days of my own discovery.

The man that the world was predicting would end up as a bankrupt
was playing with the inner reserves of his own spiritual finances,
to tell the world that it is not always billion-dollar budgets alone
that produce the best, most soul-satisfying entertainment.

Thirty-eight

S oon after the stint of inspired filming for *Guide*, I was invited by the United States State Department to visit that country as a cultural ambassador from India on their cultural exchange programme. I was to be their guest for six weeks during which time I would see the country and interact with people from various walks of life.

American people are very friendly and outgoing and I enjoyed myself meeting all kinds of people, from common men in the streets with their hail-fellow-well-met attitude to highbrows in their plush offices, smoking cigars over cups of coffee served by young attractive secretaries. I attended their cocktail parties and drove with them in their swanky cars. I met writers and artists, glamorous actors and actresses, intellectuals and thinkers.

I met the famous author Irving Stone, whose *Lust for Life*, on the life of Vincent Van Gogh, was my favourite book during my formative years, in the luxurious comfort of his home-cum-office in California. I shook his hand warmly for a long long time, as I spoke to him, looking into his eyes. In a similar vein of respect, I had held the hand of the famous novelist W. Somerset Maugham, one of the greatest storytellers of his times, when I had spotted him during an intermission of a play I was watching at the West End in London. I had run after him like an excited fan and he had very kindly obliged me. Now I found Irving Stone as generous. I met Saul Bellow, also a great novelist, in Chicago, and Howard Fast, who created a sensation in America with *The Naked God*, denouncing his early leanings towards communism, in New York. I had a cup of tea in the creative office, scattered with files and papers all over, of Elia

Kazan, the film-maker who directed Marlon Brando in *On the Waterfront* and James Dean in *East of Eden*, and later wrote a book called *The Arrangement*.

Greer Garson, the Oscar-winning actress of *Mrs Miniver* fame, and Kirk Douglas, the versatile actor, were some of the distinguished people I wanted to meet, and I was a richer man having met and talked to them. While in Hollywood, I also renewed my contacts with Frank Capra and Mark Robson, both of whom I had earlier met and made friends with in India, and visited Robert Wise on the sets of a new musical he was making after *The Sound of Music*.

I carried with me memories of the Chicago Philharmonic Orchestra all the way through my train trip to the mountains of Colorado, the rugged ridges of the Grand Canyon, and the arid white sandy desert, cactus bushes and burning heat of Arizona. I also visited Cape Canaveral, from where the mightiest power in the world conducts its space programmes; I was the second Indian, I was told, to visit it after our president, S. Radhakrishnan. I visited two American universities—Stanford and Columbia—as well, spending a day with the students. I made friends with some brilliant young growing minds, all freedom-loving and free from inhibitions, forever excited, like fresh sprouting green leaves of spring, with the early morning sunshine falling upon them.

My trip ended in San Francisco with a visit to the Redwood forests that had inspired the great American poet Robert Frost to write the famous lines that I saw in the study of Pandit Jawaharlal Nehru, written in his own hand:

> The woods are lovely, dark and deep
> But I have promises to keep
> And miles to go before I sleep
> And miles to go before I sleep.

Panditji had just recovered from a paralytic stroke and seemed more mellowed down. I had seen him earlier, for the first time, addressing a roadside election gathering, standing atop a jeep, wearing his famous light brown sherwani and the white khadi Gandhi cap that had started a trend among his party workers to blindly follow their leader by adopting it as their headgear. I was in my car driving towards Lonavala, and a mammoth gathering blocking the highway, with security men having cordoned off the area, made me stop my car. I, too, wanted to rush into the meeting, reach Panditji and be noticed by him; but constraints of the security personnel around him and my own sense of proper etiquette stopped me from doing so. I did not want to create any confusion for the crowds that had gathered there and were listening to their popular leader with rapt attention. I waited quietly until the roadshow finished, the people scattered and the prime minister's caravan rolled on ahead, reserving my intense desire of meeting our beloved leader for a later date.

And that meeting took place at Nagpur, where I was introduced to him by Krishna Menon and Y.B. Chavan, then the chief minister of Maharashtra. The organizers of the rally had invited hundreds of important people to an exclusive get-together in a private mansion to meet with the prime minister. I was there much before Panditji arrived. Everybody was so thrilled to have me in their midst that I felt big and almost Panditji-like, with so much attention and adulation being showered upon me. But the moment Panditji entered the room, all eyes switched over to him. Everybody rushed forward, breaking all rules of decorum, each one of them wanting to be the first to be seen and noticed by their idol.

Panditji paused as he made his appearance at the door, escorted by a very chosen and privileged few from the party's inner circle— looking pink and radiant, his trademark baton in his hand, an equally trademark red rose in his buttonhole, his hands folded in a 'Pleased-to-meet-you' gesture, with a touch of 'I-am-bigger-than-you-are' to his smile. I was right at the entrance. I folded my hands in total awe of him, while holding a special red rose to be presented to him, ready with a conquering smile as and when he looked at me, which he soon did. I let my charm go out to him with my hand stretched out to hand over the most beautiful flower of the evening. After bestowing just a casual half-smile on me, the other half preoccupied, with a certain superior air, he looked away towards the idolizing screams of 'Panditji ki jai', to which he seemed addicted. The flower in my hand felt terribly neglected, as did many other bouquets rushing towards him which had to be content with just being blessed with the casual brush of his hand. Soon he disappeared into the crowds, the man of the masses getting lost amongst them.

I looked at the flower I was holding which was now on the verge of withering away, when the host of the get-together walked up to me and said, 'Give the flower to me. I shall hand it over to Panditji on your behalf, for he has to leave right away by the other door.'

Later, at night, I was officially introduced to Panditji at the rally. He was sitting cross-legged on the ground, and I sat at his feet. I tried to remind him of our earlier meeting in the mansion, to which he smilingly said, 'Yes, I do remember.' Before he could say anything further, he noticed some people breaking through the barricades into the cordoned-off exclusive enclosure. Brandishing his baton, he started chasing them back, yelling 'What the bloody hell' at them in his very British accent. The masses seemed to enjoy his rebuke, and he returned to his famous cross-legged posture again, with his elbow resting on his thigh, his hand cupping his chin. It seemed he loved the mass hysteria that he created, and swam all the time in its intoxicating flow.

My last meeting with him was intensely warm and intimate. The film industry had organized a charity show in New Delhi for the Prime Minister's Relief Fund in an open-air stadium, with Panditji in attendance. He was sitting in the front row, right in the middle, with a marigold garland around his neck, and looked very serene as Lata Mangeshkar's voice rang out a patriotic number:

Aye mere watan ke logo
Zara ankh mein bhar lo paani
Jo shaheed huye hain unki
Zara yaad karo qurbani.

O people of my country
With tears moisten your eyes
And remember the martyrs
Who have laid down their lives.

It was Panditji's favourite and Lata always started her concert with a soulful rendering of the song when Panditji was present. Her singing set the pace for an evening of great splendour, and Panditji seemed in a very patriotic and generous mood. After the finale of the programme, the three of us, Dilip Kumar, Raj Kapoor and myself, got a call on stage to spend some time with the prime minister at his Teen Murti residence. We were escorted there by security guards on their motorbikes in front of and behind our limousine, and were received by his daughter, Indira Gandhi, who was then looking after the Nehru household. It was my first meeting with her. She was modest and shy, spoke only a few words, but was extremely courteous, entertaining us with cups of very special tea. Then we were ushered into Panditji's study, to be monopolized by him thereafter.

He had just recovered from an unfortunate stroke and looked mellow and somewhat resigned. He held the Big Three, as our famous trio used to be called, in his arms and was soon in a great mood, recounting his encounters with some of the great world leaders of his times. We listened to him in rapt attention, like children listening to their grandfather narrating a fabulous adventure tale. He was just like a child, taking great pride and joy in showing us some of the mementos he had received from many well-known contemporaries. We all opened up as if we had found a long-lost friend and he reacted and reciprocated in a similar fashion with childlike joy. He was perhaps looking for a moment of escape from his overburdened lifestyle that was full of having to deal with the political pressure of one-upmanship and sycophancy around him.

Raj asked him, 'We hear you used to be very popular and amorously attracted to ladies wherever you went, Panditji!'

'Not as popular as you fellows are!' was his quick retort with his very famous smile.

I had read that he owned the most charming smile and was hailed as the owner of the most photogenic face. So I asked, 'Your devastating smile stole the heart of Lady Mountbatten—is it true, sir?'

He blushed, enjoying my question and laughing it away saying, 'I love all these stories about me!'

'But they all say she herself confessed her weakness for you!' Dilip joined in, in a very humorous strain.

'People made me believe in those stories,' he laughed again light-heartedly.

I was now scanning his study with interest and asked, 'Is that the famous seat from where the prime minister of our country issues his dictates to his nation?'

He looked at the chair and said, laughing, 'Go and sit there. You'll find out.'

Panditji charmed us completely. But I could discern in him a certain sadness, of a man looking at the tragic happenings around him. The great leader who wrote about history in his *Discovery of India* while he was in jail fighting for India's independence, and made history achieving it, was soon to become a part of the history gone by. He could not hide his premonition that he was waiting for a call from his creator, from the way he laughed a little sorrowfully at times.

The call came shortly afterwards. When I was in America, I heard the news of his death. I was engulfed by sorrow.

Panditji was on the front cover of every leading newspaper in America, headlining his demise, and detailing his achievement and contribution in taking his country towards its cherished goal of a secular democracy. Very few leaders from any part of the globe commanded such an extensive and respectful coverage in the USA.

I sent a telegram of condolence to Mrs Indira Gandhi, who people called a 'dumb doll' when she took over the reins of the country. But in the long run she asserted herself to become the 'Iron Lady' of Indian politics.

Back in India, I started putting the finishing touches to the Hindi version of *Guide*. Side by side, I was working in *Teen Deviyan*, which I was also ghost-writing and ghost-directing for a friend, Amarjeet, our publicist at Navketan. It was my first attempt at direction.

During the making of *Teen Deviyan* news arrived that my father had expired suddenly at his farm in Gurdaspur. The story went that having developed a sudden craving for grapes, he sent the maid to the bazaar to fetch some; on her return she found him to have fallen into an eternal sleep.

The news hit me like a bombshell. I was absolutely still and frozen for a few moments. I called for a break in filming, went into a quiet corner and closed my eyes. I so much wanted to see him again, and indeed, I saw him, recalling my last meeting with him.

We were at a grand reception held in Bombay to celebrate the marriage of my younger sister. He looked the most conspicuous in the gathering, with his small-town manners, his customary turban on his head loosely worn in a careless style, without the arrogant 'turrah' of the normal show-off affluent Punjabi, an expensive cigarette offered to him from an equally expensive tray by a liveried waiter fixed between his little and third finger, being puffed away occasionally as he proudly surveyed the success of his son, who by now had such a following in the country.

I had asked him then to come and stay with us in Bombay, but he had said his favourite place was back home, on his own charpoy, on which he slept out in the open every night, with the same constellation of stars above him, looking down and smiling at him.

I remembered, I too used to sleep on the terrace of our house in our native Gurdaspur, my bed next to his, with him pointing out the stars to me on a dark night, trying to train my eyes on the Pole Star that shone the brightest at the tail of a group of seven stars called Ursa Major, next to another constellation called Ursa Minor. He was such a storehouse of knowledge, and was always eager to impart that knowledge to his children. And now, amidst the elitist sophistication of India's premiere city, with so many film stars around, he had stood out like a Pole Star in a starlit sky himself, with his rustic manners and the no-airs simplicity of his small-town ways.

Tears rolled down my cheeks, as I muttered, 'I miss you . . . I miss you . . . I miss you, dear . . . dear father.' I had never missed him while I was struggling to make a name for myself, never missed him as I rode the wave of success. But now, at this moment, I did not want to let him go. How could he go away without telling me? I kept crying to myself and within myself.

A few days later, again on the same sets, somebody walked in and whispered into my ears, 'Guru Dutt is dead.'

The lights were on. Everybody was ready for me to say, 'I am ready, take the shot.' Instead, I said, 'Pack up.'

The entire working unit looked at me surprised. I said loudly so that everyone could hear, in a voice that cracked with emotion, 'Guru Dutt is dead.'

Only the other evening he had invited me to his apartment. We were meeting after ages. He looked very pale and sallow. He was losing his hair. Smoking a cigarette, speaking in a voice that was weak and subdued, he said, 'Let's do another film together, Dev.'

'Why not? Get a script ready. You know I am always with you,' I answered. But it was not to be.

I could not believe that he was actually gone. I drove straight to his apartment. I was probably the very first visitor, and was ushered straightaway into the room where his body lay. There was nobody else in the room, just me and him. His face, turned blue perhaps because of the blue liquid in a glass lying next to him on his bedside table which he had drunk to kill himself, seemed to say, 'Goodbye, my friend. I have been missing you. I have to go. But you keep going!'

My heart tore into shreds. I silently walked back to my car. As I drove away, I saw the two of us together on the Poona hilltop where we had first dreamt our dreams by the fading light of the setting sun.

As Raj Kapoor, with a sad smile, stroked Guru Dutt's face, his body wrapped in white, waiting to be lit on the funeral pyre, I bade my last farewell to the greatest friend I have ever had in the movie industry, mourning his loss within myself.

Thirty-nine

Shirley Maclaine was passing through Bombay on her way back from Tokyo. A party was hosted for her at the Bombay Taj by one of the local producers. I was invited. I cancelled my shooting to meet Shirley and renew my contact with her, after the Berlin Film Festival where we had met backstage, and again in Hollywood at a post-Oscar ceremony gala dinner where I was the guest of David Lean and his Indian wife Leela, and Shirley had walked over for a formal hello.

'My coming here has a very special reason besides welcoming you to my city,' was my first sentence to her.

'Hello! How are you doing?' she responded, as we shook hands.

'I shall reserve all that for my party for you!' I said, beaming my most attractive smile.

She responded with an equally attractive laugh, and looked at the Twentieth Century Fox representative, Prabhu, her chaperone for this particular party. My hand was still holding hers. Prabhu laughed and said, 'She's here only for this evening, Dev. I have to escort her to Udaipur tomorrow. She wants to have a glimpse of Rajasthan.'

'She will go there day after tomorrow,' I said, speaking straight to her.

'But . . . he's made all the arrangements . . . bookings and all that . . .'

I interrupted her and told Prabhu, 'Bookings can be changed,' and continued, 'She is dining at my residence tomorrow. I want her to meet some more movie people.'

She did not know what to say; I was still clasping her hand. Prabhu looked at her.

'Book her for day after tomorrow, and I shall also come along, for Udaipur is my city as well,' I told him. 'If it is not a private visit for you two,' I added.

'I don't mind, if he can reschedule the arrangements,' she said, looking at Prabhu.

Prabhu looked at her, and I fired off the clincher, 'Tomorrow, you are at 2 Iris Park for dinner, that's where I stay. Shall I pick you up Shirley, and from where?'

She looked at Prabhu again. 'Ok. I shall have the air tickets cancelled,' he finally said. He had no choice. 'What time do you need her for dinner?' he asked.

'Shirley's timings!' I said.

She thought for a while and then said, 'Eight o'clock?'

'Eight o'clock,' I repeated, and finally let go her hand.

Shirley arrived at the appointed time, escorted by Prabhu, wearing a sari, with a bindi on her forehead. She looked like an Indian doll. I had invited a very exclusive group of reigning stars to meet her. They were all charmed by her.

Next morning, the four of us flew to Udaipur. I took my production controller, Yash Johar, along. He had booked us all at the exotic hotel on the lake, in its best suites. In the evening Maharana Bhagwat Singh of Udaipur, Bob to his friends, invited us to dinner at his palace. He was my friend, and had earlier played host to Pearl and Tad. While we toasted the sari-clad English maharani with a delicious local Rajasthani brew, Shirley drank deep of the splendour and princely magnificence of the centuries-old palace, with spectacular paintings hanging on the walls, and brightly coloured bejewelled chandeliers accentuating their gorgeousness.

Early next morning, as I came out of my room, I saw Shirley already dressed up and ready for the day, looking at her reflection in the waters of the lake that surrounded the palace. She smiled as she saw my reflection in the water joining hers, and our friendship grew.

I was invited by Pearl Buck to attend the premiere of the English version of *The Guide* in New York. Attired for the occasion in my own style, as I stepped out of the Sherry Netherland Hotel and into the car sent for me to take me to the Bombay cinema at Manhattan and looked at my face in the rearview mirror, I saw the black chauffeur

winking at me. His smile said, 'Wish you success for this moment.'
I reciprocated with a smiling 'Thank you' nod and tipped him
handsomely. It was not a big theatre, but full. Pearl and Tad had
invited their circle of friends, writers and playwrights and people
from television. I was introduced to them as I made an appearance
on the stage prior to the screening of the film. After the show was
over, I seemed to have impressed them, both on the screen and with
my personality. The film did not fare well, but it gave me a semblance
of recognition in a new arena. A local agent got after me to stay on
in the USA, so that he could work on some good offers for me from
Hollywood. But waiting had never been my game. The new experience
was rewarding enough. I rose in my own estimate, having tested my
potential.

I called Shirley in California, and she invited me to spend a couple
of days in Los Angeles as her guest. I stayed at the Beverly Hills
Hotel and being with her in the heart of Hollywood was a dream
come true. She took me in her self-driven flashy convertible to a very
glamorous private party where I spotted some famous faces from
American show business. She was an excellent hostess and I could
see she was reciprocating my hospitality extended to her during her
trip to my country.

While in New York, I was approached to collaborate with David
Selznick on a film to be shot in Kashmir, starring me opposite his
wife, the reputed actress Jennifer Jones. David Selznick's *Gone with
the Wind* had always been my favourite; I had seen it in Lahore
during my college days, and now tying up with the movie moghul
who produced it was a very inspiring thought. Clark Gable in *Gone
with the Wind*, and now Dev Anand from India, both in David
Selznick's films, and me co-producing with him as well! I was quite
thrilled. The clauses of the collaboration deal between him and me
were being finalized in Selznick's live-in suite at the Waldorf Astoria
when he suddenly died of a massive heart attack. The project died
with him.

I had also bought the rights of an Indian novel called *The Princes*,
written by Manohar Malgonkar, that had just won a literary award
in New York. I got hold of the William Morris agency, to start putting
together a film project with an internationally known director and

a cast with me playing the central role of the prince. It was to be a very ambitious film. The agency worked on a plan that took me to Rome and to London to push the proposition further, negotiating with a British screenplay-writer-and-director team and a famous Italian actress. In New York, I met the exceptionally talented stage actor, Sir Alec Guinness, regarding the possibility of his playing the Maharaja in the film. He was an outstanding choice and my personal favourite, after having won an Oscar for his performance in David Lean's *Bridge on the River Kwai*. I called him at his apartment in New York, as he was performing on Broadway at that time. He invited me to lunch at the Sardis at Times Square. He showed his keenness to be associated with the project and wanted to read the script. But, as ill luck would have it, the project got delayed due to certain unavoidable circumstances, and both the William Morris agency and I lost interest. My foray into my second international venture was never to be. Destiny had other things in store for me.

Forty

Back home, the Hindi *Guide* was finding it difficult to find distributors. The commercial market quoted the failure of the English version in America back at us. The numbers of wagging tongues increased manifold and started slandering the theme of the film with great gusto. The tirade against it intensified. 'It won't even be passed by the censor board,' was the new verdict passed by the gossipers. Apparently a spate of letters from anonymous senders were piling up at the information and broadcasting ministry, strongly advocating a ban on the movie from public exhibition.

Even earlier, before the release of the English version in America, the anti-*Guide* lobbyists had stormed the information and broadcasting ministry with incessant mails, to build a case against issuing a clearance certificate to the English version for its international release. According to a clause enforced by the Government of India, a no-objection certificate from the government was a necessary step for any project with a foreign collaboration prior to its release anywhere in the world.

Since the sarkari office in New Delhi was flooded with pseudo-moralistic letters from various unknown sources that were standing in the way of the movie being viewed by the audiences because of its theme of adultery, I approached Mrs Indira Gandhi, the new information and broadcasting minister, to view the film for her own judgement. She asked for the film to be screened in New Delhi, just for herself. She sat through the entire film with some of her personal friends, and did not mind my sitting along with them. I was in the front row, while she sat silently far behind. As the movie ran through, though my eyes were on the screen, my ears were behind me, struggling to catch some whisper of a comment, if any, from the minister. After the screening, I got up, waited for a few seconds and then looked behind me.

All she said was, 'You speak so fast!'

'Yes I do,' I replied. 'Did it irritate you?'

'No. It was nice. We shall send you the letter of clearance from the ministry.'

I heaved a sigh of relief, and said 'Thank you' to her. I felt morally vindicated, saying to myself, 'I am on a strong wicket.'

The greater the number of non-buyers for the film, the greater was the interest in it and the desire to see it on the part of the public. Goldie and I had matched each other's talent to make a dynamic film. His writing and directorial skills were at their peak. My own performance had never reached that intensity before. Goldie and I were confident that the film would be a revelation to the country once it saw the light of day.

When *Guide* was finally released, it opened to unprecedented crowds, with people dying to see it. In its Delhi premiere, the entire cabinet of the government except the prime minister came to watch the film, and those who could not be invited due to shortage of seats at the theatre were prepared to see it standing, or even from the projection room. Such was the excitement created by the film!

Immediately after the premiere in Delhi, we flew to Bombay for another premiere in the country's show-business capital. We had the cream of the elite amongst the audience including all the bigwigs of the movie industry. The initial reaction on their faces was that of numbness. Though they were carried away by the hugeness of the canvas, the novelty of story-telling and the great depths of characterization, they could not make up their minds to pass judgement. There wasn't a scene in the film in which the audience clapped, or in which the front-benchers threw coins on the screen, a sure proof of an Indian blockbuster. The film left them stunned. There was no cheer on their faces, only a look of puzzled bewilderment, as they stood up and walked out in silence after the last fade out. Goldie and I were at the main gate to thank them for their gracious presence at the show, but they walked out as if in mourning after a funeral. No handshakes nor a word of appreciation! Not a single hand on the shoulder of either of us, even as a gesture of sympathy for what we thought at that moment was a disastrous debacle.

As Goldie and I came back home, we kept discussing the likely verdict of the audience. From what we gauged, looking at the dumb and mute faces of the people, could it be that the film was an utter flop? An exercise in wasteful extravagance, in which we had sunk crores? Or was it that the audience was still in the process of thinking about and analysing what they had seen in those two and a half hours, trying to get to the depths of the message conveyed at the end?

Goldie and I kept debating until the wee hours in the hope of getting a few calls from the invited first-nighters, some well-wishers expressing their views. Usually, after a premiere, there is a plethora of telephone calls congratulating or criticizing the producer. But this time, calls there were none. It was as if all our telephones were dead, and the wires had been pulled out.

Curious and anxious minds, however, don't rest. We made a friend call somebody who was at the premiere show, and what he conveyed as his personal as well as the gathered collective reaction of the premiere audience was appalling and depressing. That it wasn't worth spending so much of precious time, money and labour on a film like *Guide*. That the symbol of romance that the young carried in their hearts for the matinee idol Dev Anand was missing from the film, that his popularity as the king of romance and a lover boy might suddenly wane or even die after this. That it was impossible to accept Dev Anand as a lover of somebody else's wife, turning into a sadhu and dying at the end. That the two brothers had written their epitaph with this 'great' film!

We listened to all this in utter despondency. But when we heard the word 'great' slip out of his lips, we perked up somewhat; it seemed to be the silver lining on an otherwise dark cloud. As the phone got cut off, we were ready for the future to spell out our fate.

The results at the box office were mixed to start with. Days passed into weeks, and weeks into months, and *Guide* started being talked about as no other film was. Though not much money in terms of hard cash flowed in, the film kept sending gold to the coffers of our jubilant minds, in terms of recognition of our artistic achievement. As time passed, people found more and more meaning in it, and enjoyed seeing it again and again. I have met people who have seen *Guide* thirty times or more and still want to see it again.

It was declared an all-time classic, for all ages and all eras. In Bombay, there was a danger of a drought that year; a huge poster of *Guide* showing the sadhu praying to the heavens was put up, and brought down a deluge! The film had become a legend. It won almost every major Filmfare Award. Its music, for which it ironically did not win an award, is still regarded as the finest of S.D. Burman's scores. It rose far above the stature of its English counterpart and the book. It started being seen and discussed over and over again. During its very first screening on Doordarshan many many years later, very few people were seen outside their homes. They were mostly glued to the phenomenon called *Guide* on their TV sets.

But personally for me, the most rewarding award was that I had dared to gamble on a bold subject and come away with accolades. When you are going into a territory hitherto unknown and obscure, away from the beaten path, the world often laughs at you and ridicules you. But the moment you meet with success on the same offbeat path, the same world hails and cheers you. That's the way of the world; it is very fickle minded and is always on the side of the winner. Nothing succeeds like success. Taking risks can at times be dangerous. But they are worth taking nevertheless, for without risks, there can be no extraordinary achievement.

Guide was India's official entry for the Oscars in the foreign-language category. Both Goldie and I went to America, meeting our counterparts in that country. We had shortened the film to make it look crisper, with most of the songs deleted to let the story run straight through, and had the English subtitles done in New York. Many people who saw the film there admired it. Many of them were keen to join hands with us for joint ventures. But Goldie and I were not keen. For both of us, one's creativity was not something to be shared with anyone else's. We wanted to do something bigger on the strength of our own creativity. Goldie was trying out new ideas for his next film. And I too, was growing inside, intellectually and creatively. I had started exploring more and more of myself, finding my interests, digging into my potential, trying to bring out the untapped, unknown hidden wealth inside, so that it would create its magic and dazzle everybody in the business. I wanted to go beyond stardom, and that 'beyond' was a complete control of all aspects of the thinking and final decision-making in film-making. It's only a thinking director, who thinks out and writes his own films, gives them the shape and rhythm that he has in mind, with the cast, the crew and music of his choice, who is a complete director, a complete master of the medium. I now wanted to be that director, and that master.

Forty-one

Goldie now wanted to go into the domain of suspense thrillers. He started working on *Jewel Thief*, along with a fellow writer–friend, K.A. Narayan. For this film, I suggested he should explore a new location as the backdrop, a region so far unexplored in Indian cinema.

Sikkim came to my mind. It was a kingdom to the north-east of India, with its borders touching China, Nepal and Bhutan, and was then a protectorate of India. I had visited it once, a few years ago, by car from Darjeeling, during an off-day of shooting for one of my film commitments. Not very far away from Darjeeling, it made a very picturesque journey via Kalimpong.

The clouds hung low like white cotton sheets, almost touching the windows of our car. Suddenly a clutch of them swept across the road and blocked our front view. As we steered through them, we saw on the lush-green vista up ahead a sight that captured our hearts: on a small hill was a gathering of hill-people, with the king of Sikkim holding court perched on that tiny hilltop, speaking to his subjects.

Suddenly a couple of sentries emerged, trying to find out who the intruders were. But recognizing me, they gave me a smart salute and let us pass, after I assured them we did not mean any disturbance to the tranquillity of the place, that ours was only a casual sightseeing visit. In fact, with them guiding us now, we took a more direct route to Gangtok, the capital, only a couple of miles away.

Gangtok emerged like a small decorative pearl on that breathtaking landscape, its beautiful palace nestling amongst tall green trees bedecked with pink and white flowers, bordered by lush-green valleys on both sides, and up ahead, a road winding into a thick forest, where yaks grazed, with cute Sikkimese children playing with them, basking in the afternoon sun. It all looked very idyllic, and it would look wonderful on film.

I suggested Sikkim to Goldie and together we went on a reconnaissance trip prior to the filming of *Jewel Thief*. Goldie was floored by the place, and I took pride in the fact that I had initiated the idea. The very first thing we did after we entered Sikkim through its main bazaar—with Sikkimese women in their colourful gowns walking around, knitting, and squatting here and there, chatting away with their sparkling laughter, and the tall, handsome Tibetan 'khampas', also wearing gowns and long earrings and sporting pigtails, their rosy complexions matching the pink on the cheeks of women around—was to call on the Chogyal of Sikkim, the young king who had succeeded his father whom I had seen a few years earlier from a distance, holding his durbar.

We were ushered into the palace, a modern structure done in Western style, yet retaining the architectural flavour and grandeur of its oriental hilly feel, by a couple of smartly dressed young Sikkimese army lieutenants, dressed in immaculate khaki, revolvers holstered on their thick leather belts.

As soon as we were seated in the main hall, the king made his appearance, looking very imposing in his royal garb. We stood up respectfully. My 'Your Royal Highness' was immediately responded to by his gracious, 'Mr Dev Anand, welcome to Sikkim.'

'You have a dreamland of a country,' was my answer.

'They all love it.' He felt flattered. We were now joined by the queen, the American the Chogyal had married, who was dressed similarly in a Sikkimese gown. She stretched her hand forward for a handshake.

'You are a very beautiful couple. We looked forward so much to meeting you both!' I meant every word.

The very charming combination of the orient and the occident in that mountainous kingdom, with the mysterious Tibet not far away and the ethereal Bhutan next door heightening the mystery and the mystique of the hitherto unexplored region, was going to be one of the highlights of our film.

'Who is the jewel thief?' asked the queen in a very amused way, as we sipped coffee together outside, in the neatly manicured grassy lawn.

'My director will tell you,' I said, pointing at my brother.

Goldie was in great humour. 'I cannot reveal the mystery right now!' he smiled, and we moved on, to be shown the gorgeous surroundings of the palace. Both the Chogyal and his extremely hospitable wife made splendid guides, and insisted we stayed in the royal guest house on that trip.

The army subedar stood to attention and gave a salute clicking his heels, followed by a similar action from two jawans right behind him, as I enquired, 'Is general saab in?'

Sikkim was a sensitive borderland. The Indian Army was posted all over, in full readiness, with a whole mountain division commanded by a major-general. Army personnel were deployed in all areas of the kingdom, all the way up to Nathula pass, which touched the Chinese territory. One could go all the way up to the high ranges of eleven thousand feet, as far as the barbed wire fences, but not beyond, where the Chinese army guarded its borders.

'Saab has been informed. He'll come out himself to see you,' the subedar informed me. And soon the door of the general's residence opened. There he stood, Major-General Sagat Singh in his dressing gown, looking majestic and tall, with the look of a commander who knew where all his men were at any time of the day.

'Sir!' I threw the general an army salute in my best *Hum Dono* style, and said, 'May we come in?' Goldie was with me.

'I didn't believe them. How could Mr Dev Anand come all the way here?'

'All the way! Why not? To salute General Sagat Singh!'

'Come in,' he said. 'What can I do for you?'

'Nothing. We just want to film here in this picturesque area and we want to start with you!' I said.

He laughed again, a friendlier laugh this time. 'You can shoot wherever you want, including in the areas marked "Entry Not Allowed". My men will be at your beck and call.'

Our filming was done in a very disciplined manner. The whole kingdom of Sikkim was all smiles and courtesies and participated in the joy of our filming, like in a grand jamboree, for all the days that we stayed there. We would shoot during the day and celebrate in the evenings, with the general and his officers and jawans, or with the Chogyal and his wife, entertaining them and being entertained.

On a day of rest, the general escorted me right across to the border, to have a look at the Nathula pass, in an Army Jonga jeep. The weather was severely cold, and as we drove higher and higher, it snowed more and more. By the time we reached Nathula pass, it was freezing.

Sharing mugs of hot steaming tea amidst the banter and high spirits of the jawans who were overjoyed and jubilant at the presence of a popular movie star in their midst, gave a very significant meaning to the tag of stardom that I wore. One of the jawans gave me his thick overcoat, another his big army boots for snow climbing, yet another his winter fur cap to keep my head warm, and another still a pair of leather gloves to keep my hands from freezing, so that I could comfortably climb to the ridge through the six-inch deep snow that had just fallen.

The moment I reached the top, I could see Chinese soldiers across the barbed wire fencing, peering through their binoculars, their guns pointed towards the Indian side of the border, as if ready at all times for a showdown at the slightest provocation. The Indian officer accompanying me, too, took out a pair of binoculars from his pocket and passed them on to me, so that I could have a good look at the enemy post across.

'We look at each other every day like this, to assure each other that nothing is amiss, on this highly sensitive and explosive spot,' he said. 'They even play Indian film songs at times.' He allayed all fears of even an accidental gunshot being fired from across the border, and encouraged me to go ahead and view whatever I wanted to.

While looking through the binoculars, I waved at the Chinese soldiers, who were strutting around in their uniforms, then zoomed into the portrait—dug in the snow—of the great Chinese leader Mao Tse-tung wearing his khaki uniform and a red badge, smiling his enigmatic smile. I smiled a wry smile back at him, and could feel the Chinese soldiers zooming into my face through their binoculars. I panned my binoculars and saw a black dog wagging its tail at me. That moment stayed in my mind, and I later utilized it in *Prem Pujari*, the very first film that I directed. I had a set built depicting Nathula, out of pictures taken of it, for a sequence in which soldiers on both sides of the border fire at each other. A black dog gets killed in the crossfire, wailing and wagging its tail, as the unwilling soldier on the Indian side, played by me, shouts hysterically, 'I kill you. You kill me. I kill you back. You kill me back. Where will it all end?' It was as if I was screaming the futility of war and violence to the world.

I brought in my favourite actor Ashok Kumar, who had given me my first big break in *Ziddi*, to play a very important role in *Jewel Thief*. It was perhaps a desire on my part to pay him back for his generosity to me in my earlier days. Not that he needed it. But psychologically, it rounded off a professional relationship. It took Goldie a little time to convince Dadamoni to do a negative role. But Goldie was a great convincer and Dadamoni a great sport. The three of us came up with a suspense film that people have always remembered.

After the last day of the filming of *Jewel Thief* at Gangtok, the general brought out his army band in its full martial glory, to stand by and play as he himself, with his officers of the mountain division, all in their glittering uniforms and war medals, joined the members of our unit, exchanging salutes. The Chogyal and his queen were part of the revelry too, dancing and drinking the health of one and all, and looking forward to the day when the great splendour of Gangtok would appear on screen for the world to look at and admire.

Later, General Sagat Singh was one of the first to enter East Pakistan with his paratroopers during the 1971 war, and was instrumental in the liberation of Bangladesh.

Jewel Thief became a huge hit. I flew all the way from Darjeeling to Delhi to attend its premiere at the Odeon Cinema. The crowds were jumping up and down with delirious joy as I alighted from the car outside the theatre, crazily picking me up on their shoulders, pinching me all over to make sure I was real, loading me with garlands, grabbing and shaking my hands, falling all over me. Suddenly, a hand brushed my hip pocket. I checked for my purse, and found it missing. But I did not react, for the euphoria of the moment was too immense to cry over a meagre sum of fifteen thousand rupees, lost in the enormous wave of goodwill and popularity. Stardom cannot be earned or bought at a price. I let the pickpocket dance away in joy with my cash-filled purse.

Forty-two

Movie-making is a great adventure, an adventure of the mind, soul and body. In a split second your mind crosses millions of miles, weaving together stories and characters from anywhere in the world. Your stories can be set anywhere at all. Which means a thinking writer is constantly on the move, always contemplating on the theme he is focused on, always alive to what is going on around him, living every day with the hope of achieving a brighter tomorrow. As you live for tomorrow, your present is enriched too with hope and optimism; this is real living.

I consider myself lucky that my destiny threw me into a whirlpool of such creative activity after I hit the big time as an established star. I opted to pursue my flights of fancy so that I could make maximum use of my imagination, to let my mind fly into whichever direction it chose, and explore whatever subject it wanted to flirt with. As a director I have always picked up subjects that are relevant to our times, things that attract my eyes and my ears from today's headlines, problems and ideas that affect our daily lives.

India went to war with Pakistan in 1965. That conflict became the subject of my very first directorial venture *Prem Pujari*, a film about the people of a peace-loving, non-violent nation suddenly forced to face aggression and violence. It is the story of an unwilling soldier who, by family tradition, has soldiering in his blood, but by his own temperament and thinking abhors war or any kind of violence. He loves beauty, loves life and nature, and chases butterflies like a schoolboy. An eternal dreamer, he refuses to pick up the gun when commissioned into the army and is court-martialled. But, leaving his past behind, he does willingly pick up arms to fight for his loved ones and his beloved soil with great bravery when his hometown is invaded by the enemy.

The canvas and span of this story took me to various places both near and far, first for location-hunting and then for filming. It was travel, fun and adventure all the way, as exciting and thrilling as it could be.

Retired Lt. Colonel Montgomery Kee (Monty) of the good old British army in India was now back home in his country. Scottish by birth, he had settled down in London. I had first met him when he was a commandant in the Khadakvasla Defence Academy. He had helped me and Chetan shoot a certain part of *Funtoosh* at Khadakvasla lake, then under army control. That's where I also met General Thimayya—nicknamed 'Timmy' by his colleagues—the chief of army staff.

I persuaded Monty to be a part of the *Prem Pujari* unit during my filming abroad. We had been together earlier professionally, for he had supervised the war scenes shot for *Hum Dono*, and had, therefore, had a taste of movie-making. He also had an international driving licence, and I wanted to drive into parts of Europe, exploring locations for the film. While driving I could stop anywhere at will and explore a spot that might meet the requirements of the script, not having to depend on the whims of the driver of a hired vehicle. Besides, Monty knew London like the back of his hand. And London was one of the locations of the film as well.

We hired a car in London, drove to Dover, put it on the boat that carried us to the coast of France, from where we drove first to Paris, and then to Le Touquet, a town by the sea.

Marlon Brando was to be filming on that location, we were told by the hotel staff, as we checked in for the night. We were lucky to have found rooms at that late hour—it was close to midnight. Soon after, a very attractive girl arrived at the counter with a bag in her hand. She too needed overnight accommodation. The hotel management had nothing to offer her, for the only two vacant rooms had just been booked by us. There was no other place for her to go. Her only choice was to share a room with one of us. This was quite common in Europe. She was asked to choose between me and Monty.

He walked up to me after signing the register and handing over our passports to the receptionist. I was reclining in a chair at the corner. He said, 'You don't mind sharing your room with a sensationally good-looking girl, do you?'

I looked at her. Her figure and the dress that she wore were absolutely stunning. 'Why?' I asked, still looking.

'Because she insists on staying in the same room as yours!' said Monty, smiling naughtily.

'Haven't you got yours? You are an old army horse. Accommodate her!' I joked.

'But you are the hero, and having looked at both of us, she prefers you,' he laughed.

I walked up to the counter. The girl was already looking at me.

'Linda,' she said, and shook my hand.

'Dev,' I responded.

'We have a common interest,' she said, 'for I'm told you are location-hunting for your film.'

'Indeed,' I nodded and looked at Monty.

'She has lots to tell you about Marlon Brando tonight. She is his secretary,' he said.

'We have a large enough bed to accommodate two persons, Mr Anand,' joined in the receptionist.

I had no alternative. There was a lot to talk about show business in the room with Linda.

'How big a star are you in your country?' she asked.

'How big is Brando in yours?' I asked back.

'Very big,' she said.

'You have just answered your question!' I said.

'Wow! Why can't someone cast the two of you in a movie together,' she remarked.

'You think about it!' I responded. She gave me her most attractive smile, and dived into the sheets on her side of the bed. I dimmed the lights.

From France we drove to Switzerland, crossing valleys and dales and mountains, singing to the majesty and grandeur of the snow-laden Alps, until we decided on a village named Gletch, surrounded

by rolling meadows through which ran a railway track along with
a motorable road. The serpentine road took you up to a small
picturesque town with a cute-looking church.

A very charming girl was working as a maid in the pension we
stayed in. She was a young student of English literature at Cambridge
University, and had taken on the job in Gletch because it gave her
the opportunity to see the Swiss countryside, while she made some
money for herself. Sitting on the bar stools in the small bar of the
hotel, Monty and I asked her for a drink.

'Any preferences?' she asked. She had a clear British accent.

'Whatever is the best here,' I said.

She looked at the bottles lined up, and pulled out a bottle of
Guinness. It had always been my favourite.

'How did you know?' I asked.

'What?' she asked back.

'That this is the one I like,' I said.

'I knew you would, because it is Irish,' she shot back with a
smile that won my heart.

'So are you!' I guessed.

'How did you know?' she asked.

'Because you have that smile,' I flattered her.

She smiled devastatingly again, uncapped the bottle, poured the
beer into a glass and offered it to me, while Monty waited. The froth
was overflowing, and she said, 'Drink it before it goes down.' I gave
her my charming smile, took a long sip and sat back, a look of
contentment on my face, while she gave Monty his drink. He asked
her what her name was.

'Jill,' she said.

I turned poetic, 'Jack and Jill went up the hill to fetch . . .'

'A bottle of Guinness,' she interrupted me and laughed. Then
she was called away by the owner to attend to some other guests. 'I
shall be back,' she said, and went away, taking a part of the flavour
of the Guinness along with her.

But she never turned up. At dinner time I saw her again. 'Jill,'
I called her, as she was attending to another customer.

'A Guinness for you, sir?' she enquired.

'No—you,' I answered. She blushed. 'You could be Swiss, you speak so easily to the customers here,' I said.

'No, I'm Irish,' she answered. 'You were right this afternoon.'

'That's why,' I interrupted.

'What?' she asked.

'I thought I could utilize your services,' I said.

'In what way?' She was curious.

'Would you be an interpreter to the Swiss people I use in my film, on location?'

'You are making a film!' she got interested.

'And have chosen this place in Switzerland!' I said.

She gave me her hand, saying smilingly, 'I shall be your interpreter.' I shook it.

She was our interpreter during the day, and after evening fell, she would be back in the hotel, attending to her duties in the bar, and in the kitchen, serving, cooking and cleaning dishes. We became friends, for both of us had the same temperament, easy-going and informal, and absolutely down-to-earth. But beyond a quick hello, we never had the time to speak to each other. I would be busy with my shots during the day, and after the day was over, she would be off to her working routine in the hotel, and would be the last person to come out of the kitchen, after everybody was in bed, wrapped up in warm blankets.

'We must talk, you know,' she said one day at dinner, as she served me.

'We must—when?' I reciprocated.

'The only time is after working hours,' she said.

'That late?'

'It's never late for me, since I get up late in the mornings and my duties don't start before twelve noon, unless you need me on location.'

I listened quietly. 'I have a room to myself in the hotel,' she continued.

'You do!' I muttered.

'Right at the farthest end, across the corridor—you may drop in for a chat.'

'I would love that, for we are leaving tomorrow,' I said.

'Knock at my door, a little after twelve—room nineteen,' she said and left.

The night was starry and silent, very Swiss, with only the sound of cow-bells tinkling, as the cows still grazed outside. I tiptoed out of my room, making sure nobody was watching, and knocked at Jill's door. It was opened stealthily. She had patches of black soot from the kitchen all over her arms, but her body was as fresh as the flowers that grew in the little garden of the hotel outside, and her voice as melodious and soft as the distant strains of a flute coming from the countryside, while the words she spoke were as intellectually stimulating as you would expect from a student of the famous college she came from.

We pledged to correspond with each other, and we did. Her language had the flavour of Keats, and a longing that made me go and meet her once again, when I was in England on my next trip. I brought her to my hotel, and together, sitting by the television set, we watched the finals of that year's Wimbledon.

Our next destination was Spain, and Madrid, where I had to shoot a sequence involving a bull-fight. And then on to Beirut, then the Paris of the Middle East, with snowy mountains on one side, the sea on the other, and a casino which was a playground of the rich and the affluent from all over the world. I did not do any filming there. I had gone all the way to meet Nadia Gamal, the famous belly-dancer, to invite her to India to do a dance number in the film.

'Men may come and men may go but I shall go on forever.' This is so true of the river Beas, as it flows through the Kulu Valley in Himachal Pradesh, thundering its torrential presence to any visitor there, climbing down its meandering route from Manali and from Rohtang pass further up, with the trout merrily swimming and floating over its pebbly base, playing hide-and-seek with its cold and crystal waters. And as you cross the picturesque valley into the awe-inspiring Rohtang, at every bend you encounter scenery that takes your breath away. In this area, I shot a sequence of *Prem Pujari* in which the red guards of Mao's cultural revolution blacken the face of the kidnapped Indian army major, as well as a couple of other scenes that needed the awesome ruggedness as much as the eerie silence of the location.

That was not my first filming trip to Kulu Valley. I had gone there earlier to participate in the shooting of *Bambai Ka Babu*, with Raj Khosla directing, and Suchitra Sen, the doe-eyed dusky beauty and immensely popular star of Bengal starring opposite me.

Sardar Pratap Singh Kairon, the powerful chief minister of undivided Punjab, made a surprise visit to meet us all when we were shooting for *Bambai Ka Babu*. During his casual conversation with us, he swore that the already carved state of the Punjab, which had been divided as a result of Partition, would not be further divided into Haryana, Himachal and the Punjab Suba, as demanded by the politic of each of these areas. If it ever happened, he said, it would be over his dead body.

And so it was. The state was further divided into three separate identities by the time we were shooting *Prem Pujari*. Pratap Singh Kairon lay assassinated, his bullet-ridden body discovered in his car on one of the highways of Punjab.

Forty-three

Punjab has always borne the brunt of the savagery, cruelty and violence of politics. *Prem Pujari* dealt with this savage aspect of humanity. The central plot takes place in Khemkaran, a town on the Indian side of the border with Pakistan which was invaded and overrun by the Pakistan armed forces. Their Patton tanks rolling into the village created panic and resulted in a mass-scale evacuation of men and women and children, who picked up whatever they could, and left behind whatever they could not, as they escaped to places safe from the onslaught and massacre.

While I was working on the script, I went to Khemkaran to make a first-hand study of the place and the happenings that took place there, to give authenticity to the war scenes. In this exercise I was very kindly helped by a friend, the inspector-general of the border police force of that area, Aswini Kumar, lovingly called 'Ashwin' by his friends. He was gentle, warm-hearted and extraordinarily helpful. He took me to the areas where I could meet with and talk to the people about their experiences of the catastrophe, with the result that some of the dialogues spoken in the film by the marauding Pakistani army soldiers and heard by the invaded civilians, were very realistic. Some were mercilessly slashed by the censors, especially the ones spoken by a Pakistani colonel so effectively played by Shatrughan Sinha, who was introduced in the film. And others sounded unpalatable to a small section of the audience. For this film that spoke of the futility and pointlessness of war was not liked by some fundamentalist elements in a certain community. It seemed to hurt the sensitive core of their hearts, which was evident from the damage they did to the seats of the auditoria in the areas dominated by their population. They slashed the upholstery, broke the furniture, and propagated a boycott of the film. I seemed to have made them very angry, and I thought I was on the verge of losing my stardom.

The activists of a certain political party in Calcutta, too, forcibly walked into the projection room of the main theatres where the film was running, and had its screening stopped at the point of revolvers, striking terror amongst the audience. The exhibition of the film was thenceforth terminated immediately.

Perhaps politics was playing a dirty game with me as well. The United Front was in power in West Bengal, and the Marxists were not kind to my film. The distributor of the film in Bengal had an instinctive hunch that trouble was in the offing at the release of *Prem Pujari* in his territory. He had, therefore, organized a pre-release screening of the film especially for Jyoti Basu, then the home minister of the state. I was present at the screening in Calcutta, in a private preview theatre, and was very kindly introduced to him and his family.

After the screening was over, as I stood up to thank him for the very valuable time he had taken out from his busy schedule to have a look at my film, he casually nodded, and went away with his family without passing a single comment about the film and my work in it, good, bad or indifferent.

On the third day of the film's release in Calcutta, the activists of a political outfit saw to it that the film, which was drawing full houses, went off the screens all over West Bengal.

I was then attending the marriage ceremony of Prince Birendra of Nepal in Kathmandu as a special royal guest, having been personally invited by King Mahendra for the week-long celebrations. I got a call from my Bengal distributor regarding the unfortunate incident. I felt very disturbed, and immediately on my return from Kathmandu, flew to New Delhi to meet with the home minister, Y.B. Chavan, whom I knew personally. But there was nothing he could do, except giving me a few kind words of consolation, and the assurance: 'I shall look into the matter.'

I let bygones be bygones, and closed the chapter in my mind as a sorrowful affair; but my heart still did not relent on what I had said in the film. For honesty and truthfulness are at the core of an artist, and stardom loses its glitter when coated by unrealistic phoney performances. Temperamentally, I forget my setbacks in a jiffy and prepare myself quickly for the next challenge with renewed energy. I started working very fast now on my next creative effort. I had hit upon an idea that I fell head over heels in love with.

Forty-four

I was at the palace in Kathmandu when I received a message to say there was a telephone call for me from Christian Doermer, a German documentary film-maker who was in Kathmandu. His name rang a bell. He could only be the handsome young German actor I had met in Berlin in 1962. Since he had come to know I was in Kathmandu, he wanted to meet and renew his contact with me.

Both of us, adventurous in spirit, went in the evening to a mysterious joint called The Bakery, the meeting place of hippies at night. The hippie cult had caught the fancy of the jobless, lazy, frustrated, fun-seeking youth of the world. They went wherever opium, hashish, marijuana and LSD were available in plenty, and not forbidden, seeking to pleasure their senses with the revelrous smoking, dancing and singing bouts, blending their personalities into one another, sitting around with vacant looks on their faces as psychedelic colours streamed through their drug-induced consciousness. Kathmandu was one of the hippie centres of the world at that time, and The Bakery was so famous that it had even been written about in *Time* magazine.

Christian and I walked down a hill and through narrow and dark alleys to reach a spot from where we could watch the hippies. My German friend stopped me from going further, saying it was not proper to intrude into the domain where all the hippies, at that time, were afloat on their psychedelic fancies. They would not welcome any outside intrusion, which was likely to turn them violent, abusive, even ready for a physical attack. So it was best to watch the spectacle from a distance.

What we saw was sheer cinema. Long-haired hippies, many of them men, unshaven and bearded, with garlands of yellow marigold flowers around their necks and saffron tikkas on their foreheads, were huddled together, some sitting cross-legged, others lying flat on their backs, looking up at the starless sky, as if in meditation, with their female companions lying in their laps, or with their heads resting on their chests, their skirts flying carelessly into the air that smelt of hashish. They were all smoking chillums, one chillum being passed on from hand to hand in turn.

A single candle flickered away, casting its shadow on the naughty doings of some. A giggle and a subdued mixture of tittering male–female laughter came from a corner. A moaning sigh of a female came from another, as she went through the ecstatic moment of giving herself to her male counterpart, who suddenly started doing a dance in the nude. In another corner a half-naked hippie was strumming the guitar, a cigarette dangling from his lips, his eyes closed, a garland-laden female entwined between his legs, playing with his long beard. Across from them, in a far corner, a couple lay half clad, their arms possessing each other's bodies passionately. A bearded man passed through all of them intermittently, handing over a chillum from person to person. Another sadhu-like shadow of a man was picking up flowers from a heap, and showering them on everyone.

A couple of them fell on a long-haired brown girl, her blouse loosely worn over her breasts, partly revealing her young firm breasts, her bra undone, as she played with the grass on the ground, enjoying the sweet smell of marijuana. Her hand suddenly went up to the beard of her male partner, to give it a loving stroke, as his hand, in turn, came to her lips, thrusting a cigarette into them. She inhaled in a long deep ecstasy, and as the smoke was puffed out into the man's face, she lifted hers towards him, and he dissolved his mouth into hers. Next to them a couple, flat on their backs, snored away to glory in postcoital bliss, oblivious to the world.

The brown girl attracted my attention for no other reason except that she was the only dark-skinned person among them all. Her looks were Eastern as well. As she fell back from the long-drawn kiss with her partner, giggling, she uttered a word which sounded like Hindi to me. Then she turned towards a pair of spectacles lying on the ground right next to her, about to be trampled upon by the sadhu passing around chillums.

'Bob, mera chashma,' she said, quite clearly this time. There was no doubt that she was Indian.

'What the hell is she doing here, amongst strangers, away from her own community, her identity?' The question crossed my mind rapidly. It seemed like a great story—very unusual, revealing something tantalizingly, yet hiding much more, worth unravelling and digging out. She could be the subject for my next film, I thought, a subject not dealt with in any Indian film so far. I instantly wanted to find out more about her, and to get to know what she was all about, and what the chillum-smoking group that surrounded her was like.

I asked the barman of the Soaltee Hotel if he knew about a certain attractive Indian girl who spent her nights in the company of foreigners visiting Kathmandu. He immediately reacted and gave me the details about her. Kathmandu is a small place; word spreads quickly. Everybody living there knows about everybody else. The barman said the girl was from outside Nepal, and was living with her Nepalese boyfriend. He assured me that I would find her waiting for me next day, if I visited his bar when it opened.

Next evening, as I walked into the bar, the barman saluted me and pointed at the girl sitting on a bar stool in a quiet corner of the bar, with her back towards me. I handed over a handsome tip to him and walked towards her. She, sensing somebody approaching her, turned, recognized me instantly and stood up saying, 'Hi, you wanted to meet me?'

'Naturally, the most popular and attractive person in Kathmandu,' I replied.

'I am a great fan of yours, and so is my mother,' she reciprocated.

'Where is she?' I asked.

'Montreal, Canada.'

'And you—'

'Holidaying in Kathmandu,' she said.

'A great place for that,' I said. She laughed.

'Your name?' was my next question.

'Janice.'

'Janice?'

'Originally Jasbir, but Janice is my acquired name!' she giggled. She told me her story, hesitating to open up in the beginning, but confiding in me slowly. She had run away from her mother in Montreal. She said she was a rebel, belonging to the new generation, that there was a generation gap in the world that couldn't be bridged, and to derive her own share of happiness from the world, she had quietly walked out of her home, having quarrelled with her mom, stealing a sum of money she needed for the present trip, which she said was her rightful due from her parents who did not look after her needs.

'And your father?' was my next question.

'He's divorced from my mother and now lives somewhere else,' she said briefly. 'Somewhere in Punjab.'

I listened attentively, and she added as an afterthought, sounding bitter, 'But I don't care. I . . . I really don't want to know!'

I offered her a drink. 'Not now!' she said. 'Not at this time.' It was seven in the evening.

'But I must take your leave now. Can I have your autograph?' She produced some paper from inside her blouse.

'For you or for your mother?' I asked.

'For me,' she said smilingly.

The moment she left, the story idea and Jasbir, its central character, had formed themselves in my mind. I would call the film *Hare Rama Hare Krishna*.

When I went to bid farewell to King Mahendra after the seven-day stint of celebration, I didn't have to wait long in his elegant room in the Narayantithi palace, where he often met his favourite visitors. I was ushered in by his aide. We shook hands and the warmth of the grip spelt out the intensity of our friendship.

'I'm grateful,' I said.

'And what else?' he asked, smiling, as he sat on his royal chair.

'If you allow me to say, your majesty . . . I have a story idea in my mind that has just cropped up, that could only happen in Nepal.'

He was in a mood to listen.

'Of a movie that represents a new world phenomenon, the young, reckless people,' I continued.

'You mean the hippies?'

'Yes, your majesty. It is a great thought for a film, and I want to make it here,' I sought his reaction.

'Go ahead. Is your script ready?' He was equally receptive.

'I wanted to seek your permission first,' I said.

'It is your thought, your movie. Why my permission?' he asked.

'Permission to shoot here. Wherever the script demands,' I said.

'Granted, just let me know when,' he was with me.

'The script is all here, inside,' I said, tapping my forehead. 'With your encouragement, it shall be on paper quickly.'

'Have you been to Pokhara?' he asked.

'I have heard about it.'

'Would you like to extend your stay and visit it? It is very quiet and peaceful there, good for your type of work.'

'I'd love that,' I said.

'There is a very stylish hotel there, owned by my younger brother, Prince Basundhara, called The Fish Tail, against the backdrop of the majestic snow-capped Annapurna range. It will be ideal for your writing,' King Mahendra said. 'I shall give you an inspector of police as your bodyguard and guide, a real Gurkha. He will know where to take you, and when.'

'Thank you, your majesty. Now you must be left alone, to attend to your kingdom's needs. May all the gods of Nepal be with you.' My inner prayer went out to him and we shook hands again.

With Inspector Thapa by my side whenever I needed him, and a bearded young Cuban and his wife excellently managing the Swiss-designed circular Fish Tail lodge, situated by the side of a small river, with a view of the majestic mountains on one side and a flower-laden forest on the other, I was in the perfect setting to lay the foundations of the story named after the chant that the flower children were chanting when I encountered them at The Bakery. I finished the first draft of the script in just three days.

When I went back to Bombay and announced to my staff that my next film was named *Hare Rama Hare Krishna*, they all wondered whether it was a mythological. The audience also had the same question in their minds when the film was announced to the world. But they came to know when it was being made that it was perhaps the most modern story of the day!

Forty-five

The search for the actress to play Jasbir alias Janice in *Hare Rama Hare Krishna* started in right earnest. Nobody in the industry wanted to play Dev Anand's sister in the film, everyone wanted to play the romantic lead opposite me, though the sister's part was bigger, better and central to the theme. It was to carry the film on its shoulders; anybody who'd do it and do it well was bound to walk away with the honours. I decided to cast a new girl, Indian in looks but with a Western upbringing, someone who would not hesitate to smoke or to wear outfits that would accentuate her whimsical, carefree, to-hell-with-the-world attitude. I was sure that somewhere a great star-in-the-making was waiting, an untapped, unknown talent from amongst the heap of young hopefuls.

I was doing a film with Mumtaz for my brother Goldie called *Tere Mere Sapne*; together we made a good-looking pair. She was friendly, very amiable, an easy-going, uninhibited co-star. We responded to each other exceptionally well on the sets. She had a long desire to be cast opposite me and Goldie had fulfilled it in his film. As soon as she heard of my project to be shot in Nepal, she showed her keenness to participate in it. One evening, after having invited me for dinner at her residence, she broached the subject.

'Am I in your picture?' she asked.

'You need to change your style to get into the shoes of Janice in my film Mumsy,' I said. That's what I used to call Mumtaz.

'My feet can get adjusted to all types of shoes, and of all sizes!' she said. 'I must do your film—tell me the part.'

I gave her a brief narration of the story.

'It's a hell of a role for any girl who does it,' she said, 'but I don't think I want to play your sister.' She was quite emphatic.

'Why not?' I asked her.

'For I don't feel like one, when you are with me,' she explained. We both laughed.

As soon as the dinner was over, she touched upon the subject again. 'What about my being in your film?'

'Would you agree to do the smaller and less significant part?' I asked.

'Only if it is the romantic one,' she replied.

'In that case, let me have the privilege of asking you, "Will you be the romantic leading lady opposite me, Mumsy, in my film *Hare Rama Hare Krishna*?"' I said in great style.

She was equally stylish as she answered, 'Privilege granted!' We shook hands.

'Who is doing the sister's role?' she asked, at the same time.

'Don't know yet, but I'm sure somebody's waiting to do it,' I answered.

Amarjeet was having a small party at his apartment, and I had to be there, for he never threw a party without my presence. And this was a very special occasion. He was wooing a lady and was keen to ask her to be his fiancée, in the presence of some personal friends of repute who would raise his status in her eyes and make his effort easier.

He made the evening a little more glamorous by inviting Zeenat Aman, the newly crowned Miss Asia.

Zeenat came very appropriately dressed for the party, looking chic and mod and casual, just the image I had of my Janice in *Hare Rama Hare Krishna*. After the formal introduction, I got to know that Zeenat was a product of Panchgani convent, before she went to California for a year on a scholarship.

As she sat in front of me, she was a picture of self-confidence, radiating a devil-may-care attitude. She was wearing a broad belt round her waist over a pair of slacks, a small purse hanging from it in front. I was wondering what was inside it, when her hand went there. She took out a pack of expensive cigarettes. Her other hand went into her handbag, to take out a golden lighter. She had a style all her own, not bothering who was looking at her. She took out a cigarette and put it between her lips. That was the moment her eyes met mine, for I was constantly watching her and her bearing. She smiled an attractive girlish smile, and stretched her hand towards me, offering me a cigarette as well. I smoked very occasionally, but I decided to take one on that occasion. Before I could pull out a cigarette from the pack, she had already taken one out for me. I put it straight into my mouth, still looking at her. She now ignited the lighter with a single flick, and put its flame on my cigarette, looking straight into my eyes. The flame of the lighter lit up her smiling eyes, putting an extra glow into them that said:

'I am your Janice, Dev.'

I puffed out the smoke on to her face which she quite liked, and instantly got busy lighting her own cigarette, smiling a broader smile.

'Zeenat!' I said. She raised her eyes towards me. 'Are you interested in doing films?' I asked.

Now she blew her smoke on my face and said, 'Only if it's a special one.'

'Can I invite you to a screen test?' was my next query.

'When?' she asked.

'You tell me.' I put the ball in her court.

'Tomorrow?' she said.

'What time?'

'You tell me!' she retorted.

'Eleven-thirty in the morning?'

'That's a date!' She put the cigarette pack back in its place, and the lighter as well.

She was camera friendly. She smiled and laughed and cried according to my directions. The camera liked her as well. On the way back from the studio, she was in my car—I had offered to drop her. She was wearing a large sexy pair of goggles that added to her appeal.

'I like your goggles,' I said.

She took them off and put them into my pocket. 'Take them as a present from me.'

'But they suit you,' I said.

'That's why,' she shot back.

I still have that pair of goggles sitting in some corner of my cupboard. Sometimes, when I open it, it comes out of its place to stare at me. I can see Zeenat looking at me again, the way she looked at me in the car that day, when she took the goggles off, so that I could own them.

I had her cast in an American film called *The Evil Within*, in which I was starring at that moment, along with Kieu Chinh, a leading lady from Vietnam. Later, I took her to Nepal right at the beginning of the shooting of *Hare Rama Hare Krishna*, though her work did not start until after a month, during which time she was supposed to watch Mumtaz perform in front of the camera, for her own edification.

The filming of *Hare Rama Hare Krishna* was a mammoth affair. It was done on a gigantic scale, with a unit eighty-four strong invading Nepal to shoot the first film of its kind non-stop in Kathmandu. The hospitability of the Nepalese people was exemplary, with the kingdom's capital agog with excitement, living day and night with the phenomenon called *Hare Rama Hare Krishna*. The king's support, moral as well as emotional, carried the film through to its successful completion in a period of ten weeks.

The mahurat was performed with great fanfare at the Soaltee Hotel by one of the ministers of the royal cabinet. The casino of the hotel was repainted in psychedelic colours by two young Australian girls who were in town as tourists. Indeed, the entire filming was like one huge celebration. I worked three shifts a day like an inspired man, working in the morning, afternoon and at night, depending on the requirements of the scenes, shooting day for day, night for night. There wasn't a place where the camera with the latest zoom mounted on it did not travel.

We received hearty support and cooperation from the local inhabitants. Even in Bhaktapur, the former capital of Nepal, which was communist dominated and had anti-Indian sentiments at that time, people came out in full force to participate in a dance number by Mumtaz, shot at its main square. It was as if the whole township was on a mission. All the housewives from their homes, kids from their schools, and men and women from their work, from wherever their offices or workplaces were, were on a holiday with Mumtaz, as she danced her way through their hearts, for three successive days, with the sun shining in benevolent warmth on all those whose spirits were enlivened and their joy unlimited.

And in the evenings as the bells tolled, the chants of the devotees invoked their deity fervently, praying for the speedy completion and success of the film. Muslims are not allowed inside Pashupati, one of the most famous and important Hindu temples in Kathmandu. But the high priest made an exception in the case of Mumtaz, for she was playing Shanti in the film. And as Prashant (played by me) and Shanti, for a sequence in the film, took part in the Mahapuja there, accepting the blessings of the gods residing in the inner sanctum, after having tied the nuptial knots in their presence, the whole town reverberated with the resonance of the great moment.

At Swayambhu, the spectacle of Buddhist monks chanting slokas sitting in long rows with their yellow and saffron robes, reacting to the whirring of the cameras capturing them in the full glory of their benign smiles, was as outstanding as the scene where the hippie Janice, in western slacks, holding a thali of marigold flowers, suddenly put a vermillion tikka on the forehead of a man she gets fascinated with, without knowing he is her long-lost brother. The crowds gathered to watch the filming at Swayambhu, their faces beaming with joy, their cameras clicking to catch the stars, their hands raised towards them for autographs.

One day, I spotted a young man, standing on a platform alone in a corner, looking at the magic being captured by the movie cameras. Someone came and whispered into my ears that it was the young Prince Gyanendra. I walked up to him, to invite him to come behind the camera to witness the filming from up close. But he insisted on not creating a disturbance, and preferred standing aloof, all by himself.

I had to pack up early that afternoon to fly out by helicopter to see a new location for the next day's shooting, only a few minutes away on a hilltop, which I did. Later, in the hotel, as I wanted to look at my script for a few embellishments to be added to the scenes to be shot next morning, I found it missing. A frantic search ensued. We searched high and low, but to no avail. My assistants were on tenterhooks, for being so careless as to let it go missing. Without the script in my hand, I was a cripple. Rewriting out of memory would be an arduous task, and a waste of precious time, every second of which was worth a lot of money.

I banged my forehead in utter helplessness, and suddenly, in a flash, I remembered where I had left it. I had the script in my hand when I flew to the hilltop. I must have forgotten it there, at 8,000 feet above sea-level! If so, it had to be retrieved straightaway, before nightfall, before it got picked up by someone and thrown away, or got blown away in the heavy winds, or flew down into the deep ravines surrounding the hilltop. Everybody said it was a very windy spot, and chances were that it had been swept away already. I had to rush there immediately to find it myself.

An impossible task except by helicopter, and that too before nightfall. The only helicopter available in Kathmandu was the one I was using, and that belonged to the Unicef. I called them, but the pilot was not available then. Somebody said the American Mission owned a helicopter, but it was shut at that time.

Prince Gyanendra came to my mind, for the only other helicopter in Kathmandu belonged to the king. The palace could come to my rescue. I called the secretary on duty there and explained my predicament. In a matter of minutes the royal helicopter was ready for me, thanks to the courtesy extended by Prince Gyanendra.

The evening shadows were about to lengthen as I flew over the hilltop. I looked down at the place where I had rambled the same afternoon, and I saw my most precious belonging of the moment lying entwined between a couple of twigs, its pages fluttering in the breeze, as if calling out to its owner to come and rescue it.

After I finished filming with Mumtaz, which took four weeks, I started with Zeenat. She was totally prepared, and waiting to be shot. By the time we were picturizing 'Dum maro dum' at the famous Kashtmandap, the busiest thoroughfare in the heart of Kathmandu, she had already become a practiced actress, in her element in every scene. She was in another world altogether, smoking away her chillum along with the other—real—hippies around her.

Every morning our production man would wander the streets of Kathmandu, picking the hippies up from their slumber in hideouts and hutments, tempting them with money and hash to come over and act as bit players. They would swing and dance and smoke merrily the whole day long, enjoying the feel of being actors in a film that represented them. By the evening they would either just sit and stare into nothingness, not reacting to anything at all around them, or turn violent, picking up fights over insignificant nothings. They earned good money from the film, enough to indulge in activities of their choice, and were just themselves in the film, just like the thousands of Nepalese people, who, having drunk their local brew, swayed to the rhythm of '*Dum maro dum*', with a dozen guards of the royal mounted police keeping constant vigil lest a brawl broke out in the excitement of intoxication.

The song rang through the length and breadth of Kathmandu, signalling the beginning of its popularity all over the country and the world. It brought the young and extremely talented music director R.D. Burman, S.D. Burman's son, into the limelight. It made a cult figure out of Zeenat, who started symbolizing the new young, mod, reckless generation, seeking adventures of the flesh and the spirit. For me, it was a great experience interacting with the hippies at very close quarters, as their director. Many of them opened their hearts and exposed their souls to me.

Hare Rama Hare Krishna turned out to be memorable for many reasons. Much, much later, after the release of the movie, I got a letter from the father of a girl in America, thanking me for making a film in which he could see his missing daughter participating in a sequence. She had left home, not leaving a word about her whereabouts for her parents. They were desperately at a loss to know where on earth she had decided to disappear to. The film helped them find her, for she had participated in it. They got to know from the film she had to be in Nepal, or somewhere close by in South East Asia. They followed her trail, and ultimately found her in Kabul.

As I finished filming, and the unit was packing up to come back to India, I went and spent one whole afternoon at The Bakery, where all the hippies congregated in the evenings. There was no filming taking place at that moment, no music playing, no hustle-bustle of any sort, no hippies anywhere around. Just an empty space of quiet calm—a wild grassy knoll outside a dingy used-up dormitory.

I remembered the night when Christian Doermer had brought me to that place from where, standing on the edge of a small winding pathway, I had seen the real Janice swinging in the lap of her lover.

I had recreated Janice in the film, in the form of Zeenat, for the world to remember her for a long time—and Janice's story had ended as the film ended. Reflecting on this I dozed off in the warm bracing rays of the sun, the soft cool breeze playing on my face.

I must have slept for hours, for I was tired and exhausted after ten weeks of non-stop mental and physical exertion. The strain was over and I was in a peaceful dreamless slumber. A musical note from a guitar woke me up. Evening had fallen, and the shadows of the night were about to be lit with the 'atmosphere' of the place. I looked around. My stars, the hippies of Kathmandu I had worked with, had gathered around me, and were on the verge of starting their celebration.

I blinked my eyes and saw a blooming red rose in front of my face. I looked at it and then at the person holding it. A young European girl—she must have been just past her adolescence—looking as beautiful as the early pink dawn on a cloudless day.

She said, 'I wish I was in your film. They have all told me about it. And this is on behalf of all of us!' She gave the flower to me.

I looked at all of them, and then back at her, and was sure she was a new entrant into the crowd. I took the flower, then laughed in a spirit of camaraderie. They all laughed back together.

The young girl then took out a chillum from her bag and started smoking.

As I entered the palace to thank the king for his gracious and kind hospitality, the same flower was in my buttonhole. 'That's a beautiful flower!' he remarked. 'Come again to Nepal,' he added.

'I shall come back with an invitation for you to be my country's guest at the premiere of the film in our capital, hopefully with the prime minister and her cabinet attending, to give you a reception that the sun and the moon and the stars will keep gazing at with envy!' I said, with tears in my eyes. His eyes became moist too. He shook my hand and we parted.

But before the film could be released, my eyes fell on a newspaper headline one day that carried the worst possible news: 'King Mahendra of Nepal dies of massive heart attack.' I could do nothing but weep silent tears.

Forty-six

My heart had been won over by the royal family at the Narayantithi Palace in Kathmandu. Earlier I had befriended the Chogyal of Sikkim. Now my thoughts dwelt on the kingdom of Bhutan, the last of the triumvirate of hill countries. Bhutan could not be left unvisited.

The reputed journalist Desmond Doig, a friend of mine, was my guide as we travelled by car from Phuntsholing, the township that separates India from the mystery kingdom. The occasion was King Jigme Singye Wangchuk's coronation, the biggest event the tiny peaceful kingdom nestled in its quiet cosy corner had seen in a long time. A group of international guests, from the media as well as from the political spectrum were invited, and Desmond and I were part of that group. Goldie was accompanying us, along with our cameraman. Their mission was to shoot a documentary on the king and his palace.

We drove to Thimpu, the capital of Bhutan, after a long stopover at Phuntsholing, climbing upwards on the zig-zag road, looking down at the sprawling expanse of flat green with rivers snaking through below us, stretching as far as the eye could see. Monasteries, zsongs as the Bhutanese called them, stood like icons of spirituality on top of the hills. Both men and women of the local population wore stockings and kilts, reminding one of the Scottish highlanders. Bows and arrows were seen in abundance, as the Bhutanese indulged in their favourite sport. Young kids looked like dolls in a fairyland, amazed at the sudden onslaught of foreigners on their soil, and married women carried babies on their backs, safely ensconced in their haversacks which were part of their body wear.

Thimpu valley won over your heart, but Paro valley, on the other side of the mountains, was so picturesque and breathtaking that Switzerland, the country I love the most for its beauty, paled into insignificance in comparison, so overwhelming was its otherworldly quality.

Entering Thimpu was like walking into a dreamland. The king's palace was a veritable oriental castle, surrounded by floating clouds of mist, making you feel you were treading the skies. The mood of festivity in Thimpu combined local colour and an international flavour, since so many visitors had gathered together from all over the world to pay homage to the young king on the day of his coronation. Our camera captured the magic of it all, and after the ornate ceremony, I walked to the king who sat on his throne to tell him that my humble present to him on that historic occasion was locked up in the camera that captured not only his handsomeness in all its glory with his subjects singing hymns in his praise, but also the atmosphere in which the solitude of the divine was in constant communion with the peaceful minds surrounding it, in complete contentment.

He nodded happily. I thanked him again for his hospitality and for the comforts provided during our stay in his heavenly land. He nodded very happily this time, with a broad grin which was both innocent and gracious.

Desmond Doig gave his voice to our documentary on the king's coronation, and it was sent to him as soon as it was ready, my gift to a memory that I have always cherished, with a passionate desire to shoot a film in Bhutan one day.

Forty-seven

After *Hare Rama Hare Krishna*, Zeenat emerged as a role model for all young college-going girls of the country, a cult figure who inspired the new generation to follow her lifestyle. The '*Dum maro dum*' girl was a superstar. But a star with a sister's image, not that of a romantic heroine.

To take her out of that mould before it stuck to her permanently, I planned *Heera Panna*, again a very youthful, contemporary film about a roving international photographer, a young female model and an air-hostess. This time my locations were set in Hong Kong and in south India. The film took me to explore the rugged, rocky, desolate vistas around the main highway between Bangalore and Madras. The gigantic black rocks fashioned by nature's inexplicable whim, with the sexy Zeenat swinging amidst them in a hammock in a colourful bikini in the scorching heat of the sun, the only human being in that awesome vastness except for the professional photographer clicking away with his Hasselblad, made for some very exciting scenes.

There is one particular moment from the shooting of *Heera Panna* that is deeply etched in my memory. In a certain scene, the red cap I was wearing was to fly away with a gust of wind, as I sang a song romancing Zeenat, and I was to chase it until I held it in my hands again. But it so happened that as soon as the cap flew off my head, with a little help from an invisible string tied to it, a real dust storm started raging. The cap took off like a jet, caught in the whirlwind. It started dancing in mid-air, with me following it, dancing to its tune. Another violent gust blew it away further and it fell on the bulging breasts of a village belle at the roadside. She picked it up and put it on, her hair flying in the wind, looking very smart. Zeenat screamed with delight, and the other onlookers laughed boisterously as well. The village belle suddenly felt shy, threw the cap up in the air, and it flew straight into my hands, with me snapping it up like a fielder in a game of cricket. 'Well caught!' shouted the crowd. The rustic girl dissolved into the dust storm, and I went back to my Zeenat-serenading:

> Panna ki tamanna hai, ki heera mujhe mil jaye
> Chahe meri jaan jaye, chahe mera dil jaye.

The strains of the melodious song, composed by R.D. Burman, resounded so deep in the vast valley that the whole country was soon to fall in love with it, as they were with the eyes of Raakhee, who played the third role in the film. The charm in them was devastating, their enchantment as enticing to the camera as Zeenat's tempting figure. Together, the two of them made a smashing combination.

Zeenat, who by now was known to the world as Dev Anand's discovery, was becoming more and more my responsibility. There was a wealth of talent stored inside her, which was yet to be tapped. *Hare Rama Hare Krishna* and *Heera Panna* were just not enough; she needed a larger canvas, with more varied and colourful shades of paints with which to draw her portraits.

I wanted to shoot in Nepal again. *Hare Rama Hare Krishna* had been restricted to the Kathmandu valley. I now wanted to go to the mountains of Nepal, into the heart of the wild natural beauty of its valleys and its plush meadows, and its mystical, ethereal quality, to capture what no one else had captured on celluloid.

I have always had an affinity with the mountains, and this liking had increased all the more ever since I met Tenzing Norgay in Darjeeling during the shooting of Nasir Hussain's *Jab Pyar Kisi Se Hota Hai*. Tenzing invited me home for breakfast and later took me to his mountaineering institute, and instilled in me a strong affinity with and a longing for the mountains, as if my spirit belonged there.

So I planned *Ishq Ishq Ishq*, a musical set in the mountains, a format that gave full play to the exploitation of all the elements that

the majesty of the Himalayan mountains had to offer. I travelled by
helicopter all over Nepal, to look for the best locations in the country.
Each trip was the experience of a lifetime.

Imagine yourself flying by helicopter through the middle of snow-
capped mountains, so close that you could jump out and land on
them, then landing in the valley, thousands of feet below, with
yaks grazing on the green fields and the local Tibetan farm-owners
entertaining you with steaming hot cups of tea, made with yak's milk,
before the helicopter took off again, for another destination.

Imagine yourself landing at a height of 14,000 feet above
sea level and then walking down a thousand feet to Namchi
Bazaar, the village of Tenzing Norgay, and making a sudden
appearance among the local sherpas huddled together by the
blazing fireplace, humming along with their hilly-billy songs and
participating in their revelry, being occasionally offered a puff
from a beedi to keep you warm from the biting chill of the
slashing winds outside.

Imagine yourself trekking all the way to a glorious mountain
top, with your camera equipment carried alongside by hardy porters,
crossing range after range that offer more and more breathtaking
views of the splendour of the valleys down below, before you finally
reach the top, breathless yet exhilarated, to exclaim to your inner
self looking at the view all around, 'This could only be the abode
of the gods!'

And then sleeping in sleeping bags in tents, on bitter cold nights,
with the winds howling and night animals brushing past the canvas
of your tent outside, as you watch the flickering candle next to you
go out, enhancing the drama of the moment—and waking up to the
chirping of the early morning birds calling your attention to the
colours of dawn, asking you to capture its enchanting magic on
camera for the world to wonder at.

Great thrilling moments of excitement, never experienced by
those with temperaments alien to the spirit of adventure!

A location where we camped for days for filming was Shyangboche,
14,000 feet in height with no human habitation around. We stayed
at a Japanese-built expensive hotel, meant primarily for affluent
trekkers. As we sat by the fireplace in its common room in the evenings

after the day's work, we could see, if we were lucky, four of the tallest mountains in the world including Mount Everest on a moonlit night, their snowy white tops glistening through the huge glass windows.

A handsome young man sitting next to me by the fireplace had a faraway look in his eyes as he enjoyed one such moment. His name was Shekhar Kapur, and he was my nephew. Today he is an internationally renowned director, but *Ishq Ishq Ishq* was his first film as an actor. It was also the first 'mainstream' film for Shabana Azmi, who was equally hypnotized by the extraordinary beauty of those lofty mountains.

It is quite rare to see the sun or the moon on Mount Everest, but both these heavenly bodies were kind to us during our filming. One morning, the sun threw its orange rays so artistically on the mountain that a whiff of a cloud, transparently clad, started spinning around it in an attempt to kiss it and then engulf itself into its bosom. It did succeed in doing so, but not before we had canned the most spectacular shot with Zeenat Aman and Kabir Bedi secretly romancing each other against its backdrop, the mighty peak keeping a vigil over the lovers.

If you ever happen to see *Ishq Ishq Ishq*, look out for that shot of Mount Everest with a sweetheart of a cloud spinning around it—a very rare sight indeed!

The wintry sun used to be scorchingly hot in the afternoons, and the nights were so bitingly cold that even electrically heated blankets were not warm enough for our chilly shivers! As we got up in the mornings, our fingers would freeze, making it difficult to open the taps of water for our daily morning necessities. It was around the middle of December, and the temperature was minus fifteen degrees at night, but the sky was so unbelievably blue in the mornings that it was a sheer joy for cinematography.

One day, we had to fly across to a neighbouring hilltop to film a sequence, only a couple of minutes away by helicopter. We hopped over to finish the entire schedule to our compete satisfaction, working the whole day through. The place was Thyangboche, the first base camp for mountaineers venturing to climb Mount Everest. Its spectacular monastery looked like it had come straight out of a fairy-tale.

As we finished filming there, and were ready to fly back to our base, divided into batches of four for each trip in a single helicopter flying to and fro, mist started descending on us. Visibility decreased rapidly. Soon we couldn't even see each other's faces, and it was impossible for the chopper to take off.

'Are you there?' I asked Zeenat.

'Floating in the clouds; and you?' she said.

'Swimming in them!' I answered.

And as if from nowhere, flakes of soft cotton wool started falling on us. As we shouted 'Wow' to one another, blankets of snow had already covered us all.

The romance of hide-and-seek was in the air, and we all decided to stay back on location for the night, in the few rooms inside the monastery. Outside, the snow fell steadily through the night, and inside the unit huddled together, our teeth chattering with cold. We discussed Edmund Hilary and his team who stayed in the same rooms for days and days before the weather outside gave them the chance for their first assault on the still unconquered Everest.

Next morning, the sky was spotlessly blue again, and the heat intense as the sun started climbing. The helicopter, having shaken off the thick layers of snow, was back on its wings—and all of us were on top of the world.

A very expensive motion picture, shot with a unit of more than a hundred people flying up and down the world's tallest mountains in one of the most adventurous ventures tried in the country, *Ishq Ishq Ishq* was my biggest disaster at the box-office. But it was the most inspiring and exhilarating experience for my own growth and enlightenment.

The film taught me resilience. A broken nose sometimes makes a great boxer. I had my nose broken in this film, but I came out unconquered and more invigorated, sharper in my senses and more creative in my thinking. Soon, very soon, I thought, I would move on to another idea, another project, even bigger and even more challenging.

Forty-eight

Zeenat and I started being linked with each other in the magazines and newspapers that people hungry for gossip love to read. For, while she was the adorable painting that they loved to watch, admire and emulate, I was the painter who had etched that painting. The colours were mine as was the finished drawing on the canvas. While she as a person was God's creation, her image was of my making, and together we became inseparable in the public eye.

Whenever and wherever she was talked about glowingly, I loved it; and whenever and wherever I was discussed in the same vein, she was jubilant. In the subconscious, we had become emotionally attached to each other.

At the silver jubilee celebration of *Hare Rama Hare Krishna* at a theatre in Calcutta, as Usha Uthup, the famous pop singer, sang the '*Dum maro dum*' number on stage and reached the crescendo of her rendering, she pulled Zeenat, who was sitting in the audience, on stage; Zeenat in turn pulled me on stage too, so that together we could sing along with Usha. The audience in a moment of spontaneity also jumped up on stage and the song became a chorus of over a hundred voices. The maddened crowds picked Zeenat up on their shoulders, raising her heavenwards. I felt proud of her, and yet, at the same time, I felt a stab of jealousy; of possessiveness as well. How could they own her in that way? She was my prized possession! I knew it was a stupid thought on my part, but I couldn't help it.

A couple of years later, after the premiere of *Ishq Ishq Ishq* at Metro cinema, Raj Kapoor kissed Zeenat in full view of the invited audience, congratulating her for her sparkling performance in the film. That must have made her evening all the more sparkling. Again I felt proud of her, as much as I admired Raj Kapoor for his honest and spontaneous reaction. Complimenting her was indirectly complimenting her mentor, and I inwardly saluted my contemporary film-maker for his sound judgement. Yet, I was jealous of him for making advances on what I considered my sole possession, my discovery, my leading lady, and desiring her with a kiss.

Time moved on. Suddenly, one day, I felt I was desperately in love with Zeenat—and wanted to say so to her! To make a honest confession, at a very special, exclusive place meant for romance. I chose the Rendezvous at the Taj, on the top of the city, where we had dined together once earlier.

No setting could be more appropriate, I thought, than a quiet candlelit table in the corner, the candle throwing its gleam on Zeenat's face, just as the glow of her cigarette-lighter had lit up her face when I first met her. The dimmed lights of the city below, shining out of the darkness, would certainly light up the romance of the moment.

I called her up to say, 'Zeenie, I want to go out on a date with you tonight.'

'But aren't we already going together to a party tonight?' she asked me.

'Of course we are. But let's just go there only for a brief while, say Hi to the gathering, and then quickly disappear!' It was an order, but very lovingly conveyed.

She was quiet.

'H-e-ll-o!' I said.

'Yes, I am listening.'

'Is that a date?' I asked.

'If you so desire. See you then!' And she hung up.

I picked her up. Together we went to the party. It was on in full force. The first person who greeted Zeenat from a distance was a drunken Raj Kapoor, with a gallant drawl, 'There she is!' He threw his arms around her exuberantly.

This suddenly struck me as a little too familiar. And the way she reciprocated his embrace seemed much more than just polite and courteous. She quickly bent down to touch his feet, and then gave me an embarrassed look. Raj grasped my hand in a very tight grip, like never before, as if trying to make amends for some wrong he had done, suddenly overflowing with affection.

A hint of suspicion crossed my mind. A couple of days earlier, a rumour had been floating around that Zeenat had gone to Raj's studio for a screen test for the main role in his new movie *Satyam Shivam Sundaram*. The hearsay now started ringing true. My heart was bleeding.

'You are breaking your promise,' Raj was now telling Zeenat in his drunken joviality, 'that you will always be seen by me only in a white sari!'

More embarrassment was writ large on her face, and Zeenat was not the same Zeenat for me any more.

My heart broke into pieces. I wanted to leave the party at once and go off somewhere alone, to be just by myself, so that I could swallow the humiliation thrust on my ego.

But a struggle within me transformed itself into a 'to-hell-with-it-all' attitude, and prompted me to say goodbye to a relationship which, though it had been non-committal emotionally on both sides, had been honest all the same. There was no space in it for professional dishonesty.

The painting I had made of her started showing signs of cracking.

'How long do you intend staying here, Zeenat?' I asked her.

She looked at Raj, as if seeking his permission to leave.

'Let her stay here, Dev—and you too—enjoy!' he said in a drunken drawl.

'By all means,' I said. 'Enjoy, Zeenat. Call me up later, when you feel like it!'

'But aren't we suppose to be going to the other place together?' she casually asked.

'Doesn't matter!' I said.

The rendezvous had already lost all meaning in my mind.

I sneaked out of the place, quietly apologizing to the host.

The evening delivered a blow to my personality, and my dominating spirit. I had decided on the spur of the moment to tell Zeenat for the first time how much I loved her. And that there was an idea in my mind of another story that would put her on a pedestal as never before, the highest so far. But that was never to be.

And so be it! I quickly detached myself, convincing myself that I had blundered, taking too many things for granted. There was no need for me to let any rancour germinate in my mind against Zeenat. I had prepared her for the world, and she was free to go into the arms of anyone who would help her further her ambitious dreams.

A group of chanting devotees was passing by my car. I sat listening to the sound of cymbals and bells.

Hare Krishna Hare Krishna
Krishna Krishna Hare Hare
Hare Ram Hare Ram
Ram Ram Hare Hare

I closed my eyes. Zeenat still remained beautiful in my eyes, with an honest soul. And Raj a passionate film-maker.

I opened my eyes. A streak of lightning seemed to flash across my mind and inspired a new thought. I started pursuing it. A new chapter was thrown open before me, its first pages slowly unfolding.

The idea of a new film was coming slowly into focus.

The family man: with wife Mona and the children

Speed thrills: driving off in his green convertible

Guide (1965): the exuberance of '*Aaj phir jeene ki tamanna hai*' (above); the dramatic conclusion—the media interviews the guide turned saint who is on a fast, as his estranged love Rosie (Waheeda Rehman) appears on the scene (below)

Jewel Thief (1967): with Vyjayanthimala (above); and
with Helen (below)

Prem Pujari (1970): soldier, pacifist, lover—the many faces of the hero
in his first directorial venture

Hare Rama Hare Krishna (1971): with Zeenat Aman who played Jasbir
turned Janice, his sister (above), and with Mumtaz, who played
his lady love (below)

Two trademark looks: *Jewel Thief* (1967) and *Gambler* (1971)

'Pal bhar ke liye koi humen pyar kar le'—with Hema Malini in
Johny Mera Naam (1970)

Tere Mere Sapne (1971): with Mumtaz (above)
and brother Vijay Anand (below)

With Zeenat Aman in *Heera Panna* (1973)
and *Ishq Ishq Ishq* (1974)

Des Pardes (1978): the crusader (above);
'*Tu pee aur jee*'—with Tina Munim (below)

At Nathula Pass looking across the border to the Chinese post (above)
and shooting in Kathmandu for *Hare Rama Hare Krishna* (below)

Directing Aamir Khan (above) on the sets of *Awwal Number* (1990) and shooting in San Francisco for *Love at Times Square* (2003) (below)

With daughter Devina and
granddaughter Gina

With son Suneil in *Anand Aur
Anand* (1984)

At the old Navketan office

On a visit to Tirupati

Forever young: in *Hum Naujawan* (1986) (above) and shooting in
Inverness, Scotland for *Main Solah Baras Ki* (1998) (below)

In Kutch shooting *Mr Prime Minister* (2005)

With Amitabh Bachchan—a sameness of shirts

Crossing boundaries—after alighting from the Lahore Bus,
with Nawaz Sharief and Atal Bihari Vajpayee

With idol Ashok Kumar, and Vijay Anand, who directed them both in
Jewel Thief

Location-hunting in Croatia for his new film: in Pula (above)
and in Motovun (below)

Forty-nine

I needed to get away to a new environment. I hadn't seen my son Suneil for a long time. He was studying at the American University in Washington DC. I took a flight to New York, boarded an Amtrak train from Grand Central station, reached Washington, hired a car, and soon we were running into each other's arms. The embrace lasted for a long time. Our eyes were moist with emotion.

Suneil showed me around the university campus, taking pride in introducing his movie star father to his fellow students, who were all in their college blazers, wearing wreaths of welcoming smiles on their young excited faces. Then he gave me a guided tour around the well-known streets of the American capital in his car.

I wanted to buy a pair of goggles. Suneil took me to the best optician's shop that he knew. I picked up a particular brand that I liked. He picked up a brand that he liked and said, 'Papa, you buy two, one of your choice and one of mine.'

I felt good and cared for by my son. 'And you . . . you pick up two that you want for yourself,' I told him.

'No, Papa,' he said, 'I don't like wearing goggles. Whenever I do, I shall buy them.' He knew his mind.

He took some money out of my pocket, paid for the goggles, and put the rest into my pocket, giving the flap a pat and closing the button on it, making sure that the couple of hundred dollars did not fall out carelessly.

I brought Suneil with me to New York, and took him to Broadway to see a musical. Then together we walked back to Pierre Hotel on 5th Avenue, arm-in-arm, me humming and he whistling the notes of a particular number sung on the stage that we had liked.

'I'll sleep on the same bed with you, Papa,' he whispered partly to me, partly to himself, and sneaked into my bed. We held each other close.

Next day when he was about to leave for Washington, he had tears in his eyes. 'Don't go if you don't want to,' I kissed him.

'No, I must, Papa. I love you.' And he left after hugging me again.

These were great fatherly moments for me after the brutally harsh working schedule I had thrown myself into all these years, that kept me away from my family. But I suppose that's the price you pay for the hard work you have to put in for the world to acknowledge an 'achievement' in your field.

Flying back from New York to Bombay, my eyes fell on an editorial column in a newspaper. It was on illegal Indian immigrants in England, the theme of *Des Pardes*, the movie I had already started working on.

Fifty

I was singing the song '*Bullet, bullet, bullet*', set to a catchy tuna by R.D. Burman, which was being picturized on me. As I reached the last note, and the director Vijay Anand said 'cut', a female voice loudly said 'Very good' from behind the camera, making itself heard among a chorus of claps.

I looked and found a group of girls clapping, and the one who had loudly applauded me stepped forward to say, 'Lovely shot!' Before I could say 'Thank you', she already had come out of the group holding an autograph book.

'Sorry for the intrusion! But can I have your autograph?' she said.

I looked at her. 'Why not?' I said, and took the autograph book to oblige her. It was brand new. Flipping through its empty pages, I remarked, 'Mine shall be the only autograph in your entire autograph book!'

'I bought it especially for you,' she said.

Flattered, now scribbling my name stylishly, I asked, 'You're from Bombay?'

'Very much,' she replied.

'You're in school?'

'Not any more.'

I looked at her.

'I was in Aruba only the other day and won the Miss Photogenic contest there,' she said with pride.

'Then you should give me an autograph as well!' I said, handing her back the autograph book.

She laughed.

'What next after the photogenic contest?' I asked.

'I haven't decided yet.'

'Most of the girls who take part in beauty contests are ambitious.'

'I am not.'

'You should be. You are unfair to yourself otherwise.'

'Lots of people have said that to me.'

My mind went back to the script I had just finished. Something clicked somewhere.

'Ever thought of being in the movies?' I asked.

'I don't care.'

'What do you care about?'

'I haven't decided yet.'

'Would you care to come for a screen test?'

'For which film?'

'I'm asking you.'

'If you insist.'

'I do.'

She was screen tested. The two tests of the other two girls were already lying in my editing room. I saw them all together one after the other, closed my eyes in deep concentration for a few moments, and the smart fresh-faced sixteen-year-old with a beautiful smile, Tina Munim, was selected to play the leading lady in *Des Pardes*.

I invited her to visit me on the sets of *Janeman*, which Chetan bhaiji was again wielding the megaphone for, working with the trio who had just woven their magic together in Mohan Kumar's *Amir Garib*—Hema Malini, Premnath and Dev Anand.

While choosing the title for the film, Chetan had kept on throwing various names in the ring for general consensus, when I had jumped in with *Janeman*, the most endearing word that lovers the world over address their loved ones with. *Janeman* was launched with the recording of the title song '*Janeman . . . janeman*,' inspiringly written by Anand Bakshi and melodiously sung by Kishore Kumar, to the tune of composers Laxmikant–Pyarelal, who were working for Navketan for the first time.

'Who is the *janeman* in the film?' asked Tina of me very innocently, as both Chetan and Premnath whispered to each other, 'Cute girl', and wanted to know who she was.

'I shall reveal that when I open my bag of suspense,' I remarked.

The theme of *Des Pardes* had to do with illegal Indian immigrants in England. I shot extensively in that country with the help of a very friendly and influential young Indian leader from East Africa, Praful Patel. There was almost a month's filming to be done inside a pub, for the film's story revolved around a British drinking joint, owned by one of the main characters. It was a difficult task to persuade a pub-owner there to let us do the filming inside his establishment for that long a duration. So, like we so often do in films, I had to recreate a very colourful pub with a lot of character in a Bombay studio.

I pub-crawled in London day after day, accompanied by a photographer, to take pictures of the pubs that I fancied, to build a replica in the studio. Finally, my eyes fell on The Prospects of Whitby in East London. I took photographs of the pub from various angles, and gave the entire material to my art department in Bombay. It took almost a month to erect an exact copy of the pub, including that of its exterior, to match the actual Prospects of Whitby in London, where the outdoor scenes were to be shot.

The pub recreated in the studio looked so realistic that an English couple, who visited the sets as tourists from abroad, immediately remarked as soon as they entered, 'Isn't that Prospects of Whitby in East London?' My art director won an award for the authenticity of his creation.

One of the outstanding features of *Des Pardes* was its music. Rajesh Roshan marked his first film for Navketan with an inspired music track that was one of the best of his career. And the blue-eyed executive of Navketan, Amit Khanna, was discovered by the world as a good lyricist with an easy-flowing pen.

I lined up an array of established actors for *Des Pardes*. Besides Pran, who played my elder brother, the British pub owner, Ajit played the villain trying to usurp the pub in collusion with his sweetheart, played by Bindu. Prem Chopra played another negative role, of a man forging and selling illegal passports. Funster Mehmood took charge of providing humour in his own characteristic style, while Amjad Khan, fresh from his huge success as Gabbar Singh, drew all the applause as he played Buta Singh, serving liquor at the bar in his very rustic style to the customers with a glad eye for Tina Munim all the time.

Tina was acting as a bar girl in the film. In one of its sequences she was made to sit in a bikini inside a huge rotating beer barrel overflowing with red wine, with hordes of pub-crawlers watching the spectacle from down below, drinking as deeply from the innocence of her smiling eyes—more intoxicating then the stuff she was swimming in—as from the trickling streams of wine from the barrel. That musical sequence—'*Tu pee aur jee*'—was a big hit in the movie, and Tina became a roaring success, establishing herself as a new young star on the horizon.

Having Tina next to you was as good as having a sparkling glass of red wine being offered to you. She was naughty, mischievous and frivolous, a cute girl that everyone was fond of. She was quite shy, but when she gave her shots, the camera loved her.

Fifty-one

History races faster than the seconds of the clock, as it writes its own memoirs of the annals of mankind. Indira Gandhi was riding a high as the prime minister of the country during the Emergency. The 'dumb doll' was now asserting herself in such an authoritarian way that every politician around her paled into insignificance, humbled into total submission by her dictates and commands. She was seen by her party hierarchy as the sole symbol of Indian politics. She had broken away from her parent political party, the Indian National Congress, and formed her own Indira Congress, flaunting the palm of her hand with the lines of her destiny on it as the party's symbol, thereby conveying, perhaps, that India's destiny was linked to hers and vice-versa.

'Indira is India, India is Indira' was the slogan they all lived by now. Nothing was seen and talked about beyond those six words. Indira's younger son, Sanjay Gandhi, had grown into a pampered young 'prince', who was reported to be indulging in extra-constitutional activities by running the government on her behalf with the help of an inner circle.

Infamous for his population control drive, Sanjay was already being named as the successor to the 'Iron Lady', while the press and the public gossiped about his mother, who was busy consulting the 'swamis'. The youth wing of the Indira Congress was building Sanjay up as the new young avatar of Indian politics, who would take the country to heights hitherto unknown and undreamt.

A very charming young lady of the youth wing of the party was visiting Bombay to meet with some important film folks popular with the masses, to invite them to New Delhi to attend a youth rally led by Sanjay Gandhi. She charmed me into accepting her invitation.

While in Delhi, I found my friend and colleague Dilip Kumar there as well. Evidently, he had also been invited. All the bigwigs of Indira Congress, inside and outside the government, were of course present in full force.

What I saw was an overzealous, over-passionate exercise being conducted by Congress stooges to sanctify Sanjay's succession to the gaddi. All of them were bowing to him obsequiously with folded hands, in utter servility, to hear his utterances, or his command.

As we sat waiting for the proceedings to begin in that chaotic jungle of political mumbo-jumbo, we could occasionally hear a lone voice shout from the stage, 'Desh ka neta!' This would be followed by a hand gesture to the audience, goading it to say in full-throated unison, 'Sanjay Gandhi!'—which nobody did except a couple of sycophants, again from the stage, to the utter amusement of observers like me! It clearly seemed a planned strategy to have Sanjay accepted by the masses at a time when the rule of law and all norms of fair-play and democratic functioning were stifled. I immediately disliked the spectacle, and laughed it away, seeing some very famous political heavyweights in their own right in the Congress party reduced to bit players much against their own better judgement, not having the guts to speak out the truth, genuflecting before the young fellow, whose only qualification as a politician was the blessings of his mother.

I had heard about such political goings-on in Delhi. But now, I saw them with my own eyes. 'Shame on the politics of the country,' I thought to myself. Wasn't there a leader left with any vision to move this great nation forward except an overambitious tree planter who introduced a reign of terror and the culture of wheeling-dealing into the political system? The Emergency had been declared for the sole purpose of keeping the ruling party in power and strengthening its hold on the country which had once boasted of being the largest democracy in the entire world.

As Dilip Kumar and I walked out after the proceedings were over, we were asked to go to the television centre to say a few words about the Youth Congress, with a special reference to the dynamism of its leader. It seemed their propaganda machinery was functioning on almost Fascist lines, trying to use every possible means to bring the image of Sanjay Gandhi into adoring focus.

While Dilip also hesitated to go to the TV centre to participate in any propaganda in favour of the Emergency, I vehemently and vociferously opposed the suggestion, with the result that not only were all my pictures banned from being screened on television, but also any mention of or reference to my name on an official media was forbidden, along with Kishore Kumar's, who had also refused to go and sing in one of their programmes. My conscience revolted at this dictatorial act, and I called the information and broadcasting minister in Delhi and sought an appointment with him. He received me very politely, and guessing the nature of my business, brought up the subject of my non-cooperation with the government on his own.

'What's your problem?' he asked.

'I am seeking an answer in my disturbed mind,' I said.

'To what?'

'To the state of affairs in our country.'

'What do you mean?'

'Are we living in a democracy or in a police state?'

'A democracy.'

'Then why are these calls being sent to us? To appear on TV to propagate the Emergency?'

'Isn't it a good thing to speak for the government in power?'

'Under compulsion?'

'No, by your own sweet will.'

'How can the government pressurize one's "will" into "sweetening", if the "will" thinks to the contrary?'

'Don't do it, if you don't want to,' he said after a pause.

'That's exactly why I sought this meeting, to tell the authorities that nothing should be forced on our conscience.'

'I repeat—don't do it.'

'Thank you, minister,' I said, and we parted cordially.

Back in Bombay, I met Nargis, who was very close to the Gandhi family, casually at a party. She started cajoling me into not going against the government circular of appearing on television whenever asked.

'I don't agree with your convictions!' I told her.

'You are being unnecessarily stubborn!' she said, and we left the matter at that. But I knew I had become a marked man for the Sanjay Gandhi coterie.

Fifty-two

The pro-Emergency lobby enforced strict discipline amongst the masses and the rank and file of the government offices through certain legislative measures. It did a lot of good to the country. But the fact was that the soul of the people was smouldering, their spirit stifled by an iron hand. They were dying to break the shackles, and the lava inside them was gathering momentum, soon to explode into a spluttering volcano. It just needed a single matchstick to light it up. And that matchstick was provided by Indira Gandhi herself. Overconfident and blinded by her sense of power, and misled by the sycophant brigade that surrounded her and by her propaganda machine, she suddenly lifted the Emergency and declared general elections.

'Rebels' and 'traitors' put behind bars and languishing in jails, opponents escaping the clutches of the law by going underground, came out to fight the elections. The whole country was alive again, crying for liberty and freedom, in a more vigorous and volatile way than ever since India had achieved Independence.

The number of 'traitors' to the country marked by the government were legion. Many of them who had had the means and the money to flee the country now came back as heroes, soon after the nation was liberated from the yoke of the Emergency. Ram Jethmalani, the famous criminal lawyer, was one of them. He took the first flight back from the USA and sought election from a constituency in Bombay, contesting for the newly formed Janata Party. During the crucial days prior to ballot-casting, he approached me to participate in the gigantic rally to speak for him and the Janata movement—inspired by Jayaprakash Narayan—against Indira Gandhi. The moment was a climax to the nationwide build-up that would either overthrow or finally buckle under the pressure of the Iron Lady in power.

It was a momentous decision for me to take. A majority of the movie industry was for Mrs Gandhi to stay in power. On the strength of her sustained political propaganda and the charisma of the power that goes along with a ruling leader, she had psychologically overpowered all the big charismatic stars to fall under her spell. And a notion was doing the rounds of social circles throughout the city that no one would go against her in perhaps what was the most dramatic election India was facing since the dawn of freedom.

When Ram Jethmalani left the suite of the hotel I was maintaining for my business appointments, I was on the horns of a dilemma. Already a marked man in the eyes of the authoritarian rule, my participation in that do-or-die rally of Jethmalani's, perhaps the largest and the most watched, almost meant tilting the scales in favour of the fiery lawyer, and therefore, imprinting a slap on the face of Mrs Gandhi's regime. And if the tables were turned in Mrs Gandhi's favour in the elections, there was a possibility of all my artistic activity being throttled to the point of annihilation by the vengeful forces represented by Sanjay Gandhi, which would doubtless start to work overtime against me and my interests. *Des Pardes* was yet to be finished—I had to go to England again for location shooting. My son was studying in the university at Washington and if the wrath of the government fell upon me, it would spare no effort to finish the man who dared to raise his voice against the tyranny that had been imposed on the nation ostensibly 'for the benefit of the people'.

I told Ram to give me a day to decide my course of action. And the night that followed was one of the most difficult ones I have ever spent, since I had to take one of the most crucial decisions of my life. I kept strolling in the garden behind my residence until dawn, when sleep overtook me. When I woke up, my mind was made up. I rose to the occasion, and the ovation I got at the rally for my presence in it and the short humble speech that I made reaching out to the masses at that historic moment, in the biggest gathering I have ever faced, was one of the most touching and exhilarating experiences I have ever had.

I made the headlines of several newspapers the next day and was proclaimed a real hero, for I spoke for the wave that was sweeping the country and swam at the forefront of the current that was about to herald a new dawn.

When the election results were declared, the Janata Party won an overwhelming majority, decimating the Congress party and Indira Gandhi's stranglehold on the country. The Emergency was buried for good—not even its ghost would ever appear again on the political horizon of the country. I was hailed by my countrymen for taking the lead on behalf of the movie industry, totally on my own initiative. I was invited to attend the huge gathering of the Janata Party at Rajghat, New Delhi, where we walked to pay homage to the father of the nation, at his samadhi. As I stood next to Atal Bihari Vajpayee, Lal Krishna Advani and Jayaprakash Narayan, surrounded by a sea of our countrymen, basking in the glory of their victory over the bonds of repression and yesmanship, I could visualize the great Mahatma laughing at the antics of some of the political players in his country, but shedding tears as well at the state of affairs. I was later invited to the conclave of the latest kingmakers of the country, in which the future prime minister's name was to be decided and announced. The crown fell on Morarji Desai.

I had first met Jayaprakash Narayan, who set in motion the wheels of the movement that had displaced Mrs Gandhi, at Nalanda, the site of the ancient Indian university, now in ruins, where I was romancing the 'Dream Girl' Hema Malini for the blockbuster *Johny Mera Naam*. We were suspended in mid-air in a cable car, unmindful of the cheering crowd below, as the electricity went absent without leave and the ropeway we were on came to a standstill. When we climbed down eventually to face the camera for another shot, somebody from the film unit pointed at a white kurta-pajama-clad, simple-looking man with spectacles, who was watching the filming from a distance, saying it was Jayaprakash Narayan.

I didn't believe it was him. He had a stick in his hand, his generous and benign smile beckoning me towards him as I looked his way. He looked like an ordinary villager, a passer-by who had suddenly stopped on the way to his fields, listening to a song being played to the antics of a couple of players in front of a movie camera, out of sheer curiosity. But somehow, he looked distinguished in a very undistinguished sort of way. I rushed to him, greeting him with folded hands out of respect for the man I had heard and read so much about, requesting him to come over and meet the other members of the unit. But he politely declined, saying he would only be a disturbance to the working rhythm of the shooting crew. Instead, he invited me to his Sadaqat Ashram in Patna, which was nearby, to spend some time with him, which I did the same evening.

And now I had the privilege of sitting with the same beloved leader of the masses, as he along with his other colleagues was taking a final decision as to who the next prime minister of the country should be, with leaders from every party in the cobbled-up coalition to choose from, now that Indira Gandhi had been ousted from power.

Fifty-three

The Janata government fell within a few years, long before it could complete its term. It did nothing for the country, except to emphasize that politicians were a pack of greedy fools, a motley crowd of self-seeking opportunists, small puny men with narrow outlooks, rabble-rousers at best, placed on the seats of the august Houses of Parliament with no worthwhile agenda in front of them for the progress of the nation. The Janata leaders delivered nothing of the promises held out in their manifesto. They behaved at all times like school-going braggarts who had yet to make the grade for higher studies, preoccupied as they were in quarrelling and squabbling amongst themselves, playing games of one-upmanship, and working only for power and for self-gain, not for the people. They failed to prove to the electorate that had chosen them as their representatives that the state of Emergency they had dislodged was really an evil, a throttling machine that stifled the breath of a free nation. Instead, by their misdeeds and inefficient functioning, internal bickering and infighting, they gave the man on the street an impression that India would best be governed by only the Nehru–Gandhi clan, which, it was popularly believed, had fought and secured for the country its freedom from the foreign yoke, and that it was best for the country to go back into the grip of the 'Iron Lady', for it was only with the iron rod that the country could at all be ruled.

Mrs Gandhi, beaten, isolated, and left alone to mend her own fences with her back to the wall, was shrewd enough to see the writing on the wall. She started working overtime with the cunning of a politician, forcing the Janata government to fall into its own trap and self-destruct. Elections were declared much earlier than the scheduled time.

The face of the Janata Party having been smeared, we in the movie industry got disillusioned and disenchanted with the leaders we had supported to form the new democratic government, no one more so than me who had been at the forefront of the Janata upsurge. Some of us met one evening over coffee in a hotel suite to discuss which way the political scenario of the country was headed, and an epic idea took birth.

Why not, for a change, and for the sake of the country we loved, form a political party that would transform the ugly slushy shape of things and give it a new shape as magnificent and glittering as a grand film?

The assembled gathering picked me to lead the proposed party. If MGR could spell magic in Tamil Nadu, why not me in Bombay, leading a movement not only at the state level but through the whole country?

The decision of the people gathered together fired my imagination. The nation was in a vacuum and waiting. I would raise its stature to the best in the world, socially, economically, politically. I accepted the challenge and was elected the president of the party, which we named the National Party of India, the determined motto of which was to help elect only those people to the Lok Sabha who were the most qualified in their respective fields, and therefore the most deserving.

We had our first rally at Shivaji Park. It was packed to capacity with a very responsive crowd, ready to vote for our ideology. Our next plan was to hold another rally at the Ram Lila grounds in Delhi. Mrs Gandhi, a whisper told us, was in Bombay the day our rally took place, and was trying to send us a message to join hands with her. But our die was cast, and we were confident of winning hands down; joining hands with an autocrat was absolutely out of the question.

I started dreaming about the fulfilment of the dream I had embarked upon. Ideas started surging into my head in quick succession, of reform and progress for the country and the vast number of people who inhabit this great land. A fusion of the ancient with the modern! A forward leap, while retaining the profundity of the values that have sustained our centuries-old culture and civilization! I started drawing up a blueprint of my plan of action, while my colleagues were preparing the party manifesto.

We began to hunt for the best brains, the best talents, the best thinking minds, irrespective of their caste, creed, status or religion. I had a plan for transforming India. A total renaissance! We would keep pace with the latest international trends. Illiteracy would be eradicated. New social norms conforming to the best in our society would be set. Every working man would wear trousers. The dhoti, the national dress, great for leisure wear, would be shunned for official functions. No official dignitary would ever again be seen taking the salute at a flag march in a carefree, careless attire like a dhoti, ill-manneredly flying up in the breeze, exposing the naked and not very presentable shape of his legs, proclaiming to the world that he still swears and lives by the fashions of the obscure illiterate village that he belongs to, as he struggles to put the folds of his unruly dhoti back in its place! Villages would be transformed into neat clean small towns flashing with electricity and gushing merrily with water facilities, and towns into metropolises with skylines to match the best in the world.

India is the largest democracy in the world, and as free as UK or the USA. It has a great numerical strength, next only to China, a strong moral and intellectual fibre, and unmatched cultural traditions. It would be a dreamland for the world to look and wonder at. All men and women would be equal. While retaining their local dialect, they would all compulsorily be taught Hindi, the national language, besides English, which is internationally accepted as a means of communication. Farmers and labourers, coolies and aristocrats, would all move around in cars, waving at each other in a spirit of bonhomie. And the intellectual elite would be in charge of running the country, showcasing the strengths of a new nation that would dazzle with prosperity and overflow with joy.

It was the utopic vision of a visionary, and I wanted to make it happen if I joined politics.

Next day, when I went to the National Party office, I found hordes of young people from all walks of life and from different parts of the country waiting for me. The concept of the party had enthused them all and had fired their imagination. I listened to them all, then went inside and sat in my chair, enquiring if Nani Palkhivala, the famous jurist, economist and lawyer who was with us on the stage at the rally at Shivaji Park, along with Smt Vijayalakshmi Pandit, had agreed to be one of our candidates from Bombay. I was told he had sent a message that while he'd love to be nominated to the Rajya Sabha, he was reluctant to fight for a seat in the Lok Sabha. A similar message came from another great personality who had also been approached to be a candidate. This was the first jolt to our enthusiasm. I asked if the party manifesto we had so vibrantly discussed and finalized had gone to the press. I was told a few changes were being made by other party colleagues and it would take another couple of weeks before it was published. The initial momentum had obviously slackened, and laziness had begun to set in.

The elections were only six weeks away. It would be a Herculean task to finalize all-India candidates and get ready to fight the great battle ahead in such a short time, and it was no use fighting if we could not emerge victorious, with a mandate to be able to bring our dreams to fruition.

The inertia already visible amongst the early enthusiasts dampened my spirits. I started thinking it was no use taking a hasty plunge. Outside, the youth of the country was waiting to be enrolled in the party. It was best not to give them the promise of a hope that would later disillusion them. I went out to tell them that we had to hold on for a few more days before we announced to the world that we were fighting the elections. As they felt let down too, I walked back to my seat inside. As I sat down it was not with the same verve and zeal with which I, along with many of my other colleagues, had got the ball of the National Party rolling. Something somewhere had cracked. The elections were round the corner and we were stupidly not ready yet. With a deep sense of sadness in my heart, we decided to wind up the show for the time being, and told all our supporters to canvas and vote for the outside candidates that they fancied.

And that was the end of the National Party. It was a great idea that was nipped in the bud.

I decided to canvas for Atal Bihari Vajpayee, and went to address his rally along with Goldie at the Ram Lila grounds in

Delhi. Vajpayee was perhaps the only winner in Delhi where the Indira Congress came to power with a thumping majority.

Even as Indira Gandhi was celebrating her victory and forming the government, her son Sanjay, who had also regained his seat as a Member of Parliament, died in a plane crash while flying it himself. I was filming on the sets, and a lieutenant of mine came and whispered the news of the tragedy to me, adding that if he had been alive and in power again, he would have been very vengeful towards me. I laughed the whole matter away saying I did not believe in what he said, for how could the grandson of a great democrat like Pt. Nehru be so unlike him!

Later, I sent a note of condolence to his mother, also congratulating her for becoming the prime minister once again.

Fifty-four

The release of *Des Pardes* in New York took me to that great city for the umpteenth time.

Tina had bid goodbye to me at Heathrow airport; for she was flying back to Bombay after having attended the London premiere. She shook my hand warmly and said, 'Think of me while you are in New York!' She didn't have to say this, for she had always been on my mind, being my leading lady, and so much a part of the film.

As I met the audience coming out after watching *Des Pardes* at the Queens theatre, everyone expected her to be with me, and I told them all, 'She's very much here. Can't you see?'

Perplexed, they wanted to know where. Playing with my fans, I pointed at my heart and said, 'Right inside. Can't you see, she is smiling and waving at you? She came all the way only for this—only for you!' They all enjoyed my style, and cheered.

Then, from nowhere, a trio of young girls cut through the crowd, grabbed my hands and looked at me with cute broad grins and awe on their faces. They kept smiling, not knowing what to say.

'Hi,' I broke the ice.

They picked up courage, and planted kisses on my face simultaneously. 'We want to meet you!' they said, all together.

'Of course! You are meeting me, aren't you?' I said.

'But not like this. In your hotel or wherever you are staying,' was their chorus again.

I laughed. 'Where are you staying?' they continued.

I looked at my host, the distributor of my film, Giri Raj, with an expression of 'Shall I, or shall I not?'

'I want to meet you in your hotel,' one of them entreated again.

'Come to the Pierre Hotel tomorrow,' I had to say.

'What time?'

'Late afternoon, sometime around three.'

They all came, unescorted, with autograph books. I met them in the lobby of the hotel. All of them were Indians born in America, smart kids, in a very, very American way.

As I was languorously signing away autographs, one of them said, 'I want to act in your film.' It was the one who had yesterday insisted on meeting me at the hotel.

I looked up at her. She was very earnest. 'How old are you?' I asked.

'Thirteen, will be fourteen soon.'

'A beautiful and innocent age,' I remarked. 'But perhaps you are a little too young just now.'

'When then?' she asked.

'Be in touch,' I said casually.

'How and where?' was her eager question.

'At my Bombay address.'

'Write it down!' She pushed the autograph book back into my hands.

I did. 'But I am not making any promises,' I added.

'And remember my name—Richa,' she said.

'Richa,' I repeated.

'Richa Sharma,' she emphasized.

I nodded, and looked at the other two. 'Enna!' one of them said. 'Abha!' said the third one.

'We are all sisters,' said Richa.

It was a sweet, innocent meeting. They left happy and satisfied, full of joy and vitality, the incomparable boon of that age.

A year later, while I was doing *Lootmaar*, I was back in New York, this time as the chief guest at a very well-attended beauty contest in one of the five-star hotels of Manhattan. There I met some members of the Indian elite of America. It was an eye-opener for me.

People who had migrated to the United States from India were sophisticated, doing extremely well in their respective fields, contributing towards the economy of that land as much and as well as the local Americans. They owned establishments and properties, were in the forefront of business, were held in high esteem, and had integrated into the mainstream of American life. It was for the first time as I circulated in the big hall that I became aware of the large number of Indians who had settled down in America. I had known a few of them as strugglers in India, who had left the shores of their country seeking greener pastures abroad, and were now American citizens, speaking and behaving the American way, prosperous and affluent. Their kids had grown up in Western standards of education and were as smart as their Western counterparts, and in a very fascinating way, spoke American slang but also tried to retain something of the country of their origin, inherited from their parents as cultural values, in their bearing.

I was impressed with their talent, academic as well as artistic. I also discovered that the Indianness of the Indians and their background of the mystical East fascinated the American mind. There was a fad amongst quite a few of them to get hooked on the spiritual values of the East as enunciated by some gurus.

Suddenly, I was tapped on my back, and as I turned, a young American girl with a rudraksha mala around her neck, wearing a pale orange sari and holding a small dibba containing saffron, was waiting to put a tikka on my forehead. Along with her was a young Indian swami, a tikka on his forehead as well, and a similar mala around his neck and wrists. They seemed inseparable, and were lovers, I was told. The swami was from an ashram set up by an Indian religious sect there.

'I know you from my Indian friends here,' said the American girl. 'And our guru said, when you meet Dev Anand, put this tikka on his forehead with my blessings.'

I submitted my forehead to her. Her index finger caressed it with a soft stroke of saffron powder and a sudden spirituality was in the air. A nucleus of a thought flashed across my mind. My next film *Swami Dada* was being born in a quick moment of creative contemplation.

From across the room, and from behind the American girl whose magical finger had set my thoughts in motion, a face was beaming a smile at me through the bunch of eager fans. I looked at her. Her smile was devastating. She was now rushing towards me with a flower in her hand.

'Didn't I see you on stage a little while ago?' I asked her.

'Yes!' she answered with a twinkle in her eyes.

'You looked superb, and your singing was even more so!' I meant what I said.

She had sung two songs, one in English and the other in Hindi, so eloquently and with such ease that I hadn't been able to resist enquiring from the guest sitting next to me, 'Who is that girl, with such a captivating melodious voice?'

'You'll meet her soon,' he had replied.

The young girl's name was Ananya Mukherji. Her image stayed in my mind.

Back home in India, with the basic idea of *Swami Dada* having germinated inside me, I kept working on it when I was not filming *Lootmaar*, which was now nearing completion. *Swami Dada* dealt with an Indian godman and an American girl who was charmed with him and his Indian spirituality. *Lootmaar* was on the violence that was rearing its ugly head all over. I had repeated Tina Munim in it. She had by now grown into a mature and seasoned performer. She was also accepting outside assignments and was busy professionally.

Unfortunately, there was no scope for her in *Swami Dada*. But she was very keen to be cast in the film. I struggled within myself to accommodate her, even toying with the idea of planning another film that would give her full scope. But then she suddenly disappeared from the scene, and though she was always in my thoughts, I never wanted to pry into her personal and private life.

Quick flashes of her kept coming into my memory. Tina inviting me off and on to join her and her group of young friends in bouts of disco-dancing. Tina with her parents and a doting brother inviting me to her family get-togethers, with everyone thrilled to have a known film star amongst them. Tina sitting by the fireplace in a hotel suite in Simla, along with the other unit members of *Lootmaar* in the evenings after a day's hard filming, looking prettier and prettier every day with the glow of the red embers accentuating her sunburnt complexion. Tina firing the bullets off the revolver that she handled as a part of her character in the film, scaring away the birds along with her five-year-old nephew who played my son in the film.

Everybody in Navketan missed and remembered Tina. But she

had moved on to do her own thing, to adventures beyond the film world. And one day, I heard from her that she was getting married and that I was a 'must' on the list of her special invitees. A very glamorous-looking invitation card arrived announcing her wedding, to be followed by a reception later to bless the most important couple of the time, Anil and Tina Ambani.

I was not in town on the auspicious date. But I was present in both the ceremonious occasions in spirit, with all the good wishes and blessings I could muster for the most beautiful girl that I had the good fortune of introducing to the world, and to her charming husband.

I sent a handwritten note along with a bouquet of the choicest flowers to the wonderful couple who complemented each other so well—he shining through the wealth of the nation, and she glowing as the purest of gold.

Fifty-five

I was in New York again, for the casting of *Swami Dada*. I was looking to cast a young American girl in the film. Giri Raj— my host and distributor for *Des Pardes* who had by now become a friend, promised to help me do the casting in New York. He advertised in the newspapers and gave me a call to come over and interview the girls and make a final decision from the host of girls who had responded to the ads. The exercise took me six long weeks before I could make the final selection.

I stayed at the Grand Hyatt on 42nd Street, and the interviews were conducted every day in a room of Giri Raj's posh office on 5th Avenue. The number of young girls who had applied was unbelievable: young students from college campuses, working girls, young struggling actresses from the stage and members of the SAG carrying their cards, all aspirants to stardom, up-and-coming models looking for an avenue to show their talent and hit the headlines. Many of the young, attractive girls were working in cafes and bars as waitresses, serving at the tables, waiting to be noticed and discovered by popular personalities from show business, directors, writers and stars who frequented those places.

I met many of them in my search for the one I was looking for, talked to some hopefuls for hours, getting to know their minds and their personalities. I found one thing in common to most of them. They were all keen to go abroad, to gain an experience of and exposure to the world. From the long list of girls I interviewed every day I set aside a few. Then one day an old friend of mine, an ex-Miss India residing in Boston, sent me a copy of the *Boston Globe*, asking me to look at the cover girl on it. It was a very bewitching photograph, and she made a strong case for herself. The look in her eyes seemed to say, 'Come over.'

To achieve my goal, I could go as far as the North Pole. Boston, the romanticized city of my dreams, a university town harbouring great intellect, was just a hop across from New York. I made the trip at once. A meeting with the 'cover girl' and her promoter, an old lady in a modelling school, had already been arranged, and I found myself face to face with the fifteen-year-old Lynn Sweenie, Irish by descent. There was an instant rapport between her and me.

She agreed to come to New York and spend a day there for a photo-session under my supervision. The local photographer, an Indian I knew, took some great pictures of her. She and I spent one whole evening walking together on the streets of Manhattan, I acting as her guide, for she was strictly a Bostonian, having set foot in New York only once before. We dined at the Four Seasons, famous for its starry clientele, and next afternoon she was back with her mother in Boston, waiting for a confirmation from me.

And over the next few months, the Sun-n-Sand Hotel in Juhu saw a pretty young American blonde with sky-blue eyes stepping in and out of the hotel premises holding a walkman in her hand, its earphones plugged into her ears, carefully listening to the dialogues she was to deliver in the film recorded in my voice with the proper pronunciation and articulation, as well as the song she was to lend her lips to, rehearsing all the time, as she walked, sat for a coffee at the restaurant, or lay by the pool after a cool swim in its waters.

She enjoyed wearing a lehanga, doing up her hair in a braid, putting on a tikka and singing keertan. Her hands folded in a prayer singing hymns, her face radiating innocence, she looked like an angel. I named her Christine O'Neill in the film, retaining the Irish feel of her descent.

While Lynn represented the youthful innocence of the West, the young and fresh Padmini Kolhapure, in one of the early films of her career, symbolized the innocence of Indian girlhood. When both of them were in the same shot they made the picture frames look very beautiful.

Swami Dada was one of my more mature works both in subject matter and execution and some of its captivating moments have always stayed in my mind. One particular scene from the climax is indelible from memory. Naseeruddin Shah, the wonderful thinking actor, playing a hired killer, is sitting camouflaged on the branch of a tree with a loaded gun aimed at the Swami who is at a distance, mesmerizing his flock with his sagely utterings. Shah hesitates to pull the trigger as he sees a star and crescent covering the muzzle of his gun as if descending from above, and simultaneously hears the azaan, the call to prayer. He turns his gun on the villain—played brilliantly by Kulbhushan Kharbanda—who had hired him to kill the Swami, and shoots him dead, thereafter saluting the Swami in deep respect.

During the shooting of *Swami Dada* I went to New York two more times, first for a brief spell of filming there with my American leading lady, and then as a Grand Marshal of the Indian Independence Day parade. The latter was a grandiose affair. The title Grand Marshal has a military connotation, while in fact it is a civilian honour, bestowed that year on a most unmilitary man like me, who had been rejected for an army commission at Dehradun in 1942. Being the Grand Marshal in New York's Independence Day parade meant leading the Indian contingent through the streets of Manhattan lined with men and women dressed in their fashionable best to a flower-bedecked rostrum, with the tricolour fluttering on it alongside the American stars and stripes, and shaking hands with Mayor Ed Koch, to exchange greetings of bonhomie between the two countries.

Mayor Koch was a popular man amongst the New Yorkers. He turned up in a khadi kurta, and I appeared in my saffron kurta from *Swami Dada* with a matching shawl draped around me. Standing on the rostrum together, we received the ovation of the citizens, mostly of Indian origin, with a small sprinkling of American bystanders and curious foreigners. As Koch greeted the waiting crowd in Hindi, saying 'Namaste' with folded hands, I threw a few petals on his face from a traditional Indian thali bedecked with diyas, incense and flowers, held by a sari-clad lady.

When I reached the Grand Hyatt, the red light on my telephone blinked a few messages. One of them was from Richa Sharma, the teenager I had met four years ago at the *Des Pardes* opening and later at the Pierre Hotel. She had been writing to me off and on, reminding me about herself and her ambition, and had recently sent me some of her latest photographs. She called to say it was urgent that I should call her, and left her number as well. I called her back. She did not believe initially that it was my voice, and was speechless for a few moments. Then she insisted on meeting me again before I left New York. Sensing her extreme keenness, I asked her to come over to the Grand Hyatt the next day at noon.

At twelve sharp the next day, my doorbell rang. I opened the door to find a ravishing-looking young girl in a designer suit and a felt hat, with a bag slinging on her shoulder.

'Recognize me?' she asked, with an enchanting smile. I kept looking at her in silence.

'You said twelve o'clock,' she said.

'Richa!' I laughed, still staring at her.

'Take my hand and you may kiss it!' she held her hand out to me.

I looked at her delicate fair hand with well-polished nails.

'You may, I repeat,' she said, still holding out her hand, 'for it is my birthday.'

'It is!' I exclaimed with joy, and kissed the hand as delicately as it deserved.

'And you must know that today I am eighteen!' she said.

'You are!' I continued to stare at her.

'And can do my own things, my own way, without any parental guidance, or approval!' She sounded very American.

'That calls for a celebration!' I said.

I put my arm around her, and we walked up Fifth Avenue to Rockefeller Center for a delicious decaffeinated coffee, with lots of cream in it.

Fifty-six

S uneil had done his business management course in America, and was now back home. Born with a silver spoon in his mouth, he had had things for the asking, and being my son I wanted him to be somebody who the world would remember for his achievements, greater and better than his father's.

A degree in business management was his choice, and I was happy at the thought that after having done that, he would not only run the empire built by his father, but also expand it with the moving times. On his return from the States, I gave him an independent room in the Navketan office. He had his own visiting card printed in the American style. I felt good and satisfied at his preparing himself to take over the reins of the office and control the spendings on the budget of the films we were making.

But soon he had a different dream. Secretly, he started harbouring an ambition to be a star, to follow in his father's footsteps and be known to the world as a worthy son of his father. A very logical and natural ambition! Why hadn't I thought of it myself? Maybe because he never thought of it himself either, or else why should he have opted for business management? Why didn't he openly say that he preferred his father's profession to any other, in which case the doors in that direction would have been flung open to him at once to enter and try his destiny? But as I understood it, his sudden desire to be an actor had probably arisen from watching his daddy's fans swooning and falling all over him!

Without taking me into confidence, he joined an acting school and started taking lessons in his spare time. I did not disapprove and waited for the right moment when I would ask him to unfold his future plans to his dad. He brought it up himself one day, adding that he also had a student colleague who was very keen to be introduced to me. I asked him to bring his friend along the very next day. The meeting was fixed for late in the afternoon after I came back home from a lunch date with a friend at the Taj.

Driving back from the hotel the next afternoon, as I stopped my car at a crossing waiting for the green signal, I saw a billboard with a very handsome young man on it, advertising for cigarettes. His personality looked so striking that the indigenous cigarette he was holding between his two fingers seemed much stronger and better than the most expensive cigarette brands flashed across the globe. The dash and the raw youthfulness of the figure in the photograph, with a smile as arrogant as a reed in a jungle, was so outgoing that it went straight to my heart.

'Papa!' shouted Suneil as he heard my car entering the gates. As I parked it, he wanted me to meet his friend, waiting outside in the lawns. A tall well-built but slim young man with a white handkerchief around his neck, his shirt buttons open at the front, stood up looking at me in great awe and respect. His mannerism conveyed there was some Dev Anand hidden inside him somewhere.

I immediately thought of the cigarette banner I had noticed at the Bandra crossing. Here was the fellow in the flesh.

'I think I know you already,' I remarked.

He smiled a boyishly shy smile.

'Aren't you a salesman for cigarettes?' I asked.

'Yes, a model,' he said.

'I am sure the best in town,' I flattered him.

He blushed to the tips of his ears.

'Jackie Shroff, Papa,' said Suneil to me, introducing him.

'Nice meeting you, Mr Jackie Shroff,' I shook hands with him.

His hand was trembling slightly, and after the handshake, he hid it in the pocket of his faded jeans.

I asked him about his ambition, to which he replied, 'To be a shade like you.'

In other words, to be an actor and a successful one at that. I gave him an audition and did a photo-session with him for the young lead in *Swami Dada*, and had almost finalized him when Mithun Chakraborty suddenly jumped into the fray, willing to do the role

at whatever cost. It was offered to him. He was an up-and-coming
star with a potential to hit the big time, and the greed in me to add
a known face to the cast of *Swami Dada* opposite Rati Agnihotri,
a rising star who had just hit the headlines then, carried the day.
Jackie Shroff was left in the lurch.

But he was not really keen on playing the young romantic lead.
His mind was more set on doing a negative role. He did not care
even if he made a small insignificant appearance in that sort of a role
in my film. He ended up playing Shakti Kapoor's sidekick, smoking
away throughout the film, standing next to the villain.

But that insignificant part meant a lot to Jackie. Handsomely
photographed, he won a lot of young damsels' hearts in the auditorium
with every whiff of smoke he puffed out from the cigarette dangling
between his lips. He also caught the fancy of Subhash Ghai who cast
him as the main lead in his next film. And Jackie was a star now
competing with Dev Anand!

Suneil, my son, on the other hand, was marking his time until
Anand Aur Anand was planned. I decided to introduce him in the
role of a son to a father played by me. Making his appearance on the
screen for the first time, he performed admirably under my direction,
looked boyishly charming and handsome, as I used to in my early
days. He was very much in control of himself, and histrionically
efficient whether he performed in scenes of light-hearted romance
or in emotionally wrenching outbursts. He danced and sang on
screen better than I did, especially excelling in his action scenes. He
is a lover of action and, on his own, had gone all the way to Hong
Kong to learn the art of kung-fu from a local well-known master.
After the release of *Anand Aur Anand* he was picked up by a producer
for a film to be shot in Chicago. Another film was planned for him in
Navketan, our own banner, under the able direction of Vijay Anand.

I was certain Suneil was on his way to stardom. But unfortunately
for him he was being constantly compared with his father. For him
to be able to overshadow his father was a difficult task. For people
to whom Dev Anand was the ultimate as a romantic star, his son
had to be even greater in order to be idolized and worshipped.

Both Smita Patil and Raakhee were with Suneil in the film, both
very big stars and seasoned actresses, and wonderful human beings

as well. I had always admired Smita Patil as an actress of outstanding ability. When I approached her with an offer to do a picture with me and play my secretary-cum-mistress in the film, she jumped at the very thought of it.

Raakhee is a darling of a star with soft and extremely attractive features, and eyes as docile and embracing as a cat's. Whenever I have approached her with a role in my movie, she has been ever willing, no matter how long the duration of the part and of what substance.

Amongst the three great stars, Raj Babbar being the third, Suneil was pitted against the best in the industry. He came out triumphant histrionically, though box-office-wise and in terms of mass appeal he did raise a question mark, to which only his own destiny has an answer.

Destiny has its own choice of timing to offer to each individual, if at all it decides to smile on him or her. Each person has to go by its dictates, no matter who he or she is, how capable or proficient. I am confident, knowing my son's tremendous perseverance and will-power, and aware of his passionate desire to make a name for himself in the eyes of the world, and be one up on me, that he will one day come out with an ace that the world shall remember. And who better to bless him than his own father!

Fifty-seven

I have had some great female co-stars cast opposite me—all the popular actresses of the day, women of stupendous beauty and charm, whose photographs were at the bedsides of young admiring men while they slept, dreaming of them. They have all played my sweethearts on screen, women who I have wooed and embraced, their sensuality arousing the erotic desires of the cinema audiences. Whether I was in the garb of Raju, the swindler and the spiritualist in *Guide*, the policeman Johny in *Johny Mera Naam*, the war-ravaged legless Major Verma and his lookalike Captain Anand in *Hum Dono*, Prashant, obsessed with his separated sister in *Hare Rama Hare Krishna*, a reckless flamboyant gambler in *Gambler*, a street-smart *Taxi Driver*, a paan-chewing *Banarasi Babu*, a barman serving drinks in a London pub while waiting to avenge his brother's murder in *Des Pardes*, a funster in *Funtoosh* or a universally popular Romeo, the women swooned as I smiled, and secretly made love to me in their thoughts, as I ran around my leading ladies, romancing with them. And since romance is the most endearing feeling in every heart, young and old, the one feeling that gives meaning to the humdrum monotony of people's lives, I was their role model, 'the ultimate romantic' in whom they saw everything that they dreamt about romance in their own lives.

I was swimming in the currents of that happy thought, reeling in its intoxication, as I stood humming to myself in the shower. I swirled to the rhythm of the spraying water and tiptoed dancingly out of the tub to pick up the bottle of shampoo from the table across, but my steps went out of tune with the rhythm suddenly, and I slipped on the soapy surface, took an about-turn, and fell, hitting myself hard on the edge of the bathtub. I instantly shrieked with a searing pain, and realized something had cracked inside my chest.

'What happened?' came Mona's voice from outside.

'I have fallen,' I could hardly mutter.

'For whom, this time?' she retorted, partly joking, partly serious.

'I am . . . hury . . . cannot . . . get up,' I said somehow.

She rushed into the bathroom. I was lying inside the tub, completely naked, eyes still closed, trying to stifle a groan. I hesitated to move for fear of an outburst of pain. Mona held me by my shoulders in an attempt to lift me up.

'Don't . . . it's . . . hurting . . . I'll . . . get up . . . myself . . . for I . . . know the . . . spot . . . where . . . I'm . . . hurt.'

She was suddenly worried.

'Besides . . .' I continued, 'I feel . . . awkward, being . . . naked and . . . helpless . . . I don't . . . want . . . anybody . . . to see me . . . like this.'

She stood motionless, looking at me, her concern growing.

'Please . . .! Go! Let me . . . make the . . . effort!' I said with great difficulty.

She receded into her room but kept looking at me from the opening of her door. I crawled to pick up the towel, a Herculean task; half-wrapping it around me somehow, I put all my will-power into the effort it took to stand up and walk slowly and haltingly to the other room, where I collapsed on the bed.

An orthopaedic was called—an x-ray was taken of the spine. Luckily there was no fracture, just a contusion. I had broken my ribs earlier. This time the attack was on the spine. I was in bed for twenty days, immobile and in plaster.

But my mind roamed back and forth. I had already been toying with an idea for a new script which now grew to its full strength in my mind. I worked out the structure of *Hum Naujawan*, and started thinking about its casting.

The girl with a designer suit and a felt hat on, with whom I had walked down the streets of Manhattan on her eighteenth birthday, kept coming to mind. I called Richa up from my sick bed. She was all excitement when I told her that she stood a great possibility of being cast as an Indian girl who was born and brought up in America.

'But,' I added, 'I last met you almost two years ago. Send me your current photographs, to help me make a decision.'

Within a week, a bunch of huge sexy blow-ups were lying on the table in my bedroom. Mona glared as I kept looking at them. Then she quickly picked them up, almost snatching them away from my hands, and kept them on a high table in a corner, away from my gaze and my grasp. I silently resented her act, but she walked away, saying, 'Your soup is ready and it's time for your medicine!' And the door banged with a thud.

I crawled out of the bed slowly to pick up the photographs and give them a second look. Then I kept them back again, this time in the drawer of the high table, so that nobody else could pry upon them.

A few days later, Richa Sharma was born to the world as the star of *Hum Naujawan*. As the film finished, she met the most important man in her life, Sanjay Dutt, and destiny gave her life another direction.

Sanjay Dutt dwells in my heart as a young lad sitting on my lap, reluctant to be pulled away from that cosily entrenched luxury, when both his dad, Sunil Dutt, and I drove home together in my car after having witnessed a wrestling match involving the famous wrestler Dara Singh at the Vallabhbhai stadium. Sanjay looked so much like his mother, Nargis. I had no idea then that one day I'd be instrumental in bringing 'Sanju Baba' a bride from America, in the form of my leading lady of *Hum Naujawan*.

Tabu played my teenaged daughter in the film. She was a very sweet kid, and performed her role with great verve. But she cried at the mention of her rape scene in the film, though she was spared the torture of facing the camera to enact the scene, since I used a duplicate in her place and took only her close-ups to convey the impact of the rape that was so crucial to the unfolding of the plot of the film.

A very popular college principal's teenaged daughter is raped by a roguish, pampered and spoilt son of an important political figure, studying in the same college, in *Hum Naujawan*. That traumatic incident becomes a strong dramatic element in the film as the rapist, played by Atlee Brar, is panic-stricken at the sudden death of the young girl while he is in the act, and burns all the evidence of rape, accidentally setting fire to the cottage where the rape was committed.

Even as we finished filming the sequence, news arrived that Prime Minister Indira Gandhi had been shot dead by her Sikh bodyguards. The entire nation, shocked at the brutal assassination, grieved at her demise, and also wondered at the root cause of such an outrage.

But that was what the cold-blooded politics of the country was all about, I said to myself. Indira Gandhi had angered the sentiments of a certain religious community, and in a fanatic moment of religious fervour, members of that community took their revenge on her for her 'misdeeds'.

I called off the filming, sat in a corner and reflected, what sort of leadership is it that needs to be protected by guns? And what more danger to a well-known popular leader can there be than being surrounded by gun-men all the time, for their so-called protection, when that 'safety measure' can so easily backfire?

With immense sadness at Indira Gandhi's death, I saw in quick succession all the images of her that lived and lingered in my mind.

My first meeting with her was at her father Prime Minister Jawaharlal Nehru's residence at Teen Murti, mentioned earlier. She was getting to know the quicksands of Indian politics then, playing the charming hostess to the greatest political luminaries from all over the world when they visited her father.

I remembered having met her again with the famous poet Harindranath Chattopadhyay, brother of the great freedom fighter Sarojini Naidu, when we had gone to the PM House to meet Pt. Nehru, but ended up meeting only Indira Gandhi. I was on my way to the States for the release of the English version of *The Guide*, and presented her with a copy of *The Princes*, the very well-written novel by Manohar Malgonkar, the rights of which I had bought for filming. I still don't know whether she ever had the time to read it, being caught in the whirlpool of politics.

I met her again after she was made the information and broadcasting minister in Lal Bahadur Shastri's government. I was then the president of the Actors' Guild of India, now defunct, and had sought her audience in a deputation that also included my colleagues Dilip Kumar and Raj Kapoor. She was very amiable and hospitable, and receptive to the film industry's problems, but spoke very little. In fact, every time I met her, she was more of a listener than a speaker. And every time I wondered whether the title of 'the dumb doll' given to her by her political opponents was based on factual reality. I got more and more convinced that it fitted her like a glove. At the screening of the English version of *The Guide* for her governmental approval and clearance for its worldwide release, the only two sentences she spoke to me, as mentioned earlier, were 'You speak so fast!' and 'We shall send you the clearance certificate soon.'

Once, at an international film festival gathering in New Delhi, I walked up to her to invite her to my party for the delegates at the Imperial Hotel. The only sentence she spoke, besides exuding a charming bashful smile, was 'I shall try to be there', but she did not come.

Another time, her very close confidante and a friend of mine, holding a very responsible post in the Central government, arranged an informal meeting between me and Indira Gandhi in her office. I spent more than half an hour with her, and again carried the impression that she talked very little and was mostly a quiet listener, betraying no reactions, positive or negative, on any topic.

It was a very cordial and pleasant meeting. We were both at our charming best. When the meeting ended, she said, 'Come and attend our annual Congress session in Bombay,' to which I replied, 'I'd love to.' Together we went down by the elevator. Then I held open the door to the car for her. She got inside and waved at me, and I kept waving till the car vanished in the distance. I went back to my car fully convinced that I had left a deep impression on the most important person of the country.

I did not manage to attend the all-India Congress session in Bombay, for I happened to be out of town filming, but always looked forward to another meeting with her, which never took place.

When Indira Gandhi declared the Emergency, her image shattered in my mind, like in the minds of the majority of her countrymen. Probably she had become a prisoner to her coterie of advisers and fortune-seeking friends, in her aloofness from the people that mattered.

After she lost the 1977 elections, she was sidelined completely.

She was seen landing in Bombay in a civilian aircraft, along with many other ordinary passengers. There was no official at the airport to receive her, no bursting of fire-crackers, usually associated with the public appearances of popular political leaders in our country. Away from the public eye, she became a loner, but a loner with great guts and an inherent strength of her own. She came back to power with a thumping majority that was a slap on the faces of the opposition.

Now that very great lady, made of iron and steel, was no more. Her body, bullet-ridden, lay in the dust, spattered with blood, as her party members mourned and the country was plunged into sorrow.

Over the next few days, her countrymen saw her dead body, wrapped in white, kept on ice for everyone to pay their last respects to. Then it went up in flames, as her funeral pyre was lit by her only surviving son, Rajiv Gandhi. Along with the poignant last image of Mrs Gandhi, shown over and over again on national television, was that of her white kurta-pajama-clad son and inheritor, who drew sympathy from his grieving countrymen with every whiff of smoke from the pyre that darkened the political future of the land. As the sympathy wave for the hapless son of the assassinated prime minister reached a crescendo, he was announced as his mother's successor. The young westernized pilot of Indian Airlines was now at the helm of his country's destiny, with a single quirk of fate.

A hesitant prime minister at first, but having recorded a massive victory in the elections that followed Indira Gandhi's death, Rajiv Gandhi started learning fast and on his feet. Totally inexperienced in the game of politics and its jugglery, it took him a little time to understand the whys and hows of the Indian political scene. But being well educated and groomed in style, and always aware of his family background and its contribution to India, he felt strong enough to rise to the occasion, and took no time in introducing reforms that would lead the nation into the twenty-first century.

Ironically, I never had the opportunity to meet Rajiv. Though I was invited to release a book on him written by a professor of history in New Delhi, Rajiv could not find time from his busy activities to give me an audience, and I returned to Bombay only having praised the young dynamic leadership of the new prime minister, who had the courage and strength, and age on his side as well, to take India forward with its head held high.

Fifty-eight

As I drove home one evening, I found my daughter Devina standing next to a boy in the compound.

After having passed out from Woodstock in Mussourie where she went after her intial schooling at Wellham in Dehradun, Devina wanted to study French in Switzerland. I went all the way to Switzerland to put her in a Swiss boarding school.

She did not like it there and after a while expressed a desire to go to the Isle of Wight in England to learn photography. She had decided she wanted to be an investigative photojournalist, working for international magazines like *Time* and *Newsweek*. She wanted to go to Boston for a higher degree after she finished at the Isle of Wight.

I was happy with her doing what she wanted to do. But, while she did go to the Isle of Wight to finish the course, she did not go to Boston. Life had taken a new turn for her. She started going out with a boy she had known from school. Suneil noticed it and mentioned it to me. But being liberal by nature, I did not pay much heed to it, for I knew my daughter well. If she ever got seriously interested in a boy, she would confide in me. I'd be the first person to know.

And one evening, as I drove into the compound, I found her standing with a boy, talking to him in confidence. As I got out of the car, they both confronted me.

'Hi! What's going on?' I asked.

'Papa, I want you to meet my friend,' Devina said.

'Hello!'

'Hello sir.'

I kept looking at them, waiting for the next bit.

'We want to get married, Papa.'

I stood still for a second, trying to get my head around the idea. I felt I had suddenly aged by a few years.

'Why?' I asked.

'I love him—and he loves me,' she said.

'Are you sure?' I said.

They both nodded.

'Are you absolutely sure that if you marry my daughter, you have all intentions to make her as happy as she wants?' I asked her friend.

'I'm sure,' he responded.

I asked Devina the same question.

'I'm sure, Papa,' she responded similarly.

'Then I will not stand in your way,' was my answer.

I felt very heavy inside with the added burden of an emotion that I found hard to cope with.

Devina got married in great style. She embraced me and cried on my shoulder when she was leaving with her husband for her new home. I too cried part of that night.

She gave birth to a baby girl a year later and proudly showed her to me when I visited her in the nursing home. 'She's quite something like you as well, Papa,' she said. There was a mother's joy in her as she said that. I felt good for her and blessed the child.

A few years later, Devina drifted away from her husband, and the couple agreed to go their separate ways. Devina came and broke the news to me, and cried on my shoulder again, as she embraced me. I remembered she had cried just like that as a child when I left her alone at the Woodstock school. I cried with her too, and consoled her.

Her little daughter, whom all of us affectionately called Gina, was standing beside us, looking at the play of emotions between father and daughter. Tears were trickling down her cheeks as well. I kissed her, and she hugged me tightly.

A pianist was playing a heart-rending strain on the piano on the TV. I knew that Gina was also learning the piano at Woodstock.

'Are you as good at it as he is?' I asked her.

'Not yet, but I shall be,' she said.

I liked her answer.

'The day you tell me that you are good at it, you will find the best piano in the world waiting especially for your beautiful fingers to play on it,' I said, ruffling her hair with affection and then putting it together in a cute little pony tail.

She enjoyed this, nodding in total innocence.

I kissed her again. 'And you shall play and I shall listen, and forget all about this,' I said, patting the cheeks of both my granddaughter and daughter. 'And let life go on, and enjoy it as it comes to you,' I finished, and they hugged me again.

Mona was wiping a tear too at the far end of the room.

Fifty-nine

As *Hum Naujawan* neared completion, Tabu was getting more and more ambitious. When I was driving her home after pack-up on her last day of filming, she looked at my reflection in the rearview mirror with a mischievous twinkle in her eyes and said, 'Don't I deserve to be a leading lady now? Cast me as one.'

I gave her a pat on the cheek and replied, 'Sure! You deserve to be the best leading lady ever, for you have grown very, very beautiful. Just one more year and you shall be in the news.'

'Will you cast me?' she wanted to be assured.

'I will,' I answered.

But before I could, I heard she was already being launched by someone, and soon she was a star. I felt proud, and prouder still when her stature grew with every film she acted in, and every passing year.

Once on a flight to New York, I was looking outside my window at a rainbow when I felt a soft fragrant rustle of a feminine dress slip into the vacant seat beside me. It was Tabu. She was on her way to perform at a function where I was to receive an award. After very warm hellos, she talked of the maturity that the experience of life had given her, of having 'grown up' as a woman, and of a vacuum in her life.

'Have you met your man yet?' I asked.

'Not yet. But I have learnt a lot, all by myself. Look, I am travelling alone,' she said.

'You are not alone, am I not beside you?' I said jokingly.

She gave me a flirtatious smile.

'Let's meet in New York, after the fuss of the award is over,' I said in a very light vein.

'Yes let's,' she answered with the same light-hearted eagerness.

'But I am going to Chicago after that,' she added hastily.

'Take me along with you to Chicago.'

She laughed and said, 'Why not? Let's go together to Chicago.'

'I shall call you then—to know when,' I rounded off the conversation.

But it never happened. I never called, and she never took me to Chicago.

On the same trip to New York, I was looking out at Central Park from my hotel room, watching the autumn leaves flying and dancing in the breeze, their golden spectacle enhanced by the kisses of the setting sun, when my phone rang, and across the line came a voice full of love and romance.

'I was told you are in the hotel—guess who it is,' was the tenderly spoken sentence.

'How can I forget a voice so familiar?' I replied with the same tenderness.

Adding more romance, the voice continued, 'I am feeling romantic, Dev saab!'

Intrigued and charmed, I asked, 'Where are you?'

'Very close to you,' came the sweet answer.

'I can already feel that,' I was responsive. 'But tell me how close!'

'Almost next door—I'm speaking from Manhattan,' she said. Has she suddenly come chasing me? was my immediate thought.

'Can I come over?' she was asking now.

'Why not?'

'Straightaway?'

'Straightaway!' I braced myself for the occasion, looking at my face in the mirror.

'Very prim and proper to meet the lady,' I chuckled to myself.

A few minutes later came a knock of soft knuckles on the door. I opened the door to see her smiling.

'That's the most beautiful smile I have ever seen on your face!' I gallantly complimented her.

'So, give me a flower,' she said, looking at the crystal vase on the table with lovely multicoloured flowers in it, as if waiting to receive her in the room.

'And the best one in the bouquet,' she added.

'Do you really mean it?' I was as excited as she was.

'Yes!' she blossomed out in a smile.

I sat down on the sofa, looking intently into her eyes, and said, 'It is so nice to see you feeling so romantically inclined, Meenakshi!'

'Y-e-s, I am! I just got married!' said Meenakshi Seshadri.

The cat was out of the bag, and I, wonderstruck, asked, 'What do you mean, just married?'

'This morning!' she said.

'This morning?' I repeated. 'Big news—a surprise, and a very, very pleasant one! Congratulations!' I rose, holding out my hand towards her. She grasped it, thanking me.

'I had to get away, to break the news to someone I know, respect and admire, and I knew you were in the hotel!' She was all happiness.

It was very Meenakshi-like, I thought. That mystery of a girl whose love-life was never known to anyone for she had none, or so people thought.

I went and pulled out the most beautiful flower from the vase and offered it to her.

'I feel honoured, Meenakshi, to present the very first flower on this great occasion to you on behalf of the movie industry,' I told her.

She held the flower, feeling the joy of the moment, as I added, 'And let mine be the first party to be thrown in honour of both of you, when I get back to Mumbai, to break the news to the industry that the charming lady and great actress who shunned everybody, as she romanced her way to stardom, is finally hooked—'

She interrupted me, kissing the flower, 'By an Indian doctor in America.'

'God bless you both!' I held her hand that was holding the flower and kissed it.

A graceful and exquisite dancer, I had cast Meenakshi opposite Jackie Shroff in *Sachche Ka Bol-Bala*. The role gave ample scope to her extraordinary talent. Jackie too had become a big star by then, and while he played the young romantic lead, I played an upright journalist who got romantically linked to Meenakshi's elder sister in the film, played by Hema Malini.

Sachche Ka Bol-Bala took me to Delhi for its all-India premiere. The University of Delhi threw a big reception for me. So did the Press Club of India, which then made me its honorary member.

Sixty

Cricket is a game invented by the British, and patronized by the lords and ladies of the Empire, as they lounged around in their luxurious clubs over glasses of ale and wine or frothy beer, lazily watching their favourites hit sixes, or getting out for ducks. It was a legacy passed on to the colonies they ruled. And as time went by, the game grew into an extremely popular sport, with the cricketing heroes, wherever they were, being lionized and idolized by innumerable cricket-loving fans.

Cricket can be a painfully slow game that demands all of one's leisure to watch it, in a holiday mood. But since the inception of one-day cricket, the game has become an exceedingly exciting fare. I was watching a one-dayer in a suite regularly maintained by me at the Sun-n-Sand Hotel. It excited me so much that I was glued to the TV for as long as the match lasted. Breathtaking and spectacular, it ended in a fashion similar to a suspense thriller, and an idea for a movie suddenly struck me. I called it *Awwal Number*.

It was about two great cricket players, one on the verge of retirement and the other a fresher on the threshold of superstardom. I did a script with me playing the role of an ex-cricket legend, now the chairman of the selection committee.

Though in one of my early starrers called *Love Marriage*, I did play a cricketer, hitting sixes in a sequence, the film was not based on the game itself. *Awwal Number* was planned to be all about cricket.

Aamir Khan's first film had just been released, and since he was a talented fresh newcomer joining the ranks of the young rising stars, I cast him as an up-and-coming young cricketer.

For the role of the star on the decline, my choice fell on Imran Khan, the former Pakistani captain, who had just announced his retirement from the game. Very photogenic and handsome, Imran was one of the greatest names in cricket. I thought it was a casting coup. I had met Imran briefly in Bombay when he had come to play one of his first Tests as a member of the Pakistan team. The best way for me to get in touch with Imran in London was to contact him personally. I took nobody in confidence, and purely on a personal initiative, found out his telephone number from a cricketer friend of mine, and dialled it. There was an answering machine at the other end. I left my name and number and waited for a reply. No reply was forthcoming for a few days. But I didn't let the matter rest there, and called his number again, this time from Bangalore, which I was visiting for some personal work. Luckily, Imran answered this time. I told him who I was, to which he politely said he had received my earlier message, and was apologetic for not responding as he was involved with some county cricket that had taken him outside London.

'What can I do for you, Mr Dev Anand?' Imran was very courteous.

'Everything—about what I am thinking of at the moment,' I replied.

'And what is that?'

'I believe you have retired from cricket, and I have read that you have started to model!'

'Yes.'

'So why not extend your field of activity to another direction?' I posed the question.

'And that is?' he asked.

'Will you act in my film and do the role of a fading cricket star? It will catapult you to stardom of a different kind,' I proposed.

He was speechless for while. Not a word came from him, with me anxious and eager for his reaction.

'Are you there?' I broke the silence.

'Very much!'

'So?'

'You have bowled me over, Mr Dev Anand. But I don't think I am a good actor!'

I was happy that I had succeeded in putting the thought in his mind, and said, 'Maybe I can help you make up your mind if I see you personally.'

'But Mr Dev Anand . . .'

'I need no answer right now, Imran!' I interrupted. 'Don't take any decision either for or against my proposal until the time I see you.'

'When?'

'I shall be on the first flight available,' and I hung up, very much in keeping with the impulsive trait in me, and the desire to take quick decisions.

I booked myself on the next available flight to London, checked in at the Portman Hotel in the West End, and the first move I made was to call Imran from my room. Imran was bowled over once again.

'I said I was going to meet you in London. Would you dine with me tonight?' I fired off the first salvo.

'Why don't you come over to my apartment, at Soho?' was his reply.

'When?'

'Whenever you want!'

'Let it be now. That's why I am here.'

He gave me his address. I took a cab and found his brother in his Pathani salwar-kameez waiting to receive me at the entrance to his apartment. Imran was hospitable and obliging, a gracious host, warm and friendly, the sign of a great sportsman.

I narrated the story of *Awwal Number* to him with a special emphasis on the role I wanted him to play. But he seemed a little nervous at the idea of facing the camera for a professional acting assignment.

'It'd be fun holding the premier of the film in Pakistan, with you as its star,' I tried to enthuse him. He listened with interest as I spoke. 'You are already very big all over world. The film will further enhance your status, in India as well. I assure you, you'd be in the same league in the movies as Amitabh Bachchan in our country,' I said with total conviction.

'But General Zia-ul-Haq wants me to join his cabinet as a cultural minister,' he countered.

'That's great! You can do both. Be a cultural minister, as well as a star,' I tried to convince him.

He was still in two minds, and kept harping on his political ambition.

'Let me leave the script with you. Go through it. If it succeeds in making up your mind, let me know,' I said.

He agreed.

I concluded by saying, 'I shall feel honoured having cast Imran Khan in a movie that my country would love to see.'

'But Mr Dev Anand . . .'

I cut him short, saying, 'And if you still persist in not wanting to be a film star, I shall delightfully accept your "No", yet be happy at the thought that at least I succeeded in approaching the man I desired so much for the key role in my film.'

I thanked him for the time and hospitality he had given me, and left.

Next evening I received a packet at the Portman Hotel, with my script wrapped inside, and a note that said 'No' to my proposition.

The role I had approached Imran for went to Aditya Pancholi, who did a very good job of it. Both he and Aamir were extremely watchable. The movie saw the audience chilling out and thrilled to see Aamir Khan score his first century in the last ball of the last over. Fans screamed in delight as he hit the last ball high for a sixer to reach his most-coveted century that also won the match for his team. The CCI stadium in the movie echoed with a resounding cheer as the ball fell into a hat raised skywards by a spectator, and the crowds went berserk with hysteria.

Awwal Number was to find some resonance years later in the Oscar-nominated film *Lagaan*, which Aamir produced. Aamir was new and fresh when he did *Awwal Number*, and he was cast opposite another newcomer called Aarti, whom I had renamed Ekta.

Ekta got married to the handsome actor Mohnish Behl, who was the famous actress Nutan's son. He also did a film with me, directed by my brother Goldie. When I met him on the sets for the first time, as a co-star in the same film, I looked at his eyes and 'Nigahen mastana', the very melodious song I had sung with his mother in *Paying Guest* on a moonlit night on the sets of a lonely terrace of a house, came to my mind. The audience had swooned over both of us, as I had on Nutan!

They say my films are ahead of their times. *Awwal Number* certainly was. I had combined the theme of sports with terrorism, the order of the day. In a sequence the prime minister of the country visits the stadium to watch the final moments of the match, only to be whisked away from there when the security sends out alarm signals saying that the LTTE is planning to blow up the stadium.

The mention of the LTTE was ordered to be removed from the film by the Central Board of Film Censors, since it was politically sensitive. I had to exchange its name for a fictitious one belonging to an imaginary terrorist organization. But the fact that I had not been indulging in wild fantasies when I had mentioned an LTTE attack was borne out soon after the film was released, when Rajiv Gandhi was assassinated by a suicide bomber belonging to the LTTE.

Rajiv Gandhi was mercilessly and brutally eliminated from the political scene, not by deadly bullets, as his mother had been, but by a human bomb, a monstrous creation of the present times.

Human killing is always an act of cowardice. But a suicide-bomber associates bravery with the act, to kill for a cause that the killer fervently believes in, whether it is born out of a bigoted political faith or religious fervour. It is the latest invention of terrorists, and cannot be contained by any security force. It can happen anywhere, wherever fanaticism rules.

Rajiv Gandhi became a victim of suicide-bombing, as the shocked nation wept. I had never met him, but my heart cried too. How I wished I had met him in the most romantic moment of his life when he tied the knot with his Italian lady-love Sonia. If only I had responded to the invitation sent to me by Mrs Gandhi to attend his marriage reception in New Delhi. But I was out of the country then.

Now when I heard of the diabolic act by his assassins, I prayed to God to give strength to his wife to bravely bear the cruel blow that fate had struck.

Sixty-one

Rajiv Gandhi always fought his political battles from the constituency of Amethi in Uttar Pradesh. That constituency has always been safe in elections for the Gandhi family, except once, when Sanjay Gandhi lost to a local princely man, who was later involved in the alleged murder of a famous badminton star whose wife he later married.

These facts inspired me to spin a fictionalized story around the incident for my next film *Sau Crore*, a murder mystery and a political thriller. The film took me to Switzerland once again after *Prem Pujari*.

I was flying back from San Jose, California, after attending a function in which I was the chief guest and an awardee, to New York, thinking about my new film. Suddenly, Ananya's face came flying out of the clouds, floating past the aircraft window. I had heard her sing her magical notes on stage years ago, and had been thoroughly enraptured. Since then Ananya had often been in my thoughts.

I called her number from my suite at the Plaza Hotel in Manhattan. Her father picked up the phone. I spoke to him about the reason for my calling. Excited at the thought, he said, 'Speak to Ananya,' and passed the phone on to her. After a small pause, I heard her say hello.

'It's me, Ananya, Dev,' I said.

'Hi, we think of you very often,' she replied.

'I, too, about you.' She laughed.

I came to the point, 'When do we meet?'

'Where are you?' she asked.

'Waiting for you!' was my answer.

'Where?' she asked eagerly.

'At the Plaza Hotel. This evening?'

'Mummy! Papa!' I heard her call out excitedly. Then a pause, before she said, 'I'll come there. What time?'

'You tell me!' I left it to her.

'Six o'clock this evening?'

'Fine—see you.' I gave her my room number, and asked her to call from the lobby.

As we sat talking on the sofa, I told her about the role I wanted her to do, that of a French-bred Indian girl in Switzerland. It suited her well, and would open a window to show business for her. She loved the concept, and told me about the ambition she had been nurturing to be a singer of great distinction, and hit the charts one day.

I reciprocated by offering her a song in the film, to be sung by her in her own voice. Her eyes danced with joy. She had beautiful eyes that needed to be kissed. I held myself back, and said, instead, 'I look forward to doing some mutually rewarding work with you, Ananya. How do we proceed?'

'Oh, there is nothing to proceed with,' she said. 'I am in your film, and you are my co-star and director—and together we go to Switzerland.'

She came all the way to Switzerland, alone, without a chaperon, unprotected except by her strong mind and clean conscience. Her parents came to see her off as far as London. From London, I took charge of her, as a friend, guide and her director.

Together, along with our film unit, we went to Staad, a beautiful spot in nature's most beloved country. While there, during the days we shot amongst breathtaking locales, with clouds and mist and sunshine, and lush-green meadows and rolling hills and wildflowers. And after dusk fell we would be together again, either by the fire in the wooden chateau we were staying in, or strolling with our thick jackets on across the village promenade, eating cherries, sometimes tramping across unknown vistas of the countryside, exploring them as much as each other's thoughts. At night, she would bring me a cup of hot milk with two teaspoonfuls of Swiss honey in it, and then we would retire into our own rooms. I would get up as the morning sun shot its rays through the partly open shutters on to my face. I would religiously go and knock on her door, right at the end of the corridor. Always a couple of knocks together, after which she would say, 'I'm up.'

And time flew.

It was the last day of our filming there. Nature did not like the idea of our going away. Clouds hung low as if in protest and raindrops fell intermittently. Mist danced about and covered the lens of the camera every time a ray of sunshine smiled through the overcast sky. Suddenly, lightning struck, followed by thunder, and the drizzle turned into a burst of rain. An umbrella was thrown towards me. I held it and hid Ananya from the merciless onslaught of the weather. A wooden bench lay across, beckoning to us. We ran over and sat on it, our faces underneath the umbrella, the pitter-patter of rain over our heads sounding like the beat of drums.

Another flash of lightning, and I looked into Ananya's eyes. They were dancing the same way they had danced at the Plaza Hotel, on the sofa.

'I feel like humming,' she whispered over the sound of thunder.

'Hum,' I egged her on. She hummed a ditty in English, and then in Bengali, as the winds whistled and the trees rustled, the wet flowers danced like Swiss maids in colourful costumes, and the lightning threw its shining glare on Ananya's face in a psychedelic pattern. They were moments of great poetry, probably the greatest I have experienced.

Ananya finished her song, and Nature now turned merciful. The clouds lifted, the mist dissolved, and the sunshine was back in its full glory. Our filming schedule was complete.

From Switzerland, we came back to London, where Ananya's parents were to join her again. They were staying somewhere outside London. I went all the way to Waterloo station to see her off.

Ananya had her dreams, and she deserved that all of them should come true. But the fondest dream that overtakes a young girl, aching to turn itself into reality, is to be in the arms of her life partner, the man of her dreams. She was going steady with someone when she came to shoot *Sau Crore* with me, and they were soon married in America.

Along with Ananya, I had Fatima Sheikh, another newcomer, as the other leading lady of *Sau Crore*. The Muslim name of the actress incurred the wrath of the Shiv Sena leader, Bal Thackeray, who ran the government of Maharashtra by remote control. A distributor of my film in a small territory called me to say that Shiv Sainiks, the militant cadre of Balasaheb's political outfit, were creating trouble, stopping the film from being screened in theatres since it allegedly featured a Pakistani actress.

I rushed to Balasaheb's residence and shared a beer with him, while Manohar Joshi, his most favourite lieutenant at that time, watched with interest. Sitting relaxed in his armchair, taking sips of the cool beverage and holding a cigar in his hand, Balasaheb was the Godfather incarnate. I remembered the first time we had met, when he had come to greet me at my Juhu residence after watching *Guide*.

Many years later, he had invited me to the inauguration of his daily mouthpiece *Saamna* and took pride in my sharing the platform with him, as I spoke praising the 'free and fearless' Marathi newspaper that would henceforth keep the readers informed of the happenings in the state and the nation in relation to the views held by the party. He seemed very friendly, and the way we shook hands indicated a lifelong affection for each other.

Now as I sat 'pleading' my case before him, insisting that Fatima was not a Pakistani but a Muslim born and brought up in secular India, and that he had been misinformed by his overzealous, ultra-patriotic musclemen, he was quickly convinced and politely assured me that he'd see to it that no wrong was done.

'And cheers to that,' I raised my glass of beer to him, amused at the thought of an autocratic strongman actually ruling a state of democratic India, and giving it the populist slogan 'Maharashtra for Maharashtrians'.

Sixty-two

I answer my telephone myself. I am accessible to all those who want to call me. There is no secret code or undisclosed number. Anyone who wants to speak to me can do so, though the discretion always lies with me as to who I want to speak with and who I would like to avoid, once I answer the telephone and find out the reason why the person is calling. My response to the callers depends on my own judgement. Which means that I don't ignore any calls, and am indifferent to no one. This approachability makes me happy, since I get to know everyone who calls, and also know what they call for. There are a lot of blind calls as well, anonymous callers to whom I also react in an anonymous way, changing the style and tone of my speech over the phone to suit the moment, happily enjoying that game of hide-and-seek.

Quite a few callers play my songs over the telephone when they call, and I get to know the extent of my popularity from the comments they make in the background in hushed whispers. The callers include men and women of all ages and professions, but young girls mostly! Some sparkle with their laughter, some giggle in mischief, sometimes shy, sometimes bold. I like listening to them, whether they love me, hate me or try to make fun of me. It gives me a great insight into the human mind.

I don't sleep in the afternoons. Some people are fond of a quick nap after lunch; I am not. It seems like such a waste of time. Sometimes when I am tired or overworked, or haven't had a good night's sleep, I tend to doze off in my working chair. And that's the best sleep I enjoy, sleeping all dressed up, half-reclined in the chair.

I had dozed off in this fashion one afternoon, and the phone next to me kept ringing. I let it ring, enjoying the ring in the dream

I was in. It stopped ringing after a while, and then suddenly started ringing again after a few moments, not stopping this time. I could feel its resonating sound even in my sleep. Involuntarily my hand went to the receiver, picked it up to bang it down hard and stop it from ringing, when I heard the giggly voice of a girl through the earpiece, coupled with another equally giggly voice that said, 'It's picked up!' I woke up abruptly, opening my eyes, receiver in hand, listening to another girlish voice say 'It's pi-ck-ed up' in a drawling, naughty whisper. The hush-hush tone intrigued me. I put my ear to the receiver.

'I think he's listening,' came the girlish drawl again, in a sexy whisper.

'Yes I am,' I said in a deliberately grotesque voice.

There was an outburst of giggles now, followed by another whisper, 'He's acting!' This was followed by a girl speaking in her natural voice, but with a foreign accent.

'Mr Dev Anand!'

'Who's that?' I also came back to my real voice.

'Somebody from France,' said the girl.

She did sound French, and very like a teenager. A few words in French followed.

'What does that mean? I asked.

'They mean that I want to meet you,' she said.

'Sure! Why not?' I was enjoying this.

'Can we meet now?' she asked.

I could, but I said, 'Not now, I'm afraid—maybe tomorrow afternoon, around 2.30 p.m.?'

'That's a date!' she said. I put the phone down.

Next day, at the appointed time, a couple of cute-looking young girls stepped into my penthouse, opening the door very softly.

'Comment allez vouz?' I tried to speak French. That was the only French sentence I knew. It means 'How are you?'

'Very well, thank you,' came the answer in English.

They were both dressed in body-hugging continental attires, quite revealing—as if they had stepped straight out of the pages of *Vogue* magazine.

'That's a smash hit!' I remarked.

They looked shy.

'Your dress!' I clarified, to one of them. 'Very Parisian!'

They looked even more shy.

'How is Paris?' I enquired conversationally.

'But I am not from Paris. I am from Germany,' one of them said.

'Germany?'

'But I speak French too.' I realized she had been the one on the phone.

'What brings you to me?' I asked.

'You!' She was bold now. 'Handsome and debonair!'

'Why did you lie that you are French, on the telephone?'

'I enjoyed saying it!' she laughed. Her English accent was soft and sweet. 'But we are Indians, and live in Germany,' she continued.

'So you speak German as well?' I asked.

'It's my mother tongue! I was born in Germany!'

'How old are you?'

'Fourteen.'

'Your name?'

'Mink.'

'Mink?'

'Mink Singh!'

'And what brings you to India?'

They looked at each other and smiled. I smiled with them.

'Can she be an actress?' the other one asked about Mink.

'Sorry for my bad manners. I did not ask you to sit down,' I answered.

Their smiles bloomed out. 'Sit down!' I repeated, and sat down too with them.

They giggled again, looking at each other, at the partial success of their mission.

'And what's that for, now?' I asked.

'You did not answer my question. She wants to know!' Mink's friend spoke again.

'She hasn't said so!' I said, looking at Mink.

'Can I?' now Mink picked up courage.

'It depends on . . .' And I paused.

'On what?' she was eager to know.

'On . . .' I kept looking at her, as if I was scanning a photograph.
'What?' she insisted.

'If somebody . . .' I paused again, my look still fixed on her.

'Wh-at?' she prolonged the word, becoming self-conscious.

'If somebody has a role that suits you—the way you are!'

She blushed and looked at her friend for some assurance and then looked back at me.

'Actually my mum wants to speak with you—she is a great fan of yours. Would you be willing?' she changed the topic suddenly.

'It's always the mother who comes first,' I thought, 'then the daughter.' Girls who loved me and longed for me after seeing my films have now become mothers, and have, in turn, passed their own dream to their daughters, who come and see me now with the same intensity of feeling and adoration!

She waited eagerly for my answer with the expression of an innocent child on her face, as if waiting for a toy to be handed to her. 'Tell your mum to give me a call,' I said.

Her mum's call came the next day. 'I am Mink's mother, Mrs Singh, from Germany. Can I come and meet you sometime?'

I was about to respond, but she went on. 'With a present I have for you from Germany.'

'Do come and see me, but only on condition that you don't bring any present,' I replied.

She laughed very charmingly.

'I shall come with my daughter,' she said.

Both mother and daughter came to see me, dressed in the latest fashionable clothes, competing with each other in style. They had several rings on their fingers, of different hues and designs, as well as a clutch of bracelets and necklaces. The entire room glittered.

Mink ended up playing the second lead in my next film *Pyar Ka Tarana*.

Sixty-three

'Saab! A saab keeps telephoning, and leaves his number every time, always insisting it is very important,' said my chowkidar one evening as I got back home.

'Did he mention his name?' I enquired.

'There on the table, saab! I wrote it three times. Three times he called!' he said.

I looked at the slip of paper. He had written 'Copenhagen' along with the caller's name.

'Copenhagen!' I muttered, and then forgot about it, leaving the paper next to the rest of the mail piled up on the table.

As I entered the gate of my studio the next day the accountant standing at the far end asked me if I would like to take a call from Copenhagen, which the operator was holding.

'Copenhagen again,' I muttered to myself, and said, 'Tell the operator I shall speak to him.'

The caller was Harwani, whose name was on the slip of paper lying near the telephone at home. His voice was subdued, and very meekly he said that he was interested in getting a film directed by me in Denmark.

'But I don't work for anybody outside my own fold, Mr Harwani,' I told him politely.

'But you do meet people, don't you?' he asked.

'All the time,' I said.

'Can I, then, meet with you?'

'Certainly.'

He came a couple of days later. He was dressed in a suit and was well spoken, but timid, the expression in his eyes hidden behind the thick spectacles he wore all the time. He was carrying a briefcase, which I later discovered he always carried. He was extremely respectful, and I was polite in return.

'Mr Harwani, I make films only for myself. I don't make them for outsiders,' I repeated.

'Don't treat me as an outsider. We all love you. Have you ever been to Copenhagen?' he said.

'Not in a long time. I have never visited the Scandinavian countries properly.'

'Visit them now, on my invitation. Not only Denmark. I shall drive you to Sweden and Norway as well!'

The invitation was tempting and I answered, 'The moment I have a little spare time, and am in a holiday mood, I shall let you know.'

A first-class air ticket arrived soon from Copenhagen. Harwani had been insistent, behaving as if he was some long-lost friend, and I gave in. He had left several glamorous fashion magazines from Denmark, which his briefcase was filled with, for me to look at. There were photographs of trendy models wearing the latest Scandinavian designs in fashion, laid out and printed in great artistic style. As the magazines lay open on the table, speaking of the élan and class of the Scandinavian countries, I was enticed.

In Copenhagen, Harwani was at the airport to receive me with a lovely bouquet of the finest fresh flowers. A red carpet was laid out for me. He drove me to the best hotel in the elegant city, and booked me into its best suite, with its windows opening out to the great expanse outside.

Harwani left on my table a packet of Danish kronas, in case I needed money to spend until I exchanged my own money into the local currency. The next day he took me home to meet his family, which consisted of a very hospitable wife, a son and two lovely daughters, the elder one very pretty. She opened the door as he rang the bell, and instantly said, 'Hi, I am Pinky!' in a very European style.

'Hi Pinky'! I responded in a star-like manner. She was a loyal fan and so was her entire family. They had just seen *Hum Naujawan*. The son joined us soon, and they all took me for dinner to a very popular place called Scala, full of merry-making people, with nothing but laughter and the zest for living on their faces. Later we went to

Tivoli, the city of magic and fantasy, of joy and entertainment that Walt Disney must have been inspired by

I had been to Tivoli earlier, holding Saira Bano's hand, romancing with her in *Pyar Mohabbat*, directed by Shankar Mukherji. While shop-gazing on the streets there, I had come across a cap that went on to create a cult for itself.

My *Jewel Thief* cap was bought in Copenhagen.

And the same 'Jewel Thief' was in the city again, exploring it anew.

From Tivoli we went to Christiana, for which Copenhagen is famous as well as infamous. It is full of drugs and drug peddlers, and throbbing with a young crowd living their lives fast and under the cloud of an eternal smoke that keeps them intoxicated with themselves, and away from the worries of the world. It all makes a very colourful picture, half-naked bodies with long beards and old arty jewellery, free in their minds and freer with their bodies, everyone enjoying the fruits of the free-for-all kingdom legalized by the Danish government.

In one day, I captured the essence of Copenhagen. Some of the women were so beautiful that one wished one was King Henry VIII of England, who had so many wives.

A couple of days later, we drove to the border of Denmark, a couple of hours away. We took a ferry and soon we were in Sweden, in Stockholm, the home of Ingrid Bergman, Greta Garbo and Ingmar Bergman, each a movie legend. I felt a natural rapport with the place.

I stood silent for a while at a road-crossing, where the traffic was fast. Right across, the gold of the sun was melting into different colours as it sank in the ocean, lighting up tiny specks of clouds as well. The lights in the street were suddenly lit, turning the square into a psychedelic fantasia. Short skirts and low-necked blouses, high-heeled shoes and sexy-looking sandals worn on long beautifully shaped legs, manicured nails, the hooting of horns and the banter of young girls, all centred around a huge poster of a ravishing nude, with frontals that spelt paradise for the young males milling around and with half-open painted lips that looked ready to swallow up all that is heaven on earth.

Back in Copenhagen, a trip to Norway was planned. Harwani drove like a seasoned driver, and I was like a curious child wanting to see, imbibe, learn and enjoy all that was once in my imagination and was now a reality, passing in front of my eyes as a panorama. The road was snowbound at places, trees denuded of leaves for the winter was right ahead, lonely isolated villages with dim lights eyeing you through the mist shrouding the wooden houses and sideway inns.

My mind was racing with new ideas, faster than the speedometer of the car. Ahead of us, though far away, was the North Pole. But first Oslo, the capital of Norway, where we stopped. There were very few people on the road, which glistened with snow. We went to a Norwegian pub, our bodies shivering as we got out of the heated car, our hands and noses and ears in danger of getting frozen. There was a warm sound of joy and laughter emanating from the pub as we stepped in. It seemed the entire young crowd of Oslo was huddled together there, with glasses of wine clinking, hands clasped in hands, rosy cheeks and pink faces looking like they were part of the vibrant portrait of a great romance. Our entry drew curious glances. 'Hi,' I called out to be welcomed, vaporous fumes flying out of my mouth to mingle with the jollity of the atmosphere. Half the gathering responded with a 'Hi' in a chorus, and the other half raised their glasses, inviting us for a drink. A Norwegian girl made a loud remark. I could not understand it, but her expression conveyed everything. I took off my cap, ruffled my hair and waved at her. There was laughter all around that lent great warmth to the gathering that had come in from the freezing cold outside.

Back in Copenhagen, I had made up my mind to shoot a film in Denmark. It would be a new experience.

'Give me a couple of months to get ready. I shall let you know,' I told Harwani.

When an idea takes birth, it has to be given time to grow. I start living with it, in both my conscious and subconscious states of mind. The nucleus has to take the shape of a story before I can plan the structure and the schedule.

Anita Ayub came into the picture suddenly. She was a Pakistani girl on holiday in India, the first and probably the last from that country to win a title in a beauty contest. She had deep blue eyes and a Snow White-like complexion, brown hair with a touch of gold in them, and a figure that could be kept in a showcase for people to admire. A real Punjabi Pathan. She came to see me as a fan, and ended up as the star of *Pyar Ka Tarana*.

There was another girl to be cast in the film, besides of course Mink whom I had already finalized for the second lead. She had to be a girl from Denmark. I made my second trip to Copenhagen to try and find her. Copenhagen was full of girls, immensely pretty and as fresh as roses. An advertisement had already appeared in Danish newspapers and I, too, had been on Danish television, talking about my wish to shoot a film there. Some people had started recognizing me in public places. Girls started turning up in large numbers for interviews. English is popularly spoken in Denmark, so there was no difficulty in communicating with the young crowd. They were all free and uninhibited, with strong sophisticated personalities.

Many of the Danish girls were quite tall, the height enhancing their appeal and elegance. One of them, who sought an interview, was six feet eight inches tall. As she stood next to me, talking in fluent English, carrying her height on her feet with assured charm, I couldn't take my eyes off her. She was sixteen or seventeen, broadly built yet delicate looking, her auburn hair combed back from her broad forehead and knotted, with apple-red cheeks and an angelic smile. She was God's special creation, specially chosen to stand tall among all the other pretty women. As she walked out of the room after an exquisitely feminine 'Thank you', I kept looking at her legs long after they made their exit, entering the chambers of my fantasies. I thought I could plan a full-length feature film around her. But in *Pyar Ka Tarana*, I couldn't find a place for her, especially opposite Manu Gargi, son of the famous playwright Balwant Gargi, whom I had already signed for the male lead.

I told Harwani to take me to a dancing place that the young crowd of Copenhagen frequented the most one evening. There I saw a girl sitting amongst her group of friends. She was in the full bloom of youth, smiling away in great abandon, capturing the attention of everybody around her. Very innocent looking and fresh as a morning flower, she caught my eye. She seemed right for the part I had conceived.

As the waitress came round to serve me my drink, I asked for a sheet of blank paper, and scribbled a note to the young girl. The waitress handed the note over. On receiving the note, the girl looked at me. I waved at her. She nodded and graciously walked towards me.

'You are a beautiful girl. I couldn't help wanting to be noticed by you, through my move,' I said.

'Some of my friends at the table have recognized you. You were on television a couple of days ago,' she said.

'I was. Did you watch it?' I asked.

'No.'

'Won't you sit down?'

'I have my friends there. You wanted to meet me?'

'I am sure you must have guessed why!'

'Perhaps.'

'If approached, would you be interested to act in my film?'

'I have never done any acting.'

'Would you, now? It's a good part, for somebody like you!'

She half-nodded.

'You'll love doing it, and the world shall watch and admire you,' I enthused.

She nodded again, but asked, 'Will I be able to act?'

'That's my responsibility—that is, if we both agree to begin with.'

She smiled enchantingly.

'Come over to the Scandinavia Hotel, to my suite,' I said, and scribbled the number down. 'If you've finally made up your mind.'

'Can I bring my father with me?'

'Anybody you want.'

The girl's name was Maja Riis, the first name pronounced Maya. She was Swedish by birth, but working and studying in Denmark. Her father worked in Denmark as well and drove back every day to Stockholm where he lived. He was a charming educated man. I took Maja down to the lawns of the hotel, and took a short video test of hers to see how she looked and behaved in front of the camera. And the next day, after having assured myself, I asked Harwani to add her to the list of *Pyar Ka Tarana*.

The Danish portion of *Pyar Ka Tarana* was shot non-stop in Copenhagen, on some of its best locations: in the streets, in public entertainment places, inside Tivoli, in a boat along the harbour, and in the outskirts of Copenhagen, in open fields, and in a village with a windmill. Filming was done with people going about their normal business, on the beaches, where young uninhibited girls lay naked basking in the sun, and in a swimming pool, with them diving into the water with just their panties on. Nobody bothered or took note of the cameras as they rolled, catching them in their natural element. It is an open society, its doors welcoming all those who want to enter its gates, in the same spirit and with the same freedom of mind.

One of the best features of the film was the opening sequence which covered the annual Danish festival in the streets of Copenhagen, where women with sensuous figures flaunted their sex with nothing on except scanty bras and bejewelled transparent panties, dancing in total abandon, competing with one another, marching in processions, shaking their breasts and hips to the beat of the rhythm that enhanced their provocative nudity. As people around feasted their eyes on nature's most delightful wonder for man, a woman, my cameras went wild and the dancers wilder, knowing that they were being captured on film.

The making of *Pyar Ka Tarana* was an enjoyable experience, except that it led to some unpleasantness between the two partners. I realized later that I had made the biggest blunder of my life by joining hands with somebody as my partner in business, for while you can carry the burden of your own conscience, you cannot carry the burden of somebody else's conscience with you. Making the film was an absolute labour of love, and artistically satisfying, but the business aspect of it was deplorable. When two minds get together, one of an artistic bent and the other financial-minded, caution is the watchword.

Sixty-four

Newspapers all over the country carried a lead story on gangsterism. Some rich jewellers from Mumbai had been invited to Delhi by a fake businessman from abroad to negotiate a deal involving crores of rupees. After they arrived in Delhi he set up an appointment with them in his luxurious suite in a five-star hotel, from where they never returned. Their long absence from the hotel they were staying in came to notice and the world got to know that they had been kidnapped and taken to an unknown destination.

This news item, blown up to sensational proportions, set me thinking. It became the theme of my next film called *Gangster*.

Part of the filming for the project took me to Antwerp in Belgium and to Luxembourg next door, the future financial capital of the soon-to-be-formed European Union, a free city, completely independent and the centre of European unity.

Gangster dealt with jewels and diamonds, and Antwerp, the capital of the diamond industry of the world, has some of the wealthiest Jews and diamond merchants who buy and sell fortunes there. It is a very beautiful city with a population that has many Indians rubbing shoulders with the richest of business tycoons in the world.

I was filming a sequence in a magnificent square, adjoining a very picturesque church. Seeing the movie crew and the camera performing its magic, with me moving up and down, giving instructions to Mink in soft undertones and gesturing towards the crowds, a bunch of adorable European girls sitting in a sidewalk café showed interest in being part of the filming. Seeing their enthusiasm, I chose the prettiest of them all to do a small scene with Mink, who was supposed to play a saxophone in the shot. The girl performed not only with great verve but also brilliantly, besides looking ravishing on camera. Everybody around gave her a big ovation, and as she blushed crimson, I gallantly walked up to her to give her a peck on her cheek in appreciation of her work.

'I want to do more,' she said, very enthused.

'Your name?' I asked.

'Jane,' she said, blushing.

'For the time being, it's just this much, Jane!' I thanked her, patting her on the back, and got busy with my next shot.

Next day, we drove to Luxembourg for another sequence. As I got busy arranging the camera placement, I saw a swanky car parking alongside.

'Do you mind parking it a little further away please? This area is in the range of my camera angle,' I requested the lady at the wheel.

'Recognize me?' she said, and then laughed.

'Jane!' I exclaimed, very pleasantly surprised. 'What are you doing here?'

'Following you!'

'You are a darling.'

'I am driving to my hometown, Amsterdam. Interested in filming there?'

'Not for this film!'

'In case you ever are, I am there. I have inherited a palatial villa and a fortune from my dad, who died last year. Ideal for filming!' she said excitedly. She was a millionairess, I suddenly realized.

'Thank you, Jane, for your kind gesture!' I said.

'And this is my card,' she passed on a gold-embroidered visiting card. I took it, looked at it.

'And when you are through with the present filming, you are welcome to visit me. It is a great drive, not very long, all the way to Amsterdam,' she continued.

'Thank you, Jane.' I kissed her card.

'Bye then,' and she moved on, throwing me a flying kiss with a delicate, subtle flourish of her hand. 'Think of an Indian film in Holland!' And she blew me another full-blooded kiss, leaving me looking on as her very expensive car vanished around a bend.

Sixty-five

I returned to Mumbai and got involved in a stupid controversy, because I did not see eye to eye with the points of view of the people responsible for creating it in the first place.

A popular actor had allegedly publicly slapped a media photographer representing a famous film magazine that had made some slanderous remarks about the actor having made sexual advances towards the younger sister of a leading lady on location of a film's shooting. The photographer did not take it lying down and reported the matter to his senior editors who in turn wrote a malicious article against the actor in their next issue, exposing his alleged misbehaviour with the girl in more detail. Being a gossip magazine, they added some extra spice to the entire episode. The actor overreacted. Instead of ignoring the article as stupid trash that gossip magazines are sometimes prone to print, pandering to cheap public tastes, he retaliated by creating a lobby for himself in the Actors' Association, which openly sided with him and lined up the affiliated associations of the movie industry to issue a circular to all its members banning the entire press from visiting any film studio, as well as ordering them not to give any statements or interviews to the fourth estate.

The president of the Actors' Association made the matter worse by going on air and making a statement on a TV channel saying that the acting fraternity was a group of 'social outcasts' who if maligned by the press as well would have 'no face to show to the world'.

When I watched the interview, my conscience revolted at his having referred to all his colleagues as 'social outcasts'. I thought the statement degraded the status of the acting community, was not in good taste, and certainly hurt my own dignity. I have always held my head high when it comes to social respectability. I was also in disagreement with the order passed by the association against the press. I gave vent to my honest feelings when the press approached me for my views. I said that the press in the country was free and independent, that it enlightened the public, and that every field of activity especially show business needed the press to talk about it and take its product to the world.

It was an honest interview, but it seemed nasty to my colleagues, for besides backing the press I had violated the joint resolution passed by them to boycott the media. They started a slander campaign against me saying that I was totally indisciplined, snootily independent of everybody, and always riding a high horse in a world of my own making. In a mood to chastise me and teach me a lesson for my irresponsible behaviour, they banned me and my work, ordering all film associations not to cooperate with me in any sphere of my professional activity. In other words the movie industry excommunicated me, and made me an 'outcast'.

A very prominent producer and director, and a Member of Parliament, was recording in my studio when this happened. He immediately stopped his work and walked out, dutifully responding to the association's order. My studio stopped functioning.

I laughed to myself at the comical step taken by such famous people of high mental and creative calibre. It seemed to me that they were writing a great farce and acting in it themselves, for their own entertainment.

The shutters of my studio having been downed, I called for an explanation from the associations concerned. After a closely guarded and hurried meeting amongst themselves, the president of the most important producers' association telephoned me and asked me to present my case to a committee constituted from representatives of the movie industry. A date was fixed when I was to appear before the royal durbar of the movie industry, and had to speak for myself.

I felt very important. They made me sit on a chair singled out for me, with everybody else lined up against me, sitting in a semicircle around me on my left, my right, and ahead of me, with faces that were stern and aggressive, glaring at me, ready to pounce upon the man who had single-handedly reached thus far, had made a place for himself without any 'party politics', and now dared to defy the mighty association.

I looked around and saw some of the most important names in show business—huge stars, box-office wizards in film-making, heads of workers' federations, along with the head of the producers' association, who had a lot of political clout in the state of Maharashtra. After the initial accusation fired at me by the president of the Actor's Association, I, the accused, was asked to speak in my defence. I spoke non-stop, explaining my stand, justifying my actions with all the forceful power of conviction arising out of my conscience.

There was silence. I ended by saying, 'I want you all to remember, my dear colleagues, that I am what I am on my own steam and strength, my own inner power, my own creative talent, my own dedication and hard work. I depend upon nobody. I make my own films, born out of my head and my heart. If you don't allow me to make them here, I can make them anywhere else, in any country, because with the kind of creative knowledge many of you, including myself, are gifted with, we can function in any part of the globe. I want you to know that I am fully prepared for that.'

Expressionless faces stared at me. They inspired me to add, 'I am a part of you, a small cog in a big wheel. But if you insist on not accepting me as I am, as a part of you, then I can be larger than your whole wheel.'

They were still silent. I gave them a broad smile, and walked out.

Outside, the press wanted to know the outcome of the melodramatic trial. I laughed and said nothing, went straight to my car and drove away.

With the press I became a bigger hero. But before the controversy could get out of hand, a compromise was struck: I was to speak no more against the resolution, and the studio would open again. Suneil and my studio staff convinced me to agree to this, for the studio was shut and the workers out of work. The ban against the press too died a natural death very soon.

Sixty-six

The release of *Gangster* coincided with the golden jubilee of my career. Half a century of being in the starry firmament of show business, first as a leading man, subsequently as a writer–director as well, and having introduced some sterling new talent to the movie industry in the form of stars, writers, directors, lyricists and music composers, made me very charismatic in the eyes of the world. I felt, however, that the achievement was not significant enough, for the standards I had set for myself were indefinably high. The sky was far, far above, and the more you climbed towards it, the farther it got.

Everybody everywhere wanted to felicitate and honour me on the occasion of my golden jubilee. I had to choose who I would prefer first. The decision was tough, for they were all equal in my eyes, and all their eyes were full of admiration for me.

My choice fell on Poona; I said 'yes' to the mayor when he approached me. For Pune, as it is called now, had given birth to my career. Pune was my fortress, my citadel. Its lanes and by-lanes on which I had tramped while I smelt the first fragrance of success, its main street on which I had cycled for hours and hours together buying books and magazines to satisfy my hunger for knowledge, its rocky hill behind the Prabhat Studios, now the Film Institute of India, which I climbed almost every evening, walking through its tall overgrown wild grass and looking down at the village of Khadakvasla, now known for its college of training for the defence forces, its residents who always had a smile for me whether I was travelling by tonga or walking into a restaurant for an omelette and a few pieces of baked bread or buying deliciously ripe bananas from a cart after dinner at the Lucky Irani restaurant, to gobble up at least half a dozen in one go—all these memories were forever fresh and sweet in my mind.

I deliberately opted to go to Pune by train, and not by car. I wanted to travel by the Deccan Queen, for that was the train I had travelled by when I first went there for my screen test. I chose a second-class compartment for my journey, for it meant that all my fans, many of them poor, could sit next to me, and swarm around me with eager eyes of adulation and affection, their hands thrust into mine for handshakes. I talked to them all, to the commonest of the common, listening to and answering all their inquisitive queries about myself and my future plans. Everybody was as keen to narrate his or her own tale to me, as to listen to mine of success.

The train kept halting at various places, where people had gathered to cheer me, to have a glimpse of me, with flowers or bouquets in their hands. Some greeted me just with a humble 'namastey' with folded hands, or a quiet look of reverence, ready to touch my feet like that of a god. I stood at the doorway, waving and smiling, my ego totally crushed by the simplicity of my people, as they ran alongside the train to touch my feet, hold my hand, and throw petals on my face.

'I love you, my countrymen!' I kept saying in my mind, 'more than you love me. I have given you nothing yet. I want to give you more and more. And I shall not rest before I do!'

Pune gave me a reception fit for royalty. It seemed all its inhabitants, tens of thousands of my loyal fans, had pledged themselves to line up the streets, to greet me with open arms as I drove down the city in an open jeep, offering my salutations to each and every one of them. Mayor Shirvalkar drove me to the stadium where I was to be presented my 'maan-patra', my 'roll of honour', in a decorated tonga, with men and women dancing to the trot of the horse that neighed joyously as multicoloured firecrackers lit the sky, heralding my arrival at the venue.

While in Pune, I paid homage to Lokmanya Tilak, one of the pioneers of India's freedom movement, and also visited the educational institute Symbiosis with my friend Nana Chudasama at my side. In my own humble way, I tried to inspire the students there to always aspire to the greatest heights in their dreams, and to believe in their ability to make those dreams come true.

I paused for a few moments at a street at the foot of a hill that has the majesty of a temple overlooking it. It had showered its blessings on me half-a-century ago, whenever I crossed it. I let its vibrations come to me in total silence, my eyes closed as if in meditation. People stood silently around me as well, knowing how precious the moment was for me. We are all one with our gods!

Later the city of Lucknow honoured me by giving me a public reception, with the governor in attendance. And then Bhopal, where I landed from Indore in a special aircraft belonging to the chief minister's brother. At Indore, some of my fans had come all the way to the airport to give me a hero's welcome. Fans who had been writing to me religiously for years, Jayant Srivastav, Rama Joshi and Raju Guide—who had named himself after his idol—were some of the many who jumped onto the aircraft before I got off it, overloading me with garlands. This was a prelude to the great welcome awaiting me in Bhopal, where the city had erected seventy-two arches on the way from the airport to the place where I was staying—the number of arches coinciding with the number of years I had spent on earth.

The Delhi state government held a reception for me in a hall that glittered with the elite of the city, its mediapersons and its luminaries, all of them flashing big smiles. They hailed me with one voice as I, wearing a rusty orange trench coat, threw a huge garland of marigolds, earlier put around my neck by the hosts, over the arc-lights into the audience. The garland was received with a roar of appreciation as scores of hands rose clutching at it.

Madras, now Chennai, honoured me as 'the Hero of the Century' through the *Indian Express* chain of newspapers in a stadium with thousands of people respectfully clapping in unison, with childish enthusiasm and juvenile awe on their faces. They were in for a pleasant surprise, when they saw and heard a man who looked and sounded younger, in manner and in spirit, than many of their university students.

Anandalok magazine in Calcutta, now Kolkata, were equally exuberant in celebrating me in their midst. It was a moment of great

artistic fulfilment when I received my award in the land of Swami
Vivekananda and Rabindranath Tagore.

The north-eastern states were a whistle stop away from Kolkata.
I had once been to Shillong, filming there with the vivacious Sharmila
Tagore, but had not gone beyond. Now I flew to Aizawl, the capital
of Mizoram, nestled snugly in the midst of thick forests. In a reception
for me there, I crowned a Mizo girl in a beauty contest in the main
stadium, before being driven away to share a very hospitable cup
of tea with Chief Minister Laldenga at his residence. Manipur and
Nagaland were not far away either. Word had spread of my presence
in the area—and I was equally keen to touch the hearts of people
there as well.

Driving out of Mizoram towards Manipur, as the view outside
opened up, I heard the voice of the late S.D. Burman.

Wahan kaun hai tera, musafir, jayega kahan?

Who waits for you there, O traveller, where are you off to?

The driver had switched on the radio.

I smiled with a nostalgic sentimental smile, silently saluting the
soul of the great musical maestro whose homeland was around these
parts.

I reached Kohima in Nagaland, and went straight to its war
memorial first, where the graves of hundreds of army soldiers, Hindus
and Muslims and Christians, fighting on the side of the British against
the Japanese in World War II, stood. They spoke as much of their
bravery in having rebuffed the enemy back at the cost of their own
lives as of the combined strength of their communities that could
overthrow and conquer any might if they stayed united.

Back in Mumbai, sitting on the sofa in my penthouse, I was
reflecting upon the euphoria created by the celebrations, my eyes
resting on a painting by Van Gogh hanging on the opposite wall,
when the door opened.

And there stood a tall, slim, silvery-haired, long-bearded,
bespectacled man, a stick in his hand, a bag hanging from his shoulder,
his feet bare under crumpled slacks, radiating a warm smile.

'Husain saab!' I jumped from my seat.

'Congratulations for a glorious career,' said M.F. Husain.

I beamed a smile of gratitude.

'I wanted to present myself,' he continued, resting his artistic frame in the chair under the Dutch painter's famous painting after my handshake.

'How's the world around you?' I asked.

'Same as always—calm as well as volatile.' He was fiddling for something in his bag.

'Tea, coffee, or anything I can get you, Husain saab?' I tried to play the host.

'I see a part of you in me, Dev saab.' He had now taken out a blank sheet of paper, and a couple of crayons from inside his bag. He started drawing as he continued, 'Your carefree creative restlessness—all very colourful.'

The world-famous M.F. Husain's spontaneous desire to come all the way to see me purely on his own personal initiative raised my status in my own eyes, and his signature on the colourful sketch he drew of me with a few quick bold strokes remains permanently engraved in my heart.

Sixty-seven

The Association of Indians in America also invited me to honour me for my services to the movie industry on the occasion of my completing fifty years in films. America and Canada were agog with excitement, and effusive in their outpourings of love and affection for me. The expatriate Indians felt elated interacting with a man they had seen and admired in the movies once upon a time when they were in their homeland.

I travelled from one state to another, meeting people and talking to them in groups or on public platforms, and receiving keys to various cities from their respective mayors. It was all a very rewarding experience for me, and gave a nice shine to my armour of achievements. I kept growing inside, constantly adding to my knowledge.

In Austin, the capital of Texas, with its picturesque hills and breathtaking landscapes, the mayor encouraged me to start my business there, as he graciously offered me the key to the city at a public reception.

In San Francisco, I announced on the stage that one day I'd honour all those associated with Navketan for the last fifty years in a city of my choice, a very flamboyant sentimental statement born at the spur of the moment. The people in the jam-packed hall delightedly screamed with one voice, 'San Francisco should be the place!'

I went on to Los Angeles, the city of angels, where Hollywood reigns, the thought of which had been my inspiration during my formative years. Its inhabitants stood up to cheer me when I said I was in the midst of a dream I had long lived with and was now inhaling the fragrance of a place that had inspired my own creative work.

Atlanta gave me the girl I cast in my next film, a Muslim from a rigid orthodox family, but such die-hard fans of mine as to allow their daughter to go in front of the camera under my direction.

In Las Vegas I was given a plaque and a wreath of honour, with an invitation to visit the most flashy of its casinos and glamorous shows whenever I wanted throughout my lifetime.

In Dallas, the Indian motel owners from all over America, hundreds of them, had a field day watching *Gangster* in a big hall, and later lapped up every sentence of my speech honouring their contribution not only to the Indian society in America, but also to the American economy.

The next city on the tour was New Orleans, where all the Indian settlers lined up on either side of the red carpet spread for me at the entrance to the reception hosted in a mansion, giving me a heart-warming ovation as I stepped out of the limousine.

On to Washington DC, where the entire Indian community toasted my health and well-being and progress, while one of them, having seen *Gangster* earlier, stood up condemning the blatantly shot bold rape scenes in the film; I discovered, to my amazement, that Indians abroad are sometimes more Indian than the Indians back home.

In San Diego, as I entered the theatre in which *Gangster* was being screened, with my friend and fan Dr Parvin Syal, young Afghan girls surrounded me with a charm that combined the rustic and the rugged of the Afghan mountains with the modern sophistication of an American city.

In Bakersfield, California, a granary town, the mayor informally walked into the gathering of fans around me to pin a brooch on my sweater, welcoming me to his city—a green insignia that I still have not removed from my green cardigan, for it matches its colours so well, adding to its elegance.

I went on to Vancouver in Canada, where Indians have risen to grand success and sit side by side with their Canadian counterparts in the legislative assemblies and the parliament of that country. They honoured me as songs from my films played in the background, and I regaled them with anecdotes relating to the great Indian entertainment industry and its gossipy sidelights.

My next stop was Victoria, also in British Columbia, where Sikhs from the British regiments in India went with Queen Victoria and never returned to the country of their birth, making British Columbia their home, having loved the picturesque place and its cool bracing climate. I was deeply moved by their hospitality and affection.

The day I was leaving Victoria to take the ferry to Vancouver, leaving my heart behind with my new friends, Jesse Gill, my host, took me to breakfast with an Indian couple whose dream of having me over at their beautiful home was fulfilled. They feasted me with hot delicious parathas made in the Punjabi style, especially cooked by the lady of the house with her own hands. She was in her mid-forties, but I could see the longing of a teenager in her as she rushed into her room like a schoolgirl wanting one more favour. She brought out a magazine, yellowed with age, a thirty-year-old issue of *Filmfare* that she had preserved for the day when she would succeed in taking the autograph of her favourite movie star. The magazine carried a blow-up of mine on the front cover. It immediately took me back three whole decades, and I froze for a couple of seconds. Then I took my Mont Blanc pen out of my pocket and signed my name on it. She said 'Thank you' in such an adorable way as if she was still in her teens, like she must have been when she bought the magazine.

Toronto sang and danced to the rhythm of the musical numbers from my various films, ending with '*Dum maro dum*', as it celebrated my birthday on 26 September. The gathering was in a frenzy, as cameras clicked and flashed all over, recording the moment.

'And this one is after thirty years, Dev saab!' said a voice from behind a flashing camera, clicking me along with a lady standing next to me. I looked at him. 'And that's my wife I have clicked you with!' he said jovially.

'We have a photograph of you with us on our wedding day!' she was saying, happy and excited like a child. She had the photograph in her hand, and showed it to me. It showed a young Punjabi couple with me smiling away between them; it dated back to the days of *Guide*. I remembered the moment in a flash, with Mr and Mrs Senger, married in Kapurthala thirty years ago, holding my arms again, in a faraway country where they had settled down. It is a small, small world.

Another memorable incident happened on my Canada tour. An ardent fan had been writing to me consistently for fifty years, first from Delhi, and then from Toronto, where he migrated along with his family. When he read in the newspapers that I was visiting his city, he entreated me in a letter to do him the honour of sharing a cup of tea with them at their residence. Since I had a lot of affection for him for his never-wavering loyalty to his favourite actor, I accepted his invitation. I drove to his apartment and shared a few moments of joy with his family. For them it was as if the god they worshipped had suddenly appeared in their midst and their prayers were fulfilled. As I bade farewell to the family and took the elevator down, the mother came rushing down the steps all the way from the third floor and thrust a sealed envelope into my hands. I tried to open it and see what it contained, but she stopped me from doing so, saying, 'This is a long-nursed desire in my heart, to one day meet the man I've adored and worshipped for forty-five years. Please open the envelope only after you reach your hotel.'

Her eyes were moist with emotion as she said this. I raised my hand clutching the envelope to my forehead as a gesture of respect for her sentiments, sat in my car and drove away. When I opened the envelope I found that it contained a small moorty of a deity along with a thousand Canadian dollars, and a few lines written in her hand that said, 'This small moorty is to always protect the man I worship—always keep it close to you. And the money is an offering, also to the man whose image is like that of a god to me! Please do not refuse this offering from a devotee to her god.'

A thousand dollars coming from an Indian middle-class home was probably a good portion of their lifetime's savings. It was like spending a fortune to have a darshan of the idol they adored. I imagined them, sitting in front of the little temple they had installed in a corner of their small sitting room, their eyes closed, their hands folded, their lips moving in fervent prayer as images of me from my films passed through their minds.

I telephoned her, thanking her for the deeply touching gift, but also telling her that I was returning the money—for only by returning it could I turn their gesture into a million dollars' worth! That the amount would be better utilized in the temple of their humble domesticity, and that only then would the moorty of the deity she had presented me be better propitiated.

From Toronto I travelled with my host Kush Agnihotri by car to Quebec and Montreal, both very French in language and character, where the sidewalk cafés remind one of the left bank in Paris. Then to Ottawa, very British, where the Indian High Commissioner threw a cocktail-cum-dinner party and popped the corks of its best champagne with such delightful gaiety that the Indian saris in the gathering mixed with the western skirts to toast a man whose songs had regaled them from his earliest films to his latest. It was a classy Indo-Canadian extravaganza.

The receptions held for me in America were in celebration of the still growing phenomenon of a man who had more than half a century ago started with nothing, but had dreamt of scaling the dizzying heights of success, much like the Indian immigrants abroad. I enjoyed meeting them all, men and women who had left the shores of their homeland as virtual nonentities, and were now very important people in their own fields in a new country, flourishing and prospering, owning estates and mansions, and holding positions that were the envy of even the local inhabitants. I learnt from them, and from their achievements, like a student. Life teaches us at all levels. People who inhabit the Earth are teachers as well as students, learning from each other all the time. Each in his or her own way, from an ordinary coolie to a multimillionaire, from an uneducated vagabond to a learned professor, from an ordinary mechanic to a top industrialist, gives to the other that something that the other does not have. And one keeps learning, in a non-stop process that has no limits. There is no such thing as the last milestone. Every time you reach a landmark or a goal, another one comes into view up ahead in the distance.

Sixty-eight

During my whirlwind tour, a young girl kept following me, wanting to speak to me, but never finding the chance to do so. People would not let her come close to me and whenever she managed to reach the place she thought I was staying in, I had left for another destination. Ultimately when she did succeed in reaching and confronting me she was utterly speechless.

A picture of innocence, she kept looking at me, quite out of breath, full of words, but no words coming forth from her lips, bursting to say something but not picking up the courage. 'Take your time,' I said.

She closed her eyes for a few seconds to gain her composure, then, opening them, could only manage to say, 'I can't believe it!'

'Believe it. For hasn't your belief, if it was to meet me, brought you thus far, face to face with me?' I bucked her up.

She nodded, closed her eyes again, opened them after several seconds and said, 'I want to meet you alone!'

I laughed. People around me, amused, moved away, giving her the chance to have a private word.

'Not here. They'll all make fun of me,' she said.

'Nobody will. Who are they to make fun of anybody? They are all funny themselves,' I tried to give her confidence.

'Yes,' she nodded. 'They never let me come close to you!'

'But I am so accessible! Don't you see?' I said.

She nodded again, 'I am happy I followed my heart and insisted.'

'Now say what you want to say,' I said encouragingly.

She closed her eyes once again, and after a few seconds murmured in a barely audible tone, 'I can't.'

'Don't then, if you can't,' I was on the point of impatience now.

Her eyes still closed, she now mustered courage and said, 'But I must.'

I discerned tears rolling down her cheeks. She wiped them, eyes still closed.

'I have only one ambition,' she suddenly said, opening her eyes.

'What is it?' I asked sympathetically.

'I want to be in a film opposite you!' she finally blurted out.

I had a hearty laugh, at the innocence of her statement, at the impossible dream she was harbouring. Her innocence was now showing all over her face. Even her nose that seemed a little crooked earlier seemed to blend with that innocence, looking just right on that face.

'You are a very beautiful girl, you must know that,' I pampered her. She smiled a heavenly smile. 'And you deserve much, much more. And much better than your dream!' I continued.

She was eager to hear more. 'And one day you will get sweeter fruits of life than your current obsession,' I finished. She looked reassured.

'Go back home,' I said, 'to where you came from. Let time go by. And if, later, you still think the way you think now, I'd love to hear from you.'

She had no answer.

'Ok?' I asked.

She finally nodded, saying, 'Yes.'

'I can see an autograph book in your bag, dying to be taken out,' I said, looking at one that was almost falling out of her bag. She smiled with total adoration.

I took the autograph book before it fell to the ground, looked at her and asked, 'Do I have the privilege of signing my name on one of its pages?' She nodded, with a winning blush.

'And I shall also give you my address in India, you can always write to me.' I scribbled a few more lines underneath my autograph, then put the autograph book into her bag, closed it for her, and made sure she had a smile on her face when she finally left.

The girl could not have been more than sixteen.

This incident of a teenager obsessed with a burning desire to act opposite me, a much, much older man than her, a star whose image she couldn't get off her mind as it possessed her completely, took hold of me, never leaving the innermost recesses of my mind throughout my trip to the States.

I was in Atlanta at a popular dancing joint, when a group of young girls came running to me with autograph books. The prettiest of the lot was the first to step forward, and she naughtily held forth the palm of her hand in front of me, while the others took out their autograph books.

'An autograph!' she said.

'A very cute hand!' I remarked, looking at it.

'You may read it!' she said with equal aplomb. There was mischief in her eyes and the innocence that only young age has.

The idea of a teenage girl falling in love with a much older star was lurking in my mind. My eyes suddenly became a camera screening the possibility of this particular girl in that role. I wanted to keep watching her expressions further, with her hand extended towards me. So I planned my lines to let the moment linger for as long as possible.

'But this hand of yours . . .' I said and deliberately paused, watching her.

'What?' she asked.

'Your . . . hand in front of me . . .' I looked quickly at her hand and back at her.

'Yes, what?' she asked curiously.

'Why . . . is it in front of me?' I asked very slowly.

'For an autograph!' she repeated, smiling like a little naughty girl this time, as her companions giggled.

'But . . . for that you need . . .' I purposely stretched my lines, pinning my gaze on her.

'What?' she said again.

'What do you need . . . to sign an autograph with?' I asked.

'A pen!' she said.

'Where is it?' I asked, my eyes still on her.

She laughed looking at her friends, and then back at me as one of them passed on a ballpoint pen to me.

'No. Let it be. I shall write on it without a pen,' I said. My eyes were noting the fast-changing expressions on her face. She was now blushing very charmingly.

I ran my index finger down the palm of her hand, scribbling 'Dev' in slow motion, and asked her, 'Did you make out what I wrote?'

She blushed crimson and said, 'Y-e-s,' prolonging the word fascinatedly.

'I have not just written my name. I have engraved it on the palm of your hand, and the pen can go back to the pocket it came out from.' I took the pen that the girl was holding and handed it back to its original owner with all the charm of the star the girls had come to meet so excitedly.

She laughed now and clapped her hands, her tresses falling on her forehead. She swept them back into place, becoming self-conscious, and said, 'I wish my mom was here!' Then she ran away, giggling, stopping suddenly midway to look back at me, and then disappearing from the scene.

The camera of my eyes had registered all her movements. She had passed the test so naturally that she needed no screen test after that. Meanwhile, the story for the film was taking shape in my mind.

A few minutes later, when we were sitting in the lounge, she again passed right in front of me, this time deliberately giving me an impish smile of a little familiarity.

Later, as I got into the car to go back to my hotel, she brought a couple of flowers, and held them out to me, one, a very large one, and the other very small, both very selectively chosen.

'For you!' she said.

'Thank you!' I said.

'Can I meet with you in Atlanta again?' she asked.

'I wanted to ask you the same question!' I answered. My hosts gave her the name of the hotel and the number of the suite I was staying in. She wrote it down in pencil on the same palm of her hand, as her friends giggled again!

Next morning she called. I knew she would. 'Hello!' I said as I picked up the phone.

'Hello,' she said, enticingly.

'I know who it is. I forgot to ask you your name!'

'Shiasta!'

'Shiasta! Would you do a film with me, if I asked you?' I came straight to the point.

'Yes!' There was an instant excitement in her voice. 'Can I come and see you?'

'Come over,' I said. She fitted the role I had in mind exactly.

She was an altogether different girl when she came this time, wholly keen and charged with determination.

'But you are too young to make an independent decision, Shiasta,' I said. 'Would your parents allow you to do a film?'

'With you, yes.'

'What if they don't?'

'I shall defy them'

'I wouldn't like that. You said something about your mom last evening at the disco.'

'She'd love to speak with you.'

'Connect me to her!'

She did. 'Hello!' came her mother's voice, subdued, as if expecting my call.

'You have a very sweet darling of a daughter,' I began.

She listened quietly.

'She has given me an idea for a film that I would like to do with her.' I did not beat about the bush.

There was no answer from her.

'Are you listening?' I asked.

'Yes, Dev saab!' she said.

'Will you allow your daughter to do a picture, directed by me and starring in it too?'

'I have brought her up all these years only for you, Dev saab!' she said. 'Take her along.'

I was swept off my feet by her answer.

Shiasta's father was equally flattering. 'We are a Muslim conservative family, and wouldn't have allowed our daughter to step out of home for a career in films,' he said. 'But for a man like you, whom we adore and respect, I find no problem in sending Shiasta wherever you want to take her.'

The parents reposed their complete confidence in me. And I

felt very responsible towards Shiasta whom I gave the screen name 'Sabrina', after another pretty teenager I met in Atlanta, also of Indian origin, whose ambition in life was to be an astronaut. American kids are determined and independent minded, and on their own ever since they come of age. They take their own decisions about how they want to lead their lives and brook no interference, even from their very own, when it comes to making up their minds about their future.

As the story of *Main Solah Baras Ki* was taking shape, I saw a role for another girl in the plot. Naturally, she too had to be new, so that the two girls could complement each other. It was best to have her from America as well, and my thoughts went back to the evening in Vancouver spent with my fans felicitating me.

A girl had danced to a number from *Guide* on stage. As her performance ended and everybody clapped, she walked up to me with a bouquet of flowers. I stood up and clapped, egging the people along for an encore. They lustily cheered her again. I picked up a flower from the bouquet, kissed it and gave it to her, in appreciation of her performance. She bashfully accepted it and ran away into the wings, while I put the bouquet in front of the gentleman seated next to me, saying, 'You have some great Indian talent in your country.'

'We can export it for you if you need some,' he said in the same spirit. And, in fact, that is what happened. Neeru, the girl who had danced to '*Piya tohse naine lage re*' was the second teenager I cast along with Sabrina in *Main Solah Baras Ki*. She was vivacious, sensuous, overwhelmingly confident and extremely ambitious, and went about achieving her goals nonchalantly, a great formula for success. She joined me for dinner with her family in the hotel I was staying in next evening. Earlier in the day, she had taken me along to a modelling studio for me to have a look at some of the most glamorous photographs taken of hers by the photographer who owned it. The blow-ups were very impressive, flattering her youthfulness and figure. Very provocatively sexy and pretty, she wanted to be prettier on screen, with all the razzle dazzle that goes with stardom, every star wanting to look and be proclaimed the prettiest. Neeru wanted to be in the league of the famous and did not mind in the least being cast in the second role after Shiasta. She radiated the confidence of a winner wanting to be recognized.

With two young girls in the film, the triangle had to be completed by a male newcomer. My hunt was on, and one day a popular guy from the modelling circuit looked through the door of my penthouse, wanting to come in and be interviewed. Jas Arora's eyes and smile had something that gave me positive vibrations about him, and I cast him as well in *Main Solah Baras Ki*.

Sixty-nine

Neeru and Shiasta, whom I now called Sabrina, made a very youthful twosome in the film. To match their freshness, I needed an exclusive unexplored place to shoot in, where no camera crew from India had set foot before.

I chose Scotland, and went location-hunting there. It was just the right place; there was magic in the scenery everywhere, in its countryside, its towns, its valleys and dales, in Edinburgh—which I thought was the prettiest city in the world—and beyond. My whole being was excited. Totally energized in mind and spirit, I was raring to go on my new creative pursuit.

I walked all over like I was in a dream, exploring not only new locations, but also a hidden part of me. One day I saw a great vista emerging just around a bend. I rushed forward in my excitement and suddenly tripped over my shoelaces that had come undone. I fell with a thud over the cobblestones, straight on my chest. The impact of the fall was strong enough to black me out for a few seconds.

A couple of my associates got me back to my feet and anxiously asked, 'Are you ok?'

I had badly bruised my knee and the palm of my hand, and it took me a while to recover, but I was brave enough to murmur, 'Oh, that's nothing,' partly to them and partly to myself, and bent down to tie my shoelaces as soon as I had got up.

'Let's move on!' I said spiritedly.

My mind made up about Scotland, I stayed on there all by myself, putting the finishing touches to my new script. I chose a place in the hills called Pitlochry, booked myself a room in a village hotel. I would walk miles and miles every day to the little townships and into the woods, looking out for filming locations, sometimes taking trains to other Scottish towns to look around the countryside. One such trip took me to Perth.

I had been there once before, about five years ago, on my first trip to Scotland. I had gone to Waterloo station to see Ananya Mukherji off after filming with her in Switzerland for *Sau Crore*. From there I took off for a little holiday for my fatigued mind and body. I had requested my travel agents in London to book me in a quiet serene place somewhere in Scotland, which I was keen on visiting. They sent me by train to the cute little town called Pitlochry, on the way to Edinburgh. It was in the middle of meadows and hills and dales that Scotland is famous for, its countryside immortalized by John Keats, the great English poet.

While there, I saw all that John Keats must have seen in his times, besides a few more embellishments that the modern times had added. I walked along the paths, imbibing of the nature that had so inspired Keats to go romancing with his pen. Strolling around the thick woods smelling of pine, inhaling the fresh air, I could see how easy it must be to want to break into verse in these parts.

I took trains from Pitlochry to other Scottish towns on that vacation. One of the towns I visited was Perth. Perhaps Perth, the Australian city, was named after this Scottish town; or was it the other way round?

Walking out of the secluded railway station in Perth, with not a soul on the street, no sound whatsoever except the stamping of my high leather boots on the cobblestones, I had an interesting encounter. A station wagon passed by me, and then suddenly stopped. I kept walking. Suddenly a voice called, 'Dev saab!'

I thought it was a figment of my imagination and kept walking. The voice called again, this time louder, 'D-e-v s-a-a-b!'

I abruptly stopped and turned around. A man's face peering out of the window on the driver's side was looking at me in wonder and amazement.

'Dev saab!' he repeated, sounding awestruck.

'Yes,' I nodded.

The man jumped out of the wagon and ran towards me.

'Dev saab!' he said for the fourth time, as he stood in front of me, just stopping short of embracing me, with the excitement of a child on his face.

I smiled at his thrilled state, which came from having recognized a movie star.

'You! Here?' was his next utterance.

'Why not?' I answered.

'But . . . how come?' He could not believe his eyes.

'Why not?' I repeated.

'But nobody knows!' He was flabbergasted.

'And nobody should,' I said.

'But—I was only just now—we were watching you—on the video—I'm amazed—thrilled—happy—you—must get into my wagon—right away—I shall take you—wherever—you want to go!' he gushed forth, without stopping to breathe.

'I want to go nowhere. I just want to walk wherever this road takes me,' I said.

'But . . .' he interrupted, pointing at his wagon.

'And I don't want it known that I am here,' I concluded, cutting him short.

'But . . . but you must come to my place. You . . . you have to!' He was not in a mood to let me go.

I smiled.

'Not many people there. Just four or five members of my family, they won't believe that I met you! Of all the places—here! In Scotland! In this wilderness!'

I laughed.

'We are all great fans of yours, and I'm sure you will not let us down.' His excitement was mounting.

'But . . . not now,' I said.

'Where are you staying?' he asked.

'At . . . a few stations away, in a hotel,' I said.

'I shall come to pick you up!' he insisted.

'Give me a call first,' I gave him the hotel card. 'What's your name?' I asked.

'Arif, I'm from Islamabad.'

Next day, as I was exchanging pleasantries with some of the guests staying in the hotel, Arif walked in and said, 'My car is outside, Dev saab, waiting . . . whenever you are free.'

Seeing the eagerness in his eyes, I got into his car.

As we drove along that lonely countryside road, with forests on both sides, the car hurtling and bumping over the grassy pathway, a queer thought crossed my mind. 'What if he kidnaps me? Nobody would know. The entire world would be ignorant of my whereabouts. And he could demand a huge ransom, or kill me!'

Some Azad Kashmir militants had kidnapped an Indian diplomat recently in London. The news had made the newspaper headlines. The kidnappers had killed the diplomat after holding him captive for some time.

It was a strange thought, but not without logic. Arif was a Pakistani, and India–Pakistan relations were far from cordial. It was careless on my part not to have informed the hotel doorman where I was going and with whom. He could have at least noted down the number of the vehicle I was travelling in. In a slightly panic-ridden voice I asked Arif, 'How far is it?'

'We have reached. Another minute, Dev saab!' he said, jolting the car over a thick growth of grass. Then he pulled up in front of a house. I saw his family waiting at the door, and heaved a sigh of relief.

Arif had a small ground-floor tenement that accommodated his family. Seeing me in the flesh, his wife Ayesha was in complete shock. They were all completely bowled over by the fact that a movie star from India, whom they had seen on screen and admired and held dear in their hearts, would come, out of the blue, to their house, after only a brief encounter with Arif on the road. The news could make headlines in the newspapers of their country and Arif hailed a hero!

They served me a most delicious Pakistani spread, and I relished every morsel of it, not having had the luxury of good home food for days and days together while rambling in Scotland. And I cursed myself for my mean thoughts about Arif.

Arif encouraged me to do a film in Scotland. And promised to provide all possible help.

Now, five years later, I was in Perth once again, walking down the same street, cobbled as it was then, and just as deserted. I stopped at the spot where Arif had hailed me from his station wagon, remembering the moment; just then a vehicle passed by, and stopped as it crossed me. I heard a voice call, 'Dev saab!' I looked up to see a familiar figure jumping out of the car and rushing up to me.

'Dev saab!' he repeated, and before I could say anything, joyfully added, 'It's me, Arif!'

'Arif! Again! How are you?' I responded with the same surprised joy.

He embraced me with a warm Punjabi hug, and I reciprocated with the same warmth. I looked at the vehicle he was driving. It was a car this time, one of the new models in vogue. He had become more affluent.

'What a coincidence!' both of us said in unison. We were both wonderstruck. The same place, the same spot, the same time, the same unexpected encounter! 'Who willed it?' we asked each other.

'Allah!' he said, looking skywards. 'But what brings you here again, Dev saab?' he asked.

'Didn't you say, then, that I should make a film in Scotland? My unit is arriving in a few days,' I answered.

'Then I am your production man, Dev saab! You ask for anything, and me and all my folks will help you!'

Big chunks of *Main Solah Baras Ki* were shot in Scotland. The Scottish people were very thrilled and happy that their country was being captured on film for an Indian audience for the first time. After I finished filming there, leaders of a Scottish council held a special dinner for me and my unit. After mutual thanksgiving, a Scottish silver cup, with the emblem of their council embossed on it, was presented to me as a gift from the Scottish people. I kissed it, as I kissed the Scots in my mind for their wonderful help and cooperation extended to me. We had formed a great bond of friendship with each other.

Seventy

Ladakh is another place that is alive in my memory when I think of the days when *Main Solah Baras Ki* was being shot.

Ladakh is a part of India but another world altogether—pure and ethereal, with vast expansive valleys and desert landscapes, soft ashen-red rocks, and other-worldly monasteries perched high from where the chants of Buddhist monks float down like ghostly music, just as the Indus river in all its majesty flows down the Indus valley.

The highest mountain pass in India is located in Ladakh. It is so spectacular and divinely awesome a place that it literally takes your breath away. You start getting out of breath as you reach there, some feel suffocated and dizzy, because of the lack of oxygen in the air. There is a mountain post of the Indian army there, with a major general as its commanding officer, who sits side by side with his second-in-command, keeping vigil on the high frontiers of India, with the Pakistan border on one side, and the Chinese on the other.

I saw some of the most fresh-looking, beautiful girls in Ladakh. The origins of the Aryan race, it is said, were somewhere there, in the central Asian valleys. One Ladakhi girl, of a pure Aryan race, with the freshness of an early morning flower with dewdrops on it blooming away at the caress of the first rays of the sun, was so stunningly beautiful that I could have just stayed there, writing a script and shooting a film on her!

The head Lama of the Thicksey monastery extended all his hospitality to us, and allowed us to shoot the prayer meet there, with cute-looking Ladakhi faces, men and women, young and old, lining up on the monastery parapets, silhouetted against the glistening snows of the high mountains behind. The magical strains of the bagpipers of the region accompanied by the drum beats of the dancing ladakhis, were in direct contrast to the azaan of the mullahs that reverberated in the precincts of Ajmer Sharief in Rajasthan, where another sequence of the film was picturized.

Thousands of people wanted to shake my hand and be photographed with me in Ajmer. They lined the street and hung out of the balconies of their houses as I stood in an open jeep in front of the Ajmer Sharief dargah. Sabrina, being a Muslim, joined them in their prayers, as they prayed for the well-being of everyone who was part of the unit of *Main Solah Baras Ki.*

The colours of Rajasthan, its orange–yellow sunrise and sunset, the colourful ornaments worn by the young rustic maidens, and the multicoloured turbans of the menfolk, as well as the great sweep of Jaisalmer, its golden fort and its sand-dunes, all combined to make the film very pleasing to the eye. I was quite happy with its outcome, with its grandeur of locations, its innocent theme, and the three young newcomers enacting the main roles.

To give the project an extra push I approached the star of the millennium, Amitabh Bachchan, to lend his magic touch by releasing the music cassette of the film. He graciously accepted my request.

Together, we drove in his van, closely guarded by his security men, to the venue of the function, where waiting cameramen swooped on us, clicking away photographs of the very rare appearance of the two of us together.

Amitabh wore a check shirt, his collar buttoned up. Was it a coincidence? Or was it a deliberate act on his part, having known that I was also wearing a similar check shirt and it was my usual habit to button up the collar? It was no use guessing; we both secretly admired each other, eyeing each other's shirts and the way we wore them!

Having prepared *Main Solah Baras Ki* the way I wanted to for the audience, it was now time for its first screen test by the sentries of the censor board, before it could be released. The 'censoring' of a man's creative effort is the most dramatic element of the whole process that goes into the making of a film. While the film is being reviewed by a committee, its creator often sits outside the theatre, holding his breath, his hands clenched and fidgety, smoking away like a chimney if he is a smoker, or restlessly strolling away up and down and consuming cup after cup of tea or coffee, waiting for the verdict to be delivered by the censor board, which will determine whether his film can be shown to the general public in its entirety, or whether it needs to be cut, excised or indeed mutilated so that it doesn't offend the moral and cultural norms of the nation.

Those few hours of waiting are the culmination of an artist's work and labour, intellectual as well physical, spanning a year or even two. His destiny at that moment is completely in the hands of the committee sitting in the dark auditorium, who can pass or hold back the film at their discretion from the millions of people waiting to see it.

My moment of reckoning had arrived. I was called in to face the board that had just seen *Main Solah Baras Ki*. As I stood before them, all of them holding back their real feelings about it and putting on deadpan expressions, one comment was unanimously and spontaneously expressed on behalf of them all by the regional officer—'A good, sensitive, innocent film'—to which their heads nodded together.

'Thank you!' There was a sign of relief on my face.

'But,' the regional officer continued, glancing at the written notes in front of her, 'a few cuts are required.'

I tensed up slightly.

She raised her face and said, 'A little more sensuous than necessary,' and paused.

I waited for the next bit. 'A bit too much of sex,' she was now saying.

'Where?' I asked.

'In the scene that has a hint at nudity,' she looked at her papers again.

'Where is it?' I wondered.

'A teenage girl is asked to lower her blouse,' she read her comment. I now knew which scene she was referring to, and butted in.

'But she doesn't—nor is she asked to do it—to a point of revealing her breasts.'

'But a teenager, and at that growing age!'

'But . . .' I started, but before I could continue with my argument, she was talking about the next suggested cut.

'And of course, more serious and objectionable, that drinking scene of yours!'

'What's wrong with it?' I really was at a loss.

'We don't allow alcohol! And certainly not in the hands of Dev Anand. It sets an example for the youngsters. They hero-worship you!'

'They all know that even Dev Anand drinks at times—socially,' I refuted her argument.

'No! That has to go. It does not look nice. A great hero like you, holding a glass of whisky!' she was emphatic.

'But I do that. It's natural. Don't thrust your morals on me!'

'No, it has to go!' she was now obstinate.

'But that's an important scene. Kindly don't cut it,' I now pleaded. She smiled; they all did.

'And the other cut as well,' I continued with my persuasion, 'it's a very innocent shot, certainly not crude or vulgar!'

She nodded, as if in acceptance of my pleadings, and said, 'A good film! Come and take your certificate tomorrow. You may send someone. You needn't take the trouble yourself.'

'I shall come myself, this film is my baby, and I have to hold it in my arms and take care of it,' I said.

The next day, I was at the censor office, sitting in front of the officer. She handed their letter over to me, suggesting the same cuts argued the previous day. I read through the letter, and pleaded my case again, with fresh arguments. She was very sweetly adamant and said, 'If you don't agree, I shall recommend another screening committee for your film.'

The film went to the revising committee. They too admired the film, and waived a few insignificant cuts that made no difference to the film. But they insisted that the major part of the drinking scene had to be slashed, while agreeing to retain a semblance of it. I perseveringly fought for it. They finally yielded to my viewpoint and agreed to let it go without any cuts for public exhibition, if I compromised by shortening the scene involving the young girl asked to lower her blouse. After a great deal of bargaining, both parties were happy and I went back satisfied that at least the drinking scene would not be affected by the scissors of the censor board.

But when I got the final letter, duly signed by the officer, I did not find the cut of the drinking scene having been waived as discussed and agreed upon by the revising committee. It ordered slicing off a big chunk of the scene, thus disturbing the rhythm of my own performance. It infuriated me.

Sitting in the car going back to my studio, with the censor verdict in my hand, I thought the censor board was being very high-handed, autocratic and authoritarian. After having agreed to waive a cut, it was still included in the letter handed over to me. They were toying with my film, I thought.

My mind went back to my earlier film *Gangster*. I had to go as far as the tribunal with a sitting judge of the high court viewing it, and he passed it in its totality, giving me an 'A' certificate, while all the earlier committees had insisted on giving an 'A' certificate with lots of cuts that would have hindered the flow of the film.

I could have taken a stand on this film too and fought till the end, but I was committed to a date for the film's premiere in aid of the Prince Charles Benevolent Fund in England, at the Majestic theatre in Leicester Square. Time was running out. There was no recourse left except to accept the cuts, which I did.

But inside, I was angry with the functioning of the censor board, its outdated, outmoded code, out of tune with the times, and the inconsistency of its verdicts, varying from film to film. I was in a mood to hit back and retaliate. The creative process in me intensified and I decided to tell my country what I thought of the censorship system and its laws in today's context. Another film was in the making in my mind; I would call it *Censor*.

The rough storyline and a hazy sketch of the characters started being drawn on the canvas of my mind. I needed absolute isolation to help my thinking process. I drove to Mahabaleshwar, which I always do when I want to be completely by myself, and booked myself in my favourite old-world-charm hotel, Frederick's. The hotel promises all that I need, quietitude and no disturbance, and a view as far as the eye can see. The hotel always puts me up in my desired room, the absolute last room beyond which there is no other, and a room that, therefore, has no neighbour.

I started writing furiously. Ideas flow as my pen feels the touch of paper on its tip. I don't type for I can't, and when I'm writing, time ceases to be. I forget all about thirst or hunger. The flow of words dictated by the onrush of thoughts are food and drink to me. My excitement is what sustains me.

The doorbell rang at 9.30 p.m. and was ignored. Half an hour later, a loud rap sounded on the door like a danger signal. 'Saab, are you coming for dinner or shall I bring it here?' It was one of my favourite waiters, familiar with my whims and habits.

'I shall come,' I responded, realizing my fingers were showing signs of fatigue. I decided to abandon the flow of my thoughts for the moment, and opened the door.

It was dark. A faint light glowed somewhere in the distance between me and the dining hall, on a lamp post. I jumped down the steps in front of my door, in a hurry to quickly go, eat and come back, and hit against a big stone boulder, lying carelessly on the ground. I fell flat on my chest.

It was a severe fall that could have been fatal. The sound of it resonated in the emptiness of the dark night. But there was nobody around, nobody came to my aid. I gathered together all my inner strength and got up, limping carefully to the dinner table, gradually becoming aware of where the hurt lay after the initial stunned sensation. It was between my ribs and abdomen, and it was my third fall injuring the same area.

Back in Mumbai a few days later, as I was coming back home one evening with a few books and notebooks in my hand, a voice called me from behind, from a balcony in my neighbourhood, as I stepped out of the car. The voice belonged to a young schoolgoing fan and I always looked back and responded as she waved in girlish enthusiasm. But this time, burdened with the reading material in my hands and lost in my thoughts, my foot slipped over a slab of stone as I absent-mindedly tried to turn to the source of the voice. My books and notebooks slipped out of my hands and in an attempt to catch them before they fell on the stony surface, I stumbled and fell bang on my stomach and chest, stifling a painful shriek.

'Uncle!' screamed the girl, concerned about me, but I, putting on a brave face, responded 'I am fine,' with a flying kiss of elderly affection. This was the fourth fall of the series, within a reasonably short span of time. The very first one was the result of a blow delivered by Dharmendra, my colleague whom I have always loved and admired, on the sets of *Return of Jewel Thief*, in which he was co-starring with me. (The second fall, of course, was in Scotland.)

He was to throw a punch at me, and I had to take it. The timing was perfect. But my foot tripped over the pebbly gravel scattered all over the ground as I gave the proper jerk to my face, registering the hit. Tumbling down, my other foot slipped on the pebbles as well, and in an attempt not to fall over and hurt a couple of female bit players sitting behind me, I took a somersault, landing on a block of stone that injured me badly. The impact of the fall was not only hard on my chest and belly, but my nose too started bleeding.

People participating in the scene were panic stricken. But I got up and kept on shooting, and went to the doctor for the dressing of my nose only after the scene was finished properly.

The bandage had to be on my nose for more than ten days, and when it was finally removed, the injury left a scar, a mark on the bridge of my nose, and a little crookedness, which I still carry.

Seventy-one

The world premiere of *Main Solah Baras Ki* was held in London. The elite of the Indian community was present. Sabrina flew in from Atlanta, Neeru from Vancouver and Jas from Mumbai, to hold one another's hands on stage, greeting the premiere audience as I introduced them to the invitees and the press.

The cocktail party that followed the show was very much in keeping with the spirit of swinging London. There, suddenly, I recognized a young girl who was walking up to me with a dazzling smile; she held out an autograph book with my signature and my address on it. It was the same girl I had met in the States, the girl who had wanted to act opposite me, the inspiration behind the main character of *Main Solah Baras Ki*. She had left America to join an arts' college in London. When I asked whether she was still hung up on her acting ambition, she said, 'Thanks to you that phase of my obsession has been left behind. I am very happy now in London. I am painting the world!'

Main Solah Baras Ki did not fare well at the box office. There must have been some discordant note in it that the audience did not take to. A movie is like the combined notes of all the instruments that play melodiously and in total harmony in an orchestra. If a single note of any one instrument goes out of tune with the rest, it breaks the flow, creating displeasure.

Something must have gone wrong with *Main Solah Baras Ki* that made it unacceptable to moviegoers, for which I, as the conductor of the orchestra, have to take the blame, though there are many aspects that can contribute towards the non-performance of a film. The factor of newcomers being accepted or rejected by the audience also plays an important part in the success of a film.

And, of course, besides its making, the distribution and exhibition sectors, along with the publicity for the film, are key factors that can make a film a flop or a runaway hit.

And after all is said and done, it still needs the blessings of heavenly grace! When a good film becomes a hit, the heavens are clearly on its side. And if it does not, it is probably because the gods must have taken umbrage at some discordant notes in its symphony.

The chapter of *Main Solah Baras Ki* was over. The pages of a new one were being written. The past had gone by, the future was beckoning. My new film *Censor* was now the focus of my concentration. Its sequences were being drafted and redrafted in my mind, ideas were being born, developed and demolished, to be born again, while I was still in London in the aftermath of the release of *Main Solah Baras Ki* and its premiere in Glasgow.

One evening, I came out of Churchill Hotel where I was staying, and walked on, immersed in my thoughts. Oxford Street was a little way ahead, vibrant as always, full of movement, as if all of humanity was out on a shopping spree. I immersed myself in it, moving along with the crowds, lost in my thoughts.

Suddenly, I felt a pang of pain in my abdomen. I stopped walking, and it subsided. I moved forward again. A few minutes later, I had to stop again. The pain persisted. I felt like sitting down, but made an effort to rush back to the hotel.

My younger sister who lives in England was waiting for me in the lobby, with my brother-in-law and a nephew of mine, who is a very well-established surgeon in Surrey. I told him about my pain. He took me to my room, inspected me and hinted at the first signs of hernia. I was alarmed, but not scared, for, as he put it, it is a common ailment that results from a tear in the abdomen.

All the physical falls I had had in the recent past one after the other had left their impact, now resulting in this painful ailment. The injury demanded immediate attention to save me from further risk. The surgeon suggested a quick surgery. As I gave him a long look, he said, 'Half an hour on the operation table, and next day you'll be back in Oxford Street, doing your shopping!'

But I had to get back to Mumbai. I had accepted to be the chief guest at the opening of the international film festival of India in

Hyderabad, and the date was not far. The healing of the abdomen would certainly take much more time than the surgeon had suggested to humour me. I postponed the surgery.

Back in Mumbai the same evening, I had a searing pain in my abdomen again. I groaned, and lay flat on my bed. The pain gradually subsided as I kept pressing the part of the abdomen that hurt, and finally vanished.

But I was now worried, restless and nervous. The festival function in Hyderabad was the very next week. What if a similar attack of pain suddenly struck me while I was on stage, facing the gathering with a microphone in my hand? All I needed was to be careful, I told myself to shore up my own moral strength—and leave the rest to chance!

Seventy-two

Hyderabad welcomed me with open arms. The stadium where the film festival was inaugurated was jampacked. My speech, futuristic in tone and content and full of optimism, was hailed by the crowds that gave me a standing ovation. A chorus of voices of female fans reached my ears from the far end of the stadium saying, 'We love you!' 'And I have always loved you all!' I reciprocated with a resounding voice. A renewed ovation followed.

Chandrababu Naidu, the chief minister of Andhra Pradesh, accompanied me in his personal car on the way to the venue where the festival delegates and important dignitaries of the state were assembling for lunch. While exchanging views with him, admiring his state for the rapid progress it was making in electronics and his own personal achievement as a progressive chief minister, we formed a good rapport. I had met his father-in-law N.T. Rama Rao, an actor of my generation, many years ago at an awards function as well, before he floated his political party Telugu Desam, and had found him impressive.

At lunch, the secretary of the information and broadcasting ministry asked me why I had planned a controversial film like *Censor*. My answer was that the film would not hurt anybody, but it may open the closed minds of the authorities, who should be aware of the growing openness of Indian society, especially the youth. India is a strong nation, and instead of getting bogged down by orthodox, conventional stereotypes, our nation must keep pace with the fast-moving times. Sitting in a small village in India, one could now watch all that was happening around the world. Satellite television had broken all barriers of accessibility and communication. The doors to the world were wide open to us, and Indian society must open up too. While retaining its own identity and culture, it had to imbibe the best of the outside world for its own growth and progress, discarding some of its hypocritical, irrelevant norms and sentiments that sometimes went in the name of culture and heritage. My attempt at making a film like *Censor* was only a step in that direction, debunking the outdatedness, and forcefully advocating the need to walk in step with time.

My argument appealed to his educated, intelligent sense, and he congratulated me. Meanwhile, I was congratulating myself for not letting the hernia disturb and inconvenience me during my public appearances in Hyderabad.

But it certainly had to be operated on. I could not live with the thought of a physical disability that would cause me pain at any time and retard the pace and rhythm of my creative work.

Any good surgeon in Mumbai could do it. But the grapevine would spread shock waves across the country, saying that the 'evergreen', 'forever young' man of unstinted energy, gifted by the gods with 'eternal youth' in the minds of his countrymen, was not, after all, what they took him to be, but an ordinary mortal like them all, who could be laid low by a mere hernia.

I decided to let the myth continue, and not disturb my hard-earned aura. I took a flight to London instead and landed up at my sister's residence, called my surgeon nephew, and gave him the reason for my arrival. He registered me in a hospital in Surrey.

A couple of days before my date with destiny, he drove me to his home. The drive from Walton-on-Thames to Farnham, where he had a beautiful mansion amidst wooded surroundings, had always been refreshing since it followed a scenic route through the famous English countryside. But this particular drive had a special dramatic element attached to it. I was being driven to Farnham to be thrust into the hands of the Healers. Never before had I thrown myself at the mercy of doctors, becoming totally helpless and looking up to them for succour. But now, a team of doctors was going to submit me to a state of complete docility; they would throw me onto a stretcher, gaze down upon me, examine me from the inside as well as outside, draw up a list of my strengths and weaknesses, then put me under the knife, cutting into me however they saw fit. I would neither be able to protest nor cry. I felt weak and helpless at the thought.

But then, being a man who loved new experiences all the time, I was also excited at the thought that I would be travelling into the land of the unknown once I was made unconscious.

I visited the hospital I was booked in a day before the operation, for routine blood and heart tests. 'You are a very young man!' said the middle-aged nurse who conducted the tests.

'Sure, miss,' I replied, and we grinned at each other.

The next day I was back in the hospital, for my exclusive date with my new friends-to-be, my nurses, my surgeon and his assistants.

I was stripped of all my clothes and of all my belongings, and made to wear a white cotton gown. I was like any other patient anywhere in the world. My only identity tag was a cotton band tied to my wrist proclaiming on it my name, age and my surgeon's name. Both he and his two assistants, one of them in charge of anaesthesia, came to see me in my ward to instill a little confidence in me.

During those hollow moments of waiting, as I lay still, looking up at the ceiling, I was in a world devoid of feeling, steeped in nothingness. I tried to divert my mind, and thought of Hampshire, quite close to where I was, the land of Jane Austen, whose books I had read during my honours degree course in English.

My surgeon nephew and Eileen, his Irish wife, had driven me there, before they brought me to the hospital. Jane Austen's cottage, where she lived, worked and died, is now a monument to her. The table she wrote on, the pen she wrote with, the chair she sat on, and the window through which she looked out to the outside world, have all been maintained just as they were some two hundred years ago. As I paid a visit to that glorious past, I reflected how it was once the present. And the present never dies. It only takes on a new shape, becoming what was a second ago the future, as time ticks away.

The clock on the wall in my ward was ticking away too, and two nurses entered now, saying their hellos together. They wore light blue uniforms, with their hair elegantly groomed and styled in the fashion of the day. They were carrying small knick-knacks and tools, and a razor.

'How often do you shave?' one of them asked.

'Every day! Though I did think of growing a stylish beard once. Would I look good in one?' I asked.

'I guess so!' said one.

'I have to think about it,' said the other, and signalled to me to lift my gown and bare my body.

I looked at them enquiringly.

'We have to shave you!' one of them said, and before I could open my mouth to say anything, the other one had raised my gown on her own, and clutched the razor in her hand. They proceeded to shave the hair off and around my groin.

I closed my eyes out of shyness, and opened them only after they had finished their job.

'A few more minutes!' they said, and walked out of the room with the regimented gait of trained nurses used to their jobs, working in a very efficient hospital. As soon as they made their exit, four nurses, male and female, all in green headgear and white gowns, pushed into the room like soldiers on duty, and started wheeling the bed I was lying on out of the room and into the operation theatre.

'Theatre! Again!'

So many theatres I had visited over the long span of my career, wherever my movies had been released. But this one was the most dramatic of them all, with dazzling lights of green and red indicating happenings of acute suspense.

'Would my performance in this one be a hit or a flop?' I asked myself. I had always resigned myself coolly to the fate that befell each of my performances, always enjoyed the verdict pronounced on them. And I would enjoy this one as well, I whispered to myself, as the anaesthetist smiled over my face, preparing to put me out. The nurse injected something, and I was drowned instantly into a state of nothingness, my being transported into total unconsciousness, into unknowing.

There was no pain, no joy, no ego, no self, no wealth, no power, no feeling, no God, no existence!

About an hour after having left the world, I opened my eyes again. They opened themselves with a tremendous, lazy effort. In a quick hazy flash, I saw my doctor nephew coming towards me, with the word 'theatre', written in red lights, over his head, blinking at me. He was smiling, his spectacles perched on his nose, as his words, 'It's all over,' boomed into my ears.

I mumbled in my thoughts, 'But it's just begun! My life!'

Seventy-three

I was wheeled back into my room, given another injection, a painkiller, by the nurse who wore a pendant that hung low around her neck. It came very close to my face as she bent down to administer the injection. After which she left. But the pendant stayed frozen in my sight, getting bigger and bigger till it dissolved into a similar one somewhere in the depths of my memory. I found myself in a world of myriad colours, a romantic phantasmagoria that only the whistling birds in the woods could provide music to.

The birds were flapping their wings and twittering, and butterflies zoomed in and out of sight.

The pendant reappeared, more tantalizing now, as I dug my face into her bosom. She pressed it closer, her warm silky hands clasping me as she gasped for breath in pain mingled with ecstasy.

I slid down lower. She sighed and moaned.

I came, and hid myself between her legs.

'Oh! My darling!' she whispered, kissing me all over the nape of my neck, and then rolling over, revelling in the wetness that was trickling down her naked body.

'I love you!' I said. 'I have never come across such an exquisite body.'

'I was waiting for you,' she said, digging her body into mine, in an embrace that Adam and Eve would envy.

Birds sang around us. The cornfield crackled as we ran in its midst, with the sun playing hide-and-seek from behind the tall stalks. She pulled me down again, and I lay over her. The sugar-cane plants drooped in obedience and covered us with kisses.

A golden ray of light shone its torch over us and passed, as the sun started setting. We responded to its signal and tiptoed out of our paradise, holding hands as we walked into darkness, leaving the buttons of her torn blouse behind in the fields, as a souvenir of my very first romance.

Who was she? It did not matter, for she suddenly dissolved into another being, sitting in front of a mirror in her make-up room.

'You look beautiful in the mirror,' I said admiring her.

She smiled seductively, putting a little more rouge on her cheeks, and looked at me, taking up the blood-red lipstick to caress her lips.

'That invites a kiss!' I approached her.

'I'll never let you,' she answered, turning towards me, with a look that desired a thousand kisses.

'I shall,' I said, looking into her eyes.

'When?' her eyes asked.

'Later!' my eyes replied.

'It will never be, for we are not going to be together again. This is the last day of our filming together, and we are both going our own ways,' she said into the mirror and stood up.

I gave her my hand. She gripped it. I pulled her towards me.

'The shot is ready!' came the assistant director's dull voice, from outside the door, with a knock on it.

'Coming!' we both responded from inside the make-up room.

With a mischievous laugh she dissolved into the mirror. The mirror cracked and shattered into a hundred shards, each reflecting all the colours of the spectrum, filling me with their sensuousness. Another image appeared, pigtailed and naughtily dressed, cycling towards me.

'I am here, all the way from the other world, to wish you good health and a speedy recovery,' said her balmy voice.

'How did you come to know I am in a hospital?' I asked.

'Didn't our hearts meet? Never to let the feeling go?'

'Yes, I remember! We made a pledge to each other.' She was the mama who pampered me, and I was the child, lying beside her, feeling for her bosom all the time, while she fed my intellect. 'She the sermon and I the pages she wrote into,' I was whispering to myself, as the birds flapped their wings again and lulled me to sleep once more, with a butterfly closing my eyelid and resting on it . . .

'Wake up!' She was tickling me.

And we were running, faster and faster, in the back lanes behind tall buildings that were shooting up amidst the rubble and shrubs. A thorny twig came flying into sharp focus and entangled itself in the folds of her sari. She slipped and fell, taking me down with her. We rolled over each other. Her sari came off, and all that was left was the fragrance of two bodies clinging to each other.

'I have written a million letters to you . . . open my soul to read them,' she said, kissing me goodbye. And she disappeared into the setting sun behind the Kanchenjunga, its golden hues turning into a torrent of sea waves that splashed across my face.

The white foam receded gradually, leaving me nestled in the warmth of the velvety femininity of her bosom. She lowered her large dark eyes and consumed me in their depths.

'I dreamt of the most precious ring for you,' I whispered.

'How precious?' she was hardly audible.

It couldn't be more precious than this moment. We were entwined in ecstasy. The midnight stars winked above us. Then they came dancing down in hundreds, and I became one of them. A beautiful ring dangled before me. It touched my face gently in a caress. Then it went flying into the breeze that came from the rustling pine trees, stopping for a moment, and then hurtling down, in slow motion, into the roar of the Arabian Sea, into its bottomless pit.

A door was rudely slammed on my face, and I woke up with the thud of it ringing in my ears.

Hazily I saw the door of my hospital room opening. The same nurse, looking sexier with her pendant outlined against her beautiful neckline, beamed a smile at me.

'How are you feeling?' she asked.

'I was dreaming,' I said.

'Dreams are beautiful, aren't they?'

'You are from here?' I asked.

She nodded, 'Very much. British. But born and brought up in Hong Kong.'

'Hong Kong!' I closed my eyes.

Click-click-click-click—the camera followed her as she came running through blossoms and petals and rays of sunshine, and glistening shadows and whistling winds. Click-click-click-click—

every time the camera clicked, she kissed the lens, and every time she kissed the lens, the world kissed her back. Click-click-click-click—the roll exhausted itself inside the camera.

The spool was rewinding, and the door creaked. The hospital door was opening again, the nurse looking through it.

'You have beautiful eyes,' I was telling the nurse, but she was gone.

'Gone!' I mumbled.

'No, I am not. I am right beside you,' and she laughed like the tinkling of a piano. The piano notes rose to a crescendo, blending into the call of nightbirds as we stood on a rock in the darkness of Malabar Hill.

Our bodies were united in a lingering kiss, my hands searching into the female fragrance of her skirt, hers caressing my waist in an attempt to unfold my manly delight.

A horn sounded. A car screeched to a halt by us. A policeman banged his wooden baton on the ground!

The wheels of the car we were in rolled off the cliff, and as we dropped endlessly, her voice was like a song that said, 'I wish you were not married,' with a longing that would always remain unfulfilled, growing softer and softer until it finally became a ripple in the sparkling wine.

The glasses clinked. Logs of wood crackled in the fireplace. The soul of Jigar Moradabadi was at its romantic best on her lips, as she recited him. Sparks from the molten lava turned into fire within us, blazing like a red furnace. A constellation in the sky outdazzled the rest and shot itself into extinction. Then clouds floated over the stars, covering them.

I pulled at the pallu of her sari, and we went down on the rocks by the rising waves of the sea, sheltered by the green growth around us. Our hearts beat fast as she lay on the grass, like a queen giving her kingdom to her king. 'If God has made anything the most ecstatic on earth, it is this, it is this, it is this,' was the eternal refrain of her being, as glow-worms blinked around us in the darkness of the night, both spying on us and keeping vigil.

The glow-worms turned into neon signs, blinking outside in

the street, as she cuddled close to me on the silky smooth bed. A ball of fire sprang out of a pale yellow neon sign, piercing through the transparent curtains and blinding me.

'Open your eyes,' she whispered. I opened my eyes to look at her. She was suddenly covered in total darkness. 'Recognize me?' came her voice.

'Who?'

'A woman,' she whispered huskily.

'Which one?'

'The conqueror of all men!' she breathed. And a sexily diffused light switched itself on, outlining her as she hovered above me, the two pinnacles of her conquest, with a rosebud on each of the peaks, protruding in their arrogance, shining like giant marbles.

'Of course,' I whispered too, like a humble slave, 'where were you until now?'

'Never away from you. Ask yourself. Am I not always in your thoughts?'

'Always!' I half-whispered to myself, as she bent down to dissolve into me.

The curtains fluttered inwards and began caressing my face. The neon signs turned into twirling Flamenco dancers, tapping their heels. The music soared, enveloping both the lover and the beloved in a Spanish den.

'Rub me! Rub my back!' I said sensually, my eyes half closed in slumber.

The soft drumming of her soothing fingers on my back gradually turned into the hum of an aircraft engine. The plane landed in the middle of a psychedelic mist, on top of a mountain eternally covered by snow.

'Ben Nevis! In Scotland! Haa—it's cold. It's snowing outside. A blizzard!' I thought.

'I am freezing to death,' she said, her teeth chattering. She pressed her body close to mine.

'Are you warm enough now?' I was shivering too.

'No! Not yet!' She was hardly audible.

'Now!' I crushed her to my chest.

'No . . .' It was a prolonged sigh. Our bodies merged into each other. We had no separate entities any longer.

Highlanders! Bagpipes! She emerged from the midst of the music, dangling her bag, removed her sunglasses and jumped straight into my arms. 'I am feeling sexy!' she said, and slipped into my bed, pulling the sheets over us. Her warm breath mingled with mine, her tongue tasting the wholesomeness of me.

'Sleep, my darling, sleep,' she sang a lullaby, and as I closed my eyes in deep slumber, she tiptoed out, leaving me in the lap of my mother.

'Rest, my darling, rest. You need rest. And I am here, watching over you, to protect you,' my mother said.

'But I miss you, Ma, I have always missed you!' I sobbed, for she had disappeared again.

I was still sobbing, and the woman held me in her arms, making me forget my sorrow. 'You are mine! You are mine!' she said, and covered me with kisses.

'Take me!' she moaned.

'What if you conceive!' I said, anxious.

'A beautiful conception! Let it be!'

The sun rose heralding the dawn. She was fast asleep. 'I must leave!' I whispered.

'Your home is here!' she said in her sleep.

'But I must go!'

'Go, but come back, my darling!' And her image evaporated into thin air.

Suddenly, a shooting pain erupted in my groin. It felt like my insides were being slashed with a knife.

My eyes opened with a jerk, as the pain whipped inside me. The nurse on night duty was looking kindly at me. My eyes saw her blurred image, and my lips formed a name—'Nancy', the name of the nurse with the pendant around her neck.

'No, I'm Juliana,' the nurse said. 'I took over from Nancy who was here earlier.'

'She was so sweet,' I said to myself, struggling to open my eyes.

'Am I not as sweet as Nancy?' she smiled.

'You are, too!' I tried to smile. 'Oh! It hurts when I move.'

'You need a painkiller.' She had the pill in her hand, and poured some water into a glass.

'How long have you been in this hospital?' I asked, trying to brave my pain.

'For quite some time. They say you are from India. My husband was in Calcutta working as a manager for a British firm,' she said, putting the pill into my mouth, followed by water.

'Oh yes! Calcutta!' I mumbled.

Mumbling had become a part of my being, and every time I mumbled I went into a delirious past.

The crowds threw her up into the arc-lights, with a shout of 'Encore'. She disappeared in the dazzle.

A pair of spectacles dropped on the ground.

'Pick it up!' I murmured. Juliana, who was still at the door, reacted. 'What?' she asked, coming towards me.

'The specs!' I murmured, my eyes closed.

'Are you feeling all right?' she was asking. I half opened my eyes, and saw Juliana watching me in the half-light.

'You were dreaming!' she said. I tried to smile. 'It was just a dream,' she said reassuringly, and walked away.

'Juliana!' I stopped her. She turned towards me.

'It seems like I'm taking a trip through my past!' I said. She listened silently.

'Along with such wild imagination!' I added.

'It's all these strong medicines inside you,' she tried to explain.

'I relived so many of my forgotten memories,' I mused, 'along with an added fantasy.'

'Go back to them again!' she said. 'I am here—outside. Press that red button when you need me.' She was very sweet.

'Thank you, Juliana,' I said. She smiled benevolently.

'What's the time?' I asked.

'Ten-thirty at night.'

'Oh! I thought it was nearing the dawn!' I said. She laughed.

'Stupid of me!' I mumbled. 'The dawn has yet to arrive. Good night, Juliana—I'm drowsy.' And my eyes closed again.

A tornado of a wave swept over me, and Mona was running on the sands of Juhu beach. I ran fast to catch her. 'Come on! Catch me if you can!' she laughed.

I had almost caught up with her when I tripped and sank in the sands.

Exhausted, face upwards, with the rays of the sun blinding me, I shouted, 'Mona!'

'Come home whenever you want! I don't care!' she shouted back, and ran on.

'Don't you?' I asked.

'No, no, no!' she shouted.

'Don't I come home every night?' I asked. But she was a speck in the distance by now.

'Don't I sleep in my own bed every night?' my lonely voice echoed. But she was nowhere to be seen.

'Don't I have breakfast with you every morning and dinner with you every night? Don't I?' But she wasn't listening.

'Don't I embrace Devina when she comes home from Mussoorie, to the same house where we have lived for years and years? Don't I hug Gina, my darling granddaughter, and shower her with kisses, when she comes home on vacation from Woodstock?' I went on relentlessly. But Mona was nowhere to be seen.

I chased after her, and found her sitting on a rainbow, singing:

Phailee hui hain sapnon ki baahein
Aaja chal de kahin door.

Dreams have spread their arms wide open
Come, let's fly far, far away.

She was enjoying the song all by herself.

'Isn't all that I have yours, Mona? Or Devina's or Suneil's?' I screamed.

But Mona hurriedly sneaked into her room and closed the door, like she always did. She would lock herself up with the maidservant or with her beautician friend from the parlour, or her Jewish friends from Israel and Christian faithfuls from all over, and start indulging in her religious rituals.

Suddenly a scream of hers rent the air in the dead of night. Suneil and I banged the door open. She was being assaulted by a burglar, struggling to free herself from his clutches while stopping him from injuring her body with the razor blade he was carrying. Suneil grappled with him and snatched the weapon from him, but not before he received a slash on his face that made it bloody in an instant.

'Have peace, my son, peace,' I fondled his hair as he received stitches on his face. 'I love you,' I said, kissing the top of his head, 'more than I love anybody else, my son! I want you to be bigger and better than your father! Much, much bigger!'

The temple bells started ringing. Chants of prayers flowed into my room from the Hare Krishna temple nearby. It was dawn. I could not waste so much time, sleeping in bed. Life is so short, and there is so much to do. 'Get up,' I commanded myself in an abrupt murmur, and opened my eyes.

I saw Bonie, my sister, and Raj, my brother-in-law, along with my surgeon nephew Avinash and his wife Eileen being led into my room by Juliana, who was holding a flower.

'And this one is to your dream from last night!' she said, offering it to me.

I smiled like a baby out of its cot. As the big bouquet of flowers, held by my family, started spreading its fragrance, the room started smelling like a fresh garden.

'Mona called, and asked you to call her. So did Goldie and Suneil and Devina and everybody else, all those who know you are here.' Bonie sounded happy and relieved.

I sat up, ready to move out of hospital. Through the chinks of the door to the bathroom, I could see my clothes folded on a chair, my overcoat hanging from a hook, all waiting to be reworn. I had temporarily given them up for the hospital gown.

'I kept them all ready,' said Juliana. 'Would you like to change?'

The sun shone brightly outside. It threw its rays through the branches of a tree, filtering through the glass window and lighting up my face. I found Nancy standing outside the door as well, holding another bouquet on behalf of the hospital.

Back in Farnham, in my nephew's sprawling country home, I convalesced for a week, totally cut off from the outside world. Walking slowly among the tall trees, along winding pathways strewn with leaves, with the smell of early morning dew in the air, and the embracing warmth of the first rays of the sun kissing the morning chill off my face, helped me recuperate fast. I started feeling fresh and alive, as if I had had some sort of rebirth.

With all the time to myself, and left with my own thoughts, I often rambled backwards, remembering things that I rarely thought about because of the constant rush of work. Now, with the forced rest, I could at long last contemplate on some personal, insignificant nothings that once were so precious to me.

Suddenly a desire to speak to my new leading lady in *Censor*, whom I had fondly nicknamed Heenee, came to the fore.

Heenee knew I had gone abroad, to England, but did not know which part of England, for that was a well-kept secret. I had promised to be in touch with her soon and the time was now. In fact, it was my first conversation on the telephone as I broke my silence to the outside world after a long period of hiding.

I did not reveal that I had been operated upon—she might unwittingly spread the word around. I gave another reason for my absence, saying I was rewriting the script of *Censor*, and that I was in a remote place, far away from civilization in the wilds of the English countryside, where no telephone facilities existed. A harmless lie to a girl who was very much in my thoughts.

Seventy-four

My best moments with myself are when I am in front of my mirror in the bathroom. It is there that ideas come rushing to me, as I look at my own reflection.

I was enjoying some such moments, my fingers relishing the feel of the soft shaving foam spread over my face, when there was a buzz on the bathroom extension. I ignored it.

There was another one, a while later. 'Let it ring!' I said to myself, and continued shaving.

The telephone buzzed again. I stopped shaving, picked the receiver up and kept it aside, not in the mood for any incoming calls. But now the chowkidar's voice came through the door.

'There is a call from the government, saab,' he said.

'Put me on!' I said, picking up the receiver.

The caller was an official from the ministry of external affairs, wanting to know if I was willing to accompany the prime minister on his inaugural bus ride to Lahore, Pakistan.

I loved the idea and said, 'Yes, I am!'

'In that case, please fly to Delhi tomorrow. The arrangements for your travel and stay in Delhi will be intimated to you in a couple of hours,' said the official.

I was to shoot the next day. Rubbing the shaving foam off my face with the towel, I rushed into the bedroom, put on my clothes and drove to my studio to announce a postponement of my working schedule.

My staff looked at my face wonderingly. Looking at the same expression on the face of each one of them, I wondered too.

'Why are you looking at me like that?' I asked them. 'Do I amuse you?'

'No sir! Your face!' said one of them.

'What's wrong with it? I am only—a little excited!' I said.

They all laughed. 'It's your beard, sir,' one of them picked up the courage to say.

'My beard!' I retorted. 'I don't have a beard.'

'You forgot . . .' another one said.

'What?' I asked.

'To shave!' said another.

'I did?' My hand went to my chin.

'Show that mirror to sir,' said a third. They turned the small mirror on the wall towards me so that I could see my face.

I discovered that I had shaved my stubble only from one side. The call had come midway through my shave, and I had, in haste, rubbed off the shaving foam with the towel, leaving half my face unshaven. I looked at myself in the mirror and laughed just as my staff had done.

Going by bus to Lahore seemed a great idea. I hadn't had the luxury of travelling by bus for I couldn't recall how many years!

And to Lahore, fifty-five years after I left it! It would be my first visit there after the creation of Pakistan.

And I would be going with the prime minister of my country!

I rode on wave after wave of excitement as I shaved off the other half of my daily stubble.

I took the evening flight to Delhi. There was a government official waiting at the airport, to take me to the hotel I was booked in. Next morning I was driven to the ministry of external affairs, where some of the other members of the delegation invited to go to Lahore with the prime minister had already reported. They included great cricketers like Kapil Dev and Kirti Azad, distinguished newspapermen like Arun Shourie and Kuldip Nayar, and Javed Akhtar, the famous lyricist. Official cards and badges were handed over to each of us, and our passports collected. We were then ushered into a bus that would take us to Hindon air force station in the outskirts of Delhi. From Hindon, an air force plane took us to Amritsar.

Amritsar is to the Sikhs what Mathura and Kashi are to Hindus, Mecca to the Muslims, the Vatican to the Catholics, and Jerusalem to the rest of the Christian world. The Golden Temple, with the constant chants from the Granth Sahib, pilgrims with their heads bent in reverence, the crowded bazaar, and a seventeen-year-old boy, with a prayer in his heart for his dying mother, sweating in the sultry summer day, standing in front of a Sikh sherbet vendor who saw the sun rising on his forehead and foretold his rise to stardom—the images flashed through my mind. It had all started here, way back in 1940.

I got off the aircraft with the rest. We walked into a shamiana, our hands folded in a namaskar. Sardar Prakash Singh Badal, the chief minister of Punjab, received us with the same gesture. A member of the legislative assembly from Gurdaspur, not far away from where we were meeting, reminded me of my birthplace. A fresh wave of emotion took hold of my heart.

Was the Tibri canal still flowing the same way it did more than half-a-century ago? Was the railway phatak still there, on the way to the canal from the town? And the electric poles, which told us how far away the train was, when as kids we put our ears to them, fascinated by the sound of the approaching train reverberating inside them, were they still standing? And the Jhoolna Mahal, that shook as we sat on its wall, was it still shaking just so?

I rattled off questions like a non-stop machine gun to the member of the legislative assembly from my hometown, with the curiosity of a child.

'They are all there. Everything that you mentioned,' he answered laughingly. 'But the most important thing is not there!'

I looked at him enquiringly.

'The most important son of Gurdaspur, who the town is proud of!' he said.

Soon we were on the bus. It had been decorated specially for the occasion, like a bridegroom travelling to a wedding, with all the excitement and festivities accompanying it.

Destination, Lahore!

Seventy-five

T here were three buses that took the delegation to Lahore. They moved together like a caravan.

I was seated in the first bus, with Prime Minister Atal Bihari Vajpayee sitting ahead of us all, right next to the door. The seat next to him was kept empty. Behind the prime minister was his family, and adjacent to him was External Affairs Minister Jaswant Singh, who would be the first dignitary to alight after the prime minister. I was seated right behind him, along with Vijay Malhotra, the Bharatiya Janata Party MP.

A little political colour was now being added to my personality in my own eyes as I travelled with this delegation on a political mission of great importance. I felt more responsible, more patriotic, to be a part of this historic journey from my present homeland to my past.

The bus rolled on. Atalji, a man I greatly admired, was leading us all to meet with unknown people across the border, in a land that was once so well-known to me. Images of Atalji flitted through my mind. My first meeting with him was when he had come over to my place at Iris Park, Juhu, along with Nana Deshmukh. They both held key posts in the Jan Sangh, and were in Bombay for their annual political rally. I found Atalji extremely warm-hearted, with a firm handshake and a free laugh.

During the Emergency, he was arrested and sent to jail. Just before that happened, I bumped into him at Delhi airport. He was waiting for his car, and I for mine. His laughter had the same zing and a hint that conveyed, 'Don't be surprised if I am arrested soon!'

After the Emergency was lifted and the Janata Party won the elections, I was with Atalji at the celebratory rally at Rajghat. Later, when he was the minister of external affairs in the Janata government, I broke bread with him at his official residence in New Delhi, finding myself a part of his very affectionate family, munching away snacks, cracking delicious nuts and juicy jokes over hot cups of tea. Atalji's laughter was the central attraction of a holiday afternoon.

When the Janata government fell and elections were announced, I found myself facing a crowd of thousands at the Ramlila grounds in Delhi, where I went all the way from Mumbai to canvas for Atalji. And when I celebrated my golden jubilee with a lavish party at the Leela Kempinski, inviting the two hundred best Indians of my choice from different fields of activity, Atalji was amongst the very first I invited. He called me to apologize for his absence due to a prior commitment elsewhere, while wishing me more and more success in future.

When the BJP came to power and Atalji was announced to be the prime minister of the National Democratic Alliance government, my heart danced with joy, and he reciprocated with a personal 'Thank you' letter after he received my congratulatory note.

Now the same Atalji was sitting in a bus heading for a destination across the border, on a mission that was to seal the future relationship, recently turned sour, between the two neighbours. As I looked at him from behind, he seemed alone in the greatest moment of his destiny, with such a monumental responsibility thrust on his shoulders. I terribly, terribly wished to share his burden in whatever humble capacity I could. Suddenly, I was invited to go and sit next to him for five minutes. I quietly slipped into the vacant seat next to him. We sat silent for a while. Then I gripped his hand and pressed it, saying, 'We are all with you. Do whatever you've dreamt about doing, with a conscience that represents the country's conscience!' He smiled deeply, looking at me. His famous laugh was missing, but that smile expressed it all. I let go his hand, and came back to my seat.

Outside, on the road, people were lined up on both sides, cheering as the buses rolled across. Women held up their tiny tots, small flags in their hands, raising them to salute the prime minister going on his mission. Slogans for the prime minister and for his success rent the air. In between, wherever people recognized me through the window of the moving bus, they screamed with delight, waving and jumping with joy.

Joyous screams cheered us as the bus slowed down. We were nearing Wagah, the border town. There was an air of expectancy and suspense in the bus. And sudden silence outside, as the bus halted.

Thick wooden barricades were lifted, letting in a sudden stream of people. Atalji alighted from the bus, followed by his foreign minister. There was an uncontrollable melee, stamping of feet and sound of bodies shuffling against one another and rushing together towards the meeting point. The retinues of both the prime ministers and their security guards, together with the followers of each, were trying to get the closest to the scene of action, with bugles blaring on both sides of the border and shouts of people greeting the most historic moment of the decade.

I could not see what was happening, but from the noises and the screams that came into my ears, as I helplessly waited for my turn to get off the bus, I could make out the drama being enacted. Prime Minister Nawaz Sharief was receiving our prime minister. I jumped into the crowd outside, not wanting to miss the action. A chorus of voices screaming 'Dev Anand!' immediately filled the air. Hands waved, a cheer went around, and I found myself in the midst of their hearts.

Nawaz Sharief looked at me and smiled. I reciprocated warmly. We shook hands, and he exclaimed, 'You are from the same college as me! Government College, Lahore!'

'Yes,' I replied.

I did not let go of his hand, and held Atalji's with my other hand, standing between them. Then I joined their hands by putting Atalji's on his and pulling mine out, and said, partly to them and partly to the excited faces around, 'And these hands should never separate!' Everybody cheered and clapped. The cameras had a rollicking time capturing the moment, and front-paged the photograph in every newspaper.

We returned to the bus, this time without Atalji, who had been flown to Lahore from Wagah by helicopter. We were in a Pakistani bus now. The crowds were cheering on the roadside on this side of the border as well, waving Pakistani flags at the visitors.

Lahore seemed completely unfamiliar now. My searching eyes had to strain to look for the known landmarks that had stayed in my mind from the passing panorama. I found them transformed. Their location had not changed, but the sweep of generations and a new regime had put their stamp on it, making them appear alien to my eyes. I was trying to look for my college and its surrounding area, my head peering out of the window. I saw the cannon, still intact outside the museum, still pointing in the same direction, and felt somewhat reassured.

I was ushered into my hotel suite. A Pakistani room boy saluted me, then asked for my autograph. It seemed to me that I was in my own country. 'What's your name?' I asked.

'Abdul,' he said. We have so many Abduls in India as well.

Nawaz Sharief hosted a big reception for the Indian prime minister and his delegation at the Lahore fort, a location that gave the historic moment a memorable touch. He shook hands with all of us at the main entrance. He made me stand next to him, holding my hand for a long time, and the TV cameras caught the two of us together for the country to see, as if carrying a story about two students from the same college, separated for a long time, now meeting again, to become inseparables.

'I have got to meet you on a more personal level as well, Sharief sahab, outside my official status as a member of the Indian delegation, before I leave here,' I told him.

'Of course! After all, isn't this your city?' he said.

At dinner, I was seated at a table at which some of the close associates of Nawaz Sharief were also seated. I could make out from their conversation that it was the inner circle of the Pakistani prime minister. Both the prime ministers were on stage, seated next to each other on a long table, along with their ministers and secretaries. Both read out their speeches from prepared texts. A friendly note was struck for the forthcoming Indo-Pak treaty of friendship.

Next day we were taken sight-seeing, to see the historic places of our choice. I saw them all. I had never seen them so minutely when I was in college.

The following day, a news channel insisted on taking me to my old college for an interview, saying it would make a great story.

Standing in front of the college, I was transported back to my years in Lahore. I saw my college mates and my friends in both the hostels I stayed in, 'the quadrangle' and the 'New Hostel'. I saw Hamidullah Khan Burki, standing out as the best hockey player in college, as I stood on the ground on which the students still played hockey. I saw him being cheered, as he scored goal after goal.

I saw Usha Chopra in the college corridor on the first floor, crossing me, books in hand, in a sari that shimmered with elegance, innocent as ever as I said a very shy hello to her, to which she blushed with a smile that waited for me to take the next step, bolder than a mere hello, which I never did. If she was here, right now, I thought, I would just walk up to her, and say all that I could never say then. But she wasn't there. And yet, I could hear the sound of her high-heeled shoes resounding in the empty corridor.

I laughed at my childlike imagination. The news channel team asked me why I did so, probing me further. I took them to the door of the principal's room—the exterior of which was just the same as it was when I had left, still painted blue—through which I had walked out after taking my college-leaving certificate from Principal Eric Dickinson, a pipe-smoking intellectual who had perhaps left a little imprint of his English accent on me.

It was a Sunday and the college was closed. But as news began to spread that an ex-Ravian and an important star from India was visiting the college, students started trooping in. They all looked like students from any good college in India.

'This college is mine, as much as it is yours!' was the last sentence that I uttered to all of them, as I got into the car that was now to take me to a restaurant for lunch. I was late by an hour, having spent more time than scheduled at my old college. As we were eating, I suddenly heard a musical strain from my film *Taxi Driver* being played in the background. I looked behind me and saw a flautist playing the notes on his flute in a corner, and looking at me with admiration. He stopped playing as our eyes met, and walked up to me, saying, 'I have seen all your films to date, Dev saab.'

'You play the flute so well!' I complimented him.

'I can play any of the songs you have sung on screen!' he said proudly.

'You can! I like it!' I said.

'Which one do you want me to play?' he asked.

'Are you sure you can play all of them?' I did not quite believe him.

'Yes, all!' he emphasized. 'Name any and I shall play it. Your choice, Dev saab!'

'Come on, you won't be able to,' I teased him.

'Test me, Dev saab!'

'All right then,' I said, and started thinking of a song that I really liked, which he may not be able to play. Then I said, '*Shokiyon mein ghola jayein . . .*'

'Oh, from *Prem Pujari*!' he immediately said. Then he kissed his flute, and played the song as fluently as the composition itself. His playing took me back to Kolhapur in Maharashtra, where the song was picturized on me and Waheeda Rehman. The way he looked and the feeling with which he played, the flautist could be a man from Kolhapur, or from anywhere else in India.

Nawaz Sharief kept his word, and called me for a private audience with him before the famous Lahore Agreement was signed. He introduced me to his entire cabinet as well as the chief ministers of the states of Punjab and Baluchistan. The faces all around were wreathed in smiles. 'After how long are you visiting Lahore?' was a common question.

'Longer than your country has been in existence!' I replied.

'Why not stay longer?' said Nawaz Sharief. 'On my personal invitation.' There was genuine warmth in his words.

'And come to Baluchistan as well!' added the Baluchistan chief minister.

'If I stay here, I'll want to make a film here as well,' I said.

'Go ahead and make it!' they both said.

'But before that, I'd want to travel all over Pakistan, to have a feel of what's going on here now. To study the scene before I do a script,' I put forth my next wish.

'Do whatever you want. And go wherever your mind takes you,' Nawaz Sharief was utterly kind. 'I shall arrange everything.'

I listened with keen interest. 'Stay on!' he repeated his invitation.

'Not now,' I said. 'Protocol demands that I go back with the delegation, though I'd love to come back.'

'Come back then. In fact, I shall create an excuse for you to come back. I will have you invited by the Government College, as its ex-student, for a function,' he suggested.

'I'd love that!' I said.

Sharief was in a kind mood, genuine and serious in his intentions. I started thinking seriously about shooting a film in Pakistan.

But General Pervez Musharraf was attacking Kargil even as we spoke, sending infiltrators across the mountain ranges to the Indian side of the Line of Control.

Seventy-six

The completion of *Censor* was my top priority now. The film needed a long arduous process of thoughtful writing that carried a deep conviction. I wanted to put in my best writing into it, to convey everything I wanted to say. I dived headlong into it, working both behind and in front of the cameras.

In the midst of it all, a letter marked 'Top Priority' arrived one day during a break between shots. It was from the president of the World Punjabi Association in New York, saying they were holding a convention of the organization in which some very prominent Punjabis from the world over, 'achievers' from different walks of life, were to be honoured for their outstanding contribution. They had singled me out from the field of art and culture in India, and said that my award would be handed over to me by Hillary Clinton, the First Lady of America.

I usually brush aside such letters announcing honours to be conferred on me and wanting my personal presence at the award ceremonies, since they are often an excuse to get me amongst the gathering present on the occasion for their enjoyment. But this time the American First Lady's name struck a chord of interest in me. Here was an opportunity to meet Hillary Clinton. She was not only the wife of President Clinton, but also a political thinker in her own right, having contributed substantially towards the success of her husband. A very good lawyer herself, she had also won a lot of sympathy for her calm and composed stand on her husband's alleged scandalous affair with Monica Lewinsky.

I wanted to meet her very much, and sent my letter of acceptance to the organizers of the function in New York.

My daughter Devina was in Mumbai at that time. I asked her if she wanted to accompany me. She was thrilled, and her daughter Gina whistled with joy. I asked her too if she wanted to come along. She gave an immediate joyful nod, but her mother was not keen that she should travel, saying that it was good enough that the mother represented the daughter as well when she met with Hillary. Gina agreed that it was all right by her if she was 'represented' by her mom at the coveted meeting.

'And is there anything you want me to convey to Hillary, on your behalf?' I asked, fondling her.

'Tell her I want to meet her daughter Chelsea one day,' she spontaneously answered.

Devina and I stayed at the Sheraton in New York. The function was also in the same hotel, followed by a gala dinner in the banquet hall. The glitterati of distinguished Punjabis from all corners of the world were present on the occasion. They included Herb Dhaliwal, the first Indian minister in the federal government of Ottawa, and Lord Mota Singh, the Indian Justice from England. Sant Chatwal, the organizer and host of the grand evening, introduced the distinguished guests to Hillary.

Having met her a little earlier, and now sitting next to her on the dais gave me a great perspective on the lady who charmed all the guests, both with her presence and oratory. In my brief speech, while accepting my award from her, I invited her to come to India. She in her speech at the end of the function responded to what I had said, saying she'd love to come to India one day.

After the function, Devina, her cousin and I walked through the Saturday night atmosphere of Times Square, a couple of blocks away. Saturday evenings at Times Square have always left a deep imprint on my mind but that particular evening seemed very special, as if the sun was shining brightly in all its glory in the middle of the night on the square, with a mixed crowd irrespective of hue, creed, or nationality moving around in a spirit of joy, making the night its own.

The year was 1999. In less than a year, the twentieth century was to become history, and the twenty-first, the life and spirit of a 'new age', was to begin.

The thirty-first of December every year is the most memorable night in Times Square, and the coming one was going to be the last of the century, a once-in-a-century phenomenon that would tell the story of a hundred years, never to be told on another night for another hundred years to come.

It needed to be immortalized on film, I thought, and I had to do it.

I stood in front of the clock on Times Square that ticked away year after year. But time would freeze for it at midnight on 31 December, and I made up my mind to be there at that time, with my new project. I started thinking ahead, standing still.

Seventy-seven

The year was 1964. I was on my way to New York.

A very beautiful American air hostess was attending to the passengers. She passed by my seat and then stopped to look at me. Our eyes met. The twinkle in her blue eyes prompted me to say 'hello'. She enquired if I needed a drink. Her eyes conveyed another sort of invitation, more intoxicating. I smiled, and she threw me a ravishing smile in return. I said, 'Later.'

Soon the lights were dimmed. The drone of the engines combined with fatigue lulled everyone to sleep. A blanket and a small handbag were lying on the vacant seat next to mine. I removed them from there, confident that the air hostess would come and sit next to me. She did.

'To New York?' she asked.

'To wherever you say!' I said.

'New York!' she repeated.

'Where do we meet?' I asked.

'Where are you staying?' she counter-questioned.

'At the Plaza Hotel.'

'When?'

'Whenever you say.'

'Not tonight. I have a date.'

'When, then?'

'Tomorrow, perhaps.'

'Tomorrow. No ifs or buts.'

She laughed. 'Where?'

'At the Plaza. In the lobby.'

'Nine at night!' she acquiesced.

Her name was Barbara. She turned up at nine sharp. We strolled in Central Park, held hands, kissed each other in the darkness, and dined at the Plaza. Then she insisted on going. I asked her to stay.

'No, not tonight,' she said.

'Why not?'

'I have a boyfriend. He's waiting for me.' She looked at her watch, and said, 'He'll kill me.'

'I will kill myself if you go away,' I said dramatically.

She liked this. With longing in her eyes, she asked, 'Are you here on New Year's Eve?'

'Yes. That's day after tomorrow,' I said.

'Let's spend it together.'

'But your friend . . .'

'He'd be on a flight that evening,' she interrupted. 'He's a pilot, on duty that evening.'

'What if he kills me?' I asked jokingly.

'I will kill him then,' she joked back, kissing me on the cheek.

'Where do we meet on New Year's Eve?' I asked.

'Same place. Here. In the lobby. Same time. Nine o'clock!'

'That's a date. Then together we'll go to Times Square, and do what everybody does that evening!'

'Yes, honey,' she kissed me goodnight.

And Barbara was gone, leaving so much of her mesmerizing charm behind that I longingly kept waiting for New Year's Eve.

At 9.30 p.m. on New Year's Eve, I was waiting for Barbara in the lobby of the hotel. I put my hands in my pocket, and started strolling around, looking aimlessly at the flashy window displays that glittered with the wares exhibited inside. Then I went to the sofa facing the entrance, picked up a newspaper lying there and glanced through its pages at random, my eyes keeping a constant vigil on the main entrance where she would enter from.

There was no sign of her. I looked impatiently at my watch. There was no way I could call her, for she had not left her number, nor had I asked for it.

I went to the bar, my eternal watch at the main door not lapsing for a second. I was never much of a drinker, but had enjoyed a few gin martinis at a sidewalk café at Via Venito, with an Italian signorina by my side. The gin martinis had added sparkle to that evening. So I asked the barman for one.

There was going to be an extra sparkle in it this time, for by the time I finished it, Barbara, the prettiest girl in the world, would walk in.

I gulped the drink down in one go and imagined Barbara calling me, apologizing for her delay. I was a fool, I thought. I should have checked with the operator. She might have called already; I should have left a message for her with the operator about my being in the bar. I hastily went to the house phone and enquired. No one had called.

The clock in the lobby showed 10.15 p.m. Slightly intoxicated, I went back to the bar, asked for another gin martini, and gulped it down quicker than the first one. The barman winked at me and asked, 'Another one, sir?'

'No, thank you. I never drink. This was just . . . to celebrate New Year's Eve!'

'No girlfriend, sir?'

'Of course, yes. Waiting for her—the cheque please!'

I paid the bill, went back to the entrance, and lingered there for a while. Then walked out into the brightly illuminated street.

A peal of sexy laughter came from behind me, stifled into a sigh of ecstasy. What on earth am I doing, I thought, why am I wasting my time? I shouldn't have come out into the street. Maybe Barbara was looking for me right now in the lobby.

I rushed back into the hotel. I cut through a bevy of girls waiting for somebody, entered the lobby, pushed through another group of people, my eyes searching, panning from one corner to another, looking for my obsession of the moment, until I found myself all alone again, everybody else having gone.

Barbara was nowhere in sight! I felt desolate. I needed another gin martini and headed again for the bar, which was now overflowing with people. Scores of hands were stretched towards the barman, thirsty for drinks. I raised my head over them, trying to catch the barman's eye. He cast a quick casual look at me and remarked, 'I know your drink, sir!'

'But a larger one this time!' I said.

He nodded and giving me preference over the others, handed

me a glass with the drink sizzling inside. 'It'll cool me down!' I murmured, and drank it like water. It only accentuated the heat inside me. I shook my head, as my eyes became somewhat unfocused.

'Your girlfriend, sir?' said the barman, giving me a look.

I nodded and whispered 'Barbara!' as I thrust a tip into his hand.

'Nothing like being with her at Times Square, on a night like this!' He spoke what was on my mind, as he thanked me for the ten-dollar bill I had given him.

'Yes. That's where we have a date,' I said.

'Good luck, sir!' he said. But without a word of thanks to him, I was now on the move towards Times Square. Having given up on Barbara, I wasn't going to miss the midnight moment at Times Square now.

I started walking fast. Times Square was several blocks away. And the streets were filled with people blocking my way. 'Barbara!' somebody shouted. I looked around. A very handsome-looking man was calling his girlfriend.

'Barbara!' he repeated, as I stood motionless to look at him.

'He could be the guy. The pilot Barbara mentioned!' I thought to myself.

I suddenly turned jealous now, trying to spot the Barbara he was calling. A girl was trying to push towards him through the crowds. I couldn't see her face. Then she was in his arms, her face still hidden from me by the crowds and the shadows. Standing on my toes, I jumped up and down to catch a glimpse of her profile. A light crossed her face suddenly, and I heaved a sigh of relief.

It was not the Barbara of my dreams.

A tornado of people pushed me towards Times Square, thousands of people swaying to the blaring music, beams of light dancing over their heads. A little distance away, the Times Square clock stood at the centre of attention, getting ready to announce the New Year to the world.

I raced ahead, the gin and martini holding sway over me, saying that Barbara was only playing hide-and-seek with me. That she would suddenly appear from behind to surprise me with a hug, deliberately delayed, so as to be remembered all the more.

And . . . 'D–e–v!' I heard a voice scream through the deafening noise of the revellers. It rang like a bell in a temple I once visited in

Benaras. I followed its echo. 'D–e–v!' the voice repeated itself, 'I am here!'

'So am I!' I shouted back at the top of my voice, and leaped up to see her face.

It was not Barbara's! The man the girl had called was running towards her. He was another 'Dev', probably an American 'Dave'! There were so many with that name.

I let out a guffaw. The gin martini in me was making me boisterous, as I laughed at the greatest joke of the evening. I screamed out 'Barbara!' in one long-drawn breath, outshouting everybody else around me, as the clock was about to strike twelve.

It chimed twelve, and the world around me sang, 'Happy New Year!'

'Happy New Year!' I also joined in the chorus, and Barbara was lost in it, and from my mind.

'Papa!' came Devina's voice. I was back in the present.

'I was thinking—of a movie set in Times Square,' I said. 'All about love!' We crossed the street, holding each other's arms. As we walked back to the Sheraton, I was again with Barbara for a brief moment.

I had met her again four or five years later in Bombay. She was with a flying crew that was staying at the Sun-n-Sand Hotel. She recognized me as I flitted past a group of admirers in the lobby, and shot off a familiar 'Hi'.

I turned to look at her, and after a pause exclaimed, 'Barbara!'

'I am sorry for that New Year fiasco!' she said apologetically, walking up to me. 'My boyfriend suddenly cancelled his flight, and stayed back to spend the New Year's Eve with me.'

I tried to remember the past episode.

'A very possessive guy who wouldn't leave me alone for a second—even to make a telephone call!' She did her best to look bewitching again.

'Oh! I got over it long ago!' I said. 'But that New Year's Eve in America can never be erased from my mind. It was a delightfully memorable evening for me!'

'Can I invite you to dinner tonight? In your own city?' she asked.

'Extremely nice of you! Thanks! But I have a date with my wife,' I said very sweetly.

Seventy-eight

Twenty days later, I was back in the USA as a Grand Marshall again, this time in San Francisco. The Indian Association there conferred on me the title 'The Hero of the Century', and ceremoniously presented me with an elegant wooden plaque on which my name was engraved. I accepted it with all humility, but philosophically.

For in the span of a century, there are innumerable achievements of great distinction, in different spheres of human endeavour, contributing towards the growth and progress of mankind, some well known, others a little less known but equally important. They all come into the limelight, only to fade away from human memory with time, as the headlines are taken over by their successors. Men come and go, giving place to new players. The present fades into the past and the future takes over from the present, and the wheel of time moves on.

So in actuality no one person can claim to be 'the hero of the century'. With this firm belief, I received the award without debating whether I was worthy of it. The people of Fremont were happy for me and eager to honour me, and the occasion gave them an opportunity to have me in their midst. I shared in their happiness, and was honoured to be there.

From San Francisco I travelled to New York once again. Times Square was on my mind.

It was a Saturday evening, and the Square looked like a newly-wed bride, charmingly decorated with all its razzle-dazzle, billboards, neon signs, a profusion of colours, and that wonderful sense of warmth in the atmosphere.

When the same magical feel would enhance itself a thousand-fold on New Year's Eve, I thought, I would be the bridegroom honeymooning with it, capturing its once-in-a-century look, in all its glory and all its charm, making love to it with my camera.

I made up my mind. It would be a great love affair, and I would call it *Love at Times Square*.

Seventy-nine

I was racing ahead with the filming of *Censor*. But the last New Year's Eve of the twentieth century was drawing close. I had a date with New York on 31 December. I would shoot at Times Square, and save the shots in the can till I got around to shooting the rest of the story.

I proceeded to New York, booked an American cameraman, and got ready to capture the moment that would not be repeated for another century.

The whole world was there, it seemed—whites, browns, yellows and blacks, the high and the mighty, and the lowliest of the low. All the faces were lit as if by a hundred suns, in one special moment that unified the world in a collective excitement. Yellow and green, red and blue, the entire spectrum of colours danced criss-crossing against one another, as they beamed from above and from the sides, making it the most colourful spectacle ever witnessed in recorded history.

I had fixed my camera on top of a raised platform, with my cameraman David Tumblety behind it, and his assistants standing at his side looking down at the thousands of people below, who in turn were looking up at us with curious interest.

On our right, Muhammad Ali, once the world boxing champion and now a victim of Parkinson's disease which had immobilized him partially, was counting the minutes to the magic hour when his arm would be propped up by his aides to switch on the clock that would send electric currents into the atmosphere, signalling the end of the present century and the beginning of a new, dynamic one. My camera had already caught him climbing up to the rostrum slowly with the help of his supporters. There was a forced cheer on his face with a lot of physical strain behind it, as he made victory gestures to the cheering crowd.

My eyes were roving on all sides, not letting any moment of interest slip by without being recorded. Down below, the people were waving and I kept waving back at them constantly, to ensure that they understood my commands when the camera rolled and they were in the frame.

'Is that Dev Anand?' a female voice came from behind the camera, muffled by the sounds of the crowd. I did not respond.

'Dev Anand!' the voice rent the air again. I ignored it, busy as I was instructing my cameraman.

'Dev Anand!' the voice now sounded very close.

'Pan the camera!' I ordered David.

'Panning!' he responded, catching the lady in the frame. She was American, full of excitement, and waving vigorously at me.

'Zoom in to her! Catch her enthusiasm!' I goaded him on. He zoomed in to her.

'Recognize me?' She was now jumping up and down.

'Cut!' I ordered, and looked at her, trying to recognize her face, which looked familiar.

'My daughter!' She raised the hand of a girl standing next to her over the heads of the people around. The daughter, smiling away, also jumped up and down with excitement.

It took me a little time to recognize the woman. Before I could do so, she gave me a cue. 'Remember our promised rendezvous at Times Square thirty-five years ago?'

'Barbara!' I shouted, as I had shouted all those years ago over the din of the crowds. I looked at her and her daughter. The daughter looked so much like the mother did then. In fact, she was an exact replica. Both of them wore charming smiles, one a smile of youth, the other of an older woman, now greyed, yet retaining her attractive looks of yore.

'You are as beautiful as ever, Barbara,' I said, and as her face glowed with my remark, I ordered, 'Shoot them, David.'

As the camera rolled, Barbara said, 'That's my husband, her father,' pointing at somebody. 'Hi,' said an old man standing a little behind them, his front teeth missing. He was biting into a big bun of bread.

'Hi,' I reciprocated, thinking to myself, 'he could be the same boyfriend, the pilot!' He waved like a jolly old man, giving the camera a toothless smile.

'What are you making?' shouted Barbara at me.

'A story inspired by a girl named Barbara, three and a half decades ago!' I replied, for the climax of my story revolved around a similar incident as that which had taken place all those years ago in real life.

There was a sudden surge of people, a push-and-pull of great human strength. She was drowned in the sea of humanity as it flowed towards the clock. And was lost to me again for ever.

Another five minutes to go! The heartbeat of the world was ticking away with the excitement of the coming dawn. All the sadness of the century about to end was now put on the backburner in people's minds, and all past moments of exhilarating joy were lost too in the settling dust of history. Now all eyes were riveted on the clock at Times Square. There were a million people there, it seemed, everyone celebrating, and waiting for the clock to tick over, once-in-a-hundred-years smiles radiating on their faces.

My cinemascope lens kept zooming in and out of them.

'Hi!' I shouted through my megaphone to a bunch of girls who were rejoicing. They looked back. 'You all look so beautiful—all of you!' I screamed compliments at them. Flattered, they all gave their natural reactions, and became the most beautiful leading ladies on my camera.

'And you too!' I called aloud to another group. They laughed, blushed and laughed again, like they had never done before, as the camera panned over them one by one.

A torrential wave of humanity splashed towards the camera from another side. 'You are also being caught on camera!' I reminded them, yelling. They started jumping up and down, trying to touch the sky.

'Me! Me!' a young girl jumped the highest, in an effort to stand out.

'How can I leave out a girl so pretty?' I waved at her. She smiled the smile of the century.

'Zoom out,' I gave another order to David, and the wide expanse of the camera caught them all with their enchanting smiles, flinging themselves at the camera.

'Be at your most joyful,' I kept directing them, 'for this never-to-be-forgotten phenomenon is not going to happen again for another hundred years!'

And a chorus reached the stars from the glow of the lights below, melodiously echoing, 'Y-E-S!'

The shot was a winner.

From across, the bugle struck a note. All eyes turned towards the platform. Muhammad Ali had stood up.

'Five . . . four . . . three . . . two . . . one.'

A million voices sent up a single scream of hysteria as the clock struck twelve.

A phantasmagoria of lights, like a flood of colours lighting up both the earth and the sky, burst forth above the heads of the people. Trumpets blared, the heavens dropped confetti, and balloons of all hues went soaring up.

I recorded it all on film for posterity.

A young girl blew a kiss into my camera. With that, the past had waned, and a joyous new millennium had dawned.

Eighty

From euphoric joy to the depressing depths of anguish . . .
The media suddenly announced the tragedy of the new century:
the royal family of the mountain kingdom of Nepal was
decimated in a five-minute shootout in a massacre that generated shock
waves and spread gloom worldwide. I was amongst those who were
extremely grieved at the gruesome incident that had hardly any
parallel in the annals of human history.

My mind went to the very recent past when the assassinated
King Birendra was on a private visit to India, and staying at the
Leela Kempenski with his family. I had called on him and he had
agreed to visit me in my studio. He came with his full entourage
which included his foreign minister and his minister for defence,
along with his charming queen. I had first met the couple at their
wedding in Kathmandu. The young bride had now become a
wonderful queen sitting beside her husband, both of them making
a great royal couple.

The entire area outside Anand Recording Studio, all the three
roads that lead to it, became a security zone from before they arrived
till after they left, the intelligence department having made sure
that the private royal visit was as well guarded as an official one.

King Birendra's father, King Mahendra, had also come privately
to my Iris Park residence without any fanfare. Now the visit of King
Birendra bore the same informal stamp. I garlanded him and his
queen at the entrance, and we settled down to chat informally in my
penthouse. Memories of his late father were revived, and I felt very
honoured and inwardly happy having made friends with the son
of the king who had been my dear friend.

And now suddenly—

King Birendra and his queen had both been assassinated by their own son, along with several other members of the royal family, in a ghastly shootout after which the young prince also shot himself dead. The only survivors left of the royal family was Prince Gyanendra, the younger brother of the assassinated king, and his family, who were lucky enough not to be on the ill-fated scene of the dastardly act.

This annihilation of a royal household in a matter of minutes left a scar of anguish on my mind. All I could do was to send a note of condolence to King Gyanendra, soon after he was installed as the new ruler of the kingdom. Later, I conveyed my sense of deep loss to him personally when he gave me a private audience in his palace after he and his government honoured me with an award for my contribution to cinema, the first-ever honour to anybody in the field of creative entertainment given by Nepal.

This was in July 2005, when I renewed my emotional contact with the country. I paid a visit to the Pashupatinath temple, one of the most revered temples of Hinduism, once again. Standing there I looked down at the Bagmati river, by the banks of which King Birendra was cremated and the last rituals performed for his soul to rest in peace. My eyes shed a tear that dropped into the waters of the flowing river, mingling with its sorrow for the late king.

Eighty-one

With all my energies now back to *Censor*, I finished it as fast as I could, and presented it to the censor board for certification. There were doubts in the minds of many filmwallahs that the film would find hurdles in its way, created by the system against which I was raising my voice in the film. But strangely enough, the censor board was kind to me this time. The film was passed with negligible cuts to which I agreed. In fact, the entire committee had praise for my work, my courage to call a spade a spade, and my taking the lead to advocate a more realistic and mature form of censorship in tune with the changing times.

It gave a boost to my ego when one of the members of the board remarked, 'Enter the film at the Oscars.'

But for a film in India to become the country's official entry to the Oscars involves overcoming a lot of red-tapism. If the film is a huge success, it automatically creates a lobby for itself. But if it fails to score at the box-office, it is ignored and left in the cold. Its becoming a hit washes away all its faults and shortcomings, while its turning into a flop erases from public memory whatever strength it may have had in terms of artistry and style and execution. *Censor* did not do well with the masses, and was overlooked.

But I had no regrets. For though the film did not cater to the average filmgoer waiting to escape into a world of street-level entertainment, where movie after movie is made on a repetitive stereotyped platform of cheap hilarity laced with chest-beating melodrama and vulgar displays of sexuality, it certainly gave the thinking, analytical, intelligent section of the audience sumptuous food for thought for a serious, meaningful debate.

And, of course, it gave me the complete satisfaction of saying something through my medium that no other movie-maker dared to say. *Censor* also collected quite a roster of strong actors and stars in its fold, all cast in well-delineated roles. My heart went out to all the performers for their attachment to the film. Their being in the film meant that I felt like I was directing and acting alongside the best in the business, on a canvas that was as large as the film deserved.

Rekha and Govinda, both of whom were known for their starry whimsicalities, were ever punctual and completely involved in the project. In Shammi Kapoor I discovered a great actor, who had meticulously etched the details of his portrayal of the judge in his mind before he appeared on camera. Randhir Kapoor, and later Rishi Kapoor, who also did a brief cameo in *Love at Times Square*, gave me a respect so intense and touching whenever they met me, that they made me recall their father, Raj Kapoor, one of my greatest contemporaries.

Censor was now a chapter closed to me. I dived headlong into the making of *Love at Times Square*.

The New Year's Eve of the first year of the twenty-first century was close by. The film's climax had to be shot on that day in Times Square, just as its beginning had been shot on New Year's Eve of the millennium year. My preparations were afoot to shoot again in New York.

But this time filming there was not the same as the previous year. The crowds were far less, the celebrations were toned down. The security was absolutely tight and permission was not available for filming. The 9/11 terrorist attack on the World Trade Center had just occurred. There was panic all around. High alerts were the order of the day. I had to wait for a long time and use all my influence as a star from India, to be able to go back to New York at all. Once there, it was equally difficult to secure the necessary permission to shoot at such a crowded place as Times Square.

The main area around the clock that rings in the New Year was cordoned off from all sides. People allowed to enter Times Square had to go through a thorough search, including taking their shoes off for police inspection for fear of any possible gadgets igniting explosives hidden inside them. Taking the camera inside seemed an impossibility.

But my strong will power triumphed against all odds. The force of my determination prevailed and my knack for persuasion was in top form. There was a female black cop on duty, looking very seductive in her police uniform. She became receptive seeing the eager enthusiasm on my face, and allowed me to install the camera at the position I wanted. My flirtatious talk with her did the trick after I cajoled her saying, 'I shall kiss you, honey, with a bouquet for you in my hand, if you let me cover the event from an angle close to the clock.'

She smiled flirtatiously at the importance I gave her, and responded, 'Would you take a close-up of me, with the bouquet in my hand, if I let you, honey?'

'My camera wouldn't love anybody else more!' I said, summoning all my charm.

She went and whispered something into the ears of her male colleague in uniform, a big-bellied cop, also black, with a dangerous-looking weapon hanging from his thick leather belt. He seemed to be her boss. He laughed having heard her whisper, then looked at me, and said in a gruff authoritarian tone, 'But not for long. Not a second longer than required!'

'Not a second longer than required, sir!' I repeated.

Moments later, the crowds were yelling in a joyful chorus, 'Five . . . four . . . three . . . two . . . one,' as the seconds to the midnight hour ticked away. And then there were hysterical screams. Just like last year. But to a far lesser degree. There were no laser beams. No display of fireworks. No confetti.

The crowd waved at the camera, which was focusing on their joyous faces. 'I am here as well!' screamed the black female cop from behind the crowd. 'Pan this side!' I told David. David panned the camera. She saw it facing her, and threw a flying kiss at me. Her burly, big-bellied boss stepped forward to join her, wishing 'Happy New Near' to the camera.

But soon he was brandishing his baton left and right, controlling the delirious crowds which had gone berserk as a jeep entered Times

Square, with Mayor Rudi Giuliani standing on it, waving at everyone, acknowledging their vociferous cheering. Giuliani had restored the undaunted and great spirit of America back to its moral and spiritual heights after the World Trade Center tragedy. He was the hero for the crowds this year. 'Long live America', 'America is united', 'Down with terrorism' were the slogans that rang out from the bottom of the hearts of the people around me. My camera captured it all for *Love at Times Square*.

America was slowly returning to normalcy, and I could shoot my film very smoothly, from the colourful autumn leaves of Wyndham on the east coast to the mixture of cultures in San Francisco on the west coast.

The only sequence now remaining to be shot was a song number, beautifully written and composed by Javed Akhtar and Adnan Sami. I wanted to picturize it on a young charismatic star of the day. Both Shah Rukh Khan and Salman Khan came to my mind.

Shah Rukh Khan was dubbing in my studio. During a brief tea break, he came out to smoke a cigarette. As he was sitting on the steps outside the lobby, one of my lieutenants approached him to ask if he would like to go up to my penthouse to say hello to me. He thought for a second, stubbed the fag underneath his boot, and took the elevator up. I welcomed him in. He was extremely gracious and respectful, and said he would be most willing to do the number if he didn't have his backache problem, for the treatment of which he was leaving for England very soon.

'No problem!' I responded with thanks, with great warmth and respect for the actor and the human being whose status had been raised manifold in my eyes with the encounter.

Salman Khan came to see me with the same respect. He sat exactly where Shah Rukh had sat earlier. I had first seen Salman as an utterly handsome young man just out of his teens at an annual gala function of an important publication, and was so struck by his attractive looks that a fleeting thought had crossed my mind that given the right break he would hit instant stardom.

A big star now, he sat looking at me, bashful but confident, waiting for me to say what I wanted from him.

'You know why I thought of you, Salman?' I broke the ice.

He nodded respectfully and straightaway said he was shorn of his hair at that time, for he had shaved it all off, and the moment it grew back, he'd be available for the shoot. He won over my heart then, and won it over again with the punctuality and dedication he showed while performing on the set. With a red jacket and a cap to match, he danced through the opening sequence with great grace and élan.

The shooting for *Love at Times Square* was complete. I now needed to take the film back to Mumbai, to my editing and mixing rooms, to cut, trim and embellish it with a musical score, before releasing it to the public.

Eighty-two

From Mumbai to Johannesburg—from the west coast of India to the tip of the African continent! I slept past midnight in the aircraft when it was totally dark outside, and got up to see the full moon which, a few minutes later, dissolved into the rising sun, giving the skyline a radiant red-gold hue, welcoming us to Johannesburg, 'the city of gold'.

It was a soul-stirring experience, watching the sun come up over the African continent. I remembered I had experienced a similar feeling flying over the Indian Ocean where it merged with the Arabian Sea, the blue and green waters of the two waterbodies playing endlessly with each other. I was visiting Colombo then, on an invitation from the Sri Lankan government to participate in their May Day celebrations. I had come back totally charmed by the beautiful country and its inhabitants.

Johannesburg was equally charming, its inhabitants graciously welcoming and the climate cool and bracing. I was happy to have been lured into the trip by the IIFA Awards committee, who were very kindly bestowing upon me a lifetime achievement award in their third annual awards function. I was excited like a child, not so much at the award as at the opportunity to explore a new land.

But I was very disheartened when I landed at Johannesburg and found that I was not advertised in any of the posters or billboards for the awards function, while the recipients of all the main awards had been announced in them along with their photographs. Even at the Dome, where the grand event was held to a house-full audience of movie admirers, I was given only a passing reference. As I sat in the first row, I kept thinking: was my presence being deliberately underpublicized? My heart sank. I hated myself for letting myself be pushed into an 'alien' territory by the organizers of the show. It certainly was not where I belonged.

I closed my eyes, wanting to disappear from there and fly back to my own country. And then I heard Saif Ali Khan singing one of my songs on stage. As I opened my eyes, he was right in front of me, and he dragged me into the full glare of the arc-lights, as Anil Kapoor was announcing my award to thunderous applause.

I put on a brave front, and took the microphone from Saif Ali Khan's hand. There was a pin-drop silence in the audience which was waiting to listen to me. I became one with the moment, speaking lines that went straight into their hearts.

Next day, almost all the local newspapers proclaimed me the star of the evening. I read the reports while flying back the same morning to Mumbai.

Eighty-three

I was determined to release *Love at Times Square* at Times Square, and I did it. I had wanted Hillary Clinton, who was now the senator from New York, and Mayor Rudi Giuliani to participate in the joy of my effort at the world premiere there, but this wasn't possible.

I needed a big hit that would justify my unflagging drive to write screenplays and make motion pictures out of everyday happenings and thoughts that spurred me on to enlarge them into two-and-a-half-hour sagas. Sadly, this did not happen either. But *Love at Times Square* certainly did make people sit up and wonder at the creative output that kept coming from a man who had been part of the film industry for six decades and still had the passion and the conviction to keep making movies based on his own novel ideas, which were never borrowed, plagiarized or stolen.

As for a film being a hit or a flop, a lot depends on many factors that have very little to do with its quality, the most important of these being the magnitude of the budget one can afford to spend on promoting the film. After seeing *Love at Times Square*, an important American public relations lady suggested a million-dollar budget for its promotion at a grand opening in New York, where it was shot. I was convinced of her ideas, very sure that the right push could make it a smash hit in the very country where the subject matter belonged. But my stingy local distributors pooh-poohed the thought after having delved into their pockets. And I, the producer of the film, was unable at that time to shell out that kind of money, after having spent lavishly on it all on my own during its making.

The release of *Love at Times Square* in the USA also took me to Chicago. When I think of Chicago, the great American actor James Cagney comes to mind, as well as the films about the mafia of the underworld there. And of course, one of the greatest presidents in the history of America, Abraham Lincoln! An aura of romanticism was associated with Chicago in my mind.

Much before the release of *Love at Times Square*, the Indian consul-general in Chicago invited me to attend a screening of *Guide* at one of the biggest and most famous American universities, before an appreciative audience of Indian cinema. The majority of the audience were fans of mine who had already seen *Guide* several times. Meeting the man who had produced as well as acted in the film was a spiritual experience of sorts for them. Meeting with them and talking to them, answering questions arising out of their inner psyche, was a spiritual experience for me as well. I felt like a guru clearing the muddy minds of the disciples at his feet, trying to help them swim in the pure, crystal clear waters of a mountain stream. I was happy that I had gone to Chicago to meet them. The evening at the University of Chicago was as exhilarating as the cover story on me that appeared in the *Chicago Tribune*, with a photograph of mine taken by a specially commissioned photographer that showed me standing at the open window of my hotel suite, looking out at the expansive universe across.

It is very difficult to see and absorb a great and vast country like America in a short span of time. But whatever little brush I had with it, during the shooting of *Love at Times Square* and at other times, made an impression that is deeply engraved in my memory.

New York is the city of all cities. Every time you go there, there is something new to explore, to learn, a new fashion, a new fad. Everything is mega-sized in New York, from limousines to hamburgers. You walk along an avenue, rubbing shoulders with millionaires or intellectuals at every step.

North of the city, in upstate New York, while the green of summer is refreshingly lush and eye-pleasing, the rust, the brown, the yellow and the red of the leaves is equally so, and more breathtaking, as they start falling from the trees in autumn and crunch under your feet. And finally, as autumn turns to winter, the place is covered in sheets of white snow, both on the ground as well as on the trees and roof-tops, and your senses marvel at nature at its magnificent best.

San Francisco, on the Pacific coast, with its mingling of Spanish, Mexican and Chinese cultures, is a kaleidoscope of the universe. The intermingling of races and the spirit of togetherness paint an absorbing picture of free humanity.

I had absorbed it all in my system and was preparing to depart for home, when, as I sat in the lobby of the Radisson Hotel, waiting for a friend to pick me up for an evening out, someone suddenly stopped and exclaimed, 'Mr Dev Anand!' I smiled, trying to recognize him.

'Don't you remember? We met at the Indian Chancery? In Washington DC? When you were going out to lunch with the ambassador?'

'Of course!' I replied, trying not to displease him, though not very sure who he was.

'I am an Indian journalist from the UNI, based in the American capital,' he quickly introduced himself.

'Yes, yes, of course! How are you?' I turned more polite. 'What brings you to New York?'

'Aren't you going?' he asked in reply.

'Where?'

'To the Grammy awards!'

'Oh! The Grammies! Great!'

'I am here to cover the event. Do you know, both the daughters of Pandit Ravi Shankar are nominated this year?'

'Are they?' and I started thinking to myself. I had heard of one of them, the sitarist. Who was the other one? But before I could ask, he was in a hurry to say, 'It will be fun watching the sisters competing with each other!'

'Of course!' I said. And he was gone.

Next day, I read in the newspapers that one Norah Jones had won five Grammies, a very exceptional feat by a totally unknown newcomer! The news item also elaborated on her background. She was the daughter of Ravi Shankar, the great Indian musician, and his erstwhile American partner.

A second tabloid carried a statement by Pandit Ravi Shankar from India, saying that he was proud of Norah for having won, and adding that he had no hand in her musical training or her Western compositions.

My eyes were glued to the newspaper. My creative interest was aroused at the prospect of a great story based on the lives of a world-renowned Indian musician and his equally famous musician daughter from an American girlfriend. I didn't have to meet with Ravi Shankar, whom I had known very well for a long time, or with Norah Jones, for the story was certainly not to revolve around their particular lives. The nucleus of the idea of their relationship was good enough.

It would be a film of great human relationships, I thought, to be mounted on a grand scale, with Indo-American composers and a cast and crew from both parts of the world. I started exploring the dream, cancelled my trip back to India, and stayed back in New York. Going back would mean leaving the threads of inspiration I was currently hanging on to. The scripting of the film and then the finalizing of the nitty-gritty of its huge set-up was now my top priority. The project had already taken shape in my mind.

I finished the first draft of the script in about four weeks. It was a labour of love, and an inspired creation, and I called it *Song of Life*.

Excited like a child once again, I opened my heart to some friends. The word spread like wildfire, without my having officially announced the film. Ravi Shankar and Norah Jones and their families got wind of it. They resented my making a film on them, misunderstanding my intentions, and went to the press, decrying my project.

CNN headlined Norah Jones's anger, saying 'Norah Jones Disturbed!' I had to contradict it saying, 'Dev Anand Unperturbed'. Both the statements made international news.

I flew to Los Angeles and made contact with Stevie Wonder, the famous American singer–composer, who spent a couple of hours with me in my hotel suite, and started negotiating with agents both in New York and LA to further the project to a definite concrete conclusion.

But as it happens with most big-budgeted ambitious films, most of my time was being consumed by agents responsible for putting the project together, lining up the stars and the distribution companies. And 26 September, my birthday, saw me waking up from deep slumber at five o'clock New York time, responding to innumerable calls from the press, my fans, and my near and dear ones in India and abroad, wishing me and saying they were missing me on a day they all remembered very sentimentally.

I thought of my last birthday and the ones before that. It is a day when my fans, including some from outside Mumbai, keep flocking to my studio, wanting to monopolize me for every second of the day. 26 September is engraved in their hearts like their own birthdays, and they undertake their 'pilgrimage' to come and wish me on that day and to celebrate, like devotees going to their divine deity's darshan. One Arun Mehta amongst them, who remembers by heart all the memorable events of my life, refused to go into the operation theatre for his heart surgery without a photograph of his favourite star by his side. His wife was in tears, her eyes having the same adulation for me as her husband, as she narrated the story to me.

These memories tugged at my heart, and I thought of all my fans who must be thinking of me. With the sentimentality ringing in my heart, tinged with an element of homesickness, I left my script of *Song of Life* registered with the Writers' Guild in New York, and the unfinished job of finalizing the project in the hands of my friends and agents in the USA, and headed back home, planning to quickly cast and launch *Beauty Queen*, a script I had written earlier.

On my return, I met Ravi Shankar during one of his visits to Mumbai. Our old friendship was revived, the gossip discussed, the unnecessary misgivings over *Song of Life* put to rest, and the decks cleared for filming *Song of Life*, whenever it happened in the future.

Eighty-four

I t seemed that my country had been missing me. My arrival back home heralded an unprecedented series of awards for me. I found myself at the receiving end of public adulation. It started with the trustees of Jai-Hind College in Mumbai deciding to give me the first of the awards they had instituted. L.K. Advani, the home minister, was to preside over the function, with the social elite of the city adorning the evening in the main hall of the college.

This was followed a couple of days later by the Pune film festival authorities deciding to honour me for my contribution to Indian cinema. Puneites welcomed me with open arms. The reception they gave me both inside and outside the theatre where the awards function was held was rousing. 'Pune is mine, like I am yours,' I conveyed to them all after I was given the award by Sharad Pawar. 'If there is a phenomenon called reincarnation, then I'm sure my next birth will be in a Pune household.' The gathering burst into prolonged applause.

Lata Mangeshkar was very warm and generous in her compliments to me on stage. Speaking in Marathi, she said that I had reached a stage beyond any awards. As she continued her speech, I was going into a flashback mode. Images of her past started projecting into my mind in quick succession. Lata singing one of the very first songs of her film career, '*Chanda re ja re ja re*', in one of my very first films, Bombay Talkies' *Ziddi*. She was very young then, standing at the foot of a tall mountain that she would one day scale. Lata rehearsing in a recording booth, with earphones on, a notebook and pencil in hand, jotting down and underlining the articulations of the soprano and the contralto of her voice, the rise and fall of it. Lata with the musical maestro S.D. Burman, rehearsing one of my all-time favourite songs, '*Rangeela re*' from *Prem Pujari*.

Both Lata and her younger sister, Asha Bhonsle, match each other in singing. Asha is equally great in her own style and in a different genre in her range and quality of voice. They are both incomparable when one comments on Indian film songs. The musical genius of the singing sisters is always lurking in the aesthetic chambers of my subconscious.

From Pune I drove to Mahabaleshwar, to my favourite hotel, to put the finishing touches to the script of *Beauty Queen*. As I drove into the gates of the hotel and parked the car right outside the last room at the far end, I could feel my creative juices revving up. Being in a creative mood, oblivious to the world around me, is a state I love being in. I was on one such creative high, totally engrossed in my script, with raw radishes and tomatoes and carrots fresh from the fields around me to nibble on, when my phone rang.

'There is an urgent call from Mumbai that you need to take sir, please,' the receptionist said.

'Forget it. I am very busy right now!' I shot back.

'But it is most urgent,' the receptionist repeated.

'Put me on!' I sighed.

A journalist from the staff of *Screen* was on the line, the very first to utter excitedly, 'Congratulations!' I listened silently.

'Are you there, Dev saab?' his voice was bursting with excitement. I tried to guess the reason behind it.

'You've got it!' he blurted out now.

'Really?' I answered, without knowing exactly what it was that I had got.

'The Dadasaheb Phalke Award, Dev saab!' he declared, quite beside himself.

The award had lost all meaning for me, not having received it year after year, when everybody around me repeatedly whispered to one another that I deserved it.

Even the earlier award, conferred upon me a few years ago by the government, had failed to enthuse me, for I had started suspecting the very process of deciding upon the awards that smacked of favouritism and prejudice. I had got to know about the award being given to me long before it was officially announced, for I kept getting calls not only from the capital, the centre of power and intrigue, but also from other cities, saying a very big, prestigious award was on its way to me.

A little time passed, and one day a call came from a certain under-secretary of the Government of Maharashtra, asking me if I would agree to accept a national award. My immediate reaction, naturally, was, 'How can I not? Such an honour!' and in the same breath I inquisitively asked which award it was.

He said, 'Padma Vibhushan.'

My joy knew no bounds. The award was just a step lower than the highest award in the country, the Bharat Ratna, and I thanked him.

But when it was announced, it was not the Padma Vibhushan but the Padma Bhushan, a step lower than the one that was already mine in my dreams.

A cruel jolt, and a letdown! The jubilation in my mind suddenly turned to ashes. What went wrong? The thought kept disturbing me so much that finally I skipped the award ceremony in New Delhi. Though I thanked the government for the honour bestowed on me, my medal is still lying with the home ministry amongst some of its other well-preserved souvenirs. And I have no great ambition of possessing it either. For awards do keep getting rusted with the passing of years, no matter how precious they are, and gradually recede into faded memories.

The inner light that was energizing me for my new creation, as I sat in my room at Frederick's hotel, shut out from the world, was my best award. But the telephone calls kept pouring in continuously, including one from my office in Mumbai, saying the information and broadcasting minister, Ravi Shankar Prasad, had personally called to convey the news of the award to me, and wanted me to speak to him on his hotline in New Delhi.

The honourable minister had called me once earlier as well from New Delhi, in the suite of my hotel in New York, offering me the chairmanship of the Indian censor board. I had declined saying I was a free man, and therefore the last to toe a line of thinking professed by a government in power, especially in regard to its censorship policy, and any government post, no matter how high, that made my liberated spirit subservient to the dictates of the ruling class would never be acceptable to my conscience. My mind was citing the instance of my own brother, Vijay Anand, who had taken up the chairmanship of the censor board only to be thrown out after a relentless lobby was created against him by the blue-eyed loyals of the government, who wanted his blood because of the liberal views he stood for.

I had thanked the minister, however, for his kind thought about me, which he had also appreciated. Now when I called him in New Delhi, for his final confirmation of the award conferred on me, we struck a note of mutual warmth instantly.

The telephone in my hotel room did not cease ringing until well past midnight. One of the calls was from Jabbar Patel, the Marathi film director and the chairman of the Pune film festival, who I was with only the same morning before I left Pune for Mahabaleshwar. He said he was in a theatre seeing a movie when he got the news of the award being given to me on his mobile. He could not resist stopping the screening of the movie for a while, just to break the news to the viewers, and the audience had stood up in a spontaneous gesture to give a standing ovation to me even in my absence. That struck a cheerful note in me, and was a big boost to my morale. I tossed in my bed, happy with the world, with the telephone by my side, endlessly ringing in notes of joy and congratulations, especially from the media. Many of them wanted to arrive for interviews by the first available means of transport. Several did, even late at night, trying to persuade me for a midnight camera session, in my bed, so as to be the first amongst the first to break the story to the expectant world. But I was in no mood. And they all had to settle for an early morning shoot in the cold wafty breeze the following morning.

One of the questions fired at me by a journalist was whether I knew that there was a very strong resistance to me being given the award by a well-known personality, one of my own colleagues in the field, and if I did, how I reacted to it. He even mentioned the person's name. I answered I was in total ignorance of the politics involved in deciding upon this prestigious and popular award. And that it was immensely saddening to hear my colleague's name taken in this connection. And if it was true I didn't care! For I would still be as happy without the award as I was with it.

The award function at Vigyan Bhavan, and the minister's dinner that followed, as well as the function hosted in my honour by Subrami Reddy, a personal friend also responsible for introducing me to the divine presence of the Balaji Temple, were tumultuous and soul-stirring. They made me feel suddenly that I was the heart-throb of Delhi, pulsating with an aura that Delhites had lived with for as long as they remembered. I realized, perhaps for the first time, how much I meant to my own countrymen. That all my output and the body of my work for almost six decades had not gone in vain. That the love and respect they showered upon me was to the image of a man who laughed and smiled, and sang and danced and talked to them all the time in their private moments of joy and sorrow.

At Vigyan Bhavan, as images from fragments of my celluloid career spanning fifty-nine years flickered and flashed on the screen, reminding me of all my films and the people I had worked with, my eyes welled up in emotion. I tried to hide my tears lest they be caught by the cameras lined up in front of me. But the camera lenses are great spies. They clicked as I wiped a tear. They clicked as I took out a hanky to blow my nose. They clicked as I closed my eyes in the ecstasy of the moment, floating backwards on the ocean of time. All six decades of my highly active career got concentrated and squeezed into a few seconds.

Only the resounding thunder of claps woke me up to the realization that I was being watched, both on and off the screen, with all my flaws, my shortcomings, my failings, and my larger-than-life figure in the eyes of my countrymen. They were announcing my name, this time to step out and go on the stage to finally hold the trophy that would ring the climax and for them the end of my career. It was said that the Phalke award was the last and greatest award in professional achievement. Beyond that there was none. But I was determined that it would not be so. That it was only a stimulus, a national pat-on-my-back, for further and bigger achievements to follow that would be my best, more polished, more enlightened, and more satisfying than ever before. With this decision taken, and an oath sworn to that effect by my conscience, I proceeded towards the gentleman standing a little ahead of me, waiting to lead me on to the stage. I dodged him as he was about to hold me by my arm, jumped on to the stage, turned towards the audience, and paused, smiling at them, as they all rose in unison to give me an ovation that was like temple bells pealing in a divine congregation. I let the moment linger and then blew a kiss at them. The honourable president stepped out to receive me and I greeted him with folded hands, then bent my head to receive the medal which he hung around my neck.

Soon after, the world-renowned pastor Benny Hinn was in Mumbai for his congregation called 'Festival of Blessings'. I was invited to meet him along with a very select group of people, and found him extremely friendly. We took an instant liking to each other. He invited me to attend his meeting at the Bandra-Kurla ground, and I went.

After Benny arrived, with the awestruck audience going into raptures, I heard my name mentioned from the stage, at which the audience clapped. I was ushered onto the stage. Benny dragged me towards the audience, and announced to the world, 'Dev, I am your friend for all time to come.' He was superbly hypnotic on stage, with an energy that can only belong to a man of God, and I thought myself lucky to be able to experience a truly spiritual moment. He whispered, 'I am going to pray for you.' I surrendered, for when somebody wants to pray for you, you also decide to be a part of the prayer itself. I was half-mesmerized, yet aware of everything and everybody around me. I could feel Benny mumbling to himself, his eyes closed, and then found him blessing me. I felt truly blessed. Benny had no selfish motive. He had given me his prayers out of the goodness of his heart.

Benny invited me to attend one of his gatherings in America, and we fixed a date in April. Events took such a turn that I could not make it. But my date with Benny is still on the cards.

Eighty-five

A few days later I got a call saying that Goldie was in hospital, and in intensive care. I rushed to see him, but could not meet him, for he was in a coma, constantly under the vigilant eye of the doctors treating him. He stayed in that condition for days, and then passed away. It was a blow that I could not recover from for a long, long time.

My brother's death made me weep bitterly like a child. I was inconsolable when the media and the TV cameras swooped down on me, as I descended from the steps to the second floor of his residence, where his dead body lay. The body was kept in his favourite room, in which he had done most of his writing that had left such a memorable mark on the movie industry. It was bathed and wrapped in white, with a few flowers on his head, a wreath over his body, and incense burning. As I stood by his body, oblivious to the people around me, a million tears started rising from my inner depths. I closed my eyes and imagined Goldie as a child, riding piggyback on me. And then in a flash he was a grown-up film director, taking charge of my personality, directing me in his very first directorial venture. The tears rushed out, and I opened my eyes to find Vaibhav, Goldie's grown-up son, standing next to me, his eyes bloodshot with weeping as well. A quick ray of light from a ventilator above fell on Goldie's face and lit up the touch of gold that shimmered in his hair—Goldilocks, my father used to call him. My tears became one with Vaibhav's as I hugged him, pressing him close to my heart.

When his funeral pyre was lit and his body went up in flames, I stood at a distance, watching the smoke go up, mingling with the breath of the universe. The TV cameras confronted me, eager to tell the viewers how I felt about my brother's passing away. I pointed at the smoke spiralling up into the skies, saying, 'Don't you see his life's work rising into the skies? Becoming immortal? Don't you see he is not dead, but so alive in what he left behind?'

Indeed—*Kala Bazaar, Tere Ghar Ke Samne, Guide, Jewel Thief, Johny Mera Naam*, they were all immortal now. I looked at the smoke floating away, and Goldie's smiling face seemed to console me, 'Weep not, my brother! I am so much around you, and inside you. Celebrate me, all the time!'

Then I saw him disappear, giving place to a Victoria driven by a horse, with my brother Chetan sitting in it. He too was amongst the clouds.

Chetan Bhaiji loved driving in a Victoria, 'royally', as he had said when he had taken me into one on my very first visit to Bombay, the city of my dreams. I now saw him driving the Victoria, whipping the horse. While I could not be beside Goldie when he breathed his last, I vividly remembered the pangs of death when Chetan was facing the inevitable. Those few heart-rending moments before his final goodbye to the world cannot be wiped from my memory. He had lost consciousness, and was trying very hard to breathe, his chest rising and falling abruptly, his hands folded on his chest, as if in communion with the power that was hovering around him to whisk him away at any moment! He was suddenly totally peaceful, his physical suffering gone, as he jerked his head sideways, to the heart-breaking shriek of the woman he had lived with during the final chapters of his life.

I kept watching his funeral pyre until the very end, when with a snap his skull was consumed by the devouring flames. Now I saw him alive again, sitting in the Victoria, galloping into the clouds, stopping to pick up his darling younger brother on the way. Both brothers looked happy in each other's company.

Then I saw the clouds burst, and from within them appeared Mohan Bhaiji, my eldest brother, smiling, opening his arms to receive his siblings.

Mohan Bhaiji had gone to the toilet in his house in Gurdaspur, and never came out. His unusually long stay inside raised the alarm amongst the family members. They broke open the door of the toilet and found his dead body lying on the floor. All of us drove to

Gurdaspur to attend his funeral. But our arrival was delayed and by the time we reached the town, his body was being placed on the funeral pyre. We drove straight to the burning ghat, right at the moment when his son was lighting the pyre, with the whole town waiting to condole his brothers. We pushed forward to see our brother, all wrapped up in white, his soul gone from his body. Unmindful of the hordes of people eagerly watching me, I stood on a platform, at a distance from the burning body, trying to find out whether it was still hovering somewhere in the sombre atmosphere. Suddenly, a whiff of breeze blew. Dust flew. A few scattered, dry leaves on the ground created an eerie rustle. A thin haze formed out of the flames enveloping my brother's body and then vanished into thin air. His son broke into a dreadful wail, and I kept gazing at the empty sky that had taken the spirit of my brother away.

All the three brothers gone from this earth. Were they now united somewhere? Where? They all left that enigma behind. Death—the eternal enigma of the living world. Does it mean one's total extinction? Or is it a final confluence with the God we all worship?

I opened my eyes, my reverie over, my gaze falling on the body of Goldie which was now in the last stages of being consumed by the tongues of the flames. Everyone standing around had witnessed it turning into ashes. This is certainly not the way to go from the world, I determinedly thought to myself. Not with the world around enjoying the spectacle of your death!

I would, when the bell tolled for me, just want to vanish away, like a whiff of air into the breeze that blows, becoming a leaf on a branch that sways, a flicker of the flame of the fire that burns, a drop of water in a stream that flows, a joyful raindrop that bursts out of a cloud, or a particle of shining sand swept into the folds of a playful tide. I would never, never want to be seen dying . . . or dead.

'Sad! Dev saab! Very sad—say something more,' came a voice that represented many more unspoken voices. I looked at the battery of cameramen and photographers, feasting their eyes on my long-drawn mood of reflection.

I smiled at them, as my only answer, and said, 'Time to go back home!'

Eighty-six

I was looking for two beautiful girls to play the leads in my film *Beauty Queen*. Photo sessions were being held almost every third or fourth day at my favourite fashion photographer Harish Daftary's studio, looking for beautiful eyes, beautiful legs, beautiful figures, and enchantingly innocent and attractive faces. A frantic search was on to discover new talent to dazzle the world once again.

As I was in the midst of all this excitement, the news came that the NDA government in power had lost its mandate to rule the nation, having failed to get a majority in the general elections. A combination of a large number of parties, led by the Congress, was staking claim to power. The coalition was headed by Sonia Gandhi, Rajiv Gandhi's much-revered and much-maligned widow, who was making her maiden appearance on the scene of Indian politics. It made a very fascinating story for the analysts to discuss and for the satellite news channels to cover round the clock.

After Rajiv Gandhi's death, Sonia Gandhi had at first appeared along with her handsome kids at prayer meetings and the like, wanting to be seen, recognized and looked at with awe and reverence, as the last representative of the Nehru family. Having assured herself of her emotional acceptance by the masses, she picked up the courage to throw her hat into the ring of politics. The opposition started attacking her openly, saying she was a foreigner and a novice in politics, and not qualified to head a major political party. But Sonia had played her cards well, and was able to pull a surprise out of the hat in the elections, rekindling the torch of the Congress party from its dying embers.

The NDA initially expected a thumping walkover in the elections. Later, as the fever of campaigning picked up, it compromised its mindset to a slim majority. But, in the end, when the results came out, the BJP had to be content with being only the second largest party. Sonia Gandhi's Congress emerged the largest, but fell short of a majority. In order to rule, they had to depend upon the crutches of their coalition partners.

With no single party getting a majority to rule, the verdict of the electorate had set up a hung parliament. For days and days nobody knew who the next prime minister would be. Everything was in a state of limbo. Wheeling-dealing for the highest post in the country and for the formation of the government started showing its true colours. Politics became a commodity on sale in the bazaar of cunning, crookery and one-upmanship. In that tricky atmosphere of 'coalitions of convenience' and short-sighted personal gains or vested interests, the nation was on tenterhooks, not getting a clear picture of what the future held in store. Who would be the prime minister? Would he or she be from a glorious or a shady past? A known criminal in politics or an unknown political hero? An unknown novice, with no experience in handling power, or a weather-beaten player who understood all the nuances of political manoeuvring? The true face of the multi-party system, with an emphasis on so-called regional aspirations, was being exposed.

I hit upon an idea for a story. It came to me in a flash, and I sat up in excitement.

In the next few minutes it was narrated to some of my colleagues. They too jumped up in excitement. And I immediately kicked off a project that I would call *Mr Prime Minister*. *Beauty Queen* was put on the backburner and *Mr Prime Minister* got ready to be launched soon, my fastest film ever to mount the sets.

I decided to shoot it in an earthquake-ravaged small township called Bachao in Gujarat, in the Kutch area, with me playing Mr Prime Minister, a role that would be a culmination of all my experience, knowledge and maturity as a man, a citizen, a thinker, an actor, writer and director.

Revolutionary in concept and a satire on our corrupt political system, *Mr Prime Minister* was aimed at shaking the conscience of our political bigwigs out of its lazy slumber, to wake up to the realities of what pure, clean, mature and efficient politics should be in a modern democratic country.

Eighty-seven

While filming *Mr Prime Minister*, my concentration was in top gear. An inspired exercise, the momentum of the filming never flagged at any stage. I would be ready for location as the sun rose, driving 25 kilometres from where I had made my headquarters to the hilltop where the impact of the 2001 Gujarat earthquake was the maximum, with the surrounding areas bearing an equal brunt.

People would start collecting from down below where the main bazaar of Bachao was, and by the evening as the sun started to set, they were there in the hundreds, sometimes in thousands, as if climbing up to a pilgrimage—coming all the way from the neighbouring villages, townships, even cities, to participate in an event called *Mr Prime Minister*, totally involved in seeing the making of it.

Forty years earlier their elders had witnessed a similar phenomenon of filming in that very state in a place called Limdi, not very far away, where the swami of *Guide* sat praying to God for his people, congregating around him in thousands. Now, four decades later, people with curiosity writ large on their faces were swarming around the same actor, now playing Mr Prime Minister.

One of the last laps of shooting took me abroad, very briefly, for a day's filming at London's Heathrow airport, and for a couple of days to Naples in Italy, where, in the midst of a few ruined desolated spots ravaged by a calamity of nature, a few scenes were shot.

After having completed the shots, I spent a lot of time tramping up and down Naples along with my Italian escorts. It was Christmas time. The Christmas spirit was evident in the smiles on every face, in the crowds thronging the magnificent Grand Piazza and the galleries around it. Walking through the area, I lived through the entire renaissance period that had produced such great artists, architects, builders and creators, who gave our modern world an inspiration for all the splendour and sophisticated artistry we now live in. I enjoyed every step that I walked, and then, as if to participate in the joy of the humanity around, I squatted in the middle of the cobblestoned square, amidst hundreds of people wondering at its architectural grandeur.

Suddenly I heard my father smiling and saying to me, 'See Naples before you die, Dev-aan!' He used to say this often when he was tutoring me. 'I have fulfilled your dream, Dad,' I said to him in my thoughts, a little sad that in his own lifetime, he was not able to visit Naples himself.

Suneil let out a shout of joy from across the piazza, breaking my reverie. 'The perfect cap for you, Papa!' he said. He was pointing at a shop. And there was a cap there, one amongst many designed and styled in Italy, that was indeed very nice. In fact it took my breath away. I had been looking for an unusual cap in London and then in New York, and later in Atlantic City, but had not found any worthy of my prized collection at home.

I bought the cap and wore it, indulging a fond feeling that it was exclusively designed for me. It matched the scarf I was wearing so well! Looking at myself in the mirror of the shop opposite, I found two Italian signorinas watching my reflection. As their eyes met mine, they boldly complimented me, 'Handsome—artisteeque!' I felt like a young man again, turned and doffed my cap at them, saying 'Grasse' as charmingly as youth itself.

A little distance away, scores of handwritten notes were stuck on the branches of a wish-tree, praying to be fulfilled by Father Christmas. Khursheed, playing my Italian wife in the film, took a ballpoint pen and a small writing pad out of her bag, scribbled something and placed it in front of me for my autograph.

'Sign it without reading,' she said.

I dutifully followed her command. She stuck the note on the wish-tree, hoping our film would win an Oscar.

'Wishful thinking!' I smiled.

But it brought instant joy to our hearts, which went so well with the evening at the Grand Piazza.

Eighty-eight

With the European part of the filming over, the last bit to be shot was a rap sequence, both in Hindi and English, defining what *Mr Prime Minister* was all about. Both the versions were written and sung by me as a supplementary attraction to the film.

I deliberately chose a day closest to my heart for starting to picturize it—the 26th of September! Exactly eighty-two years after I had announced my entry into the world with a cry.

On the same day, sixty-two years ago, I had stood outside the Gateway of India, pledging to myself with a determined mind to one day enter and rule over my countrymen in some obscure tiny corner of their hearts. I was now in a mood to examine how far I had succeeded in my long-enduring effort, and ordered my camera crew to the very same spot at dawn, having announced to the world that I would be filming a rap song that I would be performing myself.

As the first rays of the sun lit up my face, people started trooping in larger and larger numbers from all over the city, even from outside it, participating in the joyous moment, watching me perform with the same untiring gusto, verve and keenness as when I had started my career six decades ago, still trying to reach the ever-elusive stage of perfection I'd been striving to master all my life. All the TV channels vied with one another to flash to the eager world the fast-changing spectacle of the grand show of humanity centred around their favourite movie star.

After the day's filming was over, as the sun went down, its last rays now falling on a huge mass of humanity, congregated there as if in a festival, with broad smiles of adoration on their happy faces, gazing and waving at me, I stood up on a horse-driven Victoria decorated with multicoloured feathers, doffing my hat with an intensely courteous bow to the assembled gathering.

Meanwhile, busloads of young teenagers with angelic faces, wearing school uniforms, were offloading themselves around me, scrambling out of their seats, screaming 'Dev Anand!' Their hands were raised with notebooks for a quick scribble of my autograph on their pages. A TV journalist from behind the camera shouted a question, 'Which has been the happiest and the most exhilarating moment of your life, Dev saab?'

'This one is!' I shouted back.

Another one shot back, 'And your best award?'

'This one again!' I said.

The horse vigorously swished its tail, raised its head and neighed a thunderous approval as well.

A similar Victoria waited to take me to the world premiere of *Mr Prime Minister* at Ahmedabad, from the main entrance of an open-air theatre to its huge screen.

A horse neighed again, this time commanding me to get into the buggee. I hopped on to it, and the horse trotted along amidst the deafening applause that gave way to a melodious cheer comprising only two words: 'DEV ANAND!'

The resonance of the cheer exploded into vibrations, echoing and re-echoing everywhere, scattering themselves and mingling with the breeze that blew them into all directions.

And that one single moment became an eternity for me.

All sixty years of my work, all eighty years of romancing with life was condensed into one deep breath of prolonged ecstasy, elevating me to nothing short of a spiritual experience.

I imagined I was receiving an Oscar, Khursheed's wish on the Christmas tree at Naples coming true.

I imagined that the blessings showered on me by the gods at Tirupati and at Siddhivinayak Temple in Mumbai were not in vain, and had now become the music of the temple bells and gongs resonating into an endless choir, enveloping me forever in the heavens.

There was nothing beyond that I craved for. Only that everlasting moment mattered.

I did not care whether the film was a hit or a flop, whether it was accepted or discarded, condemned, ridiculed or praised to the skies, so long as the thought and the message I had tried to convey got released into the atmosphere, for people to see and hear and react to.

Flying back to Mumbai, I was already riding high on the wings of my imagination again.

Romancing with my thoughts, moving forward forever, always looking to the future, never dwelling on the buried past—that special ray of sunshine still upon me.

Epilogue

The year is 2007.

The UPA government is still steady on its feet, in spite of some stumbling blocks that have come its way. The economy is doing well, touching a growth rate of 9 per cent and above. And the nation is getting ready to celebrate sixty years of Independence.

Our cities are getting bigger and bigger, the high-rises taller, the slums below the high-rises larger. The ever-increasing number of multiplexes and shopping malls are signs of a smiling economy. Imported cars and luxury goods shine out of the showroom windows, enticing consumers with their exclusive novelties. Technically savvy Indians are holding their heads high across the world. Instant communication, through the Internet and mobile phones, is the order of the day; man has never been closer to man, and yet their minds are so far apart. The culture of violence is growing too, with massacres of innocents by terrorists having become an alarmingly regular occurrence.

Meanwhile, show business dazzles as brightly as it can. Film censorship has become more liberal—vulgar swear words spat out by foul-mouthed riff-raff on screen are passed off as signs of 'realism', and the media of our times admires it, applauding the cinema that advocates it as an indication of its 'progressive maturity'. The reigning stars are prospering more then ever before, with their fees touching astronomical figures thanks to an unprecedented boom in television channels that promote their popularity far and wide, reaching spheres of exhibition hitherto unknown. In addition, commercial business houses and advertising agencies buy endorsements for their products from movie stars offering astounding pay-packets. As a result, the cream of the Indian stars are now counted amongst the mega rich.

It is difficult to decide who amongst them is a 'Badshah', a 'Shehenshah', or a 'King'.

I am also progressing with the times. I am happy, spending most of my time with myself. Various organizations continue to felicitate me and laud Navketan, my banner, and this makes me proud. Last year, the republic of Croatia invited me, opening the doors of its exquisitely picturesque country for me to shoot a feature film there. From Zagreb, the capital, I toured the length and breadth of the land with the joy of a child, on the hunt as always for new ideas. One day, on the island of Bojni, I came across a photograph of Pandit Jawaharlal Nehru with the late Marshall Tito of Yugoslavia, hung on the wall of a museum that preserves the memorabilia of Tito's historic meetings with world leaders of his age who visited his country. Both the leaders were clinking their glasses of wine, toasting to the friendship of the two nations, India and Yugoslavia, after having signed the famous Non-Aligned Movement document in the 1950s. I stood in front of the photograph and smiled a salute of respect to both the leaders. I imagined Panditji coming out of the photograph to bless me on my new international project to be shot in Croatia, earlier a part of Yugoslavia but now an independent republic. And I raised a toast in my mind with a deep reverence to Panditji, to his eternal spirit that keeps watching over the country he helped bring independence to, showering his blessings on it as it passes through ups and downs on its forward march towards progress.

When Heartbeats Are the Same is the name of my new international venture. I'm all ready for the journey, all excited again just like a newcomer.

Climbing uphill on a long straight road, with just the sky at the far end of it, the early rays of the sun falling on me in luminous joy, the strains of an old and familiar melody, '*Come September*', fall on my ears as the driver fiddles with the radio. And my mobile rings, one of the first calls on a day that is the 26th of September, 2006. The call sets in motion an unending chain of similar calls from back home, thousands of miles away. I respond to them all as warmly as I can. The car stops at Motovun, one of the beautiful towns of Croatia.

With the mobile in my hand still ringing away incessantly, I stand on the top of a hill in Motovun looking down at the expansive breathtaking valley below with a highway snaking through it, planning to bring my cameras here as well. A sudden breeze wafts across my face, with its cool flush of fresh energy invigorating me completely.

The soft honeyed voice of the young Croatian lady who has brought me thus far, tramping up the narrow cobbled streets from where the car was parked, floats up to me, 'Do you like it here, Mr Dev Anand?'

I look back at her smiling, and say, 'I do . . . I do.'

Gaata rahe mera dil.

My heart is singing, like it always has been—

This is a beautiful world!

Filmography

Hindi Films Dev Anand Has Acted In

Year	Film	Director	Banner	Co-stars
1946	Hum Ek Hain	P.L. Santoshi	Prabhat Studio	Durga Khote, Kamla Kotnis, Rehana, Rehman
1947	Aage Badho	Yashwant Pethkar	Prabhat Studio	Khursheed, Vasant Thengdi, Kusum Deshpande
1947	Mohan	A.N. Banerji	Famous Pictures	Hemavati, Alka, Vimla Vashisht
1948	Hum Bhi Insaan Hai	Phani Mazumdar	Maya Arts	Ramola, Niharika
1948	Vidya	Girish Trivedi	Jeet Productions	Suraiya, Cuckoo, Madan Puri
1948	Ziddi	Shahid Lateef	Bombay Talkies	Kamini Kaushal, Pran
1949	Jeet	Mohan Sinha	Rajkirti Chitra	Suraiya, Durga Khote, Madan Puri, Kanhaiyalal, Bhagwan
1949	Namuna	Hirasingh Baria	M&T Films	Kamini Kaushal, Cuckoo, Leela Chitnis, Kishore Sahu
1949	Shair	Chawla	Jagat Pictures	Suraiya, Kamini Kaushal, Cuckoo, Agha
1949	Uddhar	S.S. Kulkarni	Pratibha Chitra Mandir	Munawar Sultana, Nirupa Roy, Bharat Bhushan, Pratima Devi
1950	Afsar	Chetan Anand	Navketan Films	Suraiya, Ruma Devi, Kanhaiyalal, Zohra Segal, Manmohan Krishna

Year	Title	Director	Production	Cast
1950	Birha Ki Raat	Jagirdar	Noble Arts	Nargis, Jagirdar, Om Prakash
1950	Dilruba	Dwarka Khosla	Lotus Orient Films	Rehana, Cuckoo, Achla Sachdev
1950	Hindustan Hamara	Paul Zils	Documentary Unit of India	Prithviraj Kapoor, Nalini Jaywant, Tripti Mitra, Jairaj, Premnath
1950	Khel	S.M. Nawab	Shaheen Pictures	Nargis, Nigar Sultana, Anwar
1950	Madhubala	Prahlad Dutt	Ranjit Studio	Madhubala, Manju, Jeevan
1950	Nili	Ratibhai Punatar	Ranjit Studio	Suraiya, Shyama, Cuckoo, Agha
1950	Nirala	Shankar Mukherji	M&T Films	Madhubala, Yakub, Leela Mishra
1951	Aaram	D.D. Kashyap	Kashyap Productions	Madhubala, Durga Khote, Premnath, Talat Mahmood
1951	Baazi	Guru Dutt	Navketan Films	Geeta Bali, Kalpana Kartik, Johny Walker, K.N. Singh
1951	Do Sitare	D.D. Kashyap	Famous Pictures	Suraiya, Premnath, Kuldeep Kaur
1951	Nadaan	Hirasingh Baria	M&T Films	Madhubala, Mubarak, Madan Puri
1951	Sanam	Nandlal Jaswantlal	United Technicians	Suraiya, Meena Kumari, K.N.Singh
1951	Sazaa	Fali Mistry	G.P. Productions	Nimmi, Shyama, K.N. Singh
1951	Stage	Vijay Mhatre	Jeevan Pictures	Ramola, Kuldeep Kaur, Cuckoo
1952	Aandhiyan	Chetan Anand	Navketan Films	Nimmi, Kalpana Kartik, Leela Mishra, Johny Walker, K.N. Singh
1952	Jaal	Guru Dutt	Film Arts	Geeta Bali, K.N. Singh, Johny Walker

Year	Film	Director	Banner	Co-stars
1952	Tamasha	Phani Mazumdar	Bombay Talkies	Ashok Kumar, Meena Kumari
1952	Zalzala	Paul Zils	Art Film of India	Geeta Bali, Seeta Bose, Kishore Sahu
1953	Arman	Fali Mistry	Film Technicians of India	Madhubala, Jagirdar, K.N. Singh
1953	Humsafar	A.N. Banerji	Navketan Films	Kalpana Kartik, Chetan Anand, Smriti Biwas, Johny Walker
1953	Patita	Amiya Chakrabarty	Mars and Movies	Usha Kiron, Agha, Lalita Pawar
1953	Rahi	K.A. Abbas	Naya Sansar	Nalini Jaywant, Balraj Sahni, Habib Tanvir, David
1954	Baadbaan	Phani Mazumdar	Bombay Talkies Workers' Co-operative Society	Ashok Kumar, Leela Chitnis, Meena Kumari, Usha Kiron, Jairaj
1954	Ferry	Hemen Gupta	Film Trust of India	Geeta Bali, Premlata, Gulab
1954	Taxi Driver	Chetan Anand	Navketan Films	Kalpana Kartik, Sheila Ramani, Johny Walker, Hamid Sayani
1955	Farar	Phani Mazumdar	Unique Pictures	Geeta Bali, Mehmood
1955	House No 44	M.K. Burman	Navketan Films	Kalpana Kartik, Kukmum, K.N. Singh
1955	Insaniyat	S.S. Vasan	Gemini Pictures	Dilip Kumar, Bina Rai, Agha, Vijayalakshmi, Shobhna Samarth
1955	Milap	Raj Khosla	Film Arts	Geeta Bali, K.N. Singh, Johny Walker

Year	Title	Director	Studio	Cast
1955	Munimji	Subodh Mukherji	Filmistan Studio	Nalini Jaywant, Nirupa Roy, Pran
1956	CID	Raj Khosla	Guru Dutt Films	Shakila, Waheeda Rehman, Johny Walker, Kumkum, K.N. Singh
1956	Funtoosh	Chetan Anand	Navketan Films	Sheila Ramani, K.N. Singh, Kumkum
1956	Pocketmaar	H.S. Rawail	Black and White Movies	Geeta Bali, Lalita Pawar, Nadira
1957	Baarish	Shankar Mukherji	Alankar Chitra	Nutan, Lalita Pawar, Kumkum, Mehmood
1957	Dushman	Raj Rishi	Quatra Art Productions	Usha Kiron, Kumkum, Minoo Mumtaz
1957	Nau Do Gyarah	Vijay Anand	Navketan Films	Kalpana Kartik, Jeevan, Shashikala
1957	Paying Guest	Subodh Mukherji	Filmistan Studio	Nutan, Sajjan, Jagirdar
1958	Amardeep	T. Prakash Rao	Shivaji Productions	Vyjayanthimala, Padmini, Ragini
1958	Kala Pani	Raj Khosla	Navketan Films	Madhubala, Nalini Jaywant, Sapru
1958	Solva Saal	Raj Khosla	Chandra Films	Waheeda Rehman, Sapru
1959	Love Marriage	Subodh Mukherji	Subodh Mukherji Productions	Mala Sinha, Abhi Bhattacharya, Helen
1960	Bambai Ka Babu	Raj Khosla	Naya Films	Suchitra Sen, Achla Sachdev
1960	Ek Ke Baad Ek	Raj Rishi	Raj Kala Mandir	Sharada, Tarla, Heeralal
1960	Jaali Note	Shakti Samanta	S.P. Pictures	Madhubala, Helen, Madan Puri
1960	Kala Bazaar	Vijay Anand	Navketan Films	Waheeda Rehman, Leela Chitnis, Nanda, Chetan Anand, Vijay Anand

Year	Film	Director	Banner	Co-stars
1960	Manzil	M.K. Burman	Kalpana Pictures	Nutan, K.N. Singh, David
1960	Sarhad	Shankar Mukherji	Alankar Chitra	Suchitra Sen, Ragini, Lalita Pawar
1961	Hum Dono	Amarjeet	Navketan Films	Sadhna, Nanda, Leela Chitnis
1961	Jab Pyar Kisi Se Hota Hai	Nasir Hussain	Nasir Hussain Films	Asha Parekh, Pran, Rajendranath
1961	Maya	D.D. Kashyap	Light of Asia Films	Mala Sinha, Lalita Pawar, Helen
1961	Roop Ki Rani Choron Ka Raja	H.S. Rawail	Rahul Theatres	Waheeda Rehman, Sundar, Sahira
1962	Asli Naqli	Hrishikesh Mukherjee	L.B. Films	Sadhna, Sandhya Roy, Nazir Hussain, Leela Chitnis
1962	Baat Ek Raat Ki	Shankar Mukherji	Alankar Chitra	Waheeda Rehman, Chandrashekhar, Johny Walker
1963	Kinare Kinare	Chetan Anand	Nyay Sharma Films	Meena Kumari, Chetan Anand
1963	Tere Ghar Ke Samne	Vijay Anand	Navketan Films	Nutan, Om Prakash, Rashid Khan, Harindranath Chattopadhyay
1964	Sharabi	Raj Rishi	Black and White Movies	Madhubala, Lalita Pawar, Daisy Irani
1965	Teen Deviyan	Amarjeet	Nalanda	Nanda, Kalpana, Simi, I.S. Johar
1965	Guide	Vijay Anand	Navketan Films	Waheeda Rehman, Kishore Sahu, Leela Chitnis

1966	Pyar Mohabbat	Shankar Mukherji	Alankar Chitra	Saira Banu, Shashikala, David
1967	Jewel Thief	Vijay Anand	Navketan Films	Ashok Kumar, Vyjayanthimala, Tanuja, Helen, Sapru
1968	Kahin Aur Chal	Vijay Anand	J.M. Films	Asha Parekh, Shubha Khote
1968	Duniya	T. Prakash Rao	Time Films	Vyjayanthimala, Balraj Sahni, Prem Chopra, Johny Walker
1969	Mahal	Shankar Mukherji	Roopkala Pictures	Asha Parekh, Farida Jalal, Abhi Bhattacharya
1970	Prem Pujari	Dev Anand	Navketan Films	Waheeda Rehman, Zaheeda, Prem Chopra, Nazir Hussain, Shatrughan Sinha
1970	Johny Mera Naam	Vijay Anand	Trimurti Films	Hema Malini, Pran, Premnath, I.S. Johar, Padma Khanna
1971	Gambler	Amarjeet	Nalanda	Zaheeda, Kishore Sahu, Shatrughan Sinha
1971	Hare Rama Hare Krishna	Dev Anand	Navketan Films	Mumtaz, Zeenat Aman, Prem Chopra, Kishore Sahu, Mehmood Jr
1971	Tere Mere Sapne	Vijay Anand	Navketan Enterprises	Hema Malini, Mumtaz, Vijay Anand, Agha
1972	Ye Gulistan Hamara	Atma Ram	Guru Dutt Films Combine	Sharmila Tagore, Pran
1973	Banarasi Babu	Shankar Mukherji	Alankar Chitra	Raakhee, Yogeeta Bali, Jeevan, I.S. Johar
1973	Chhupa Rustam	Vijay Anand	Navketan Enterprises	Hema Malini, Vijay Anand, Bindu

Year	Film	Director	Banner	Co-stars
1973	Shareef Badmash	Raj Khosla	Navketan Films	Hema Malini, Helen, Ajit, Jeevan, Shatrughan Sinha
1973	Joshila	Yash Chopra	Trimurti Films	Hema Malini, Raakhee, Pran
1973	Heera Panna	Dev Anand	Navketan Films	Raakhee, Zeenat Aman, Rehman
1974	Amir Garib	Mohan Kumar	M.K. Productions	Hema Malini, Premnath, Helen
1974	Ishq Ishq Ishq	Dev Anand	Navketan Films	Zeenat Aman, Kabir Bedi, Zarina Wahab, Shabana Azmi, Shekhar Kapur, Premnath, Nadira
1974	Prem Shastra	B.R. Ishara	Nalanda	Zeenat Aman, Bindu, Rehman
1975	Warrant	Pramod Chakraborty	N.P. International Films	Zeenat Aman, Pran, Dara Singh
1976	Darling Darling	Gogi Anand	Fortune Films	Zeenat Aman, Nadira, Mehmood
1976	Janeman	Chetan Anand	Navketan Films	Hema Malini, Ajit, Premnath
1976	Bullet	Vijay Anand	Navketan Enterprises	Parveen Babi, Kabir Bedi, Rakesh Roshan, Jyoti Bakshi
1977	Kalabaaz	Ashok Roy	Pashupati Pictures	Zeenat Aman, Pradeep Kumar
1977	Saheb Bahadur	Chetan Anand	Himalay Films	Priya Rajvansh, Om Prakash
1978	Des Pardes	Dev Anand	Navketan Films	Tina Munim, Pran, Ajit, Amjad Khan, Sreeram Lagoo, Mehmood, Prem Chopra

1980	Man Pasand	Basu Chatterji	Film Unit	Tina Munim, Girish Karnad
1980	Lootmaar	Dev Anand	Navketan Films	Tina Munim, Amjad Khan, Ranjeet, Prem Chopra, Simple Kapadia
1982	Swami Dada	Dev Anand	Navketan Films	Mithun Chakraborty, Rati Agnihotri, Padmini Kolhapure, Christine O'Neill, Naseeruddin Shah
1984	Anand Aur Anand	Dev Anand	Navketan Films	Raakhee, Raj Babbar, Smita Patil, Suneil Anand, Natasha Sinha
1986	Hum Naujawan	Dev Anand	Navketan Films	Richa Sharma, Atlee Brar, Bunty Behl, Tabu, Anupam Kher
1989	Lashkar	Jagdish Kadar	Tanusree Films	Madhvi, Sonam, Neeta Puri
1989	Sachche Ka Bol-Bala	Dev Anand	Navketan Films	Hema Malini, Meenakshi Sheshadri, Jackie Shroff, Marc Zuber, Prem Chopra
1990	Awwal Number	Dev Anand	Navketan Films	Aamir Khan, Aditya Pancholi, Ekta
1991	Sau Crore	Dev Anand	Navketan Films	Fatima Sheikh, Ananya Mukherji, Raman Kapoor, Naseeruddin Shah
1993	Pyar Ka Tarana	Dev Anand	Navketan Films	Manu Gargi, Akshay Anand, Mink, Anita Ayub (Dev Anand did not act in this film)
1995	Gangster	Dev Anand	Navketan Films	Manu Gargi, Mamta Kulkarni, Anita Ayub, Mink, Rubaina Khan

Year	Film	Director	Banner	Co-stars
1996	Return of Jewel Thief	Ashok Tyagi	T.P. Aggarwal	Ashok Kumar, Dharmendra, Jackie Shroff, Shilpa Shirodkar, Madhoo, Anu Agarwal, Prem Chopra
1998	Main Solah Baras Ki	Dev Anand	Navketan Films	Sabrina, Jas Arora, Supriya Karnik, Neeru
2001	Censor	Dev Anand	Navketan Films	Heenee Kaushik, Hema Malini, Shammi Kapoor, Rekha, Jackie Shroff, Mamta Kulkarni, Ayesha Jhulka, Raj Babbar, Randhir Kapoor, Archana Puran Singh, Amrish Puri, Govinda
2003	Love at Times Square	Dev Anand	Navketan Films	Heenee Kaushik, Shoib Khan, Siya Rana, Chaitanya Chaudhary, Moon Moon Sen, Satish Shah, Rishi Kapoor, Salman Khan
2005	Mr Prime Minister	Dev Anand	Navketan Films	Prem Chopra, Milind Gunaji, Boman Irani, A.K. Hangal, Tara Sharma, Anjaan Srivastav

Index